The Origins of Modern Arabic Fiction

The Origins of Modern Arabic Fiction

Matti Moosa

An Original by Three Continents Press

First Edition
Three Continents Press
1346 Connecticut Avenue N.W.
Washington, D.C. 20036

ISBN: 0-89410-166-8
ISBN: 0-89410-167-6 (pbk)
Library of Congress No.: 81-51657

To Inge, my wife

and

To Adeeba, my sister

with great love

and

gratitude

ACKNOWLEDGMENTS

The present work would have never been possible without the assistance of many people. First of all I wish to extend my sincere thanks to the Faculty Senate of Gannon University whose generous grants enabled me to make several trips to the Middle East to do the primary research. I would also like to thank my colleague, Professor George Welch, Jr., who contributed generously of his time in reading and correcting this manuscript. To Dr. Frank F. Angotti I owe the explanation of the many ideas and themes derived by Arab authors from Western sources and also to his untiring effort to read and correct parts of this manuscript. I wish also to thank my brothers Akram Moosa and Hazim Moosa, my sister Najeeba Moosa of Baghdad and my friends William Amin and Sami Nasif of Cairo for their time and effort in trying to locate for me most of the sources used in this book.

Miss Rita Ann Nies of Gannon University library has been unremitting in her effort to obtain materials for me without which my work would have been tremendously handicapped. I am also indebted to the efficient and sharp eyed Mrs. Kay Medairy for typing the first copy of the manuscript. I am also indebted to Miss Rose Coccarelli for typing the final copy of the manuscript, and to Mrs. Kay Wojciak for her help in proofreading the manuscript.

I am particularly grateful to my wife whose patience and encouragement were a great source of inspiration which enabled me to continue with this work.

Last, but not least, I wish to express my appreciation to my friend, Professor Jack E. Tohtz of Edinboro State College for reading and correcting the original copy of this manuscript.

God is beautiful and He loves beauty

A saying of the Prophet Muhammad
in Arabic Calligraphy by Isma'il Haqqi (1942)

CONTENTS

CONTENTS

PREFACE

This book attempts to trace the genesis and analyze the development of Arabic fiction in the nineteenth century and early part of the twentieth century. It attempts to do so with a fundamental emphasis upon the cultural ethos within which new genres of Arabic fiction emerged. As such, it is much closer to being a social and literary history rather than being—and this was not my intent—basically a literary criticism. Within this context, this work attempts to deal with the question, right from the start, of what exactly is subsumed under the rubric, "modern Arabic fiction." Unlike the West, the Arab Middle East did not have a tradition of recognizable and generally accepted literary forms like the short story, novel, and drama. The development of modern Arabic literature came late and did not evolve to a reasonably sophisticated level until very recently. Accordingly, when one attempts to deal with the concept of Arabic fiction during the nineteenth century one finds it a nebulous and elusive one. This problem is further compounded by the fact that Arab writers did not have widespread viable literary modes for the sustained and intelligent representation of their ideas, reflections and criticisms of Arab society.

It was drama that appeared first via the pen of Marun Naqqash, a Syrian, in the 1840's—and it continued to dominate the literary scene in the Arab World throughout the nineteenth century. And precisely because of the protracted attention given by Naqqash and other writers to the theater only it will be given a great deal of attention in this work. This should not imply that Arabic drama ever did become a polished and multi-faceted mode of expression in the western sense. In fact, it was and remained, during the time span dealt with by this study, relatively crude. In any case, a sophisticated audience was lacking, and appreciative and serious theater-goers were few. Thus a paramount reason for the weak status of drama (and fiction) throughout this era was the almost total absence of a literate and appreciative public. After Naqqash's death in 1855, his brother, Niqula, formed an amateur troupe which traveled throughout greater Syria staging his brother's plays making a rather desperate attempt to stimulate interest in playgoing. In turn, after Niqula's death, his son, Salim, formed a professional theatrical troupe which produced not only his uncle's works but his own plays as well. Frustrated at the lack of audience reception in Lebanon, he moved his troupe to Egypt, where the drama had for some years attracted a small but steadily growing audience. Indeed, Khedive Isma'il had built a Western style Opera House in 1862, but because of the dearth of native material, the plays were overwhelmingly Western in origin.

In Egypt, Salim Naqqash and his troupe performed the plays he and his uncle had written, on a regular basis. Even these, however, were not really original. Many were eastern-style adaptations of Western dramas and Marun Naqqash's *al-Bakhil* (1847) which may be regarded as the first native Arabic drama, owes its theme and inspiration to Molière *L'Avare*. The subject matter, characters and themes of many of Naqqash's other dramas were drawn from the medieval Middle Eastern classic, the *Arabian Nights*. Thus, true uniqueness and creativity were lacking. However, there was somewhat of an exception: Ya'qub Sanu, and Egyptian Jew not only established a Cairo popular theater in 1870 but in that theater performed his own dramas which were, if not profound, at least original. The life of this first genuine Arab theater in Egypt was cut short by the despotic, Khedive Isma'il, who took offense at Sanu's play, *al-Darratan* (The Rival Wives) believing it to have been a sly criticism of his own polygamous practices. Isma'il closed Ya'qub Sanu's theater and banished him from Egypt, from whence he went to Paris and lived until his death in 1912. After Sanu the fate of Arabic drama in Egypt took a turn for the worse and nothing original was attempted until the turn of the century. Until that time, Syrian troupes, actors and playwrights dominated the theater in Egypt. Prominent among the Syrian playwrights were Ahmad Abu Khalil al-Qabbani, Sulayman al-Qirdahi and Iskandar Farah. There was little to distinguish them from previous writers. For instance, al-Qabbani's works were adaptations of Western dramas or a rehashing of the fantasies and sentiments of the *Arabian Nights*. Not until 1905 did a true Egyptian theater emerge again, established by al-Shaykh Salama Hijazi.

Another important step in the development of modern Arabic fiction were the translations from Western fiction which began to be widespread toward the end of the 19th century. Since Arab writers had only limited fictional models to build on and since there was, in addition to a lack of knowledge and technique, a lack of incentive, it was natural that Arab writers should find the translation of Western works much to their taste. Most of their translations were primarily from French because of the influence of French culture in Egypt through Muhammad Ali's contacts with France, and in Syria, through French Jesuit missions. After the establishment of the Syrian Protestant College (the present American University of Beirut), Arab writers began to translate from English as well. The translations, most of which were of second-rate romantic fiction, found a ready audience—even though they were anathematized by many Arab traditionalists as "immoral."

The impact of the en masse translation of Western fiction upon the Arabic world has had a great influence on its language and literature. To cite just two examples of this influence, it introduced Arab writers to Western literary techniques and models and it changed the Arabic language through the many words and concepts Arab writers borrowed from Western literature. Although these translations served as a source of innocent entertainment for the literate public, they were vehemently attacked by conservative elements of society who believed that not only were they a corrupting influence on the beauty of the Arabic language, but also detrimental to public morals.

No review of the rise of Arabic fiction would be complete without mention of the *maqama*. Having limited literary antecedents upon which to build a modern fictional genre, and before the introduction of mass translations from the West, some authors depended on the *maqama*. The *maqama* traces its beginning from the Arabic Middle Ages. It is based on a single anecdote and portrays the actions of a hero, usually a wandering rogue, as related by a narrator. Simple and straightforward, the original purpose of the *maqama* was, generally, not only to amuse, but to instruct the Arabs in the subtleties and beauty of their language. However, there were those who attempted to infuse the *maqama* with a more relevant content towards the beginning of the 20th century. Men like Muhammad Ibrahm al-Muwaylihi in his *Hadith Isa ibn Hisham aw Fatra min Al-Zaman,* Hafiz Ibrahim in *Layali Satih* and to a certain extent, Muhammad Lutfi Jumu'a in his *Layali al-Ruh al Ha'ir,* had some success with the form. But due to its inherent rigidity, it never developed into a viable vehicle of modern expression.

Thus, throughout the 19th century, Arabic fiction languished in limbo. On the one hand it had no indigenous inspiration, no traditional foundation, no clear-cut antecedents upon which to build other than the *Arabian Nights* and the *maqama,* both of which acted more as a constraining rather than a liberating influence. The narrow confines of these extant Arabic genres, together with the general insularity of the Arabic world at that time, obviated an evolution into more modern forms and telling themes. This difficulty was compounded by the denunciatory broadsides of Arab traditionists, the quasi-xenophobic attitude of many Arabs who were opposed to translations from Western fiction and the stubborn insistence of others who wanted to indiscriminately translate and utilize Western forms and themes solely for the purpose of profit. These circumstances, taken as a whole, precluded the growth of a worthy native modern fictional form.

It was not until 1870, that in Syria, an author appeared who in his art incorporated a semblance of originality and modernity. This was Salim al-Bustani, son of the celebrated author and enclyclopedist, Butrus al-Bustani. In that year, his novel *al-Hiyam fi Jinan al-Sham* (Love in the Gardens of Syria) appeared and can be considered rather loosely as the first genuinely Arab "novel." He was the first Arab writer who attempted to create one in the Western sense of the word. Its biggest drawback was, however, that although the book had modern characters, the theme and style were still overly imbued with the spirit of the *Arabian Nights*. Al-Bustani wrote many romances and short stories all of which had the same *modus operandi*, in that they reflected a more or less traditionist Arab approach. For instance, horses, heroes, and damsels in distress prevail with disconcerting regularity.

His plots are weak, his characters lack depth and individuality and his themes are superficial. Yet, he was the first Arab writer to be attuned to the prevailing intellectual currents and ideologies of his time, even attempting to treat socialism in at least two of his novels. He was also the first Arab writer who coined terms used until this day in the Arab world, such as *Ishtirakiyya*, for socialism, and *Ibahiyya* for nihilism.

But al-Bustani's influence had another, more immediate and, perhaps more salutary impact. He was the central figure of the Beirut intellectual and literary circle whose focal point was his magazine *al-Jinan*, and which influenced a whole generation of Arab writers who followed in his wake. The most important figure in al-Bustani's circle at *al-Jinan* was Francis Marrash. Marrash is most famous for his allegory *Ghabat al-Haqq,* but his importance lies in the fact that he was the first truly cosmopolitan Arabic intellectual and writer. He was familiar with, and wrote about the many issues of his time. Science, metaphysics, pedagogy, criticism, poetry, numerous essays, all fell within his scope and interest. He did not write much fiction, but because Marrash was one of the best informed and most perceptive and popular writers of the contemporary Arab World, his influence upon others was important.

Less important than either al-Bustani or Marrash, was the sometime novelist, Nu'man Abduh al-Qasatli. He was an historian by training and vocation, but he wrote three romances which were serialized in *al-Jinan*. They all reflect the influence of al-Bustani, taking up, for the most part, the same themes but with one big difference: he strongly advocated the democratization of Syrian society and the implementation of a parliamentary system modeled on those in the West. This work ends with Jurji Zaydan, 1861-1914, a Lebanese Christian who was an historian, wrote over twenty novels and, besides, was the editor of *al-Hilal*, an influential intellectual journal. With him the first phase on the rise of modern Arabic fiction ends. He was the first to popularize true history through fiction, and to succeed in breaking completely with many of the constraining bonds that had limited the horizons of, and obviated fruitful creativity by, those who came before him.

CHAPTER I

HISTORICAL BEGINNINGS: EGYPT

The story-telling habit is as old as civilization itself, and ancient Arabic literature is no exception. The Arabs of the pre-Islamic era traditionally related tales portraying their tribal life and embodying many aspects of their social behavior, such as generosity, self-praise, courage, group feeling, erotic love, and revenge. Most of these prevailed after the emergence of Islam and were retold, particularly to Arab soldiers in the early period of the Islamic conquests, to arouse their fighting spirit. Although the exact date of the codification of these tales is not certain, *al-Jamharah,* ascribed to Umar ibn Shabba al-Numayri of al-Basrah (789-875), was probably the first anthology which contained some stories of the Arabs and their wars with the neighboring nations before the advent of Islam.[1]

Such can hardly be considered the ancestors of modern Arabic fiction. They are completely different not only from each other but also from recent fiction, particularly the short story, in their scope, in their relation to the environment, and in their form.

Tales like those collected as the *Thousand and One Nights* for the most part tell of wonderful adventures in which the ingenuity or good luck of the hero determines the outcome. The action tends to be fabulous, with no connection to life as it is lived. The settings are usually the romantically far away, and the characters generalized types rather than individual personalities. Moreover, the form of the native tale is markedly rhetorical (as one would expect in a tradition originally oral), and the narrative tends to be episodic rather than organic.

It would be equally presumptuous to attempt to establish a relationship between modern Arabic fiction, particularly the novel and short story, and the medieval literary technique known as the *maqama.*[2] This genre was perfected by the famous belletrist Badi' al-Zaman al-Hamadhani (969-1007), who was followed by an equal if not superior master of the same technique, Abu al-Qasim al-Hariri (1054-1122). The revival of the *maqama* in the nineteenth century by Abu al-Thana al-Alusi (1801-54) in Iraq, Nasif al-Yaziji (1801-71) in Lebanon, Ahmad Faris al-Shidyaq (1804-88), and Muhammad Ibrahim al-Muwaylihi (1858-1930) in Egypt was a continuation of an old tradition rather than the introduction of new models of fictional prose. Although they lacked the essential characteristics of the modern novel, particularly development and plot, the *maqamas* of al-Muwaylihi may be considered the closest approach of the native tradition to the novel: their representation of life in Egypt in the last century is realistic, and their characters are finely delineated.[3]

Social as well as literary conditions prevented the development of the novel in Egypt. By the beginning of the nineteenth century, Arabic literature, like its culture as a whole, had reached a point of exhaustion. Several centuries of despotic rule by the last dynasty of Mamluks had destroyed any possibility of cultural vigor. Ignorant, ruthless, and perpetually engaged in their struggle for power, the Mamluks had no interest in the educational and social well-being of the Egyptians. Illiteracy became widespread, and learning found refuge only in the famous al-Azhar Mosque—the sole surviving institution of learning from the Fatimid era. Although al-Azhar helped preserve an interest in the Arabic language, its methods of teaching were archaic, and the subjects of study were restricted to grammar, philology, and the religious sciences of Islam. The study of the Arabic language was not meant to develop or encourage creative writing or generate new themes and styles; it was seen as a means to understand and interpret the Qur'an and the Shari'a.

The hostility of al-Azhar's 'Ulama toward the study of the humanities and liberal arts prevented any possibility of scientific and literary progress.[4] The inadequacy of literary expression and the lack of eloquence can be clearly seen in the work of such Egyptian writers as Abd al-Rahman al-Jabarti (d. 1822), whose style is saturated with colloquial usages.[5]

Meanwhile, the ignorant and illiterate masses found ancient and medieval Arabic folklore a source of entertainment. This material was often religious in origin (e.g. the stories of *al-Sayyid al-Badawi, Fatima the Daughter of Bari, Sayyidi Ibrahim al-Disuqi* and the story of *Our Lord Ali and the Head of the Ghul),* or it treated of the lives of heroes of antiquity (e.g. *Abu Zayd al-Hilali, Antara ibn Shaddad, al-Zahir Baybars,* and *Sayf ibn dhi Yazan).* The tales, usually told orally, were modified, and to some extent Egyptianized, to suit the illiterate audience. But, despite its popularity, folklore won neither approval nor encouragement from the so-called educated classes. They shunned it as trash, while the religiously minded Azharites thought it was beneath consideration.

Not until very recently have contemporary Egyptian writers removed the traditional curse from folklore by studying it seriously. Hence, by the end of the eighteenth and the beginning of the nineteenth centuries Arabic literature in Egypt, reflecting the general cultural decline in the country, was at its lowest ebb.

Some contemporary Egyptian writers cite the French occupation of Egypt (1798-1801) as the starting point for a new era in the cultural life of that country, regarding it as the most significant link between Egyptian thought and Western civilization since Europe's assault on the East in the Crusades.[6] This new contact, they maintain, not only awakened the Egyptians to their deplorable backwardness, but also aroused in them a national feeling. This became instrumental in the final disintegration of Ottoman rule in Egypt and was accompanied by curiosity about Western ideas and European civilization. Following the French evacuation, Egypt began to look more toward Europe than toward its native traditions in pursuit of modern ideas.[7]

In fact, however, the cultural impact of the French expedition in Egypt was insignificant. The French remained there for only three years, not even long enough to stabilize their position, let alone to modify the hostility of the Egyptians toward the "infidel" invaders. A historian of the period, al-Jabarti, bitterly criticizes and denounces the behavior of the French, especially of their women, in Egypt. Although he described the immoral French as infecting the Egyptians with their corruption, this conservative Muslim, who was utterly shocked by the French "misbehavior," was not slow to observe the good qualities of the French. He greatly admired the French sense of justice, which appeared outstanding when compared with the cruelty of the Turkish rulers. Tremendously impressed by the way the French conducted the trial of Sulayman al-Halabi, the murderer of General Klebér, he also admired the slogan of the French Revolution, "liberty, equality and fraternity."[8] Other Egyptians from al-Azhar, such as the Shaykh Hasan al-'Attar (d. 1835), the teacher of Rifa'a al-Tahtawi, also appreciated French knowledge and learning.

But Egyptian fiction was still following conventional modes and drawing from traditional sources. A clear example is the collection of popular tales written by al-Shaykh Muhammad al-Mahdi (d. 1815), a rector of al-Azhar.[9] These attracted the attention of Jean Joseph Marcel (d. 1854), a member of the French expedition, who translated and published them in French.[10] Although the Arabic versions of these tales have never been published, and are thought to have been lost, the tenor of the original text is clear enough.

The tales were divided into two parts by the French translator. The first contains the introductions by both the translator and the author, who relates his meeting, on his pilgrimage to Mecca, with a certain adventurer, Abd al-Rahman, who amused the people by his tales. Abd al-Rahman begins to tell the author stories similar to those of the *Thousand and One Nights*, such as those of the *Abbasid Caliph and the Barmecides,* the *King and the Highway Men,* and the king who after his death summoned his Vizir and asked him to help his daughter rule his country, which was in a chaotic condition. He also relates other tales, such as the *Ten Voyages* of a certain Murad and the tale of the King who blasphemed and was expelled, but then repented and was restored to his throne. He even tells tales told by animals, such as the tale of the *Two Foxes and the Gardener,* which undoubtedly bears the stamp of the tales of *Kalila wa Dimna.* Throughout these tales, the narrator relates the adversities which befall him during his adventures and which lead him finally to the Maristan (asylum).[11]

In the second part, set in the Maristan, he not only relates tales to his inmates, but also recounts tales told by them. He begins by telling of his acquaintance with the inmates, among whom were Rafif al-A'war (the one-eyed), a certain Abd al-Qadir, and Abu Bakr al-Jallab, and each in turn reveals the circumstances which brought him to the Maristan. Rafif begins with the story of his escape from Alexandretta, where he made a living by using magic until the governor of the city discovered he was a charlatan. From Alexandretta he went to Lebanon, and then to the land of Gog and Magog, and finally he reached Acre ('Akka), which was governed by Ahmad Pasha al-Jazzar, who ordered Rafif's arm to be cut off. Rafif returned to Egypt and endeavored to join the body of learned men there, but was accused of being mad and thrown into the asylum. Another character, Abd al-Qadir, tells of his relation with the girl next door; their affair was discovered by the neighbors, and he was punished for his misdemeanor by being thrown alive into the Nile. He managed to save himself and returned to his girl. Then he relates how he joined a band of robbers who captured the daughter of a Persian Shah; because of his sense of chivalry he tried to rescue the princess, but was defeated and thrown by the robbers into a well. He then managed to escape and reached a country where he became a King. The people of that country learned of that affair, however, and finally he ended up in the asylum.[12] Despite their narrow scope, rigid style, and non-realistic characters, these tales satisfied the literary curiosity of an eager but illiterate audience.

The French occupation touched the life of the Egyptians only slightly. No literary revival like the one indirectly caused by the activities of the American and Jesuit schools in Syria took place in Egypt until the time of Muhammad Ali, who rose to power after the French had left. The schools he established and the educational missions he sent to Europe in the first quarter of the nineteenth century were the main channels through which Western ideas and culture began to trickle into Egypt.[13]

Particularly instrumental in the spread of Western ideas was Madrasat al-Alsun (The School of Languages), established by Muhammad Ali in 1835 under the leadership and supervision of a pioneer Egyptian intellectual Rifa'a Rafi' al-Tahtawi (1801-73).[14] With his students, he translated more than one thousand books into Turkish as well as into Arabic. But since the majority of these were military and scientific treatises, designed to serve Muhammad Ali's purpose in creating a modern, strong Egypt, they had no immediate effect on Arabic literature.

When Muhammad Ali sent the first large educational mission to France in 1826, al-Tahtawi was nominated by the Shaykh Hasan al-'Attar to accompany it as religious adviser. This stay of a few years in Paris afforded him the opportunity to learn the language and to study French social life. His book *Takhlis al-Ibriz fi Talkhis Paris*, which appeared for the first time in 1834, gives a full description of his trip to France and of his life and observations in that country. The discussions of French customs and ways of life omit nothing which aroused his curiosity. He was particularly astonished by the progress of the French in the arts and sciences, by their prosperity and their education, and by their look of cleanliness, as compared to the Egyptians. He also found time to become acquainted with a number of distinguished French Orientalists, including Caussin de Percival, Pierre Amédée Jaubert, and Sylvestre de Sacy, some of whom made use of al-Tahtawi's knowledge of Arabic in their translations. On the other hand, al-Tahtawi learned from them and was able to read books on ancient civilizations, Greek philosophy, and various sciences. He became interested in the trends of French thought and read Voltaire, Rousseau, Montesquieu, and Racine.

Al-Tahtawi seems to have been influenced considerably by French liberal democracy and by French revolutionary ideas. During the revolution of 1830 against Charles X, he sympathized with the revolutionaries rather than the government. In fact, he summarized the ideas of the French revolutionaries, defended them, and explained them to Arabic readers.[15]

A unique figure in the history of Arabic thought in the first half of the nineteenth century,[16] al-Tahtawi was the first Egyptian intellectual who thoroughly understood Western ideals and was able to transmit them to his conservative society without prejudice. His writings and ideas created an intellectual movement whose form and substance were not only a far cry from the thinking which had prevailed in Egypt since Islamic medieval times but were instrumental in constructing a new social and cultural foundation of his country. This movement called for a re-evaluation of those archaic traditions which had impeded the progress of Egyptian civilization. Despite his traditional Azharite schooling and thinking, and his rigid religious upbringing, al-Tahtawi revealed an open mind which accepted and appreciated European ideas and civilization.[17] But, of course, such foreign notions were thought by his co-religionists to be morally harmful and hostile to their way of life.

But al-Tahtawi's importance for modern Arabic literature does not lie in his *Takhlis al-Ibriz*, or in the other seventeen books he either wrote or translated. His major contribution was the translation into Arabic of *Les Aventures de Télémaque*, by François de Salignac de la Mothe Fénelon, Archbishop of Cambrai (1651-1715). Titled *Mawaqi' al-Aflak fi Waqai' Tilimik* (The Positions of the Celestial Spheres in Relation to the Adventures of Telemachus),[18] this was al-Tahtawi's only translation of Western prose fiction and, more important, one of the earliest translations of French fiction to appear in the Arab world.

Yet al-Tahtawi's purpose in translating *Télémaque* was not primarily literary. The reason he chose this particular piece lies in his frame of mind and his condition at the time. In 1849 he was appointed as a principal of an elementary school in the Sudan. Although the pretext was that his services were badly needed there, in reality he was exiled to that country by the Viceroy Abbas I. A slanderer had intrigued against al-Tahtawi and brought to the attention of the Viceroy some of al-Tahtawi's revolutionary ideas in *Takhlis al-Ibiriz*. Wronged

and humiliated by his exile, al-Tahtawi, who could not openly criticize an unjust ruler, resorted to fiction to express his indignation and to attack despotism
indirectly.[19] In *Télémaque* he found an allegory which perfectly fitted his case
and the injustice done to him.[20] It is not surprising, therefore, that the translation appeared for the first time in 1867 in Beirut, and not in Egypt, where he
did not dare publish it.

Nevertheless, the translation has literary merit. Both the Arabic title and
the text itself show the extent to which a conservative Muslim could adapt
Western literature to the spirit and conditions of his time. Gracing his work
with traditional elegant rhymed prose and embellishing it with popular Islamic
proverbs, al-Tahtawi adhered to the original copy in its general outlines. He
apparently meant to dress his work in an Egyptian garb with Egyptianized
figures.

This effort showed at least an initial departure from traditional and static
literary models and opened a gate, however narrow, to future possibilities for
the modernization of imaginative literature.

This tentative beginning gained impetus with the Europeanization policy
of the Khedive Isma'il (1863-79), in whose reign many native and European
schools were opened, and under whose guidance the whole system of education underwent many changes which affected the development of literature.[21]
Although the Europeanization of Egypt was eventually built upon the foundation laid by Muhammad Ali, most, if not all students in the schools he
established were drawn from the feudal Mamluk families which formed the
social and political elite. The Egyptian natives were not yet interested in having
their children educated and therefore refused to send them to school unless
forced by the government.

Furthermore, Muhammad Ali was evidently less interested in education
per se than in the aggrandizement of his political ambition to create an empire.
The schools he established were meant to serve his army and support his military schemes, and to provide qualified personnel for the civil service. But in his
eagerness to provide his country with professional specialists, Muhammad Ali
gave little attention to the critical problem of establishing a program of general
elementary education for all his people.[22]

Higher education faced many operational problems. In the first place,
qualified staff members were not available in adequate numbers. Teachers
were either brought in from Europe, with all the financial problems such recruitment entailed, or drawn from the few members of Napoleon's army who
remained in Egypt. Moreover, the lack of textbooks in Arabic made interpreters necessary. Lectures delivered in French, were usually translated
simultaneously and dictated to the students.

Because of such difficulties, the Department of Education decided to
send the graduates of these schools to Europe, mainly to France, to further

their studies. To prepare them for advanced studies, the government established an Egyptian school in Paris to train them in the French language. The
future Khedive of Egypt, Isma'il, was one of the students at this school. An
Armenian, Istefan (Stephen) Bey, a student in the first Egyptian educational
mission to France in 1826, was appointed its principal. He was assisted by
another Armenian, Khalil Effendi Charakian, though most of the staff of this
school were French army officers, appointed by the French Ministry of War.[23]

The premature death in 1848 of Ibrahim Pasha, son of Muhammad Ali,
who had new plans for the advancement of the school, and the French revolution in that same year impeded the progress of this school and ultimately forced its closing. During the reign of both Viceroys Abbas I (1848-54) and Sa'id
(1854-63), the fate of the Egyptian schools established by Muhammad Ali was
sealed.[24] By 1848, the number of graduates who were qualified for the civil service had already exceeded the need of the government for employees. And the
period of peace which followed the troubled era of Muhammad Ali lessened
the demand for army officers, military technicians, and other qualified personnel who came from the same schools. In general, a conservative reaction
against influences from the West had set in. Under Abbas I (noted for his anti-
Western feelings) all schools of higher education except the Military Academy
were closed down.

When Isma'il ascended the throne in 1863, Egypt had only one elementary school, one secondary school, one military academy, a medical school, a
midwifery school, and a school of chemistry. Isma'il set out to revive the
schools which his grandfather, Muhammad Ali, had established and resumed
educational missions to Europe. Furthermore, new administrative measures
were taken. A ministry of education was established for the operation of the
schools, which now came to be known as al-Madaris al-Amiriyyah. They were
classified into three types: elementary, secondary, and higher education.
When the procedure for popular education was complete, a broad foundation
supporting more intense and specialized studies had reversed the educational
system in the time of Muhammad Ali.[25]

Isma'il also established new schools of law and the liberal arts. One of
these, Madrasat al-Idarah (The School of Administration), later became the
Law School, to which was added the old School of Languages. This new institution produced qualified government personnel and prepared the future
political leaders of Egypt.

Al-Tahtawi's liberal ideas contributed to this education revival. Influenced by French ideals, he felt that education in Egypt would be incomplete if
Egyptian women were deprived of it. The opening of two secondary schools
for girls was a brave step toward the emancipation of Egyptian women. Unfortunately, this commendable effort was destined to failure because the ultra-
conservative element in Egyptian society was not prepared to accept or tolerate
such a daring change.

Another proponent of education in Egypt, Ali Mubarak Pasha (1823-93)[26] also studied in France, where he specialized in military engineering. But his responsibilities during the short period he was Minister of Education brought him into more direct contact with specific problems. Hence he was more pragmatic in his approach than al-Tahtawi.

The crucial problem Mubarak faced was the lack of qualified teachers, mainly of Arabic, in the state schools. Al-Azhar was the only institution he could use to meet this urgent need. But its archaic and traditional methods of teaching, which had been followed since medieval times, posed another problem. Seeking to develop teachers who would use more flexible methods to suit the rapidly changing conditions of education, he determined to reform the practices of al-Azhar by introducing modern Western techniques. The idea met with bitter opposition from al-Azhar's Ulama, however, and failed to materialize.

Not discouraged by this failure, Mubarak struck upon the brilliant idea of establishing in 1872 an all-male school, *Dar al-Ulum,* to provide the future teachers for the new schools. This was to be wider in scope than al-Azhar, adding natural sciences, social sciences, and mathematics to the traditional religious and philological subjects. Indeed, it was a courageous attempt to graft a progressive and dynamic Westernized system onto a static educational scheme. To support his new schools, Mubarak established the Khedivial Library, which housed new as well as old books gathered from various collections around the country.

In addition to these empirical measures, Mubarak turned to fiction to convey the importance of education to his countrymen. He also sought indirectly to reprimand the 'Ulama of al-Azhar for their rigid ideas by writing the romance *'Alam al-Din.*[27] The title character is a young man whose father, a villager, sends him to al-Azhar. Upon completing his studies, he teaches there, and soon he gets married. One day he meets an English traveler who admires the Arabic language and wishes to perfect himself in it in order to publish Arabic manuscripts. The Englishman, perhaps thinking that the Azharite shaykh is the companion he needs, proposes to take him to Europe. 'Alam al-Din's pupils dislike this proposal and criticize their master for accepting a journey in the company of a non-Muslim foreigner. He silences them by invoking a Qur'anic verse which enjoins the Muslim believers to extend help to an infidel who appeals to them for help, in order that he may hearken to the word of God. His wife encourages him to take the trip, and finally he leaves, taking with him his son, Burhan al-Din. The narrative presents 'Alam al-Din's description of the countries and the things he saw in Europe and his impressions of a civilization completely foreign to him.

This romance unmistakably reflects Mubarak's desire for Westernization and dramatizes his attempt to show that a traditional Muslim society could find common grounds with a progressive, more flexible one. Although the

author states that both the Azharite shaykh and the English traveler are fictitious, it is clear that these two characters represent two different cultures.
'Alam al-Din is an Azharite shaykh, yet, unlike his real-life counterparts, he is
enlightened and wants to learn more about the world, even in the company of
a European and a Christian. Nevertheless, he refuses to accept wholesale
everything he has seen and learned in Europe. As a discerning individual, he
tends to accept what he thinks suitable to his Oriental taste and customs. While
appreciating the civilization of Europe, he does not attempt to sever his relations with his Muslim tradition. Rather, he comes to the conclusion that there
is a great deal of merit in the traditions of his society.

In structure *'Alam al-Din* is clearly related to the Arabic fiction of antiquity. Discursive, descriptive, episodic, and didactic,[28] it lacks the
characterization and plot of a substantial modern novel. The novelty is the introduction of a European character in order to make possible the comparison
between East and West. Like the Azharite 'Alam al-Din, the English traveler is
treated as a pawn in a chess game, ready to move only when and where the
author wants him to. His role is to explain aspects of European civilization to
his Egyptian counterpart.[29] In fact, he is more than merely a guide on a tourist
trip; he is an educated man with wide knowledge of East and West. For instance, when the two travelers board a train, the Englishman asks 'Alam al-
Din what he thinks of it. 'Alam al-Din answers that it reminds him of the Day
of Resurrection, and that the common people in Egypt think that it is moved
by the devil. And here the author fills pages and pages telling his readers
(through railways and their spread throughout the world), the division of the
passenger train into three classes of seats, the number of world passengers, and
their distribution over these three classes.

It seems remarkable, however, that this English traveler draws all his information from French sources. This could only be explained by the fact that
Mubarak himself had studied in France and also served for a time as an
engineer on the Egyptian railways. Moreover, the probability that the author
had read Rousseau's *Émile* and other similar works during his stay in France
helps to account for the particular form which his own work assumed.[30] Furthermore, the author seems to mingle fantasy with fact, particularly in recounting 'Alam al-Din's search for a wife. Instead of utilizing this theme to project
the human aspects of his character, the author discusses the virtue of marriage,
the qualifications of the bride, and the question of whether a man should
choose a rich or a poor wife, a virgin or a widow. He concludes that the poor
but virgin bride would be the best wife. In other words, the author poses as an
Islamic jurist who wants to provide the readers with sound advice concerning
marriage, and the narrative is secondary to his interest. In a few lines, the
author concludes the episode of 'Alam al-Din's search for a wife by stating
that at the end, 'Alam al-Din went to see one of his friends and married his
friend's sister.[31]

Thus the literary efforts of Ali Mubarak attempted to inject Western characters and subject matter into the static modes of Egyptian literature. Like works of the medieval Islamic period, *'Alam al-Din* did not actually break away from the Arabic literary tradition. Principally a didactic work, it did not serve as a foundation for later efforts. But it did prepare the ground for more appreciation and utilization of these models in the future.

Although the educational revival under Isma'il seemed to be a genuine effort to set Egypt on the road to Westernization, it only touched the surface of Egyptian society. Education, which had been a monopoly of the children of the Turkish and Circassian élite, was provided to a great number of native Egyptians. Yet the new schools produced for the most part only a large group of semiliterates, whose number continued to increase under the British occupation in 1882. When education was modified to provide the occupation authorities with suitable government employees, many schools, including the School of Languages, were closed down. The educational missions to Europe were stopped, and emphasis was placed on elementary and secondary training rather than on higher education. Furthermore, while the number of hours for the teaching of English increased, the time devoted to the teaching of Arabic, the native tongue, decreased.

To remedy the decline of Arabic studies and native education in the state-controlled schools, the Egyptians established private schools. These, however, eventually closed down because of insoluble financial, administrative, and academic problems. Not until 1906 was the effort made to found a university designed to shoulder the responsibility of revitalizing education and setting it on the right path. The Egyptian University was officially opened on December 21, 1908.[32]

But the educational revival under Isma'il did have an important consequence for modern Arabic literature: the theatre was introduced into Egypt. In 1868, Isma'il established *Masrah al-Komedi* (Théatre de la Comédie) and in 1869 *Dar al-Opera* (Théatre Khédivial de l'Opéra). These were probably intended less to meet a public demand than to demonstrate the Khedive's policy of westernizing Egypt. Since native literature could not provide the theater and the opera with sufficient subject matter, the borrowing of themes from European or ancient Egyptian sources became imperative. The most prominent works performed during this period were Verdi's *Rigoletto* and *Aida,* whose plot was derived by the French archaeologist Mariette Pasha (1821-81) from papyri sources. While the establishment of the theater did not create an indigenous drama, it did afford writers the opportunity to adapt or Egyptianize a great many Western plays. They could also experiment with dramas whose themes were drawn from Arab history.

As the official use of Arabic dwindled, those who could read French and English found entertainment in the fiction written in these languages. But it was also necessary to satisfy the demand for literature by the semiliterate public, which had been superficially touched by Western ideas. For readers who could neither develop a full taste for Western literature nor any longer find enjoyment in the Arab and Islamic tales of antiquity, French and English texts were translated or, better still, adapted. This activity, which had its roots in al-Tahtawi's translation of *Telémaque,* came to fruition under Isma'il.

At the forefront of this effort was Muhammad 'Uthman Jalal (1829-98).[33] Once a pupil of al-Tahtawi in the school of Languages, Jalal began his career as a member of the Translation Bureau established in 1841. From the beginning he was interested in French literature, mainly drama, and translated many palys into colloquial Egyptian Arabic verse based on the *zajal,* a popular Arabic meter in strophic form. His voluminous translations included several comedies by Molière— *Tartuffe, Les Femmes Savantes, L'Ecole des Maris, L'Ecole des Femmes,* and *Les Facheux—Paul et Virginie,* La Fontaine's fables, and several of Racine's tragedies. He also wrote a play entitled *al-Khaddamin wa al-Mukhaddimin* (Domestic Servants and Employers) in the zajal meter.[34]

Jalal's adaptations were not intended as literal translations; his purpose was more didactic than literary. He also attempted to provide the pupils of the Egyptian schools with books written in understandable and appealing Arabic, while promoting an interest in Western ideas. In order to enhance the appeal of French literature, Jalal not only used colloquial Arabic but went so far as to Egyptianize the names, scenes, and, to some extent, the themes to suit his audience. He gave *Paul et Virginie* the charming but peculiar title *al-Amani wa al-Minna fi Hadith Qabul wa Ward Janna* (Expectation and Graciousness in Relating the Narrative of Qabul and Ward Janna). *Les Fables* by La Fontaine became *al-'Uyun al-Yawaqiz fi al-Amthal wa al-Hikam wa al-Mawa'iz* (Wakeful Eyes Concerning Proverbs, Wisdoms, and Exhortations), and *Tartuffe* became *al-Shaykh Matluf* (Ruined). Jalal gave three of Racine's tragedies— *Esther, Iphigenie,* and *Alexandre le Grand*—the general title *al-Riwayat al Mufida fi 'Ilm al-Tragida* (The Useful Romances Concerning the Science of Tragedy), and his adaptations of four of Molière's comedies were published in 1889 under the title *al-Arba' Riwayat min Nukhab al Tiyatrat* (literally, Four Romances selected for the Theater).

The characters were clearly Egyptianized. For example, Tartuffe became an Egyptian Shaykh Matluf; Madame Pernelle, al-Sit Umm al-Nil; Orgon, Chalbun; and so on. Even the bailiff, Loyal, did not escape Jalal's wit; he became the ma'dhun (a person authorized by Islamic law to perform marriages) 'Abd al-'Al. In Bernardin de St. Pierre's romance Paul became Qabul (Acceptance) and Virginie Ward Janna (Roses of Paradise). Such free adaptations are typical of all Jalal's translations from the French.[35]

Jalal also meant his adaptations to be a source of entertainment. His introduction to La Fontaine's fables explained that to provide pupils with books containing amusing tales, he chose those that, in his opinion, were the most famous in the French language. The Arabic text was intended "to be an example for those who desired to be educated, since these (fables) contained parables, wisdom, and superb themes." He goes on to say that the reason he used simple language was to make them comply with the customs of al-Umma al-Arabiyya (the Arab nation).[36] Although Jalal used the term al-Umma al-Arabiyya in a literary connotation, still it should be of great significance to the history of Arab nationalism. It is a term seldom used by a nineteenth century Egyptian writer.

Jalal's literary effort reflected conservatism which retained its roots in the traditional past yet welcomed and utilized foreign literary models. This tendency was clearly demonstrated by the parables and popular sayings of everyday life which embellished his adapted works. Jalal evidently shared al-Tahtawi's belief that literature is not an art which exists for its own sake, but one that fulfills the dual functions of instruction and entertainment.[37] In presenting French literary models in simple expressive language, he used them as vehicles to convey the traditional notions of Egyptian society, with only a slight touch of the original French ideas.

What Jalal did not take into account was the fact that his literary models were designed to suit a specific audience in seventeenth century France.[38] Thus he did not always discriminate clearly between the universally human and the particular characteristics of a foreign culture, interpreted by authors whose psychology was foreign to their audiences. His adaptation of La Fontaine's *Fables* was unresponsive to the linguistic subtlety of a text intended for sophisticated French readers and stressed their simple, if not naive, didacticism. Egyptian illustrations, were often introduced into these ingenious moral parables, on the assumption that moral "saws" would appeal to readers whose entire literary orientation was didactic. Nevertheless, Jalal made an important contribution to Egyptian literature; through his efforts, the Western stream continued to flow into Arabic waters, revitalizing a literary tradition that was, in many respects, dying of stagnation.

It is evident, however, that Arabic literature in general was not profoundly influenced by the educational revival and the Westernization policy of Isma'il. In fact, these activities were mainly devoted to fields other than literature, such as the study of the Arabic language and law. This tendency is indicated by the great number of Arabic books printed in this period, most of which dealt with grammar, philology, rhetoric, Islamic Shari'a and jurisprudence, and Arab history. This revival probably reflects an effort of Egyptian society to preserve its traditions against Western influence. Nevertheless, many works in different Western disciplines, mainly French law, European history, and studies of Egypt and the Arab East, were also published.

The public press contributed little to this revival of learning. During the first few years of Isma'il's reign, it was mainly a mouthpiece for the government and the Khedive, and a sounding board for his praise. The only publication to escape his grip was *Rawdat al-Madaris,* a school journal supervised by Rifa'a al-Tahtawi. This periodical was concerned with educating and guiding students and "incidentally" encouraged them to publish some of their literary efforts in it. Even when signs of rebellion began to appear toward the end of Isma'il's reign, the intelligentsia were more concerned with political liberation than with any literary renaissance. Hence literary progress lagged behind that of politics.[39]

Although the didactic aspect of literature was of great interest to the educated element during the first few years of Isma'il's reign, by the end of this period the intelligentsia were openly demanding various kinds of reform. This change in attitude may be attributed to several factors, including the awakening of social conscience among the people and their increasing dissatisfaction both with foreign intervention in the affairs of Egypt and with their own government. The last was most manifest in the army, where native officers resented the government's discriminatory policy favoring the Turkish and Circassian minority. But the most significant factors in the changing climate of opinion were the intellectual revolution caused by the teachings of the revolutionist and radical reformer Jamal al-Din al-Afghani (d. 1897)[40] and the different intellectual activities of the Syrian immigrants who flocked to Egypt after the Lebanese massacre of 1860. These two influences affected in one way or another the intellectual and literary trends in Egypt, including the development of the writing of fiction.

Al-Afghani first came to Egypt in 1869, on his way to the Ottoman capital, but remained only forty days. Later he returned and stayed in Egypt from 1871 to 1879, when he was banished by Isma'il, whose despotic rule and Europeanization policy were the target of al-Afghani's sharp criticism. Although he left few writings, al-Afghani's liberal ideas profoundly stirred the conscience of the Muslims. He tried to revolutionize the Islamic world by constantly reminding Muslims that they were intelligent and able to manage their own affairs and to live as a respected civilized nation. He believed that the Muslims had lost their pride in their heritage and culture, and that they should do something to revitalize it. He may have even viewed himself as a kind of Messiah ordained to redeem the Islamic world from the oppression of the infidel Western conquerors.[41]

At his quarters near al-Azhar, al-Afghani lectured on a variety of subjects with great courage and eloquence. But the subject he loved to discuss continuously was the art of writing and speaking Arabic. Before fighting for their rights, he argued, the Muslims should master the secrets of the language of the Qur'an, and he was always surrounded by men of letters, poets, grammarians, and journalists—as well as people from other walks of life. To his disciples and to the majority of the people of his time, al-Afghani spoke not simply as a reformer and a philosopher, but as the "Sage of the East." No words can express his impact on the intellectual life of Egypt so truthfully and precisely as those of the famous Egyptian poet Hafiz Ibrahim:

> The influence of Jamal al-Din was reflected in noble souls, and his words were quickly picked up by attentive ears. The result was that the death sentence was pronounced over *taqlid*, and that God, through him, resurrected the language and resuscitated the remains of composition. He, may God have mercy on him, left Egypt without leaving us a book or writings from which we could learn. But he left us heads to think with and to generate ideas. As if he thought of this when he was on his deathbed, he was heard saying, while breathing his last, that 'we have left the world without leaving a written trace, but we have left traces engraved on breasts'...He left the world as did Socrates without leaving a volume of his writing. And if it were not for Muhammad Abduh, the man of the Afghan would not have been known; likewise, if it were not for Plato, the chief of the Greek philosophers would not have been remembered.[42]

Al-Afghani's many disciples believed, as he did, in the idea of Islamic unity. Though fully aware of European intervention in the affairs of Egypt and in the rest of the Islamic world, they were no less convinced that the despotic rule, whether Ottoman or not, was the major factor in their weakness. Thus the main concern both of the disciples and of their master was to arouse the conscience of the Islamic peoples and to purify Islam from superstitions. They encouraged the Muslims to liberate themselves from unjust government and to throw off the European yoke, and they sought to rally all of the Islamic countries around the Islamic caliphate as a step towards final unity.[43]

While in Egypt, al-Afghani incited young Egyptian patriots against the government of the Prime Minister, Riyad Pasha, and he also helped establish *al-Hizb al-Watani,* the first organized national group of that time.[44]

Muhammad Abduh was probably al-Afghani's most devout follower. Apprehensive about coercive and revolutionary methods of achieving political aims, Abduh believed in a gradual but constructive reform rather than in forced but short-lived changes. Hence he preferred to criticize the unjust rule of Riyad Pasha rather than collaborate with the revolutionary element in the army led by Ahmad 'Urabi (1839-1911). Abduh also believed, with some justification, that the Egyptians were not ready for a revolution, and he was particularly astonished at the radical enthusiasm of the middle and poorer classes. A revolution did erupt in 1882 but was soon suppressed, and Egypt was occupied by British forces and came under British rule.

Although Muhammad Abduh's various activities were mainly devoted to the revitalization of the Arabic language, the purification of Islam from superstition, and the reformation of al-Azhar, he also advocated the writing of the novel and encouraged novelists. It is even said that Sa'id al-Bustani (d. 1901) wrote his story *Dhat al-Khidr*, which was published in the newspaper *al-*

Ahram toward the end of 1884, under the inspiration and direction of Muhammad Abduh. Regarding the novel as a useful instrument for social reform, Abduh wrote an article in *al-Ahram* (May 11, 1881) which reviewed the most popular books of his time.[45] He found that the reading audience obviously preferred works of history, articles dealing with moral subjects, and novels. The latter he called *romaniyat* (romances), and he included among them *Télémaque* and *Kalila wa Dimna*, a book translated from the Pahlevi by Ibn al-Muqaffa' (d. 727). He also called the attention of readers to a number of short stories that had been translated by Salim Naqqash (d. 1884) and by his friend Adib Ishaq (d. 1885) and published in *al-Ahram*.[46] However, Abduh considered fiction of secondary importance, and his role in its development never exceeded the limits of encouragement or compliment.

After the failure of the Urabi revolution, Abduh abandoned politics and devoted his efforts to reforming Islam in order to restore its fundamental characteristics of purity and simplicity. He also worked to revitalize Arabic writing which had become rigid and dull. But while these efforts were a major factor in revolutionizing literary language, they caused no change in themes or subject matter. Nor did they help create new literary genres, such as the novel or play. In form, Arabic literature still reflected ancient modes.

Another of al-Afghani's disciples, Abd Allah Nadim (1843-96), attempted to use colloquial language to satirize the backwardness of the masses in his short-lived newspaper *al-Tankit wa al-Tabkit* (Raillery and Reproof). But his association with the masses remained very strong: he was the only member of the intelligentsia who adhered to the Urabi revolution to the end and, in fact, became the mouthpiece of that revolution. Although he is best known for his fiery nationalistic speeches, he is reported to have encouraged the performance of two plays, *al-Watan* and *al-Arab*, in the school he had personally established. The Khedive Tawfiq attended performances of these plays and even donated money to encourage Nadim. When the revolution failed, Nadim went into hiding for ten years. He reappeared and established a periodical, *al-Ustadh*, in 1892.[47]

The defeat of the 'Urabi revolution in 1882, which was a failure of the nationalist movement at that time, had tremendous repercussions on the Egyptian intellectuals. Pious but intellectually enlightened, they now surrounded Muhammad Abduh and, like him, were determined to serve their country in fields other than politics. Disappointed in the political development of the country, they concentrated their efforts on the revitalization of the ancient Arabic heritage. But their efforts were also restricted to the modernization of style and in no way helped create new fictional genres.

In the meantime, the Syrian belletrists had flooded Egypt with translations of Western novels of various kinds.[48] Although in the first half of the nineteenth century there was very little literary activity among the Syrians in Egypt, and what little there was had no significant effect upon the development of Arabic fiction, the situation changed after the massacres of 1860. After many Syrians had been brutally slaughtered by the Druzes, large numbers of Syrian Christians left their native land for Constantinople, Europe, and Egypt. Those who emigrated to Egypt became involved in a remarkably wide range of cultural activities, publishing newspapers, performing on the stage, writing and translating European fiction for Arab readers. They brought to these activities a knowledge of European languages, the result of their training at the missionary schools established in Syria during the early nineteenth century. Moreover, Syria's trade with Europe, the presence of European businessmen in Syria, the existence of an Arabic press, and the widespread publication of Arabic books had hastened their cultural sophistication.

From roughly 1850 to 1925 the literary activities of the Egyptians and the Syrian émigrés, particularly in the translation of European prose fiction and drama, were so intertwined that it is all but impossible to distinguish them. Indeed, so many Syrian writers (and dramatic performers) shuttled between Syria and Egypt during this period that one is uncertain whether to classify them as Syrians or Egyptians. But it is clear in any case that they not only composed original works but also translated or adapted a great many works of Western fiction, including numerous dramas.⁴⁹

The émigrés, mostly Christian, actively transmitted European literary as well as scientific thought into Egyptian society. Their effort was aided by their monopoly of newspapers and periodicals, such as *Al-Ahram*, established by the Taqla brothers, and *al-Muqtataf,* founded by Ya'qub Sarruf. In their enthusiasm, however, these Syrians failed to take into account the different cultural conditions and specific needs of the Egyptian society. Some of them —for example, Dr. Shibli Shumayyil (d. 1917) and Farah Anton (d. 1922)—went so far as to introduce toward the end of the nineteenth century progressive yet anachronistic concepts. The theories of evolution and communism were not only incomprehensible to the majority of the Egyptians but completely foreign to their society. Indeed, Muhammad Abduh entered into heated argument with Anton to defend the tenets of Islam against Anton's allegation that Christianity was more tolerant and receptive to scientific investigation than the religion of Islam.

The majority of native Egyptian belletrists continued to attempt to revive the Arab heritage. But, at best, they paved the way for the Egyptian "renaissance" which began to appear in the first decade of this century. They regarded the Syrians' translations with great suspicion, dismissing them as a cheap means to make easy profit and complaining about the degradation of classic Arabic style; the style of most of the translated novels was in fact very poor. Furthermore, since most of them dealt with love, intrigue, murder and adultery, they were considered not merely worthless, but dangerous to public morals, particularly in the undiscerning younger generation. In fact, most of the conservative writers regarded the novel not as a valid literary form but as an alien and illegitimate child of Europeanized society.[50]

By the turn of the century, however, a few Egyptian belletrists, motivated by quick profit, were competing with the Syrians in translating European fiction into Arabic. Others, like Muhammad Ibrahim al-Muwaylihi, utilized the *maqama* to criticize the social and cultural foibles of their society. This revival of the *maqama* may be considered as a counteraction to the translated European novels: it met the demand of the Egyptian reading public and, to a certain extent competed with the translations.[51]

The drama was also a target for some critics. Translated plays, dealing mainly with mysteries and love affairs, were considered not only alien to Egyptian society, but dangerous because they treated subjects completely out of harmony with Oriental and Islamic customs. Two Egyptian authors, Muhammad Abd al-Muttalib and Abd al-Mu'ti Mar'i, made this point clear in their book *Hayat Muhalhil aw Harb al-Basus*. After describing the factors that prevented the Arabs from developing the drama, and criticizing European writers for building their plays around cheap love affairs, the authors stated:

> Our Oriental upbringing and Islamic morals forbid us to accept such customs. No literary type has entered our country except this repulsive one. You do not even know what themes of amorous affairs and of the affairs of women do to the youngsters and what bad effect they would leave upon them. Therefore, our young generation, at the beginning, responded to this literary type as fun and entertainment, while our sensible men did not concern themselves with it but rather considered it unnecessary at a time when we were in dire need of fundamental works. But a thing may appear to some people as necessary while to others not necessary. This is why the dramatic art found supporters among men in the field of education, who in later years introduced it into the schools.[52]

They also set forth their plan to provide students with a series of plays based on themes drawn from ancient history, in order to stimulate appreciation of past Arab accomplishments. They insisted that they would avoid amorous subjects or women's affairs, so that their works would be more conducive to virtue.

The Christian writer, Jurji Zaydan (d. 1914), who devoted his pen to the service of Arab history in works ranging from historical novels to an account of Islamic civilization, viewed the translation of Western literature, mainly the novel, in a different way. He termed this activity a literary renaissance and compared his time with the Abbasid era, when Muslim writers translated tales from the Persian. The stories translated from French, English, and Italian, known as *riwayat* (romances), were, Zaydan insisted, meant for entertainment rather than for social or historical benefit. Zaydan noted that sensible Arab readers had welcomed these romances in the place of the tales which were popular among the common people in the nineteenth century, and which the Arabs had known since the medieval Islamic period, because they found them more plausible and more suited to the spirit of the time.[53] He found the translated novels particularly appealing because, unlike the ancient books of Arabic literature, they are presented in a very simple language, close to the understanding of the reading public, which was not educated enough to understand the florid and complicated style of antiquity.

Popular taste was influenced also by a psychological factor. During the period of despondency after the failure of the Urabi revolution and the British occupation of Egypt, the majority of the literate or semiliterate public turned to fiction to escape political reality. And at just this time the Syrian belletrists and journalists were busily engaged in the translation of Western fiction. Nevertheless, despite Zaydan's optimistic attitude, these literary forms, particularly the novel, remained in disrepute until the middle of the present century. As late as 1937, an article by al-Zayyat (d. 1968) in his weekly magazine *al-Risala*, explaining the policy of his publication and thanking his readers for their support, reflected the prevailing antipathy toward stories:

> These readers did not want *al-Risala* to be a platform of praise or a source of bias. They wanted it to retain a state of poise and dispassion and unsentimentality. They had even categorically refused to see it assign a place for stories.[54]

The writer apparently wants to voice his readers' opinion that storytelling is a shameful art. It would therefore be a disgrace to his publication.

The translation of Western prose fiction continued to grow in Egypt in the nineteenth century, although a native Egyptian novel was not created until the first quarter of the twentieth century, when the conditions for its emergence became favorable. In fact, the chief cultural development of the period was the attempt to initiate various social and educational reforms which paved the way for the birth of the future Egyptian novel. The literary efforts characterized by realism and courage, mainly in an attempt to adapt European ideas and European literary models to an Oriental society and to revitalize and modify native ideas to suit the real social conditions, were limited in theme and scope. They reflected the genuine desire of some intellectuals to educate their countrymen but could not reach the majority of the people at least until the Egyptians finally succeeded in 1908 in establishing the Egyptian University. Fashioned after European institutions, the university was intended to revive the Arabic heritage and language, which the British occupation had repressed, and to promote higher education, which had been forbidden under British authority. Meanwhile, those Egyptians who were financially able sent their sons to Europe to continue their studies. Educators like Ahmad Lutfi al-Sayyid (d. 1963) called for a comprehensive study of the relation of the individual to his society and for a scientific interpretation of human conduct which would make it more responsive to European intellectual thought and to European institutions. This program indicated that the ground was gradually being prepared for the full-scale cultivation of Western ideas, and literary models were soon reflected in Egyptian fiction.[55]

CHAPTER II

THE RISE OF THE ARAB DRAMA

IN SYRIA AND EGYPT

In ancient Arabic literature drama was simply unknown. Within Arab society in the pre-Islamic and the Islamic periods, literature centered mainly on non-dramatic poetry in a tradition that was oral but not imitative. Furthermore, the Arabs of the ninth and tenth centuries A.D. neglected Greek drama, preferring to translate Greek philosophy and medicine.[1] Even ancient Syrian scholars, who introduced the Arabs to Greek philosophy and who themselves translated many of these works into Arabic, had no concept of Greek dramatic genres. Thus, Abu Bishr Matta ibn Yunus (d. 940) in his translation of Aristotle's *Poetics* understood "tragedy" and "comedy" to mean "praise" and "satire." This misreading led the Arab philosopher Ibn Rushd (Averroes) (d.1198), to apply what he thought to be Aristotle's definitions of tragedy and comedy to traditional types of Arabic poetry, *madh* (praise) and *hija* (satire) which he supported by examples from native poetry.[2]

Some contemporary Arab scholars maintain that it was the Islamic religion which prevented translation of Greek dramas, since the Arabs thought they involved pagan gods and mythology. However, there was no contradiction between Islamic religion and Greek philosophy, particularly logic, which was equally effective in either culture: the Muslims used it to support many Islamic tenets against their opponents.[3]

Other critics maintain that dramatic composition requires objective thinking and an ability to particularize subject matter which ancient poets lacked. They contend that the ancient Arabs had no aesthetic understanding of tragedy, although they may have experienced it, and therefore could not produce dramas like those of the Greeks.[4]

Popular Entertainment

Nevertheless, it is certain that the Arabs in medieval times knew and enjoyed some types of theater. For example, the shadow play—a kind of puppet show called *Khayl al-Zill*—was popular in Egypt in the twelfth century and survived through the nineteenth century. Indeed, there was a highly developed shadow-play literature. The most popular "playwright" was Shams al-Din Abu Abd Allah Muhammad ibn Daniyal al-Mawsili al-Khuza'i, nicknamed al-

Kahhal (the oculist), who probably died in the first part of the fourteenth century. His book *Tayf al-Khayal fi Ma'rifat Khayal al-Zill* (Phantom of Imagination of the Knowledge of the Shadow Play) was edited in part and published by Georg Jacob.[5]

In nineteenth-century Egypt a Turkish puppet show called Qaragoz (black-eyed) was popular among the lower classes. This does not mean that the form was Turkish in origin and had been brought by the Turks after their occupation of Egypt at the beginning of the sixteenth century. More probably, Turkish was used in the Qaragoz plays because of the decline of Arabic and the predominance of the language of the conqueror.[6] The shadow play was also popular in Syria and North Africa in the nineteenth century.[7]

The Egyptian public's enjoyment of another type of theatrical entertainment was recorded by a German traveler, Carsten Niebuhr, who visited Egypt in 1780. When he arrived in Cairo, he never expected to see theatrical performances, but he did go to see a play of sorts. A troupe consisting of Muslims, Christians, and Jews performed in the open air on an improvised stage in the yard of one of the houses. There was a backdrop behind which the actors changed their costumes. Niebuhr asserts that although no European resident in Cairo had ever witnessed the performance of a native Egyptian comedy, he saw one in the house of an Italian. It was performed in Arabic, interspersed by Arabic music, and Niebuhr was not attracted to it because of his ignorance of the language. But he wittily noted that the role of the heroine was performed by a costumed actor who had a great deal of trouble concealing his beard.

Niebuhr also described the audience's response to the play. Apparently the heroine, a vicious and cunning woman, attracted travelers to her tent, where she robbed them of their belongings and money and then beat and expelled them. When this scene was repeated several times, some of the spectators became tired and irritated and shouted their total disapproval of such a boring and immoral act. The rest of the audience soon joined in, forcing the actors to stop the performance before the play was half completed.[8]

A similar type of entertainment was described by Edward William Lane, who was in Cairo in the 1830's. He saw low and ridiculous farces performed by actors called "al-Muhabbizun," professional comedians who performed at festivals, weddings, and circumcisions, at the houses of the rich and before dignitaries, and sometimes performed in the squares of Cairo. Their performances were crude, and, "it is chiefly by vulgar jests and indecent actions that they amuse and obtain applause."[9] The actors were mainly men and boys, for it was still considered indecent for women to appear in public. One of these farces was performed before the Pasha, Muhammad Ali, the Viceroy of Egypt, in honor of the circumcision of one of his sons. The characters were a chief of a village, his servant, a governor of a district, a Copt clerk, a fallah, and his wife. The performance was preceded by drumming, piping, and dancing, and the musicians and dancers acted in the play as simple fallahin. The purpose of this farce, it seems, was to bring to the attention of the ruler of Egypt the oppression of the peasants by government officials, particularly tax collectors.[10]

Western Theaters

Such performances cannot be considered the ancestor of the modern Egyptian theater of drama. There is no evidence that the kind of farce described by Lane had any continuity or connection with later developments, which might be said to begin with the French occupation of Egypt. Napoleon's expedition included a number of actors and musicians who performed French dramas. A few clubs were improvised for such entertainment, and one of them, the Tivoli, built within the French community, had a full stage.[11] A contemporary Egyptian writer Abd al-Rahman al-Jabarti, mentions that the French met once every ten days in a place called al-Komedi (Comedy) at al-Azbakiyya, where they watched plays for four hours during the evening. No one was allowed to enter this area unless he wore a special dress and presented an identification card.[12]

Another stage was established by the French commander Jacques Menou, who became Commander-in-Chief of the French forces after General Kléber was assassinated in 1800.[13] But that theater and the dramas performed there were obviously French. The only effect they might have had on the Egyptians was in arousing curiosity about such novelties. Had the French established a firm foothold and remained in Egypt for a long time, their theatrical activity would probably have inspired some Egyptians to attempt native performances. These, in turn, could have stimulated playwrights and indigenous dramas and eventually created an audience for a national theater.

This did not happen, of course, but the French influence appeared again under Muhammad Ali. A letter by the French Consul in Cairo dated November 8, 1829, indicates that a French stage had been established by young amateurs to entertain the members of Napoleon's expedition who preferred to remain in Egypt after the evacuation of the troops and the French teachers and technicians recruited by Muhammad Ali himself. Recruiting some young ladies, from respectable French families, these amateurs had performed two plays *L'Avocat Patelin* and *Le Gastronome sans argent*—on November 3. The performance was preceded by a verse introduction composed by one of the actors.[15]

A few years later Gérard de Nerval, reported on another theater, called "Teatro del Cairo". He attended an amateur performance announced as a benefit for the blind. The stalls were packed with Italians and Greeks in red caps, making a great deal of noise, some officers sat in front of the stage, and the boxes were filled with veiled women, most of whom wore Oriental dress. The play was *La Mansarde des Artistes*, and several major roles were performed by young people from Marseille; the leading lady was Madame Bonhomme, the head of the French reading room. Most of the female spectators were Greek, Armenian and Jewish women from high society. They were beautifully dressed in taffeta and black silk and covered their faces with white veils. After leaving the theater, de Nerval says, these women rode on their donkeys preceded by grooms carrying torches.[16]

An Italian company established at l'Okella Neuve in Alexandria was probably the first to issue instructions regulating the proper operation of the theater. And when Regnault travelled to Egypt in 1854, he went to see an Italian drama played on an open air stage. The interesting aspect of Regnault's report is that the chief actress was Egyptian, with a bronze complexion and a charming voice with which she tried to imitate the Italian accent.[17]

Other stages were established by Europeans in coffee houses, such as the Grand Orient and El-Cazar cafés, as well as in the Palais Royal; the latter is mentioned by Louis Gardey,[18] and there are also reports of a theater in the time of the Viceroy Sa'id Pasha (1854-63).[19] When Isma'il rose to power, he built the Théâtre de la Comédie in 1868, at the same spot where a hall built by Sa'id once stood, and the Théâtre Khédivial de l'Opéra.

Clearly, these stages were neither Arab nor Egyptian and had no direct effect on the development of a native theater. The drama did not become popular, because the general public could not understand the languages in which the plays were performed; furthermore, most ordinary people could not afford the entrance fee. But the European theater did appeal to members of Egyptian high society, who attended either from sheer curiosity or in search of novel amusement. In general, the social and cultural conditions which hampered the Egyptian novel probably also prevented the rise of a full-fledged Egyptian theater and an Egyptian drama. In any case, not until the Khedive Isma'il established his theaters was there any individual interest in the possibility of a popular stage.

Marun Naqqash and his Successors

Conditions were more favorable in Syria, where theater was introduced before 1870 by Marun ibn Mikha'il Naqqash. He may be rightfully acclaimed as the founder of the Arab theater.[20]

Naqqash was born in Sayda (Sidon) on February 9, 1817, to a Maronite family, but raised in Beirut, where the family moved in 1825. A precocious boy, he began to learn, besides Arabic, Turkish, French, and Italian, how to compose poetry at eighteen, and soon mastered Oriental music. He also studied bookkeeping, which qualified him for the position of chief clerk at the Customs Department in Beirut. For a time he was a member of the Beirut Chamber of Commerce, and later he became a businessman. His work took him to Aleppo, Damascus, and the rest of Syria. In 1846 he visited Alexandria and Cairo and then sailed to Italy, which had strong relations with the Arab

East. In Italy he visited many theaters and was so impressed by them that he decided to introduce the stage into his own country. Upon his return to Beirut, he formed a troupe with some friends who shared his enthusiasm. His efforts were crowned by the staging of his drama *al-Bakhil* (The Miser) toward the end of 1847.[21] This may be considered the first drama in the Arabic language.

The guests Naqqash invited to the performance at his home included foreign consuls and the dignitaries of Beirut. Soon news of his drama spread, and it was even written about in the European press. (There was no press in Syria at the time).[22] The favorable response of the audience and the eagerness of the people of Beirut to watch this novelty encouraged Naqqash to stage another drama *Abu al-Hasan al-Mughaffal aw Harun al-Rashid* (Abu al-Hasan the Gullible or the Caliph Harun al-Rashid), whose plot was borrowed from the *Thousand and One Nights*. To this performance, again in his house, either at the end of 1849 or the beginning of 1850, he invited the foreign consuls, the Turkish Wali, and a group of Ottoman high officials who happened to be in the city, as well as the dignitaries of Beirut. The guests apparently were full of praise, and encouraged by the good reception, Naqqash applied to the authorities and obtained a high firman (decree) to build a theater adjacent to his home. On this stage his third and last drama, *al-Salit al-Hasud* (The Impudent and Jealous Young Man) was performed in 1851. This theater was later purchased by the Papal Nuncio in Beirut and, in accordance with Naqqash's will, converted into a church (probably the present Santa Church standing in the Jummayza quarter).[23]

Naqqash's dramas were not as widely popular as he hoped. Only a few foreigners and a handful of educated natives appreciated them; the majority of the people, from sheer ignorance, remained indifferent. At first they had to be coaxed to attend his productions[24] by the promise that the plays would contain folk music and poetry.[25] At times Naqqash became utterly doubtful about the success of his art. As one of the characters in *al-Salit al-Hasud* (Act III, Scene 4) says, "The continuance of the theater in our country is unlikely."[26]

The brilliant career of Marun Naqqash ended when, on a business trip to Tarsus, he was stricken by a severe fever and died on June 1, 1855, at the premature age of thirty-eight. But his troupe and others whom he had trained in theatrical technique, continued to compose and perform dramas in Syria.[27] Two decades after his death, his nephew, Salim Naqqash (d. 1884), moved the troupe to Egypt, where they performed *Abu al-Hasan al-Mughaffal* in 1876.

Because *al-Bakhil*, the first of Naqqash's dramatic works, has the same title as Molière's *L'Avare*, some scholars believe that it was a translation. However, Jurji Zaydan, a contemporary, emphatically states that this was "the first drama in the Arabic language,"[28] and that Naqqash had "composed this play from the beginning to the end." But Najm goes on to acknowledge that Naqqash wrote his play after he had read Molière's comedy and made use of its characterization and humorous elements.[29] The treatment of miserliness or stinginess, which constitutes the main humorous element of the drama, shares much with *L'Avare*.[30]

The most striking feature of *al-Bakhil* is that it is written in verse rather than prose and that it is all set to music. The full title reads *Riwaya Mudhika Kulluha Mulahhana Dhat Khamsat Fusul Ma'rufa bi Riwayat al-Bakhil* (Comical Romance [or Drama] in Five Acts all of which is set to Music Known as the Romance of the Miser).[31] Whether this description was devised by the author or his brother, Niqula, who collected and published Naqqash's three plays in *Arzat Lubnan* is not important. What is significant is that the drama "is all set to music".[32] One might speculate that it was meant to be an opera, especially since the author's intention is evident from the introduction he delivered before its first performance. After mentioning his visits to the theaters in Europe and ascribing certain moral and artistic benefits to them, he classified dramas into different categories: "One of them, which the Europeans call prose, is divided into comedy, drama, and tragedy, which are performed without verse and unsung; the second one, which they call opera, is sung." Naqqash goes on to explain:

> It is most important and necessary for me to compose and translate in the first place the first and not the second type (the opera) because it is easier and more likely...But what made me deviate from the norm and follow this course is that the second type (the opera) was to me more tasteful, desirable, splendid and delightful. Secondly, my opinion, desire and earnest concern made me inclined to believe that the second (opera) would be preferable to my people and kindred.[33]

Niqula, in his introduction to *Arzat Lubnan*, noted the great care his brother took to set his dramas to music. In order to simplify the task of those who wished to perform the plays, he numbered the roles of the actors to indicate the type of song or melody to be used for each role. At the end of *al-Bakhil*, Niqula appended a list of melodies and songs numbered to correspond with the labels in the text. He explained the nature and source of each melody, some of which were based on Egyptian popular songs, others on French songs and melodies. These numbers certainly indicate that the drama was meant to be sung throughout. Thus *al-Bakhil* was not merely the first native Arabic drama, but the first Arabic comic opera.

Naqqash's use of varied dialects and speech patterns to further the development of the plot was particularly effective. Generally, the dialogue is a mixture of classical Arabic and the colloquial speech of Lebanon. For example, 'Isa uses Egyptian dialect while impersonating the Egyptian secretary, and two others imitate Turks by speaking broken Arabic. This radical device predictably drew some criticism, and even Niqula tried to justify his borhter's use of non-standard language by explaining that it was only his first drama; this, of course, misses the point entirely. Niqula also argued that Naqqash deliberately used imperfect speech in order to encourage others to compose realistic dialogue. "If it were not for *al-Bakhil's* poor language I would have not been able to compose the riwaya (drama) of *al-Shaykh al Jahil* (The Ignorant Old Man), which is filled with grammatical mistakes."[36] But these arguments are rather academic, for despite its artistic and literary innovations, Naqqash's first play was obviously well received even in the conservative Syrian milieu, at least by the literate élite.

His next venture, *Abu al-Hasan al-Mughaffal*, was superficially based on the *Thousand and One Nights* story "al-Na'im wa al-Yaqzan" (The Sleeping and the Wakeful).[37] But it departs from this source in both plot and structure. Unlike the story, it treats the problem of the movement from one social class to another. Whether or not Naqqash was aware of the social implications, the encounters of his protagonist, who comes from a low class, with the privileges of a higher class intermingle questions of social standing with the problem of appearance and reality, which is the point of the original story. Abu al-Hasan has always dreamt of bettering his lot, and his daydreams have become a reality to him. However, the Caliph and his Vizir devise a ruse to show him that the world is not as he sees it. Even when he is given the power and authority he has never had before, he faces as many problems as he did when he was poor and powerless.

Unlike *al-Bakhil, Abu al-Hasan* is only partially set to music. A notice at the beginning of the text indicates that the index of songs has been numbered the same way as in *al-Bakhil*, but it goes on to state that a line indicates the places where the song ends and the verse or prose speech of the actors begins.[38] The index of melodies at the end of the drama refers to the same French songs used in *al-Bakhil*. Thus, though *Abu al-Hasan* is undoubtedly a musical drama, its language is a combination of prose and poetry. In Western terms, it is more musical comedy than opera.

The style of this play is less lucid than that of *al-Bakhil* and uses the traditional rhymed-prose prevalent at the time. (There are also some foreign terms, characters, speeches, and stage directions). Parts of the dialogue are intolerably longwinded, especially in the first act, which treats of the love and troubles of Abu al-Hasan. Some of the characters could be eliminated without damaging the structure, the theme, or the sequence of events; for example, the role of al-Hajja, Abu al-Hasan's mother, is unquestionably superfluous. Furthermore, the author does not provide clear stage directions. A strange note at the beginning of the second act, for example, indicates that the setting is the *Saray* of the Caliph and that the room contains the royal clothes, a crown, and a scepter. But *Saray* (more correctly *Saraya*) is a Persian word for "palace," and the Caliphs of Baghdad never wore crowns or carried scepters.

Naqqash makes charming use of Molière's wit. For example, when Abu al-Hasan asks his brother Sa'id if he knows the attractive Da'd, if he visits her family, and if he has any relations with them, the scene follows the same pattern as Harpagon's questioning of his son Cléante about Marian in *L'Avare*. Cléante praises the young lady before he realizes his father's interests in her.[39] This entertaining drama must have appealed to the nineteenth-century Syrian audience, and the mere fact that Naqqash adapted a story from the *Thousand and One Nights* to the stage is evidence of his fertile imagination and prodigious originality.

In contrast, the plot and setting of Naqqash's third and last drama, *al-Salit al-Hasud*, reflects various aspects and customs specific to Syria in the middle of the nineteenth century, although it also has a Molièrian touch.[40] The characters are recognizable as contemporary types and the action centers around the practice of fixed marriages. Parental authority was dominant, but children sometimes defied it. There are three acts, and the forty-six scenes are written partly in verse and partly in rhymed prose. The latter does not seem awkward or affected; however, like Naqqash's second drama, it is only partially set to music, and the published text has a numbered index of songs and melodies.

Judged in modern critical terms, the style and language are generally inferior. At times the dialogue is lengthy and boring. To display his literary knowledge, the author incorporates into the first act a complete ode on the art of prosody, with a lengthy analysis of the verse meters and their subdivisions. He also explains the correct meanings of many terms that had been used erroneously by the public. In the third act, one of the characters, Jirjis, concludes this discussion with an intolerably long statement explaining inconsistent or defective rhyme and showing how the poet can avoid these defects. Such unnecessary interpolations not only weaken the texture but also obscure the action of the play.[41]

Nevertheless, Naqqash grants all his characters, including the heroine Rachel, a remarkable degree of freedom to determine their lives. At no point does Rachel appear to be oppressed or controlled by her father. The lively and dynamic characters are only occasionally obscured by the interpolation of unnecessary subjects. Particularly successful is the portrait of Sim'an, Rachel's fiancé, who despite his stubbornness, shows a fragile spirit.

Molière's touch is again conspicuous. The dialogue between Abu 'Isa and his pupil, Jirjis, regarding what is prose and what is verse brings to the memory a similar dialogue between Jourdain and philosophy master in *Le Bourgeois Gentilhomme*.[42] The strange and thoughtless Sim'an recalls Alceste in *Le Misanthrope*. Furthermore, the two valets, Jabbur and Bishara, who appear before Rachel and her maid, Barbara, as wealthy men of prestige remind us of Mascarille and Jodelet in *Les Precieuses Ridicules*. When Madelon and Cathos reject their respective lovers, La Grange and Du Croisy, these lovers employ their valets Mascarille and Jodelet to expose the weakness of the two ladies. To conceal their identity, Mascarille clothes himself in his master's finery and assumes the title Marquis of Mascarille while Jodelet appears as the

Viscount of Jodelet.[43] In fact, Naqqash admits through Sim'an that he has "borrowed some of its (this drama's) themes from the riwayat Ifranjiyya (European dramas)."[44]

To evaluate Naqqash's plays properly, however, one must consider the social, political, and literary conditions prevailing in nineteenth-century Lebanon. His work was not only a novelty but marked the beginning of a new epoch in modern Arabic literature. He merits admiration for his boldness, enthusiasm, and determination to break through literary tradition by introducing the theater into the Arab world. He rightfully merits the title of the father of the Arab drama.

David Urquhart, who happened to be in Beirut in 1850 and saw a performance of *Abu al-Hasan al-Mughaffal*, has provided a first-hand account of Naqqash's theatrical talents. On January 12 Urquhart searched through the narrow alleys of Beirut until he reached Naqqash's house which was teeming with people, including a Muslim judge, two muftis, and three serene looking Ulama. Urquhart describes the structure of the stage, reports that the acting was a little confused and that the singing was bad, but concludes that the production was artistically successful. Urquhart realized that the Arab spirit could be easily awakened and stimulated. He also saw that the author had gathered fair knowledge of the European stage during his trip abroad.[46]

Although Naqqash's premature death was indeed a great loss to the burgeoning stage, his pioneering efforts were carried forward in both Syria and Egypt. In Lebanon, which was part of Syria until the end of World War I, many writers and artists worked on plays for the stages established either by learned societies or by schools. Al-Madrasa al-Wataniyya (The National School), founded by the celebrated Butrus al-Bustani (d. 1883), staged several dramas, including *Yusuf al-Hasan* (Joseph the Fair) in 1865, based on the Biblical story of Joseph. In July 1896 an adaptation of Fénelon's *Télémaque* by Sa'd Allah al-Bustani[47] was performed there. The theater was also encouraged by the schools of al-Sharfa Monastery,[48] the Jewish School of Zaki Cohen,[49] the school of al-Thalathat Aqmar (The Three Moons School), and the Jesuit School,[50] among others.

An especially prominent learned society, al-Jam'iyya al-'Ilmiyya al-Suriyya, established in 1868 for the dissemination of learning and the arts among Arab-speaking people, also promoted acting, and several dramas whose themes were drawn from Arab history were performed by its members.[51]

Other plays were staged by amateurs or by charitable associations of the church, including the Rum (Greek) Orthodox Charitable Association and the Maronite Charitable Association. The latter assigned the profits from theatrical performances to help the needy of their communities, as did Zahrat al-Adab, established in Beirut in 1873, which included a group of prominent writers.[52] There was also some individual dramatic activity in Syria, with performances in private houses. For example, *al-Shabb al-Jahil al-Sikkir* (The Foolish and Drunken Young Man) by Tannus al-Jirr, was performed in the home of Habib al-Qirdahi in 1863.[53]

The plot of one drama, *al-Muru'a wa al-Wafa* (Chivalry and Fidelity), composed by Khalil al-Yaziji (d. 1889) and performed in Beirut in 1878, was drawn from a well-known folktale of Arab history.[54] According to the famous writer Zaydan, who saw the performance, this was the first verse play in the Arabic language and represented an important development for Arabic acting.[55] But it is probably more accurate to grant that status to Marun Naqqash's *al-Bakhil*.

Another drama of consequence was the loose translation of Racine's *Andromache* by Adib Ishaq (d. 1885). This was composed at the request of the French Consul and was performed three times in Beirut in 1875, the profits going to the assistance of orphan girls.[56] *Sayf al-Nasr* (The Sword of Victory), composed by Yusuf al-Asir (d. 1889), was also performed in Beirut that year, and its profits were used to purchase printing equipment for the Jam'iyyat al-Funun (The Arts Society).[57]

It is quite difficult to evaluate systematically the multitude of dramas written in the period between the death of Marun Naqqash and the end of the century. Indeed, one cannot even ascertain the number of plays translated, adapted, or composed, because a great many of them are lost, have gone out-of-print, or were printed in obscure and forgotten journals. One writer alone, Ibrahim al-Ahdab (1826-91), wrote at least twenty plays, most of them drawn from Arab history. These gained popularity as well as the approval and encouragement of Rashid Pasha the Wali (governor) of Damascus.[58]

Marun Naqqash's theatrical activity was directly continued by both his brother and his nephew, Salim Khalil Naqqash, who died prematurely in 1884. Niqula showed early proficiency in learning Oriental and European languages, particularly Italian. He was trained by his brother in business administration and when Marun went to Europe he succeeded him at the Beirut Customs. After 1852 Niqula was quite active in business, both private and governmental, besides continuing his study and practice of law. In 1877 he was elected to the Ottoman Parliament. But his other activities did not dampen his journalistic ambition, and in 1880 he established a newspaper, *al-Misbah* (The Lamp), which continued for twenty-eight years. Earlier he had edited the periodical *al-Najah* (Success).[59]

Niqula's interest in the theater came more from a recognition of his brother's pioneer accomplishment than from personal ambition. He continued the training of amateur actors and wished that his brother were still living to see what his disciples had accomplished.[60]

Completely modest, he acknowledged his brother's superior dramatic talents and admitted that he was the first to follow in his footsteps.[61] As a token of his devotion, he produced his brother's drama *al-Salit al-Hasud*. The performance was attended by the Ottoman Wali and proved to be a success. Among the actors was Niqula's son.[62]

Niqual's own dramas included *al-Shaykh al-Jahil* (The Ignorant Old Man), *al-Musi* (The Testator), and *Rabi'a ibn Ziyad al-Mukaddam,* whose theme was drawn from Arab history.[63]

Marun's nephew Salim, an active writer, translator, and journalist, proved even more fervent and ambitious in the theater. Although most of the dramas he produced were adaptations of European originals, [64] his literary and theatrical output was amazing.

Salim's major literary work was *Misr li al-Misriyyin* (Egypt for the Egyptians) in nine volumes. The first three were probably suspended and destroyed by the Egyptian government on the pretext that they contained impertinent information in their biographical accounts of Muhammad Ali and the Khedive Isma'il. The remaining six volumes appeared in 1884, the year of the young author's death. His publication of several newspapers and periodicals attests to his journalistic efficiency.[65]

Salim's substantial knowledge of the European theater is demonstrated by his article on the advantages of the theater, which gives a short account of its history. He sees its function as more than that of providing entertainment, arguing that drama should reflect the wonderful aspects of virtue and the morbid aspects of vice in order to induce people to do what is good and shun what is evil. He applies this criterion to the handling of love and amorous situations, though he seems to believe—contrary to the opinion of his contemporaries—that love was an acceptable element in drama. He neither condemns nor justifies amorous spectacles, but he contends that both the beautiful and the ugly phases of love should be revealed. If the love presented is decent, it will certainly appeal to those who admire virtue; if it is wicked, it will be condemned by those who have good taste. Even humor and comic incidents, Salim argues, should have moralistic and didactic implications. Otherwise, there is no justification for the drama.[66]

Salim keenly promoted the Arab stage by forming and training a theatrical troupe in Beirut at the request of some of his friends. The troupe followed *al-Bakhil* with a performance of Salim's adaption of Pierre Corneille's tragedy *Horace* in 1868. This was so successful that a contemporary writer reported that some European spectators watched and listened attentively until the end, in spite of the fact that there was nothing extraordinary about the acting or the scenery.[67] Salim's major problem in training the actors was to harmonize the different voices and adjust them to the musical instruments. Although his theatrical efforts were rudimentary, they were admirably successful.[68]

To continue his theatrical activity, Salim needed official or popular support. Training actors and providing plays was not enough to maintain a theater. Faced with what he called lack of "material means," he decided to move his troupe to Egypt, which offered more opportunity because of the notable cultural progress it had achieved under the Khedive Isma'il.[69] Salim contacted a few Egyptian dignitaries, who advised him to appeal to the Khedive directly, and journeyed to Egypt to convince Dranite Bey, director of the Opera, of his competence. The response was favorable, and a decree was issued permitting him to perform "Arabic" plays in Egypt. According to *al-Jinan*, when some Egyptians heard of this decision, they praised the Khedive, whose support "would enable the Arab nation to enjoy the performance of riwayat (dramas).''[70]

Salim's troupe was expected to arrive in Egypt in September 1875, but because of the outbreak of cholera it was not able to enter until the fall of the following year. Because of the hot weather, its debut was shifted from Cairo to Alexandria, where it opened the season by performing Marun Naqqash's *Abu al-Hasan* on Saturday, December 23, 1876.[71] There were twelve performers, four of whom were actresses, in the troupe, which performed Marun's other plays as well as Salim's adaptations.

In this same year 1876 Salim invited his colleague Adib Ishaq (d. 1885) to Alexandria to assist him. In Alexandria Ishaq revised his version of *Andromache* and had it published, after adding Arabic verse to some roles. He also adapted *La fille de Roland* by H. de Bornier, and another play, *al-Malik Sharliman* (Charlemagne), was probably of French origin. A rather loose translation of Pierre Zaccone's *La Vengeance* was entitled *al-Intiqam* and published in Alexandria in 1880. It is reported that the text of another play by Ishaq, *Ghara'ib al-Ittifaq*, was among his many possessions stolen in the Lebanese village, al-Hadath, after the author's death.[71]

Ishaq's adaptations of *Andromache* and *Charlemagne* were performed several times in Alexandria, and one report indicates that they were received favorably by the public.[72] However, another account says that Salim's effort was not successful and that both he and his colleague finally became disenchanted with acting, left their troupe in charge of an actor, Yusuf Khayyat, and thereafter devoted their energies to journalism.[74]

In terms of substance and style, Salim Naqqash contributed little to the development of Arab drama. All of his works were simply adaptations, and some of them distorted the originals, with little regard to the author's ideas, structure, or taste. In this sense, Salim is no different from other writers who took great pains to Arabicize even the names of the characters in what were basically French dramas. His introduction to his version of *Horace* admits that it was adapted from the French with many changes, particularly the addition of Arabic verses and music. But his use of the verb "allaftuha" implies that he actually wrote this drama, basing it on some themes he borrowed from Corneille.[75]

Unconvincing as this justification is, Salim's works were in the mainstream of Arabic fiction during the nineteenth century. All of it leaned heavily on foreign, particularly French sources. His style is actually more lucid and polished than that of his uncle Marun, although he also embellished his writing with the time-honored rhymed prose, which was considered a literary nicety at that time.

Nor do the works of Adib Ishaq constitute a progressive step toward the creation of a domestic drama. Like Naqqash and other contemporary writers, he also introduced verse and music into the adapted dramas, presumably as a reliable source of attraction for Arab audiences, and he cut down lengthy dialogues which would probably bore Arab audiences. He completely omitted some parts of Racine's *Andromache*—e.g. scene 3 of Act III, only part of which was incorporated into scene 2—and introduced a new lyric scene into Act I.[76]

After Salim Naqqash and Adib Ishaq deserted their theater in 1877, Yusuf Khayyat (d. 1900) reorganized the troupe and added a few Egyptian actors to it. He made his successful debut as director with the performance of *Sun'al-Jamil* at the Zizinya Theater.[77] In 1879 the company moved the troupe to Cairo, where it enjoyed the Khedive's encouragement and support until his wrath was provoked by a performance of *al-Zalum* (The Tyrant), which contained allusions to despots and injustice. Thinking the play was an indirect criticism of his rule and of his person, the Khedive ordered Khayyat and his troupe out of Egypt.[78] The Opera House was closed to Arab actors and performances until 1882, when Sulayman al-Qirdahi (d. 1909) and al-Shaykh Salama Hijazi (d. 1917) obtained the government's approval to resume Arab acting. However, because of the 'Urabi revolution in that year, al-Qirdahi suspended theatrical activity until 1884.[79]

Abu Khalil al-Qabbani

In 1884 another noteworthy dramatist, al-Shaykh Ahmad Abu Khalil al-Qabbani, came from Syria. He had already created considerable theatrical activity in Damascus (which had met with no little opposition and ridicule from Muslims). He was born, probably in 1833 or 1836, in Damascus to a Turkish family in Konya which had emigrated there. Like many Muslim children at that time, he received religious schooling at the Kuttab (Qur'an School), and later he chose the vocation of weighing merchandise by the *qabban* (platform scale), an activity which earned him the epithet al-Qabbani.[80] He also studied Oriental music and dancing under al-Shaykh Ahmad 'Uqayl al-Halabi, gaining marked proficiency in these arts.

Whether al-Qabbani studied acting or learned the skill through personal endeavor is a matter of speculation. Muhammad Kurd Ali maintains that his importance is demonstrated by the fact that he acquired the art of acting without formal study. He was simply told how acting was practiced in the West and was able to imitate it.[81] Perhaps he saw only one play.

This view seems incredible since acting requires more for its mastery. Another theory is that by witnessing all performances by a French troupe on the stage of the Lazarite school in Damascus al-Qabbani gathered some idea of acting, orchestration, the distribution of roles, and even of costumes and makeup.[82]

Muhammad Yusuf Najm, al-Qabbani's modern editor, challenges these theories as unlikely and unfounded. He feels that the news of Marun Naqqash's theatrical activity must have reached Damascus and that al-Qabbani had probably seen one of those plays. Or he may have met someone who saw the performances by a Lebanese troupe in Damascus; Najm notes that Tarrazi reports that Ibrahim al-Ahdab had in fact performed a drama titled *Iskandar al-Maqduni* (Alexander the Macedonian) in Damascus in 1868 at the request of Rashid Pasha, the Wali of that city. Najm also speculates that al-Qabbani may have read the Turkish translations of French dramas, but this theory seems to move along the same lines he has tenaciously striven to discredit.[83]

There is some clear evidence that al-Qabbani trained a group of his friends to act and staged with them his first drama *Nakir al-Jamil* (The Ungrateful), in the house of his grandfather, probably in 1865.[84] But the authorship of this drama raises a problem. In 1956 Najm stated that it was an original work, but his introduction to the anthology of al-Qabbani's writings says that it was adapted from an unknown Western source.[85] The text of *Nakir al-Jamil* does in fact appear to be an adaptation of Western drama.[86] The names of some of the characters (e.g. Constantine and Alexander) betray its non-Arabic origin, and neither the action nor the themes are domestic. Ghadir (meaning treacherous), who was saved from utter death on the roadside by the kind and magnanimous Halim, the Minister's son, harbors the morbid idea that he has become so indebted to his benefactor that the only way to alleviate this bond is to eliminate him. Although his plan is revealed to the King, he is pardoned at Halim's request. Ghadir remorsefully confesses his jealousy and with great shame deplores his ingratitude. The drama is somewhat reminiscent of the parable of the Good Samaritan, and the King's dream brings to mind the vision of Pilate's wife.

But since there is no evidence that al-Qabbani knew Western languages, although he apparently did know Turkish, he could not have adapted or translated this drama from its Western original.[87]

In any case, *Nakir al-Jamil* marked the beginning of an era of eventful dramatic activity which did not end until al-Qabbani's death in 1902. Information is lacking about al-Qabbani's early theatrical career, but he may have staged a number of plays before he received official support and encouragement from Subhi Pasha, the Turkish governor of Syria, in 1871.[88] His work was also endorsed by the liberal Midhat Pasha, the governor in 1878-79, who promoted the theater as a part of his cultural reform program. When Iskandar

Farah, a notable actor, was permitted to form and train a troupe he joined al-Qabbani, and, with Midhat's financial support, they rented a place in Bab Tuma (Thomas's Gate) to perform *Aida* and the *Shah Mahmud*. The public's response was encouraging, and prompted by Midhat's interest, al-Qabbani and his partner prepared more material for their newly born stage.[89]

Their activity was soon doomed, however, for when the troupe performed Marun Naqqash's *Abu al-Hasan,* it came under violent attack by both the envious and the reactionaries. The fanatic Shaykh Sa'id al-Ghabra particularly condemned al-Qabbani for corrupting the people's morals.[90] Conservatives resented the appearance on the stage of the figure of Caliph Harun al-Rashid, the Commander of the Faithful, in the person of the poor and gullible Abu al-Hasan, for they thought this denigrated the Caliph's office and person. To placate them, al-Qabbani even agreed to share the profit from his stage with them. According to one report, the Shaykh Sa'id al-Ghabra was not satisfied with his meager share and went to Istanbul to complain personally to the Sultan. A royal decree issued to the new governor, Hamdi Pasha, prevented al-Qabbani from acting and forced him to close down his theater.[91]

Disgruntled by the antagonism and ingratitude his native city had shown him, al-Qabbani appealed to a wealthy merchant friend, Sa'd Allah Hallaba, a Syrian who had made Alexandria his permanent residence. Hallaba's response was favorable, and the troupe of fifty actors journeyed to Alexandria in 1884.[92] Al-Qabbani may have also accepted the advice of the famous singer Abduh al-Hamuli, who then was vacationing in Syria and suggested that al-Qabbani move the company to Egypt, for later he set up a wooden theater near al-Ataba al-Khadra in Cairo.[93] Al-Qabbani was very active during his stay in Egypt, and his performances met with marked appreciation.

In 1892 al-Qabbani and a troupe consisting of twenty actors came to the United States to perform at the Chicago World's Fair. They spent six months in this country, and al-Qabbani then returned to Syria.[94] Between 1893-94, now in his sixties, al Qabbani taught acting in the evening at a hall made available through one of his friends and admirers. But he was apparently dissatisfied with such inactive work and returned to Egypt to resume acting. His career continued until 1900,[95] when the stage which an admirer, 'Inayat Bey, had built specifically for him was burned beyond recognition. After this disaster, the troupe was dispersed, and al-Qabbani returned to Damascus. He was penniless, but the sympathetic Syrian government allocated him an annual subsidy. He died of the plague on December 19, 1902.[96]

Al-Qabbani's output included some sixty dramas adapted either from Western sources, mainly French, or from ancient Arab tales, primarily *The Thousand and One Nights.* Only eight of these are currently available, in the collection edited by Najm, who also provides a detailed list of other adapted or original dramas performed by al-Qabbani and his troupe in both Syria and Egypt.[97] In adapting Western drama and borrowing some of his themes from ancient Arab tales, al-Qabbani was perfectly in tune with the literary activity of his time. He even claimed for himself the authorship of *Lubab al-Gharam aw al-Malik Mitridat*, an adaptation of Racine's *Mithridates*, first published in 1900.[98] It was quite acceptable, if not fashionable, for many Arab writers or translators at that time to plagiarize complete Western novels and dramas.[99]

In fact, al-Qabbani's adaptation of *Mithridates* is not significantly different from Adib Ishaq's of *Andromache*. Many scenes have been added, though the structure remains untouched.[100] However, little material is completely deleted; instead, it is utilized in new scenes which he added to the plot.[101] Some speeches have been rewritten in Arabic verse, and the popular rhymed prose also appears. Although this device is not awkward, it becomes very boring to the modern reader. The fact that the characters seem two-dimensional is not totally the adapter's fault; apart from the slave queen, Monima, the kind, chaste and decent daughter of Ephesus, Racine's original drama lacks effective character portrayal.[102]

The plots of al-Qabanni's other dramas are drawn either from the *Thousand and One Nights* or from popular Arab tales recounting the deeds of heroes, such as the famous poet-hero 'Antara ibn Shaddad. The *Nights,* of course, not only furnished Arab playwrights and story writers with plots but were also a significant source of entertainment for the public. Even before Marun Naqqash and al-Qabbani attempted to cast some of them in theatrical form, the stories were read to audiences in major cities throughout the Arab countries, particularly in coffee houses. Thus al-Qabbani's dramas derived from them perpetuated an old, rather than providing a new, source of entertainment. The technique was different, of course, though it was far from elaborate or accomplished.

Like many nineteenth-century Arab playwrights, al-Qabbani treated the historical play as a tale recast in dramatic form, disregarding both accuracy and art. The characters remain as flat as they are in the originals, and their actions reveal little about the age in which they lived. The love scene between Ghanim ibn Ayyub and Qut al-Qulub, the principals in *Riwayat Harun al-Rashid ma' al-Amir Chanim ibn Ayyub wa Qut al-Qulub,* might have been very touching love scenes, but it seems a cold debate about an impersonal matter, with the lovers eventually resigning the outcome to fate.[103]

The characters in *Riwayat 'Antar ibn Shaddad* are even paler. The courageous and chivalrous deeds of the pre-Islamic poet 'Antar or 'Antara ibn Shaddad of the Banu Abs—whose name, according to legend, was sufficient to frighten his enemies—are played down,[104] and his unremitting struggle to win the love of his beautiful cousin Abla is even more pointedly distorted. Instead of the fiery lover, he is portrayed as a jealous husband who tries to defend his wife through petty squabbles with his rival al-Amir Mas'ud rather than through his bravery and legendary prowess.[106]

The criticism also applies to two of al-Qabbani's other plays, *Riwayat*

Harun al-Rashid ma' Uns al-Jalis and *Riwayat al-Amir Mahmud Najl Shah al-'Ajam*.[106] The stereotyped characters lack the dimensions necessary for a forceful drama. Like his contemporaries, al-Qabbani lacked both literary ability and powerful imagination. And his understanding of dramatic structure was insufficient. Hence he could not mold gripping drama out of traditional material, as Racine and Corneille had.

The remaining plays of al-Qabbani are either adaptations or loose translations of Western plays.[107] In *Mithridates* and *Riwayat Hiyal al-Nisa,* (Women Craftiness) whose original is unknown to this writer, al-Qabbani left the names of the characters unchanged. In *'Afifa,* which is perhaps an adaptation of a French *Geneviève,* all the characters have Arabic names, while in *Nakir al-Jamil* (The Ungrateful), also of Western origin, some remain in their original form.[108]

Al-Qabbani's dramas are far too limited in scope to be universal. It is perhaps expecting too much from a nineteenth-century Arab playwright that his dramas should harmonize traditional and modern ideas, or even that some of the ancient tales should be used to criticize certain social ills of his time. Al-Qabbani was an imitator rather than an innovator, but he was perfectly in tune with the tradition set by Marun Naqqash. He might be considered the creator of the "Arab operetta" which influenced the succeeding theater in Egypt, especially that of al-Shaykh Salama Hijazi, and can be found to this day in the Egyptian theater and cinema. He may also be credited with introducing pantomime, a hitherto unknown art which he occasionally demonstrated at the end of his regular performances.[109]

Technically, al-Qabbani's dramas are of full-evening length. They usually consist of four or five acts, which may or may not be sub-divided into scenes. In some plays the scenes are called *juz* (part), while in others the term *manzar* (scene) is used. In the translated or adapted dramas the scene is called a *waqi'a* (incident or event).[110] Usually, each play ends with a song in praise of either the Turkish Sultan or the Khedive of Egypt, or both—and, in one notable case al-Abbas, the uncle of the Prophet of Islam.

Ultimately, al-Qabbani was more important as an actor-manager than as a playwright. For more than three decades he and his troupe performed numerous plays, and Najm's index indicates that some of these were played several times before different audiences in Syria and Egypt. This not only demonstrates the popularity of al-Qabbani[111] but also testifies to the people's interest in the theater as a source of entertainment.

The plays of al-Qabbani, like those of Marun Naqqash and other nineteenth-century playwrights are a matter of past history. They have no appeal to contemporary audiences in the Arab world, primarily because of their rhymed prose style and their ineptly manipulated plots. Contemporary Arab audiences do not even find them a source of entertainment, given the presence of movies and the emergence of more sophisticated dramas written in easier and more understandable language. Although Arab audiences still enjoy watching Shakespeare's and Molière's plays in translation, the works of their own pioneer playwrights have become a matter of academic interest.

It may be that the absence of a dramatic tradition and the non-existence of other genres in the Western sense prevented the rise of a first-rate Arab dramatist during the nineteenth century. The playwrights, who had to borrow their plots either from ancient tales or from Western dramas, seem more amateurs than accomplished writers. This lack of tradition is also felt in the plays of the famous poet Ahmad Shawqi (d. 1932) composed during the first quarter of the present century.

Although Salim Naqqash, Adib Ishaq, and al-Qabbani were all of Syrian origin, they were active in Egypt. And it was in fact an Egyptian nationalist Jew, Ya'qub Sanu, who first established a significant native theater.

CHAPTER III

YA'QUB SANU AND THE RISE

OF THE ARAB DRAMA IN EGYPT

Sanu's Life and Varied Activities

Ya'qub Rafa'il Sanu was born in Cairo in February, 1839. His family was Jewish,[1] although one contemporary Egyptian critic, Ibrahim Abduh, makes him out to be a Muslim. Sanu's memoirs, which Abduh read in Paris, do not relate an unusual story in support of this claim. His parents had lost four children before Ya'qub was born, and his mother appealed to a venerable old man at al-Sha'rani mosque to beseech God to protect and spare the child she was carrying. Like the prophets of old, the man told her that she would have a baby boy and added, "If you dedicate the child to the defense of Islam, then he will live."[2] To be sure, this account does not make Sanu a Muslim, since his mother was following a common practice of Middle Eastern women, whatever their religious convictions.[3] Although nowhere in his mémoirs does Sanu himself refer to his Jewish origin, some of his biographers have mentioned that he was brought up in Judaism, studied the Old Testament, and deserved to be called a Levite.[4] He may also have permitted his burial in a Jewish cemetery, as the records of the Consistoire Israélite de Paris show.[5] The fact remains, however, that his life and works afford no evidence that Sanu ever emphasized his Jewish heritage or allowed it to override his primary identity as an Egyptian.

At twelve he was able to read the Old Testament in Hebrew, the Gospels in English, and the Qur'an in Arabic. He began to compose Arabian poetry at an early age, and one of his earliest works was a poem in praise of the principal of his school. On his father's advice, he composed a poem praising Ahmad Yagan, the grandson of Muhammad Ali, the Viceroy of Egypt, to whom he was chief consultant. When young Ya'qub read this poem in Ahmad Pasha's presence, the latter was so appreciative of the boy's precocity, that he offered to send him to Europe to study at his own expense. Ya'qub was barely thirteen when his benefactor sent him to Livorno, Italy, where he spent three years.

Soon after his return to Egypt at the age of sixteen, Sanu lost both his father and his benefactor. He supported himself by teaching European languages and sciences to the sons and daughters of Egyptian dignitaries, and even to some members of the Viceroy's family.⁶ Later he joined the staff of the Polytechnic School, most probably in 1863. During his six years there, he must have come in contact with many students who later played significant roles in Egyptian society and government.⁷ In addition, he must have been intimate with intellectual leaders and no doubt took a strong part in Egypt's cultural awakening in the middle of the nineteenth century.

Among his varied intellectual activities were the founding of cultural societies and the establishment of several newspapers and periodicals. These interests brought him into the circle of the great reformer and sage Jamal al-Din al-Afghani and the Shaykh Muhammad Abduh, with whom he was soon on intimate terms.⁸ Al-Afghani and Abduh benefited from Sanu's knowledge of foreign languages and studied French under him. The sobriquet by which Sanu came to be known developed from this association.

Having decided to establish a journal to satirize the misdoings of the Khedive Isma'il, the three friends concluded that Sanu was best fitted to serve as its editor and left the name of the projected paper to his discretion. When he left them, Sanu soon found himself surrounded by drivers each begging him importunately to hire his donkey for the ride home. As he tried to make his choice, he heard one driver shouting, "You with the blue glasses, please hire my donkey"! Sanu admired this new epithet—and used it to name the new journal—*Abu Nazzara*. The first issue of the journal appeared in 1878, and Sanu was known thereafter, both in Egypt and in Europe, as Abu Nazzara (the man with the glasses).⁹

When the Khedive Isma'il came to power in 1863, Sanu admired him and even composed a poem in praise of the new ruler as an advocate of freedom and progress.¹⁰ For some years Sanu worked strongly to introduce the Arab world to Europe. He translated many Arabic poems into Italian and published in English periodicals numerous articles dealing with Arabic and Islamic literature. Three plays he wrote in Italian about Egyptian customs met with great success in Italy.¹¹

Sanu was soon disillusioned, and in the pages of his same newspapers he bitterly criticized the wayward and arbitrary policies of the government. His papers were not devoted wholly to news and editorials but included a mixture of cartoons, songs, letters and commentaries whose sole purpose was to satirize the tyrannical rule. Sanu was the first Egyptian to use the European technique of political cartoons, a method that proved even more effective in Egypt than in Europe.¹² Although both his cartoons and his numerous articles avoided mentioning the Khedive by name, they sarcastically referred to him as "Shaykh al-Hara" [i.e., Chief Man of the Quarter], a term which in Arabic slang is also equivalent to the word which arouses so much indignation in the breast of the freedman in Lord Lytton's *The Last Days of Pompeii*.¹³ Sanu's attack on the British occupation of Egypt was no less vehement. He carried this on not only in his publications, but also through the National Party, for which he was an influential spokesman. He may even have devised the party's slogan, "Egypt for the Egyptians,"[14] for throughout all his battles Sanu never claimed to be more than an ordinary Egyptian. He once emphatically told a reporter for the *Daily Telegraph,* "The English call me French, the French call me English, the Turks call me infidel; I am simply an Egyptian."[15]

Sanu may have been pretentious about his claim to have established the first Arab theater in Egypt.[16] His mémoirs describe Cairo in 1870 as swarming with Europeans, particularly French and Italians, and two troupes, one French and one Italian, presented many dramas in both languages on an open-air stage at the beautiful Azbakiyya park. Sanu says that he took part in all these performances, for he deeply loved those languages and the works of the great dramatists he had read. He adds that the farces, comedies, operettas, and modern dramas moved him to establish an Arab theater, only after he had seriously studied such playwrights as Goldoni, Molière, and Sheridan in their own languages. When he had gained the necessary confidence, he wrote a one-act operetta in colloquial Egyptian, interspersed with popular songs,[17] and then chose ten of his most competent pupils, probably from the Polytechnic School, to perform it. One of the boys was trained to play the romantic female lead, since local custom forbade women to appear on the stage or in public.

Sanu requested the Khedive to attend the performance of this operetta and encouraged him to establish a theater for the Egyptians who were not yet familiar with the dramatic arts. Most of them did not understand Italian operas and French comedies for which the Khedive had established two magnificent stages. The Khedive gave his permission for performance of the operetta as part of a theater concert at the Azbakiyya park, and Sanu was pleased with this official support.

More than three thousand people—Egyptians, European visitors and residents, the Khedive's retinue, and members of the foreign diplomatic corps —gathered to watch this novelty, an operetta in the Arabic language. The hall was packed with spectators, most of whom remained standing, when Sanu and his company faced an audience for the first time. He must have been deeply moved by the sight of thousands of people anxiously awaiting the performance. They were greeted with great applause, and he could hear voices shouting, "Excellent! Excellent!" in different languages, so that the hall sounded like the tower of Babel. Collecting his courage, Sanu introduced the actors, briefly explained the benefits of the theater, apologized for any short-comings in the performance,.and asked the audience to bear in mind that this was the first experiment of an Arab troupe in Egypt. In fact, however, the performance was so successful that the audience asked that it be repeated.

This experience encouraged Sanu to form a regular troupe, with two poor but nonetheless beautiful and honorable girls in the female roles. This innovation was welcomed, and the final reward came when the troupe was invited by the Khedive to perform on his private stage at Qasr al-Nil. They staged three comedies, *Anisa 'ala al-Muda* (A Fashionable Young Lady), *Ghandur Misr* (The Egyptian Dandy), and *al-Darratan* (The Rival Wives). After the performance of the first two, the Khedive summoned Sanu and, in front of his ministers and entourage, declared, "We are indebted to you for the establishment of our national theater. Your comedies, operettas, and tragedies have introduced our people to the art of the drama. Go, then; you are the Molière of Egypt, and your name shall forever be so."[18]

It is plausible that the delighted Khedive was imitating Louis XIV, who admired and patronized the dramatists he invited to perform in his palace.[19] But his delight turned to absolute fury when he watched the third comedy, which revealed how polygamy results in the disruption of the family. Apparently seeing the play as a criticism of his own polygamous practices, the Khedive again summoned Sanu and sarcastically advised him, "My lord Molière, if you have not the endurance to please more than one wife, do not provoke others to be the same."[20] Sanu was advised to drop *al-Darratan* from his repertoire or lose his theater. He chose to drop it, despite the fact that it had already had 53 performances.[21]

Nevertheless, Sanu's stage was closed forever in 1872 by order of the man who only two years earlier had called him the "Molière of Egypt." Sanu himself gives two principal reasons for this action: the resentment of the British and the hostility of Dranite Bey and Ali Mubarak.

He claims that when Isma'il asked him to perform three theatrical pieces in a great soirée attended by many prominent foreigners, the plays drew a long ovation from most of the audience, including the Khedive himself, but the British dignitaries became piqued when the chief character made a derogatory remark about John Bull. Either directly or through their agents at the Royal Palace, they convinced the Khedive that the plays presented by Abu Nazzara implied criticism of his government and policies and constituted an imminent danger to his rule and to the destiny of the country.

This accusation may or may not be justified, but it is unquestionably true that Sanu was a consistent agitator against British rule in Egypt. He rarely missed an opportunity to rail against British policies and even composed one-act comedies criticizing their behavior and their actions. One of these attributes the sudden rises and declines in the stock market to speculation by foreigners, particularly the British, in commodities such as foodstuffs and agricultural produce, which were badly needed by the Egyptian people.[23] Another dialogue, *al-Sawwah wa al-Hammar* (The Tourist and the Donkey Driver) ridicules the broken Arabic accent of an English tourist but makes no substantial criticism of the British.[24] It seems more probable that the Khedive's disenchantment came as the result of Sanu's sharp criticism, in words and pictures, of Isma'il's own policies.[25]

Sanu also complains that two men close to the Khedive—Dranite Bey, Director of the Opera, and Ali Mubarak, Minister of Education—were responsible for the demise of his theater. He claims that these adversaries used the press as a platform for attacking him. In his comedy *Mulyir* (Molière) *Misr wa ma Yuqasihi* he says with great bitterness:

> I was happy and comfortable, without worry, until the day I became engaged in the theater and in the writing of *riwayat* (romances). Then I became sick and weak. My pupils left me, my work stood idle, and I had severe critics and enemies who out of sheer jealousy attacked me in the newspapers. But I endured the machinations and vexation of my enemies for the sake of my countrymen. For example, I have been teaching at the Polytechnic School for three years, during which all my pupils were pleased and happy. But when I established the Arab theater the crafty Minister Ali Mubarak became jealous of me, especially when our Lord [the Khedive] ordered him to increase our salaries. He immediately ordered my dismissal from the Royal Schools.[26]

The same play speaks specifically against Dranite Bey, who, in addition to his duties at the Opera, supervised the Comédie Française, and who regarded Sanu's newly established theater as a threat to his own domain. One of the characters praises Sanu as the man who deserves to be called "the Molière of Egypt" because he has suffered for so long to establish an Arab theater and insists that Dranite Bey, a druggist who used to give injections to Abbas Pasha, has become the greatest enemy of his new Arab theater. However, Sanu himself has been skillful enough to outwit Dranite and provoke him to anger.[27] Again, however, it is more plausible that the Khedive closed down the theater because it had become apparent that in some quarters his "plays were regarded as subversive."[28]

Sanu's open opposition to polygamy, his criticism of the government in his play *al-Watan wa al-Hurriyya* (The Fatherland and Freedom), and his exposure of Isma'il's tyrannical actions must have goaded the Khedive to anger. The fact that Azharite Ulama joined Sanu in composing plays for his troupe to perform may have been the final blow.[29] As Ibrahim Abduh points out, "It was not surprising that Sanu's theater should have been established under these circumstances. But what is most surprising is the Khedive's toleration of this theater for two years."[30]

The energetic Sanu soon found other outlets for his literary activities. In 1872 he established two societies; *Mahfil al-Taqaddum* (The Circle of Progress) and *Jam'iyyat Muhibbi al-'Ilm* (The Society of the Lovers of Knowledge)[31] to promote literary knowledge and a better understanding of Egyptians, regardless of their religious affiliation. Muslims, Christians, and Jews alike were attracted to these societies by their liberal outlook and contributed numerous lectures on various topics, but they also appealed both to such conservatives as Azharite 'Ulama and to army officers who adhered to the principles of liberty and equality.[32] But in 1874 the Khedive ordered them disbanded and exiled some of their members to the White Nile.

Here again, Sanu sees the British as villains. They wanted him to ad-

vocate and encourage their influence in Egypt and therefore took offense when
he delivered a series of lectures on French history and literature:

> They took revenge on me and succeeded through base methods and cheap
> intrigues in intimating to the Khedive Isma'il that these two societies had
> become a center for revolution. There was nothing for the Khedive to do
> but to prevent students and learned men from attending our meetings. The
> societies were then forced to close their doors.[33]

Sanu and other Egyptians who were displeased with the Khedive's
despotic rule and his suppression of criticism of his rule in the different media,
particularly the press, next decided to keep their countrymen informed of
Isma'il's policies by translating and distributing articles, dispatches, and
telegrams from European newspapers to the reading public. Furthermore, the
members and supporters of the National Party resumed their secret meetings.
When the Khedive countered by forbidding such translations, Sanu's criticism
became even more outspoken. Incensed, the Khedive is said to have remarked,
"This foolish 'Molière' is opening the eyes of my subjects more than he should
by his lectures and poetry. If I do not eliminate him, I will never be able to rule
or be obeyed."[34]

The Khedive did get rid of Sanu temporarily, in 1874, when he went to
Europe and stayed for some time. According to Tarrazi, he was studying
political conditions and the character of the people and returned filled with admiration for the Europeans' progress and fired with the zeal to introduce
modern civilization to the Egyptians.[35] Sanu's version of the trip, though quite
vague, is substantially different. He claims that he suffered great hardships
after the suspension of his societies and that the Khedive sent him to Europe
on an important semi-official mission. Upon his return, he submitted to the
Khedive a detailed report of his accomplishment, but Isma'il prevented its
publication for many years and finally destroyed it on the ground that it was
revolutionary. He even refused to reimburse Sanu for the expenses of the trip,
which amounted to 8,000 francs.[36]

In fact, Sanu's strained relations with the ruler relaxed when Ahmad
Khayri Pasha, the Khedive's chamberlain and a former editor of *al-Waqa 'i al-
Misriyya*, convinced the Khedive to trust a man whose activities reflected the
great "renaissance" engendered by his own progressive rule. In return for his
pardon, Isma'il demanded that Sanu should be more moderate in his speeches
and writings, and Sanu consented to these stipulations. Thereafter, he tells us,
he spent his evenings at the Royal Palace at Abdin and became acquainted
with the Khedive's ministers, some of whom even asked him to teach their
children French and English.

Although Sanu resumed his custom of praising Isma'il in verse whenever
the occasion arose,[37] the truce between the two was short-lived. The more he
watched the Khedive, the more he became disenchanted with "his crimes,"[38]
and though he avoided the local press, he spoke out sharply in both private

and public circles. He claims that when Sharif Pasha, Isma'il's Minister of Foreign Affairs, urged him to introduce some reforms which would placate Sanu, the Khedive roared, threatening that if this arrogant fool did not keep silent, he would teach him how to do so. He would squash him like a bug, Sanu says Sharif Pasha reported shortly before he died.[39]

Sanu finally found a platform by asking the protection of the Italian Consulate, as many other free-thinking journalists had done. Assured of this security, he began to publish *Abu Nazzara Zarqa,* in 1878.[40] In all fifteen issues of this paper, Sanu never missed an opportunity to satirize the despotic rule of Isma'il, the deplorable conditions of the oppressed Egyptian peasant, the anomalies of the government, and the ambitions of foreign powers, particularly the French and British, in Egypt. He also filled it with diverse observations and his recollections of more than three decades. Apparently the paper was immensely popular; De Baignières says that fifty thousand copies of it, "an enormous number for Egypt," were printed.[41]

Sanu published in *Abu Nazzara Zarqa* some of his scathing one-act comedies satirizing the various conditions of the Egyptian society. He was careful, however, not to arouse Isma'il's fury by avoiding imprudent criticism of the political conditions and the Khedive's policies. One of these comedies, *al-Qirdati* (The Monkey Showman), portrayed an authoritarian ruler whose unsatiated lust for money led him to exact severe taxes from the impoverished people, even at the cost of their lives or property. Another, *Hukm Qaraqush* (The Rule of Qaraqush), showed the oppression of the poor *fallah* (peasant), particularly because of the iniquitous taxes and the forced labor imposed upon him.[43] Still afraid that Isma'il might retaliate against any overt criticism Sanu invented the cryptic Shaykh al-Hara as the chief target of his caustic ridicule. To the poor *fallah* he gave the nickname "Abu al-Ghulb" (The Oppressed One).

Sanu was no less harsh in denouncing the actions of Isma'il's ministers and of members of the royal family. *Abu-Nazzara Zarqa* became a platform for the expression of liberal ideas and an advocate of the wronged and the oppressed. Its rebellious tone must have caused some apprehension in the Egyptian "Pharaoh," as Sanu liked to call Isma'il. Sanu's defense of the French publisher Castile, who was persecuted by the Khedive after having lived in Egypt for nearly half a century, exemplifies his noble purpose.[44]

Finally Isma'il could no longer tolerate Sanu's attacks on him and his government. He was particularly outraged by the insinuations (which agreed with a current rumor) that the despotic Khedive had his own way of eliminating his enemies: inviting them to his palace and serving them poisoned coffee. He was determined to get rid of Sanu, by murder if necessary.[45] When some of his friends who were close to the Khedive realized that Sanu's life was in danger, they advised him to leave the country—and to be careful not to drink the Khedive's coffee.[46]

But the Khedive could not harm him without provoking trouble with Italy, which, like many European states, enjoyed extraterritorial privileges under the system of capitulations. It is reported that the Khedive asked the Italian Consul to expel Sanu from Egypt and suspend his journal. Sanu's version of the events leading to his deportation is ambiguous and again blames his misfortune on the British. He claims that the British Consul brought to Isma'il's attention Sanu's articles praising French culture and convinced him to get rid of the journalist at any cost.

Sanu reports that two attempts were made on his life. One day in May 1878, as he was walking at Shubra, one of the Khedive's hirelings attacked him and stabbed him. Sanu fell to the ground, and his companion chased the assailant, calling policemen to arrest him. But the policeman nearby allowed the culprit to escape, on the Khedive's instructions. Fortunately, the knife struck the buckle of Sanu's belt, and he was only slightly injured.[47] Somewhat later, the Khedive reportedly sent one of his men to shoot Sanu as he was entering his house at midnight. The bullet narrowly missed him but made a hole in the door. Sanu left the door unrepaired as evidence that the Khedive had made an attempt on his life. Some Egyptians, says Sanu, believed that he had escaped death because he had been carrying an amulet which protected him from danger.[48]

After these failures, the Khedive used more peaceful and subtle methods to eliminate Sanu. He sent Khayri Pasha to obtain the name of the minister who had apparently provided the secret information about the Khedive's private life which Sanu published the night before the suspension of his journal. Khayri, if we may believe Sanu, even tried to bribe him to betray the ministers and assured him that his journal would be protected. He pointed out, however, that if Sanu persisted in refusing to divulge his sources, the Khedive's secret intelligence network would soon discover who had furnished him the information.

Sanu was shocked to see an important man like Khayri Pasha acting as a spy for the Khedive. As he showed his visitor to the door, he said, "Tell Isma'il that if he is treacherous, I am not, and that all the treasures of the world are not worth the shadow of my honor."[49] Khayri, moved by Sanu's strong sense of honesty, embraced him and tearfully thanked God for allowing him to meet an honest man. He wished that all Egyptians might follow in Sanu's footsteps and make the tyrant tremble before them.

Sanu also felt that Khayri must have been carrying royal orders to kill him if he refused to provide information. Soon afterwards, the rumor spread through Cairo that Sanu had been shot in his bed. To the shocked people, the Khedive appeared to be a murderer and a tyrant, and he had to act to calm down the restless masses.

A few days later, Sanu writes, a group of officers, once his students, urged him to attack the royal palace at Abdin and save Egypt from the murderous

Khedive. Sanu warned them, however, that such an action would give the British a reason to occupy the country. Moreover, he argued, since he was under the protection of the Masons, Isma'il was extremely afraid to harm him.

But the Khedive of Egypt still had the power to banish him. Indeed, he did exactly this, after he had caused Sanu to lose his pupils and the support of those Europeans, particularly in the diplomatic service, who were studying Arabic under him. When Isma'il ordered his deportation, Sanu left for Alexandria on June 22, 1878. Eight days later he boarded a French ship bound for Marseilles.[50]

Sanu who embellished his brief autobiography with his very fertile imagination, makes his departure from Alexandria a dramatic event of national importance. On the day of his departure, he says, the masses became restless. Whenever his train stopped on the way from Cairo to Alexandria, women brought him fruit and lifted up their children to his compartment window, asking him to bless them. The peasants could be heard shouting, "Don't go and leave us in the clutches of Shaykh al-Hara!" On June 29, says Sanu, he was asked by his fellow citizens to visit the statue of Muhammad Ali at the Consuls' Square and bid them farewell. Here is his description of the final scene as he boarded the ship for Marseilles:

> The passage of time will never obliterate that moving scene. Under the sight of Isma'il's spies, men and women of the city [Alexandria], rich and poor, passed before me, silently greeting me and wishing me happiness in subdued voices. On the next day, about noontime, I boarded the French ship "Freycinet", which took me to Marseilles. It was an august scene. The Khedive himself wanted to see me leaving the country. He passed by the wharf in his carriage, surrounded by his guards, at the same time I was boarding the boat which carried me to the ship. The masses did not dare shout, 'Down with Isma'il!' because there were too many policemen. Instead they shouted, 'Long live Abu Nazzara!' Other voices shouted even more loudly, 'We demand a prophecy from you, O Shaykh!' I should admit that I was too perplexed to know what to say. But I felt as if I had been inspired to say, 'One year from now Isma'il will be exiled as I am today.' Circumstances dictated that this prophecy should become literally true.[51]

Sanu's whole account is undoubtedly exaggerated. Isma'il surely wanted to eliminate him, but he did not have to go through so many intrigues to get rid of one man. It is hardly likely that crowds of people, including women, who were traditionally in heavy seclusion and were forbidden to appear in public, came to the harbor in something like a popular demonstration to see Sanu off. Moreover, the account seems to contradict itself when it states that on June 29 the people who passed before Sanu greeted him in low voices, fearing the Khedive's spies, while the next day, in the presence of the Khedive himself, they shouted their approval of him.

A similar exaggeration of his own role in provoking a rebellion against

Isma'il can be inferred from Sanu's discussions with French journalists, particularly M. Jehan Soudan and M. Martin.[52] In point of fact, French newspapers contributed enormously to his egotism by attributing to him an even greater role in stabilizing the Egyptian financial situation than was given to the special Debt Commission assigned this responsibility. Once in Paris, where he feared no repression by the Khedive, Sanu vividly presented himself as a formidable Egyptian leader and revolutionary. De Baignières accurately described the aura of glory he built around himself:

> In these reports from James Sanua to M. Jehan Soudan and M. Martin, one will notice that the Egyptian Molière has adopted a role which is not exactly outstanding for modesty. But, not realizing this, he would have predicted and anticipated everything. There is perhaps in the above remarks a certain slight poetic exaggeration of which not too much should be made. These are just as common to the West as they are to the East; and from the moment when he saw Alexandre Dumas was convinced that he had personally produced the Revolution of July, and Lamartine was convinced that he was the instigator of the Revolution of February, we do not see why anyone should criticize the sincere but naive conviction of James Sanua that he was the sole author of the Egyptian Revolution, and that he had actually accomplished it singlehanded, or practically so. On the other hand, it must be admitted that the Egyptian Revolution up to this point has not had sufficient good results, so that it would not require a certain amount of courage to claim exclusive instigation of it.
>
> How, after all, could the egotism of Abu Naddara have resisted a certain inebriation when sober financial journals, especially *La Réforme Financière*, were going to assign to the actions of his patriotic pamphlet a special importance he surely had never dreamed of, and wished him well in the following terms: —
>
> 'We ask of our readers permission to present them the man who all by himself has done more for the holders of Egyptian bonds than the Debt Commission together with all the members of the Investigation Commission, the committees, and all the journalists of Europe'.[53]

In any case, Sanu settled in Paris and continued to write and to publish several journals.[54] He established relations with prominent statesmen and men of letters both in France and in other European countries. In 1901 he met with the Khedive Abbas II but refused to return to Egypt, on the ground that the country was still under British occupation.[55] In 1908, he visited Istanbul, to participate in the Young Turks' celebration of the proclamation of the constitution; for this occasion he wrote a tract in French, in rhymed prose approximating the Arabic *saj* style. His journalistic activity continued until December 1910, when the last issue of *Abu Nazzara* appeared. Toward the end of his life his sight began to fail, and he ended his days in total blindness. He died in Paris on September 30, 1912.[56]

Sanu's Plays

It is astonishing that a man of so many talents, who played a prominent part in the political and cultural movements in Egypt in the latter half of the nineteenth century, a colleague of Jamal al-Din al-Afghani, and the founder both of the first genuine Arab theater and of the first satirical journal in Egypt, should have been totally neglected by Egyptian writers. Although he has received thorough and serious attention from Western scholars and reporters, not until very recently did Ya'qub Sanu begin to attract the attention of contemporary Egyptian writers. Philip Tarrazi devoted a few pages to him in *Tarikh al-Sihafa al-Arabiyya* (1913), but this is simply a short sketch and offers no critical study of Sanu's multifarious activities.

The first Arab writer to interest himself seriously in Sanu's work was Ibrahim Abduh, who contacted Sanu's daughter, Mme. Louli Sanua-Milhaud, in Paris and obtained from her some of her father's publications. Abduh, however, was chiefly interested in Sanu's journalistic activity and paid little attention to his dramatic output.[57] In 1956 Muhammad Yusuf Najm's general discussion referred to the titles of those plays that had already been mentioned by other writers or by Sanu himself in *Mulyir Misr wa ma Yuqasihi* (The Egyptian Molière and What He Suffers), a drama dedicated to Philip Tarrazi and first published at Beirut in 1912. Najm mistakenly believed that this was the only one of Sanu's thirty-two plays which had survived, but later he discovered that Anwar Luqa had already contacted Sanu's daughter in Paris and obtained a manuscript containing eight of his texts. He hoped that Luqa would provide him with copies, so that they could be included in the series on the Arab theater he was then undertaking. But, for reasons which Najm himself could not understand, Luqa refused. Finally Najm contacted Sanu's daughter directly and obtained another copy of the manuscript, which he published in 1963.[58]

This incident should not, of course, detract from the credit due Anwar Luqa. He was the first Arab writer to deal at length with Sanu's dramas and published a brief study of them in 1961.[59] The interest of Arab writers in Sanu's dramatic works is growing, and there is already a book-length study of them.[60]

Sanu's earliest theatrical pieces, including a one-act comedy about Egyptian customs, all met with great success when they were performed on Italian stages both in Egypt and in Italy.[61] In French he wrote *al-Salasil al-Muhattama* (The Shattered Chains), an Ottoman patriotic drama which was published in Paris in 1911 and dedicated to the Ottoman Grand Vizir Husayn Hilmi Pasha.[62] He is also reported to have composed a French dialogue *Boulala,* as yet unpublished.[63] But his major contribution was his many Arabic plays—thirty-two, by his own count—several of which are now available. A great number of his dialogues and short comedies appeared in the journals he published in Egypt and Paris.[64]

These plays cannot be judged in terms of classical literature. They are written chiefly in colloquial Egyptian Arabic, interspersed with many Italian and French terms. Their language does not follow Arabic grammatical rules and often deviates widely from conventional writing.[65] Moreover, when appropriate, different dialects of the Arabic language are used, as well as different accents for non-Arab characters, especially Berbers and Europeans. Although the text of the plays is clear and intelligible to readers familiar with colloquial Egyptian Arabic, it is more difficult for others.[66]

Sanu was aware of this problem, and in *Mulyir Misr wa ma Yuqasihi* he even dramatized the question of writing in colloquial language. One excerpt from that play will convey his views on the matter:

> *Istephan:* This man [the Italian editor] is mad; no one will pay attention to what he says. We will succeed, while he will fail to achieve his goal.
>
> *Mitri:* In two words we can answer him, gag his mouth, and make him run to hide in his mother's lap. *A comedy contains what takes place and what originates among people.*
>
> *Istephan:* Well done, Mitri! Your words are like diamonds.
>
> *Mitri:* I wonder if, in their communication, people use grammatical or conventional language.
>
> *Istephan:* Never in their lives do authorities and learned men communicate with each other in grammatical language.[67]

There is no doubt that Sanu's cardinal purpose was not to give the public reading material, but to provide pieces for the stage. Another passage makes it clear that the composition of verse dramas is not difficult; what is difficult is to perform them.[68]

Sanu, it should be remembered, did not write for the educated élite, as did his contemporary Adib Ishaq, and other Syrian and Egyptian writers. He wrote for the masses, in a simple but effective language that they could understand.[69] He may also, as he claims, have written plays to satisfy his penchant for storytelling and romances, and to express social criticism in an acceptable form.[70]

His aim was not to satisfy his audience with a cheap laugh or a passing thrill, but to deliver a message to his countrymen.[71] He wanted to arouse his fellow Egyptians' sense of human dignity, [72] and to reform customs which he regarded as either inappropriate or unethical. It is hardly surprising therefore, that he emphasized social and moral themes in his works.

The humorous nicknames Sanu gave Isma'il, his son, and his ministers perfectly suited their position and behavior. "Shaykh al-Hara" was the chief of a small Hara or quarter, the smallest administrative unit in the town. Tawfiq success became "Tawqif" (impediment) or "al-Wad al-Ahbal" (the foolish lad). The Prime Minister Riyad was "Abu Rid" (a derogatory diminutive name), and the Council of Ministers was "Jam'iyyat al-Taratir" (the assembly of clowns). The oppressed peasants were given such humble but honorable epithets as "Abu Shaduf" (he who irrigates the land with the primitive shaduf), to symbolize the fallah's cultivating the land and irrigating it with the sweat of his brow, and "Abu al-Ghulb" (the oppressed one).

The cruel officials, mostly men of Turkish origin, were labeled "Kurbaj Agha" ("Whip Agha") to symbolize their ruthlessness.[73]

The use of such metaphorical language to disguise criticism is, of course, no novelty, in either Eastern or Western literature. Rifa'a Rafi'al-Tahtawi, for instance, employed the device in his translation of Fénelon's *Télémaque* to criticize the Viceroy Abbas I, who banished him to the Sudan. Once Sanu had reached Paris, where he had no fear of repression, he attacked the Egyptian Khedive and government publicly, using the real names of the people involved.[74]

Sanu's one-act comedy *al-Qirdati Lu'ba Tiatriyya Hasalat fi Ayyam al-Ghuzz Sanat 1204 A.H.* (The Monkey Showman, a Theatrical Play which took place in the time of the Ghuzz [Mamluk Turks] in Egypt in 1204 A.H./A.D. 1789), portrays the oppression of the poor and the government's disrespect for people's life and property, during the reign of the Ghuzz, who were notorious for their ruthless and unjust rule. Sa'd, the monkey showman, cannot pay his tax. The tax collector threatens to jail him and even entices him to steal if he must. Finally, he steals the tax collector's donkey, sells it, and uses the proceeds to settle his tax problem.[75] A one-act farce, *Hukm Qaraqush,* also set in the times of the Ghuzz, concerns a peasant who must submit to forced labor and must even sell his ox to pay his taxes. Sanu himself described another one-act comedy, *Shaykh al-Hara,* as a theatrical play which takes place in the time of the Pharaohs. Yet the dramatization of the disenchantment of both the people and the army with authoritarian policies is strictly contemporary in tone. Shaykh al-Hara is worried about the restlessness of the people, particularly those in the army, who have been alienated by his oppressive policies. He is plagued by fears, suspecting that there is a plot by army officers, students, and peasants to kill him and take the money which he "earned by the sweat of his brow." He trusts no one, not even his closest confidants. His repressive measures prove useless in preventing a revolt by all sections of the population. The revolutionists finally deliver the ruler to the Turkish authorities, who take him out of the country.

In this short portrayal of the unity of all sections of the population against Isma'il's rule, Sanu includes the Azhar's 'Ulama, who joined the revolt. He contrasts the Egyptians' courage, self-respect, and willingness to fight for their rights with Isma'il's cowardice, selfishness, and haste to flee the country with the money he has stolen from the people. Indeed, the play also brings to mind the revolt against Farouk (one of Isma'il's descendants) in 1952, which led to his deposition and his flight to Europe with large amounts of money.[77]

Even after Isma'il's removal from office, Sanu feared that the deposed Khedive might one day regain the throne and resume his abusive policies. This concern is expressed in *Jursat Isma'il* (Isma'il's Scandal), a comedy that exposes the ruler's intrigues to have his son and successor Tawfiq dethroned. The scene is the Grand Hotel in Paris, where the ex-Khedive is residing with some of his lackeys and wives. Isma'il lavishes substantial amounts of money on the British and Italians in Egypt, as well as on journalists in Paris, to convince both the Egyptians and the foreign observers to accept his restoration to the throne. A French journalist who plans to expose a great scandal involving Isma'il refuses a substantial sum on money to keep silent, sues Isma'il, and obtains a court order to freeze his assets. The appearance of court officials at Isma'il's hotel suite sends his harem into a panic. Realizing that he must either pay a fine or have his belongings confiscated, he uses the money originally intended for the journalist to pay the court officials. The ghost of Abu Nazzara appears to gloat over the predicament of the bewildered ex-Khedive, who cannot understand why this specter harasses him continuously.

This comedy quite plainly exposes Isma'il's infinite selfishness, his concern for power rather than for the people. The author presents himself as a ghost, symbolizing all those Egyptian journalists who have been persecuted by Isma'il. He appears at intervals to comment on an incident or encourage an opponent to stand his ground against the despot.[78]

In *al-Wad al-Mariq wa Abu Shaduf al-Hadiq* (The Playboy and Clever Abu Shaduf), which dramatizes the oppression of the peasant by the ruthless government officials, particularly those of Turkish origin, Sanu exposes the weak character of the Khedive Tawfiq and his submission to the will of his chief minister Riyad. When the Turkish official Nabbut Bey ("Club Bey," whose name symbolizes the forcible exaction of taxes) learns that the Khedive will visit his directorate in upper Egypt, he orders Kurbaj Agha to gather the peasants and make them raise money to pay for the state reception. The Agha threatens to whip with the Kurbaj everyone who fails to pay. The peasants denounce such oppressive methods and rise up against Nabbut Bey.

When Khedive Tawfiq arrives, the peasants complain and implore him for mercy, but he is not at all interested in their welfare and pays them no attention. Since they actually expect nothing from a powerless ruler, they mock and even attack him. The Khedive screams to his soldiers for help and they manage to carry him to a waiting ship. The two peasants, Abu Shaduf and Abu Qas'a, who are thought to be the instigators of the uprising, take to their horses and escape.

Although the theme of this comedy is not new, it is more effectively constructed than Sanu's other one-act plays. The action is efficiently manipulated and the main idea dexterously brought home. The worsening conditions under Tawfiq and the ignorance of the Turkish officials who disregard the peasants' plea that they have no money to pay for the celebration, lead to a logical outcome—revolt, even physical assault, against the Khedive.[79]

In *Zamzam al-Miskina* (Poor Zamzam), the characterization of a poor, oppressed breadseller is weak, but the play is largely successful in conveying the conditions of life for the poor in Egypt. The scene is Suq al-Silah street in the Old Cairo district, where Zamzam sits with her basket of bread for sale, her little child, with his face smeared with dirt, next to her. It is the end of the day, and Zamzam, who has not sold her bread, is happy to see a government official approaching her to buy her wares. The unlucky woman does not realize that the official has come to demand that she pay a fee for occupying a place on the street. She insists that she is too poor to pay such a fee, adding that she has heard that the Khedive promised to abolish this tax. The official explains that the question of taxes has passed from the Khedive's control to the foreign consuls. When she says that she will seek support among the religious leaders, she is told that the Khedive (Tawfiq) has already won them over with bribes. Zamzam refuses to pay any tax, and the official begins to beat her. Her cries for help attract a crowd of Muslims and non-Muslims, and some of them take advantage of the chaos to steal her bread. Her appeals for help are lost amid the noise, and while attempting to escape, she drops her child, who is trampled to death by the crowd.

Zamzam is caught and brought before another official, seated next to a foreign consul. She is told to pay the tax or become subject to punishment according to the law. Scoffing at such laws, which do not protect the rights of the poor, she appeals to the foreign consul to intercede on her behalf with the official so that she can be exempted from the tax. The consul does so, and the Egyptian official obeys. As she departs, the heroine mourns the loss of her child and condemns the bad times: poverty and injustice prevail, and infidel Christian consuls must intercede on behalf of the believers.[80]

Although the affliction of Zamzam and her like is carefully revealed, this ignorant, illiterate breadseller seems too politically sophisticated, especially during her argument with the government official about the intervention of foreign consuls in the domestic affairs of the country. She also displays a fair knowledge of the prominent position of the Azhar's 'Ulama, somewhat weakened by their indifference in upholding their rights. The author offers no conclusions on these matters, but leaves them to the judgment of his audience.[81]

The extant full-length dramas of Sanu do not treat political or social subjects. Indeed, their praise of Isma'il and his achievements seem quite paradoxical in view of the author's antagonistic attitude towards the Khedive and his policies. These longer dramas deal with such matters as love and marriage, polygamy, and the Egyptians' indiscriminate imitation of European customs and manners irrelevant to an Eastern society. In one of them the stock market provides the background for a love affair ending in marriage, while another sets forth the hardships the author encountered in establishing his theater and in training and caring for his actors.

Today only the eight dramas in Arabic published by Najm in 1963 and some other pieces written in European languages are available. The remainder of Sanu's dramas are known only by their titles, if at all.[82]

A lively one-act operetta, which the author summarized in a lecture at

Paris, dramatizes the adventure of a European prince in a harem in Cairo. Sanu says that young European visitors to the East have only one desire—to have an adventure in a harem, through the mediation of an Agha (chief eunuch). But the matter is not so easy as these young men would like to imagine, for harems are tightly guarded, and intruders may expose themselves to danger.

The hero of this unidentified drama is a young European prince who bets Ahmad, the son of an Egyptian Pasha, a thousand Egyptian pounds that one month in Cairo will be enough for him to carry off an adventure in a harem. When he does finally arrange to be alone with a concubine, she describes the unbearable life of the harem, in a song which contains this supplication:

> Save me, O noble son of Europe, from this gloomy palace which is like a tomb for the living. Save your loving dove from the hands of that old man who defiles her tender body with his unclean caresses, and wilts her lips with his lifeless kisses. Take me far away to your country, and I swear that I will brighten your life by my nearness to you, and by my beauty and kisses.[83]

This scene, Sanu reports, enraged the spectators, mostly Egyptians who did not wish to see a European, presumably a Christian, trying to elope with a Muslim woman.

The supplications of the concubine move the prince, but the lovers are surprised by the sudden appearance of the Pasha, the master of both the palace and the harem, with four policemen. The angry Pasha orders the policemen to bind the unfaithful concubine back to back with her lover, put them in a sack, and throw them to the crocodiles of the Nile (a fantastic punishment, since the Nile in Egypt has no crocodiles). The prince protests the Pasha's actions, calling them base and treacherous. Unmindful of these threats, the Pasha coolly inquires of the prince who will receive the winnings from his wager with Ahmad. The frightened prince not only offers the Pasha the amount of the bet, but even promises to double it in exchange for his release.

At this point, the Pasha removes his large white beard, revealing to the unbelieving prince that he is none other than Ahmad. Likewise, the pretty concubine removes her veil and, to the prince's utmost frustration, is discovered to be a handsome Syrian actor who has artfully played the role of a concubine. The officer laughingly tells the Pasha that he should not believe the legend current among European young men that they can venture into a harem without being caught. Finally everyone is invited to a sumptuous dinner party in the palace garden.[84]

Sanu's summary implies that his main purpose in writing this drama was to criticize the harem system, which was in fact a social abuse. But he appears to have been extremely cautious not to anger those Egyptians who had harems; indeed, he ends his drama by reassuring the audience that what they had heard and seen is not true, merely contrived. Without condemning the harem system, he shows the social ills and problems it produces, particularly the inevitable infidelity of the inmates, who must find outlets for their suppressed emotions. The overall drama is reminiscent of similar adventures in *The Arabian Nights*, although the scene is strictly contemporary.[85]

Bursat Misr, reveals the failure of a marriage based solely on material considerations. Ya'qub, the president of a financial company, is in love with the pretty sixteen-year-old Labiba, daughter of the banker Salim, but lacks the courage to ask for her hand in marriage. Salim in turn wants to give his daughter to Halim, a young man she does not love. Salim also considers it his duty as a friend of Ya'qub's father to see that Ya'qub marries the daughter of his chief clerk Ishaq. But when Labiba refuses to marry Halim, her father suggests that they become engaged for six months, after which she may either marry him or break the engagement. After much conversation designed to persuade her that Ya'qub is socially and financially unacceptable as a suitor, Labiba accepts her father's suggestion, but deep in her heart she is determined to marry the man she loves.

At the banquet given by Salim on the occasion of Labiba's engagement to Halim, a broker rushes in to inform the guests that he has received a telegram from London saying that relations between England and the United States have become tense over the Alabama Incident.[86] The telegram also contains the disturbing news that the value of banknotes and bonds has declined. Halim is alarmed because, just a few days earlier, he invested his money in bonds and banknotes on the advice of his broker. He is threatened not only with bankruptcy, but also with the loss of his fiancée. Furious, he leaves the banquet and goes to the stock market to find out the true facts. In his absence, Ya'qub and Labiba join hands and kneel down before her father to receive his blessing and approval of their engagement. Apparently she has convinced her father that love is stronger than money. Halim returns to tell everyone that the news they have just heard is false but discovers that he has lost both his fiancée and a marriage which would have given him money and prestige.[87]

Another drama, *al-'Alil* (The Sick Man), in two acts and seventeen scenes, uses the illness of one of the characters as an occasion to defend modern medical methods against the claims of quacks, and to praise the hot-water baths founded by the Khedive Isma'il at Hulwan. To make the drama more palatable, Sanu also introduces a love story.

Habib, a widower with a pretty young daughter named Hanim, complains of a nervous ailment caused by his shock over the death of his brother at Istanbul. When he asks his servant to summon Zahid Effendi, a famous physician at Qasr al-'Ayni Hospital, the servant, who believes in superstition more than medicine, brings instead a quack, one Shaykh Ali. Habib refuses to be attended by such a man but is convinced by his daughter that he cannot do any harm. Ali claims to have the talisman of King Solomon and boasts that he can call forth devils and jinns and imprison them in glass jugs. He tells Habib that if he wishes to recover, he should make a vow regarding whatever he considers most valuable. Habib, who values nothing more highly than his daughter, vows to give her in marriage to the person who heals him. Then Ali gives Habib a talisman, claiming that it will cure him. Habib alternately fears that the talisman will have the desired effect (in which case Ali will marry Hanim) and feels confident that Ali is a quack and cannot cure him. Finally the physician, Zahid, advises Habib to bathe at the sulphur springs at Hulwan.

Mitri, a young man who loves Hanim, hastens to Hulwan to tell the physician in charge, Kibrit Bey (Sulphur Bey) about Habib's vow and is assured that if Kibrit succeeds in curing her father, Mitri can marry his beloved. But when Habib arrives at Hulwan, he meets Elias, a friend of Mitri's, who has great difficulty speaking. Indeed, when Habib hears Elias stuttering, he bursts into laughter and feels so much better that he believes he is cured. Elias, who also knows of Habib's vow, asks for his daughter's hand. After a heated argument between the two suitors Kibrit intervenes on Mitri's behalf, telling Habib that he has been cured not because of Elias, but because of the warm sulphur waters of Hulwan.[88]

Abu Ridah al-Barbari wa Ka'b al-Khayr, a play in two acts and eleven scenes, treats another aspect of Egyptian society, matchmaking, and also deals with the relations between domestic servants and their employers. Abu Ridah and Ka'b al-Khayr, both Nubian domestics, work at the home of al-Sit Bunbah. Bunbah discovers that Abu Ridah loves Ka'b al-Khayr, but Ka'b al-Khayr loathes Abu Ridah for his laziness and asks his mistress to replace him. When Bunbah tells her of Abu Ridah's feelings, she becomes angry for she believes there are no good Berbers. What's more, she asks, if Abu Ridah truly loves her, why does he flirt with the neighbor?

In the meantime, Nakhla, a rich cloth merchant who owns four shops in the Hamzawi quarter and is in love with Bunbah, elicits the aid of Mabruka, a matchmaker, who tells him that Bunbah will not marry until she has solved the problem of her two domestic servants. Nakhla promises Ka'b al-Khayr ten silk dresses if she will marry Abu Ridah, yet neither this offer nor his joint efforts with Mabruka persuade her to accept him as a husband. In despair, Abu Ridah attempts suicide before Ka'b al-Khayr, tying his turban around his neck in an effort to strangle himself, but she remains unmoved. Then he seizes a knife, and just as he is about to stab himself, she rushes to tell him that now she is certain that he loves her. Finally she marries Abu Ridah, while her mistress marries Nakhla.[89]

The delicate subject of polygamy is treated in *al-Darratan* (The Rival Wives),[90] the play which aroused Isma'il's fury. Ahmad, the central figure, is a lower-middle class Egyptian whose friends usually call him "Malik" (King). He spends most of his time smoking hashish with some friends from the banu Shaddad. Although Sabiha, his wife of fifteen years, is faithful and devoted to him, Ahmad is captivated by Fattuma and desires to marry her. He convinces his wife that she needs a helper around the house, and that Fattuma is just the person. Sabiha reluctantly accepts, but, of course, the two wives begin to fight constantly. Ahmad's life becomes miserable, and he eventually divorces and expels both wives. But soon he discovers that although he is now free, he is lonely and unable to manage by himself. He realizes that he has made a great mistake in taking a second wife. Sabiha feels that she should have been more understanding of her husband's situation and returns to him, admitting her mistake. Ahmad is soon reconciled with her and promises not to disrupt their married life again.[91]

Another drama dealing with love and marriage,[92] *al-Sadaqa* (Friendship, but the term also implies faithfulness in love), centers about three couples. Najib and his sister Warda are orphans who have been living for four years in Alexandria with their aunt Safsaf, a rich widow who has taken good care of them. Warda loves her young cousin Na'um, who is studying in England, and they have vowed to marry after his return. She is worried because for three months she has not received a letter from him. Her brother Najb loves Taqla, the daughter of the Syrian merchant Ni'mat Allah, who is himself in love with the widow Safsaf and wants to marry her.

A young Englishman meets Warda at a party, admires her, and asks his friend Ni'mat Allah to ask her aunt for her hand. Warda naturally refuses because she is waiting to marry her cousin, who is in England. When Safsaf tries to convince her niece to marry the young Englishman on the grounds that her cousin must by now have found an English girl, Warda tearfully answers that she will never betray him. But the young Englishman tells her that he knows her cousin in England, and that in fact the cousin has become engaged to his sister and will soon marry her. Warda faints upon hearing this news but soon recovers and prepares to leave the house when her aunt rebukes her for not marrying the young Englishman. But the suitor follows her to the door and reveals his real identity. Na'um had disguised himself and played this role in order to test Warda's love and devotion. In the end Warda marries him, her aunt marries the wealthy merchant, and her brother Najib marries Taqla.[93]

In *al-Amira al-Iskandaraniyya* (The Alexandrian Princess), a drama in two acts, twenty-eight scenes, Sanu criticizes the middle-class Egyptians who indiscriminately mimic European life and customs. Ibrahim, a small merchant who lives with his wife Maryam and daughter Adila, is quite content until the day he becomes wealthy. Maryam begins to imitate everything French, even speaking French at home as a sign of her sophistication. She despises her husband because he cannot speak French and accuses him of being ignorant. She insists on his employing a French maid, believing that Arab maids are ignorant and inferior. When a simple clerk, Yusuf, asks to marry her daughter because they are in love, she cannot believe his audacity.

Maryam and Adila, her daughter, later encounter a young Frenchman,

Victor, at the theater. The next day he hands Maryam two letters. One is from his father, whom the family met in Paris, asking them to take care of his son (The father, it seems, knows Arabic because he lived in Algiers and served with Ibrahim Pasha, the son of Muhammad Ali, the Viceroy of Egypt.) The second letter is from Victor himself, asking for Adila's hand. The prospect of such a match greatly pleases Maryam: Victor is not merely French but has the title of a chevalier. Adila and Victor go to the French Consulate to be married.

While they are gone, however, Victor's father unexpectedly appears with the shocking news that his son is in France and will soon marry his cousin. Furthermore, he wrote no letter consenting to Victor's marrying Adila. When the couple return from the Consulate, the whole truth is revealed. Yusuf has impersonated Victor in order to marry her. Maryam is shocked and faints. When she recovers, her husband begins to mock her and pins on her breast a medallion recently presented to him by the government. Victor's father calmly tells her that title, decorations, and money are nothing in comparison with what man can earn by honorable conduct and a good reputation.[94]

Mulyir Misr wa ma Yuqasihi (The Egyptian Molière and What He Suffers) is entirely different from Sanu's other plays. Here the author expresses the theory that the theater should dramatize life and people[95] and also explains the hardships he encountered in establishing the Arab theater in Egypt. He apparently wrote the play to disprove the criticism of an Italian journalist in Alexandria (possibly the editor of *L'Avvenire d'Egitto*) who had charged that the Arab theater was inefficient and that the dramas were written in colloquial and ungrammatical language. The play was also a deliberate affront to the director of the Khedive's stage, who had reportedly told Isma'il, after viewing the performance of Sanu's troupe at the Royal Palace, that Sanu himself was a charlatan.[96]

The text reveals that Sanu chose certain actors to play certain roles. He may have been influenced by the Italian Commedia dell' Arte, and in fact his drama betrays the unmistakable influence of Molière's *L'Impromptu de Versailles*, which treats the problems of a theatrical company's director with his actors and actresses. The criticism of Sanu's composition and dramas recalls the play *Le Portrait du Peintre*, which Boursault wrote to criticize Molière's comedy *L'École des femmes*.[97] There is no question that Sanu wrote this play with one purpose, to praise himself and what he considers his unparalleled achievement, the founding of the first Arab theater in Egypt.

It is important to remember that these plays were written to be performed, not read. They are not so purely didactic as the one-act dialogues that appeared in Sanu's numerous journals, which were meant not only to entertain readers but also to educate them about problems of immediate concern. The fact that the dialogue is in colloquial Arabic makes it all the more difficult to understand the humor and meaning, and the text is sometimes complicated by numerous foreign terms, chiefly from Italian and French. But the humor in these dramas derives not only from subtle situations or odd characters, but also from the different accents of non-Arab characters.[98] The broken Arabic of the Nubian characters in *Abu Ridah al-Barbari wa Ka'b al-Khayr;* of the European maid Theresa in *Bursat Misr*; of another maid, Carolina, in *al-Amira al-Iskandaraniyya;* and of the Greek physician Kharalambo in *al-'Alil* must have provoked continuous laughter from the audience.

While Sanu attempts, often successfully, to dramatize life in Egypt as he sees it, the published texts do not emphasize the settings or provide accurate descriptions of them. Only in Act I of *al-Amira al-Iskandaraniyya* is the setting specified—a sumptuously furnished room at the home of one of the characters—but there is no detailed description of the home, the room, or its furnishings.[99] The first act of *Bursat Misr* is set "in the coffee shop outside the stock market," with no hint as to where the stock market is, what kind of coffee shop it is, and why the characters meet there. The action of the second act occurs "at the home of Khawaja Salim," but Sanu gives us no information about the location or type of house. Throughout the play there are intermittent allusions to places or furniture, but they have no connection with the characters or their daily lives. Although the two acts of *Abu Ridah al-Barbari wa Ka'b al-Khayr* take place in the home of al-Sit Bunbah, we are not given even the slightest information about the house which would throw some light on the life of Bunbah and her two domestic servants. The same criticism applies to all of Sanu's dramas, both full-length pieces and one-act comedies.

Unlike his one-act plays and dialogues, whose characters are drawn from the peasantry and lower classes of Egypt, Sanu's full-length dramas are peopled with middle or upper-middle-class Egyptians, sometimes of high social standing. There are bankers and physicians, merchants and actors, and even princes and pashas. They are well educated—some have received their schooling in Europe—and financially secure, for they live comfortably and can afford to employ domestic servants. But they are largely bound up in their own personal concerns, and nowhere do they seem engaged in the political and social affairs of their country, or to play any role in advancing their own society.

It is not hard to understand why these plays are peopled by such politically passive middle-class characters. When Sanu wrote and staged them between 1870 and 1872, he was moving in high society circles and enjoying the favor of the Khedive Isma'il. Himself in a sound financial position, he showed little concern for the poor classes, especially the peasants. It was after Isma'il closed down his theater in 1872, and when he had lost both his teaching position at the Polytechnic School and his income from private tutoring, that Sanu, who was in dire need of money, friends, and supporters, better understood the plight of the oppressed classes. Yet while he remained in Egypt he was unable to dramatize their tragedy for fear of retaliation by Isma'il. Hence it was only after he went to Paris that he utilized all his talents to defend the Egyptian peasants in his one-act comedies.

Although some of the characters in Sanu's longer works are petty clerks, junior bank employees, and other middle-class types, like the characters in *al-Darratan,* I cannot support the contention of one contemporary writer that Sanu defended these people or fought for their rights by criticizing the government.[100] The minor clerks Najib in *al-Sadaqa* and Yusuf in *al-Amira al-Iskandaraniyya* eventually marry wealthy young women; Sanu's portrayal of them is on the whole neutral rather than sympathetic.

To the extent that Sanu's plays express his essential attitudes toward his society, their characters do not enjoy an independent existence. These highly personal creations simply could not have been produced without Sanu. The extreme generality of the settings within a very limited section of the society also reflects the universality and significance of his central ideas. They need no specific location in time and place to be understood.

For instance, knowing Sanu's concern about the inferior role of women in Muslim society, it is not surprising to see young ladies like Labiba in *Bursat Misr,* Warda in *al-Sadaqa,* and Adila in *al-Amira al-Iskandaraniyya,* who supposedly live in a country where women have no rights or freedom, defy parental authority and marry the young men whom they love. Similarly, the parents are portrayed as conservatives who believe that they best understand what is good for their children and therefore consider it their responsibility to choose the right husbands for their daughters.

Sanu is less successful in projecting the true character of the lovers who marry these young ladies. They are pale, shy, and timid. Ya'qub in *Burst Misr* sends many love letters to Labiba but does not have the courage to ask her father for her hand.[101] Mitri in *al-'Alil* is so conservative that he calls his beloved Hanim his "sister" as an expression of respect, and when she tells him that if her father wants to give her in marriage to Habib she will refuse, he advises that she should not disobey her father.[102] Only Na'um in *al-Sadaqa* appears slightly adventurous: he goes through some difficulty in disguising himself to win his beloved Warda.

The characters in *al-Darratan*, particularly Sabiha and Fattuma, provide a believable picture of a house shared by two rival wives. The feud between them becomes intensely dramatic when each comes to believe the husband has sought to serve only her interests. The first wife, Sabiha, contends that Ahmad has married the young and pretty Fattuma not for her beauty, but so that she can help with the housechores, and Fattuma argues that Ahmad has married her for her beauty and youth, since Sabiha has become old and unattractive.[103] It is interesting that Sabiha wishes she had the right to marry again, in order to show Ahmad what having a rival in the house would mean.[104] Ahmad is in fact irresponsible and does not understand the problem which he has created. He is mistaken in thinking that divorcing both wives will settle the matter.

Sanu shows great skill and facility in handling the dialogue of his plays. Faithfully capturing both the thoughts and the life style of the class he portrays, he accurately renders idioms and nuances. He knows the language and topics of conversation of the peasants, bourgeoisie, and high society. And he is equally adept at reproducing specific speech patterns, including the Nubian accents of the servants in *Abu-Ridah al-Barbari wa Ka'b al-Khayr* and the European accents of Theresa in *Bursat Misr,* Carolina in *al-Amira al-Iskandaraniyya,* Kharalambo and Kibrit Bey in *al-'Alil,* and Mr. Higgins (sic) in *al-Sadaqa.* Perhaps outstanding among Sanu's accomplishments in this regard, however, are the representations of Ni'mat Allah's Syrian dialect in *al-Sadaqa* and Elias's stutter in *al-'Alil.*

Sanu's dramas not only attracted a large audience of Egyptians of all classes, but also provoked the curiosity and interest of the spectators. The audience became involved with the stage, sometimes to the point of participating in the action. De Baignières quotes a journalist writing for the *Saturday Review,* who praised Sanu's theater that the audience frequently made comments or suggestions to change the end of a play to suit their delight in happy endings. Sometimes the spectators would tell the actors what to do, or incite one character against another. In a love scene, for example, they would exclaim, "Let us see whether you will let your rival take your beloved away from you," or, "How can you prefer such a stupid and arrogant man to this decent and respectable young man?" When these comments came, Sanu was hiding backstage, ready to prompt the actors with the right answers to save them from embarrassment.[105]

Sanu also remarks that the quality of his audience improved considerably in the second year of his theater. Intelligent, responsive, and interested, it represented all segments of Egyptian society. But its direct interventions in the performance turned some of the most serious situations into occasions for roaring laughter. In the drama *Ghandur Misr* (The Egyptian Dandy), of which only a summary survives, Sanu did not realize that the actress he had assigned the role of a desperate lover hated the actor who was to play opposite her. But the poor actor truly loved the actress and was grateful for the opportunity to perform a love scene with her. After the actress finished a line expressing her love, the actor, taking her acting as the truth, elatedly turned to her and whispered softly, "May God bless this stage which finally humbled you and made you express your love to me before thousands of spectators." The actress became furious and, forgetting that she was on stage, slapped the presumptuous actor in the face. She turned to the audience and declared that the words of love she had whispered to the conceited actor did not represent her true feelings. "For," she continued, "I would rather be blind than love him. It is the author, the Egyptian Molière, who put these words in my mouth." Sanu says he was shocked and utterly embarrassed by the incident. But, to his complete disbelief, the audience roared in laughter and applauded. They were so amused by the feud that they demanded a repetition of this incident. And Sanu had them repeat it throughout the play's month-long run, for the poor actor thought himself fortunate to be slapped at every performance by the woman he loved. Finally, perhaps as a result of this repeated scene, the actress relented, changed her mind, and married the actor.[106]

Sanu tells another story about the audience's participation in the two-act drama *al-Bint al-'Asriyya* (The Modern Young Woman), of which only a summary survives. Safsaf, the heroine, was an adventuress who, as a result of her indiscriminate imitation of Western ideas and manners, abused her freedom and overstepped the limits set for her by society. Because of her constant flirting, her fiancé broke their engagement. She was branded as promiscuous; no man would marry her, and she was left brokenhearted and forlorn. But the audience did not like this sad ending for the beautiful and vivacious Safsaf and hissed and booed. They implored Sanu to make Safsaf marry a young man worthy of her beauty and youth. The spectators even threatened that if he refused, they would never applaud him or attend his theater. He had to bow to their wishes, even though the alteration ran counter to the play's logical structure.[107]

The influence of Sanu's theater on the conservative elements of Egyptian society was apparently tremendous. He seems even to have stirred the imagination of the Azharite Ulama, which had never before been stirred to writing fiction. Al-Shaykh Muhammad Abd al-Fattah, a learned friend of Sanu's, composed a tragedy titled *Layla*, which was performed on Sanu's stage. The performance was attended by prominent ministers, scholars, and poets, and the audience's response was quite favorable. But during a scene depicting the killing of four sons of a tribal chief by a ruthless despot, a wag slyly whispered to two newly assigned policemen in the audience that it was their duty to prevent people from being murdered. The gullible policemen jumped to the stage and arrested the "murderer" amid the jeers and laughter of the spectators.[108]

Such incidents reflect Sanu's importance as the creator of a native theater using familiar rather than classic situations. His social comedies came at a time when the theater in Egypt was controlled by Syrian theatrical companies and Syrian playwrights who as an easy way out adapted or plagiarized masterpieces of Western drama. There is no evidence that Sanu's plays were ever presented to the public after 1872, even though his antagonist the Khedive was deposed in 1879. Fear of the government's wrath or the prevalent mood for utilizing Western plays may account for this neglect. In any case, theater like Sanu's lapsed into oblivion until a famous comedian Najib al-Rihani founded his comedy theater in the 1930's.

CHAPTER IV

THE TRANSLATION OF WESTERN FICTION

Importance of Translation

During the late nineteenth and early twentieth centuries a number of Western romances, novels, and dramas were translated into Arabic. These not only introduced Arab writers to the techniques of the various modern genres but also taught them the value of characters whose actions might both represent life and make it more meaningful.

Although the influence of such translations cannot be ignored, some contemporary Arab writers are reluctant to accept the position that "the art of the Arab story is a novelty which we adopted, among other things from Western literature, at the beginning of our cultural movement in the middle of the nineteenth century through translation or imitation."[1] They argue that ancient Arab writers were quite skilled in the art of story telling. Some of them support this view by referring to the love story "Maddad wa May" (from the book *al-Tijan,* by Wahb ibn Munabbih, d. 733), claiming that its theme is as significant and universal as those of Shakespeare's *Romeo and Juliet* and Bernardin de St. Pierre's *Paul et Virginie,* although it is plainly an indigenous work of Arabic literature.[2] The chief weakness in this view is the obvious confusion of the tale or romance of the pre-Islamic and Islamic periods, as typified by the *Thousand and One Nights,* with the novel and the short story. The Arabs, like other peoples, were obviously capable of inventing and developing prose narratives, but these do not approach Western fiction as we know it today. The native tale, for instance, as it is exemplified in the *Thousand and One Nights,* shows narrative and episodic sequence. In the Western story the plot also shows narrative sequence, but the sequence is ordered by causality. In the native tale, events are generally characterized by the fabulous. In the Western story the events tend to contribute to the plot. In the native tale the characters are types—the clever or lucky hero, the beautiful princess, the wise Caliph, the good and the bad advisers, the cunning old woman, and the gullible daydreamer. In the Western story the characters tend to be first individuals with well-defined personalities, although they also represent a type. In the native tale the setting is romantic, the long ago and the far away, and the atmosphere is magic. In the Western story the setting tends towards realism, the tension between man and himself, man against man, man against nature, or man against society. Since these critics did not clarify their concept of the *riwaya,* their argument is obviously futile.

Other critics take a more moderate position. For example, Mahmud Timur, the celebrated novelist and playwright, readily acknowledges that modern Arabic fiction has been substantially influenced by translations of Western literature, although he also notes its deep roots in the Arab past. A natural inclination toward prose fiction was clearly manifested in diverse and copious works over a period of several generations, but Timur concludes that the Arab writers' Oriental nature gave their works certain characteristics different from those of Western literature.[3] Yet he also confuses the tale with the modern novel and short story when he adds:

> We have been rather quick to deny that Arabic literature is void of stories. The reason for this denial is that we have used the Western story in its particular structure and determined frame as a criterion. Then we have searched in our Arabic literature to find works of a similar form, but to no avail. How wrong we are to use such a criterion, because Arabic literature has its own characteristics and form.[4]

Another contemporary critic states boldly and without reservation that the seeds of modern Arabic fiction, which is alien to Arab society, actually came from Europe. Yahya Haqqi, who is also a novelist, maintains that the Arab first came to know the modern story through translations. He cites as evidence the translations of ten thousand European stories compiled by the head of the national library in Beirut before the middle of this century. After such an extensive exposure to Western fiction, Arab writers felt that the tales of the *Thousand and One Nights* and the *maqama* were not only an insufficient basis for the creation of a full-fledged story, but "artistic tidbits, lacking unity and demonstrating no opinion or doctrine. They depict the ancient past, but have no connection with the present."[5] Haqqi goes on to say that although the Arabic story has assumed a special form and style different from those of *Hadith Isa ibn Hisham,* it lacks that mysterious touch that marks literary art. Haqqi concludes:

> There is no harm in admitting that the modern story came to us from the West, and that those who laid down its foundation were persons influenced by European literature, particularly French literature. Although masterpieces of English literature were translated into Arabic, French literature was the fountain of our story.[6]

According to Mikha'il Nu'ayma, a distinguished critic and man of letters, translation from Western fiction marks an essential stage in the development of Arabic literature. Because of the poverty of Arabic thought and the dearth of Arab writers, there is a desperate need for foreign literary ideas and models to satisfy the needs of Arab readers. He makes an agonizingly truthful appeal:

> Let us translate. The beggar begs when he cannot support himself by the work of his own hands. The thirsty man begs his neighbor for water when his well dries up. We are poor, though we brag about our abundant wealth. Why, then, should we not attempt to satisfy our needs from the abundance of others which is available to us? Our wells have no water to quench our thirst. Why should we, then, not obtain water from the wells of our

neighbors, which are not forbidden to us? We are in a stage of literary and social development in which we have become aware of many intellectual needs. These needs were never known to us before our recent contact with the West. We have no sufficient number of pens or brains to satisfy these intellectual needs. Therefore, let us translate.[7]

Wherever the truth may lie among these diverse opinions, the fact remains that Arab writers translated numerous short stories, novels, and dramas from Western tongues. Some of those who attempted to write novels or romances in the late nineteenth and early twentieth centuries acknowledged the superiority of the Western novel and their inability to produce fiction of comparable quality.[8]

At the beginning of the present century, as Sir Hamilton Gibb rightly observes:

> The incentive was thus lacking in literary circles to the composition of works of a similar kind [sic—similar to Western fiction] in Arabic. As the demand grew, the most natural course was to meet it by translating French and English novels, instead of setting to the ungrateful task of building up an indigenous novelist literature, which involved the creation of an entirely new literary technique.[9]

The investigation of such translations is an exceedingly complex business. Many translators simply plagiarized whole novels, distorting their contents or adapting them for Arabic audiences. Often the translator failed even to furnish the original author's name or the title of the novel. Scholars have made genuine attempts to trace the origin of novels translated from French and English, but many of them were lost, published in periodicals no longer available, or issued serially in daily or weekly journals which are difficult to locate.

The task of translation was begun by the Syrians, but after the Lebanese massacre of 1860 and the subsequent immigration of many Syrians to Egypt, it was taken up by some Egyptians before the turn of the century. The cultural conditions existing in the two countries in the nineteenth century gave rise to this activity. In the period preceding the French occupation of Egypt in 1798, the social, political, and cultural conditions in that country had reached their nadir. Learning and teaching at al-Azhar were limited to religious thought and related subjects, while the proficiency of craftsmen had deteriorated to an alarming degree. Ignorance, corruption, and degeneration were part of the Egyptians' way of life. In addition, the weakness of the Ottoman state whetted the ambitions of the Mamluks, whose perpetual struggles for power had turned the country into a battleground. Apart from a few merchants and businessmen, the number of Syrians in Egypt at that time was inconsequential.

Syria was also experiencing a prolonged, tragic cultural decline.[10] However, toward the end of the seventeenth century, with the arrival of religious missions, numerous Roman Catholic monastic orders, both native and foreign, had been established. These included al-Mukhallisiyya, al-Hannawiyya, and the Maronite order. Among the cultural developments they fostered was the founding of elementary schools whose curricula, in accordance with their objectives, were fundamentally religious.[11] Nevertheless, when the French traveler Volney visited Syria and Egypt at the end of the eighteenth century, he was alarmed at the ignorance prevailing in both countries as well as in Turkey. He remarked particularly on their poverty in the disciplines of science, medicine, music, and mathematics. He claims that one group of monks at St. John Monastery in al-Shuwayr was no less ignorant than the rest of the people, although they were affiliated with Rome; indeed, he says, they considered the person who told them that the earth rotates to be an enemy and a blasphemer.[12]

Yet a group of luminaries, both Christians and Muslims, shone in major Syrian cities like Aleppo. Their literary activity, together with the introduction of printing into Syria, may be said to mark the beginning of a new cultural epoch. Included in this group were the Patriarch Makarius al-Halabi, who visited Russia in 1652; the bishop Germanos Farhat the Maronite (d. 1732), who left several literary and philological writings, as well as translations; and Rev. Abd Allah Zakhir al-Halabi (d. 1748), who established what was probably the first press in al-Shuwayr and produced a number of religious and polemic works.[13]

At the end of the eighteenth century, after Syria had fallen prey to ruthless and dictatorial governors like Ahmad Pasha al-Jazzar, the Wali of Akka, and the Shihabi princes in Lebanon, a small group of Syrian merchants, mainly Christians, prospered for a time in Egypt. But the tyrannical rule of the Mamluks Murad and Ibrahim made it very difficult for them to pursue their business, and eventually they were forced to leave the country. They returned, however, after the French occupation had put an end to the Mamluks' rule and brought relative peace and safety. A number of Christians, both Syrian immigrants and natives of Egypt, were attracted to the service of the French as translators. But the activity of these men was limited to the translation of scientific and medical books, together with official proclamations and circulars issued by the French army command. Quite prominent among them was an ambitious and active clergyman, Rev. Rafa'il Anton Zakhur Rahib (d. 1831), a Vasilian monk who was the only Oriental member of L'Institut d'Égypte established at the direction of Napoleon Bonaparte.

Rev. Rafa'il Anton Zakhur Rahib came from a Malkite (Roman Catholic) Syrian family which immigrated from Aleppo to Egypt at the start of the eighteenth century. Born at Cairo March 7, 1759, he received his early religious education and training there, and at eighteen went to Rome to further his studies. He spent five years at the Séminaire de Sàint Athanus, and two more years at one of the Italian institutions, where he studied European languages. In 1781 he returned to Sayda and entered al-Mukhallis (Savior)

Monastery, where he was engaged in translating religious books and documents. In 1782 he was ordained a deacon, and three years later he became a priest. After 1785 he departed for Rome in a religious embassy, and while there he undertook to translate some of the documents associated with this embassy. When this embassy finished its duty in Rome, Rev. Zakhur Rahib returned to Egypt, remaining there until the French occupation of that country under Napoleon Bonaparte. On August 20, 1798, Napoleon issued instructions for the formation of L'Institut d'Égypte, stipulating in Article 20 that the Institute should employ an Arabic translator. Rev. Zakhur Rahib was selected for this post, and was also chosen as an honorary member of the Institute's Committee of Fine Arts and Literature. He also served as chief translator for Jacques Menou, who became the Commander-in-Chief of the French troops after the assassination of General Kléber. Extremely active and ambitious, he was highly esteemed by many prominent French army commanders, including Napoleon himself. But when Egypt reverted to Ottoman rule after the evacuation of the French troops in 1801, Zakhur found himself greatly hindered by the Ottomans, who were suspicious of Christians who had worked for the French. Seeking to escape his dilemma he wrote to Napoleon on March 14, 1802, declaring that he was ready to devote his life to the service of the French Republic under the First Consul. We have no evidence that Napoleon answered Zakhur's letter. However, these is evidence that Sebastiani, whom Napoleon sent to study conditions in Egypt in the aftermath of the evacuation, conferred with many prominent Egyptians and presented them with pictures of Napoleon. Rev. Zakhur Rahib was among these men and apparently seized this opportunity to renew his relations with the French ruler, for on November 20, 1802, he wrote Napoleon a second letter thanking him for his gift and pledging his absolute submission to "the angel of peace". He included in this letter an Arabic ode and a translation of it into Italian. Since his letter did not have the intended effect, however, Zakhur resolved to go to France himself. In 1803 he arrived at Marseilles and sent word to Talleyrand, the foreign minister, that he was carrying documents which were of the utmost importance to the French government, though the nature and contents of these documents were not known. Upon arriving in Paris, Zakhur wrote another letter in Italian, seeking an audience with Napoleon, and his request was approved. We do not have the details of their meeting, but sixteen days later, on September 24, 1803, Napoleon appointed Zakhur a professor at l'École des Langues at Paris. Zakhur lectured on colloquial Egyptian Arabic and was also engaged in the translation of manuscripts in the school's library pertaining to Egyptian history and literature. He was also active in writing, and published *Arabes du Désert* (Paris, 1819), a three-volume translation of *al-Badou aw Arab al-Sahra,* which he had written during his time in Egypt. Two of his works from this stay in France are extant only in manuscript form: a reader titled *Marj al-Axhar wa Shubban Hawadith al-Akhbar,* and *Majma' Asahh al-Ibarat wa Adaqq al-Rumuz fi Ard Misr wa Jabal al-Druze,* a history of Egypt and the

Druze mountain. Zakhur's translation of some of La Fontaine's fables, probably the earliest Arabic version of Western fiction, survives in a manuscript
at the library of the School of Oriental Languages in Paris. After Bonaparte's
defeat at Waterloo and his exile, Rev. Zakhur Rahib lost a staunch supporter
and patron, and the new French regime, at odds with those who had supported
Napoleon, decided to reduce Zakhur's salary. Rather than accept this humiliation, he returned to Egypt in 1816 and entered the service of Muhammad Ali as
a translator. At Muhammad Ali's order, he made an Arabic translation of
Niccolo Machiavelli's *The Prince,* now preserved as MS 435 in the Egyptian
National Archives at Dar al-Kutub.[14]

Presumably this activity by Zakhur and other Syrian translators was the
first of its kind not only in Egypt, but anywhere in the Arab East. It marked
the beginning, however inconsequential, of the Arab world's direct contact
with Western learning, though a more substantial acquaintance with European
sciences and culture had to wait until Muhammad Ali rose to power in 1804.
When, through a sequence of shrewd and calculated maneuvers, he emerged as
the governor of Egypt, a new era in the history of Egypt began.

The Syrians, whose prosperity and safety were seriously affected by the
power struggle after the French evacuation in 1801, were again forced to leave
Egypt. But when Muhammad Ali had restored peace, they returned and their
numbers were swelled by new immigrants. Rev. Zakhur Rahib came back to
Egypt from France in 1816 and entered the service of Muhammad Ali,[15] who
had organized an army and established various schools staffed with European
teachers. He enlisted the services of men who knew Arabic and one or more
European languages, especially French and Italian, to translate foreign textbooks into Arabic and serve as classroom interpreters for the teachers. Most,
if not all, of these translators were Syrians and prominent among them were
Rev. Zakhur Rahib, Yuhanna Anhuri, George Vidal, Augustine Sakakini, and
Yusuf Fir'awn.[16] Such employment was imposed by the exigencies of the
educational situation, and by no means an indication of genuine literary activity; the translations were restricted to military and scientific works. During his
stay in France, Rev. Zakhur Rahib translated several of La Fontaine's fables.
This work constitutes probably the first translation of European fiction into
Arabic.[17] Otherwise, the earliest Arabic versions of Western works of fiction
were random and unsystematic, often regarded as curiosities or as evidence of
the translator's literary virtuosity rather than as projects undertaken for the
public good. An anonymous translation of *Robinson Crusoe,* produced in
1835 at Malta, may have been the work of Ahmad Faris al-Shidyaq, who had
been engaged by American missionaries there in 1834 to assist them in
translating religious literature into Arabic.[18] It was perhaps the first Arabic
translation of a work of English fiction.

Despite the efforts of Marun Naqqash to adapt Western dramas for
native audiences in Syria, no systematic translation activity developed there.

The schools established by European and American missionaries in Syria and Lebanon, together with those later founded by natives, played a significant role in enlarging the audience for fiction. Yet, according to Jurji Zaydan, the real literary renaissance did not begin until the outrageous massacre of the Christians in 1860 forced many Lebanese villagers to move to Beirut, where foreigners established large schools.[19]

As the reading public grew, Arabic journals began to appear in substantial numbers, and they attracted new readers by offering translations of Western fiction, published both in single issues and in serial form. The readers were apparently pleased by what they read; many of them bought the journals primarily for the fiction they presented. The first journal to devote a regular section to fiction was *Hadiqat al-Akhbar*, founded in 1858 by Khalil al-Khuri. A translation of Dumas *père's The Count of Monte Cristo*, made by Salim Sa'b was published serially in *Al-Sharika al-Shahriyya* by Yusuf al-Shalfun.[20] Another journal, *al-Jinan*, founded by Butrus al-Bustani in January 1870, published numerous translations and adaptations of Western fiction, including sixteen translations by its editor, Salim al-Bustani, himself,[21] as well as a number of original pieces of Arabic fiction. Other works of Western fiction were published in a number of periodicals from the middle of the nineteenth century through the first quarter of this century.[22]

In Egypt, the School of Languages established by Muhammad Ali in 1835 was the first institution to deal with systematic translations of Western books. Although, as had been noted earlier, most of the works translated were non-fiction, there are two chief exceptions: the version of Fénelon's *Télémaque* by Rifa'a Rafi' al-Tahtawi,[23] and the works of al-Tahtawi's pupil Uthman' Jalal, which were primarily adaptations of Molière's dramas. The great majority of the translations of fiction were made by the Syrian immigrants, who controlled the major journals in Egypt. Moreover, unlike the Egyptian conservatives, the Syrians were not handicapped by any belief that fiction was immoral and worthless. They were more closely associated with European idea and culture than were the Egyptians, whose relations with Europe had suffered a setback under the Viceroy Abbas I. The daily newspaper *al-Ahram*, founded by the Lebanese Salim and Bishara Taqla in 1876 in Alexandria, devoted a regular space to translations of fiction.[24] Other periodicals, including *al-Muqtataf, al-Diya,* and *al-Hilal,* likewise attracted readers by entertaining them with translated stories. While the Syrian immigrants' journals were giving special attention to fiction, *Rawdat al-Akhbar, al-Mu'ayyad, al-Manar, al-Liwa, al-Jarida,* and other conservative Muslim publications concerned themselves with political, social, and religious reforms—although the last also devoted some attention to fiction.[25]

At least until the British occupation of Egypt in 1882, the Syrian immigrants concentrated on translating French fiction because of their long-standing cultural relationship with France. In fact, this relationship dates back to April, 1649, when the Roman Catholic Maronite community in Lebanon was placed under the protection of France and King Louis XIV.[26] Translations of fiction were also made from German, Italian, Russian, and other European languages, either directly or from French versions.[27] The majority of the reading public was made up of middle-class citizens educated in various foreign schools, but they had not acquired sufficient knowledge of European languages to savor fully works written in them. On the other hand, ancient Arabic folklore, whether written down or recited by story-tellers in the local coffeehouses, was no longer appealing or attractive to the more sophisticated reading public.

Although French had been the predominant Western language in Egypt since the time of Muhammad Ali, the translators increasingly devoted themselves to English fiction after the British occupation of Egypt in 1882. To establish a better political climate for the British to train civil and public servants, the Earl of Cromer, Her Majesty's Agent and General Consul in Egypt (1883-1907) introduced the English language into the schools in 1889. He argued that English and French were no longer merely additional subjects to study, but the basic medium of teaching such disciplines as history and the sciences. He further justified his program by pointing out the lack of teachers qualified to teach in the Arabic language. "As the number of highly trained Egyptian teachers increases," stated Cromer, "instruction will without doubt be given in Arabic to a much greater extent than heretofore."[28]

Thus the translation of English fiction emanated from two sources: the Syrian immigrants who had been trained at the American school in Beirut and the Egyptian students who had graduated from schools under British control. Another factor which contributed greatly to the popularity of translated fiction was Cromer's relatively lenient policy toward the native press, which tended to encourage freedom of expression. Cromer helped to establish journals published in both Arabic and English, and supported them materially as well as morally. These journals generally advocated Cromer's policies, however, and others which received no government support either withered away or found their circulation greatly limited.[29]

Nevertheless, several periodicals established by Syrian immigrants or by native Egyptians were widely circulated by the turn of the century.[30] One of the most outspoken and courageous was *al-Liwa*, founded by the nationalist leader Mustafa Kamil (d. 1908) in January, 1900.[31] Concomitant with the flourishing of domestic journalism, the Egyptians' technical mastery of printing improved greatly, and their printed volumes rivaled in quality those turned out in Syria.[32] As a result, many more journals began to publish both stories and serializations of full-length romances and novels translated from European languages.

Just as the writers of fiction, who had to satisfy the taste of the traditionalists, were slow in moving toward the creation of a full-fledged domestic novel and short story, the translators moved cautiously to avoid clashing with the accepted moral values of their society. A brief glance at the works translated reveals that most of them came from the romantic tradition. A translator had to portray a pure and Platonic love, not a merely sensual relationship. Thus one of the works which gained wide circulation was Sir Walter Scott's *Talisman,* in a version which Ya'qub Sarruf (d. 1927), a prominent writer, translator, and journalist, prepared in 1886 for distribution to those who had already paid their subscription to his periodical *al-Muqtataf* for the following year. Sarruf was motivated to make this romance available to Arab readers both by its historical theme and by the figure of Salah al-Din (Saladin), who has become a legendary exemplar of chivalry.[33] Another early version by the celebrated Butrus al-Bustani, titled *al-Tuhfa al-Bustaniyya fi al-Asfar al-Kuruziyya,* went through several printings. Among the other works of English fiction which soon appeared in Arabic versions were Scott's *Ivanhoe* (1889), by an anonymous translator; and one of his Waverly novels, serialized in *al-Muqattam* under the title *al-Shahama wa al-Afaf* in 1890; Lord Bulwer-Lytton's *The Last Days of Pompeii* (1889), by Farida 'Atiyya; Swift's *Gulliver's Travels* (1909), by Muhammad al-Siba'i; Wilkie Collins's *The Woman in White* (1909), by Muhammad al-Siba'i; Robert Louis Stevenson's *Treasure Island* (1921), by Riyad Junaydi Effendi; and yet another version of *Robinson Crusoe* (1923), by Ahmad Abbas.[34] Though the simpler themes and language of romances gained them wider popularity, some works of artistic substance were also translated, either to suit a very limited audience or to reflect the sensitivity of the translators. Among these were Charles Dicken's *A Tale of Two Cities* (1912), translated by Muhammad al-Siba'i, and Thackeray's, *Henry Esmond* (1918), though Wahba Mas'ad Effendi's version of this latter work should probably be regarded as a plagiarism.

Translation from Russian fiction was also current in the latter part of the nineteenth and the early twentieth centuries, particularly in Palestine. This was partly connected with religion, since after the eighteenth century Russia claimed protection of the Greek Orthodox subjects of the Ottoman Sultan and the holy places in Palestine. To demonstrate their interest in the religious and social well being of their brethren in the faith in the Arab East, Russian missionaries were sent to Syria, particularly Palestine, to establish schools, religious orders, and religious societies. Most of these were elementary schools, such as those established in Hims and Baskanta, one of whose graduates is the celebrated man of letters Mikha'il Nu'ayma.[35]

The Russians also established a Teachers Higher College in Nazareth, whose students were chosen from the top graduates of the Russian-operated elementary schools. It was in these schools that many Arab students were introduced to the masterpieces of Russian literature. In fact, some of the teachers of these schools were Arabs selected to complete their higher education in Russia.[36] Thus there emerged a group of Syro-Palestinian Arabs who perfected the Russian language and appreciated Russian literature and fiction. Nu'ayma, for example, states that as soon as he had gained a fair command of the Russian language he began to read Russian periodicals as well as the works of writers like Tolstoy, Dostoevsky, and Chekhov. The masterpieces of Russian literature made him aware of the abject poverty of Arabic literature in the period around the turn of the century. Realizing the Arabs' dire need for writers who cared more for substance than for literary trivialities, he was not merely shocked by the dearth of efficient writers, but felt ashamed.[37]

Khalil Ibrahim Baydas (d. 1949), a writer and journalist, was perhaps the first translator of Russian fiction into Arabic. He was born in Nazareth in 1875 and received his early education at the Greek Orthodox school in his town.[38] He joined the Russian Teachers Higher College in Nazareth and after his graduation was appointed principal of the Russian elementary school in Hims. He was transferred to the Russian elementary school in Biskanta, Lebanon, among whose students was Mikha'il Nu'ayma between 1899 and 1902.[39] It was Baydas who paved the way for Nu'ayma to enroll in the Russian school in Nazareth.[40]

In 1905 Baydas was transferred to Haifa, and in November 1908 he published a periodical *Majallat al-Nafa'is* which was renamed in the following year *al-Nafa'is al-'Asriyya*. It was moved to Jerusalem in 1911, was suspended for two years, moved once more to Haifa and finally disappeared in 1919.[41] In his periodical, Baydas published his translations of many works of Russian fiction as well as his own fiction.

Baydas was very active in translating Russian fiction into Arabic. In 1898 alone he translated three Russian novels, Pushkin's *The Captain's Daughter*, published in Beirut, *al-Qusaqi al-Walhan*, (literally, the *Amorous Cossack*), serialized in the journal *Lubnan*, and published separately in 1899; and *al-Tabib al-Hadhiq*, (literally, *The Clever Physician*), published in Beirut. Furthermore, he translated Tolstoy's *Anna Karenina*, which was serialized in *al-Nafa'is* in 1913, and *Knyaz Serebryany* (Prince Serebryani) under the Arabic title *Ahwal al-Istibdad* (The Horrors of Despotism), published in Haifa in 1909 and reprinted in Cairo in 1927.[42]

Baydas also translated several European novels from Russian versions. To one work by Marie Corelli he gave the Arabic title *Shaqa al-Muluk* (literally The Misery of Kings), although the Russian translation by Z. Gora Viskaya, had given it another title. The Arabic translation was serialized in *al-Nafa'is* in 1908 and was published separately in Jerusalem in 1922. Another novel which Baydas translated from a Russian translation was one by the Italian writer Emilio Salgari, which Baydas gave the Arabic title *al-Hasna al-Mutanakkire* (literally, *The Disguised Beautiful Woman)*. This was also serialized in *al-Nafa'is* in 1911 and was later published separately in 1925. A Russian version of a work in German by F. Mehlbach was translated by Baydas under the title *Henry al-Thamin was Zawjatuhu al-Sadisa* (Henry VIII and his Sixth Wife) and serialized in the same periodical in 1912-13 and later published separately in Jerusalem in 1921. His translation of a historical novel, titled *al-'Arsh wa al-Hub* (The Throne and Love), was serialized in *al-Nafa'is* in 1914 and published separately in Jerusalem in 1921.[43]

Baydas's knowledge of European languages other than Russian was evidently not strong enough to enable him to translate fiction from the original languages. In fact, translating from a translation of the original was not uncommon in the Arab world; Khalil Matran's translation of some of Shakespeare's plays from the French and Ahmad Hasan al-Zayyat's translation of *Werthers Leiden* from the French are examples. However, al Zayyat's version of Geothe's story is in so beautiful and engaging a style that it has become in itself an Arabic literary masterpiece.

Baydas' approach was not greatly different from that of other translators in his time. Like Tanius Abduh, he took great liberties with the text —often to such an extent that nothing was left of it except its general outlines. In his introduction to his translation of *al-Mutanakkira al-Hasna*, Baydas states that his translation of Salgari's romance is meant to be different from the original. He apologizes that he was forced to condense and summarize a great portion of the text because such a voluminous work would be boring to his readers.[44]

Even his version of *Knyaz Serebryany*, which was translated directly from Tolstoy's original, changed, omitted, and reorganized many sections of the novel. He claimed that he intended to render it more suitable and pleasing to the readers and to emphasize its dominant theme of tyranny and despotism. Having lived under the rule of the notorious Ottoman Sultan Abd al-Hamid II, Baydas perhaps intended *Ahwal al-Istibtad* (The Horrors of Despotism), to remind his readers of conditions in their own country.[45]

Several graduates of the Russian schools in Syria and Palestine followed Baydas's footsteps. However, their translations were usually made from the original Russian. In 1902 Rafa'il Sa'd's version of Tolstoy's *Dreutzer Sonata* was first published not in the Arab world but in Rio de Janeiro, though it was published by Salim Qub'ayn in Cairo in 1904. Qub'ayn also translated Tolstoy's play *The Power of Darkness* in 1909; it was reprinted in Cairo in 1926. In 1908 Rashid Haddad translated Tolstoy's *Resurrection* and *A Prisoner of the Caucasus* published in 1908. In 1922 Anton Ballan published a series of popular tales by Tolstoy under the Arabic title *Rawa'i al-Khayal*. Ballan had been active in translating some of Tolstoy's novels and publishing them in his periodical *Hims*. In 1915 Bebbawi Ghali al-Duwayri published his translation of Tolstoy's *Family Happiness*.[46]

In the first quarter of this century some Egyptian writers translated several works by Tolstoy, including the play *The Light That Shines in the Darkness* by Muhmud Tahir Lashin. Other works of fiction by Tolstoy, such as *Assarhadon*, *Family Happiness*, and several children's stories, were translated and published in 1928. It is estimated that before 1946 no less than twenty of Tolstoy's works had been translated into Arabic.[47]

In the decades following the Second World War Tolstoy's *Anna Karenina*, *Resurrection*, and the trilogy *Childhood, Boyhood and Youth* were translated and published in Arabic. A translation of *War and Peace* was made by Baydas's son Émile and published in Beirut. Indeed, most of the masterpieces of prominent Russian writers are available today in Arabic translations.

Translations from European sources often reflected the personal taste of the translators, rather than the interest of their readers. The press and the market were flooded with the worst of European fiction,[48] and not until the first quarter of this century did translators begin to deal in earnest with the masterpieces of Western literature.

For some reason, probably the love of adventure and heroism, which abound in Arab tales, the translators took a special liking to the works of Alexandre Dumas *père*. A serial translation of *The Count of Monte Cristo* by Salim Sa'b was published in the periodical *al-Sharika al-Shahriyya*. In 1870 another translation of this work, made by Bishara Shadid, appeared in Cairo.[49] *Les deux Dianes* (The Count of Montgomery), translated by Kaiser Zaniyya, was published serially in *al-Ahram* in 1881 and reprinted in a separate volume at Alexandria in 1907; Najib Haddad published his translation of *The Three Musketeers* at Cairo in 1888.[50] Between 1888 and 1910, no fewer than twenty-five novels by Dumas *père* were translated into Arabic, including two which he wrote in collaboration with Émile Gaboriau and August W. Schlegel.[51]

Between 1875 and 1894, Arabic versions of at least four works of fiction by Jules Verne also appeared, along with works by Chateaubriand, Pierre Zaccone, Eugène Sue, and other French authors.[52] Several works by Victor Hugo and George Ohmet were translated into Arabic by Mikha'il Jarjur and published serially in the journal *Hadiqat al-Akhbar* at Alexandria in 1888. Interestingly, Jarjur's translation of the episodes of Fantine, Cosette, and Jean Valjean from *Les Misérables* (1888) appeared almost two full decades before Hafiz Ibrahim made his loose and inaccurate translation of the same work.[53] After the turn of the century there was a great increase in the quantity of French fiction translated, particularly the works of romantic authors.

The translation of French and English dramas was even more extensive, although the translators seem to have been more selective in this area. The drama had already been introduced into the Arab world, of course, and because plays were performed rather than read, they appealed to a wider audience than prose fiction. Among those dramatists most favored were Molière, Racine, Corneille, and Shakespeare. Arabic versions were also made of several dramas by Victor Hugo, Voltaire's *Mérope,* and one or two dramas by George Bernard Shaw.[54]

By the turn of the century, a new generation of Egyptians, educated under the British occupation, began to rival the Syrians in the translation of Western fiction. Two new phenomena could be observed: the establishment not only of periodicals wholly devoted to the publication of fiction, but also of monthly and bi-monthly volumes of translated fiction published either by individuals or by publishing houses, and the commercialization of translation as both the publishers and the translators discovered in it a new, rewarding source of income.[55] Notable among the periodicals and monthly volumes were *Silsilat al-Fukahat* (Beirut, 1884); *Diwan al-Fukaha* (Beirut, 1885); *Muntakhabat al-Riwayat* (Select Romances: Cairo, 1894), by Iskandar Karkus; *Silsilat al-Riwayat* (Cairo, 1899), by Muhammad Khidr and Bashir al-Halabi; *Majallat al-Riwayat-al-Shahriyya* (Cairo, 1902), by Ya'qub Jamal; and *Musamarat al-Nadim* (Cairo, 1903), by Ibrahim Ramzi and Izzat Hilmi. Perhaps the most popular of all was Khalil Sadiq's by-monthly *Musamarat al-Sha'b* (Cairo, 1904), which encouraged many writers by publishing their translations.[56]

Amazingly, almost until the end of World War II, most of the translated fiction consisted of detective and mystery stories. This does not mean, of course, that the masterpieces of Western fiction were not available in Arabic, but that they were the exception rather than the rule. The works of Arthur Conan Doyle, Ponson du Terrail, Zavier de Montepin, Michel Zevaco, Paul Segonzac, Maurice Leblanc, Mary Jules, Michel Morphy, and Charles Merouvel were widely available. Detectives and romantic adventurers, such as Conan Doyle's *Sherlock Holmes*, du Terrail's *Rocambole*, Leblanc's *Arsène Lupin*, and Zevaco's *Pardaillan* were very popular in the Arab world in the 1930's.[57]

Of course, these popular translations were not made for any literary or aesthetic purpose. They brought their translators quick fame and easy living and provided a semiliterate, unsophisticated audience with temporary diversion. Because they were mass produced by men with little or no literary finesse, they were in most cases superficial and erratic; moreover, they were badly printed on inferior paper and priced low enough—no more than a dime for an individual member of a series—to be within the means of nearly every reader. Although it is impossible to cite the names of all the translators of fiction of this sort, we should mention Niqula Rizq Allah (d. 1915), Tanius Abduh (d. 1926), and As'ad Khalil Daghir (d. 1935) were the most prolific of them. Tanius Abduh alone is said to have translated no less than seven hundred works of fiction into Arabic.[58]

In many instances the translators of Western fiction took extensive and sometimes unwarranted liberties with the original text of a work.[59] Ya'qub Sarruf not only changed the title of Scott's *Talisman* to *Qalb al-Asad wa Salah al-Din* (The Lion Heart and Saladin), but also admitted that he had taken the liberty of omitting, adding, and changing parts of this romance to suit his audience's taste.[60] Another translator, Muhammad Kamil Hajjaj, summarized the works of no less than twenty Western writers and published them at Cairo in two volumes under the title *Balaqhat al-Gharb*.[61] Other translators changed the titles and the names of the characters as well as the contents, in order, they claimed, to make the translated work more acceptable to their readers and more consistent with the native literary tradition.

An interesting case involves a romance titled *Tuhfat al-Murid fi Ziwaj Odette bi Farid*, translated by Muhammad Lutfi Telegrafji (a telegraph operator) published in Cairo in 1888. His introduction justifies his alterations by pointing out that when he saw that many writers had compiled volume upon volume of histories, exhortations, aphorisms, tales, and poetry for the common benefit of their readers, he too found it expedient to present a "strange tractate" based on an English version of the original French work. He changed the Western names to facilitate their pronunciation for the "Sons of the Arabs," a generic term applied to all Arabs; hence this is a "love story between Odette and a Christian young man whom I have chosen to call Farid."[62]

Some translators had the audacity to plagiarize the whole works without mentioning the name of the author or even the language of the original. In 1918 there appeared *Mukhtasar Sirat Henry Esmond* (A Short Biography of Henry Esmond), by the renowned man of letters Wahba Mas'ad Effendi, a member of the staff of the Great Coptic College in Cairo. Dedicated to the Director General of the Coptic Schools in Egypt, this work was branded by Latifa al-Zayyat "an audacious thievery."[63] Al-Zayyat gives several more instances of outright plagiarism, including Hafiz Awad's version of Frederick Marryat's *Japhet in Search of a Father*, which was published in the *Musamarat al-Sha'b* series. Awad gave new titles to each of the five installments, justifying this division on the grounds that each of the component parts should be considered as a separate work of fiction.[64] Another translator, Abd al-Qadir Hamza, plagiarized a French novel which he called *Dahaya al-Aqdar* (The Victims of the Fates) for the same series.[65] Such unethical practices made it very difficult to establish the source of some of the translations of Western fiction. Henri Pérès, who meticulously compiled a substantial bibliography of works translated from French, found it impossible to trace the origin of many romances; finally he gave up his investigation and listed many as anonymous.[66]

Still other translators tried to legitimize their plagiarism by mentioning only the language of the original work, concealing the name of the author. The editor of *al-Hilal* criticized these translators in unequivocal terms:

> We blame translators, and particularly those who translate romances, for suppressing the names of authors. What is the wisdom of doing so? If these translators claim these works to be their own, we could then say that they want to ascribe these works to themselves. But when they admit that they have only translated these works, would it not be better if they affixed the name of the author, who has consumed his brain and spent nights in

research and exposed himself to bitter criticism and reproach in order to write a romance? He even probably paid for the publication of his romance, without making a profit. Should not his right in writing his work be preserved as we preserve our right of publishing these works?[67]

The Quality of the Translations

Since these translations were mass produced by men who were motivated by monetary rather than literary considerations, it is hardly to be expected that they should be flawless. In fact, they are often poor, principally because of the translators' utter disregard for the literary essence of the works with which they were dealing. Tanius Abduh was perhaps the most irresponsible of all: according to writers and journalists who knew him personally, Abduh did not really translate but Arabicized what he read. He never adhered strictly to the original or tried to convey its meaning. He translated anywhere and everywhere, regardless of his circumstances—in a coffeeshop, on a sidewalk, on a train, even on the flat roof of his house. He was, if we may believe one contemporary description, a walking library. A writer and journalist, Salim Sarkis, says that Abduh carried with him sheets of paper in one pocket and a French novel in the other. He would then read a few lines, put the novel back in his pocket, and begin to scratch in a fine script whatever he could remember of the few lines he had read. He wrote all day long without striking out a word or rereading a line.[68]

Another writer, Karam Milhim Karam, says that in translating, Abduh never adhered to the text of the original, but merely summarized what he had read, using poor and inartistic language. Karam does not agree with Abduh that the poor language of his translations should be excused on the grounds that it was easier for the common reader to understand. Moreover, Karam says, Abduh's shoddy translations cannot be justified simply by his claim that he was too anxious to make a living from them to have sufficient time to concentrate on their quality.[69]

More qualified writers were able to make translation a respectable literary craft. They were more conscientious in choosing the works they dealt with and in conveying the spirit of the author in an artistic Arabic style, with relatively little loss of the original sense. Some of them even took pains to write introductions providing a brief account of the author and his period, his purpose in writing the work translated, and the aesthetic value of his work.[70]

Muhammad al-Siba'i (d. 1931), who spent a quarter of a century translating works from several European languages, belonged to what has been termed the "modern school" of translation, which included Ahmad Hafiz 'Awad, Ibrahim Abd al Qadir al-Mazini, Muhammad Badran, and other graduates of the Higher Teachers' Schools, known for their proficiency in both Arabic and European languages.[71] Al-Siba'i was born in Cairo in 1881, to an Egyptian father and a Turkish mother. After graduating from the Higher Teachers' College, he spent some years in teaching, but was unable to endure the rigid regulations of the state schools. Thus, he resigned his position to venture into the field of writing. He began his new career by writing in *al-Jarida* in 1908 and later in *al-Bayan,* a periodical founded by Abd al-Rahman al-Barquqi in 1911.[72] His first translation of the French *Cariolenes,* appeared in 1912. Among the works of Western fiction he translated were masterpieces of French, English, and Russian literature. His noteworthy translations from English included Dickens' *A Tale of Two Cities,* Thackeray's *Henry Esmond* (in collaboration with his younger brother Taha), and Shakespeare's *The Merchant of Venice.* From the Russian authors he generally chose realistic writings of wider variety than those translated by Khalil Baydas.[73] His contemporaries, such as al-Mazini, considered al-Siba'i a very meticulous and capable translator who not only captured the spirit of the author but made the work thoroughly enjoyable to the Arab reader. He deserves high praise for having chosen to deal with the best of Western fiction, for he was genuinely concerned with the aesthetic and literary development of his audience. Near the end of his career, however, al-Siba'i grew despondent, saying that the writing profession had become barren and that his pen had become as undignified as a beggar's flute.[74]

Other writers carried on the process of adapting Western fiction which had begun in the nineteenth century. Among these, Mustafa Lutfi al-Manfaluti (d. 1924) is one of the most important literary figures in the Arab world in the late nineteenth and early twentieth centuries. His exquisite (if somewhat sentimental) treatment of his material made him not only the master of a distinct Arabic style, but also the founder of a literary school.[75] His popularity among Arab readers, young and old, was challenged only by the cryptic and highly sentimental writings of Gibran Kahlil Gibran (d. 1931), whose *The Prophet* and other early writings in English were translated into Arabic by Rev. Antonius Bashir.

Al-Manfaluti was born in 1876 in Manfalut, Egypt, to an Arab father and a Turkish mother, both of fairly high social standing. At the local *Kuttab,* a primary school attached to a mosque, he received a firm religious education and, like other children, learned parts of the Qur'an by heart when he was barely eleven years old. He spent ten years in study at the religious university of al-Azhar but became disenchanted with the traditional subjects taught there and found in the lectures of the modernist al-Shaykh Muhammad Abduh what his perplexed soul was yearning for. As he admits, he was influenced strongly by the bold, revolutionary teachings of Abduh, especially by his new approach to the exposition of the Qur'an and to the works of pioneer Arab writers.[76] His main interest was not in cultivating religious studies but in absorbing all he could of various literary works.

Disregarding the peculiar notion held by many ultra-conservative Shaykhs at al-Azhar that studying literature or even acquiring a little knowledge of it was "an act of idleness and a temptation of the Devil," al-

Manfaluti read the works of ancient and modern Arab writers voraciously. His reading about the pre-Islamic period became so imprinted in his memory that the Arabs' tribal life, their tents and camels, their wars, their loves and other emotions became utterly real for him.[77] He read in translation whatever he could obtain of Western fiction, chiefly the works of the romantics and of the neo-Arab writers in America who had been influenced by the American romantics. The influence of romanticism, however slight, is nonetheless real in the writing of al-Manfaluti.

His life, however, was neither cheerful nor enjoyable. When his master al- Shaykh Muhammad Abduh died in 1905, al-Manfaluti, despite his differences with and criticism of Abduh, grieved greatly. To assuage his sorrow, he returned to his native town and remained two years in semi-isolation, busying himself only with an article for al-Shaykh Ali Yusuf's journal *al-Mu'ayyad*. Later, *al-Manfaluti* was supported by the nationalist leader Sa'd Zaghlul Pasha, who gave him a job as an Arabic editor at the Ministry of Education. When Zaghlul was transferred to the Ministry of Justice, al-Manfaluti went with him but was dismissed from his position as soon as Zaghlul was out of power. He continued to write for local journals until 1923, when Zaghlul procured for him a position as a clerk at the Egyptian Senate. He did not enjoy this new post long, however, for he died the following year.[78]

Except for the severe but highly disciplined attack against the literary conservatism of Mustafa Sadiq al-Rafi'i (d. 1937) by modernist writers like Taha Husayn, Ibrahim Abd al-Qadir al-Mazini, and Abbas Mahmud al-Aqqad, no other Arab literary figure had come under such heavy critical fire as al-Manfaluti. Both al-Mazini and al-Aqqad in their book *al-Diwan fi al-Adab wa al-Naqd* were intent on destroying the image al-Manfaluti had created among the enlightened Arab readers.[79] The controversy over al-Manfaluti's literary skill and achievements was stirred up not only by his writings and ideas, but by his temperament. His emotionalism, his impatience, and most of all his limited education made him unaware that he might simultaneously be a conservative and a liberal, a reformer and a reactionary, a moralist who condemned suicide and an author who showed some of his characters taking their own lives.[80] Hamilton A.R. Gibb has rightly observed:

> As a religious reformer, he attacked conservatism and its sanctuary, the College of al-Azhar, and condemned saint worship, the derwish orders, etc., but went out of his way to insult his master Muhammad Abduh, and having blamed him for introducing modern interpretations of the Koran, went on in the very next paragraph to make drastic interpretations himself. Together with a fervent Islamic patriotism, which led him at one time to condemn all Western studies and at another to protest against Armenian massacres, he betrayed on almost every page of his work the influence of Western currents of thought. ...In essay after essay he preached the duty of charity (*ihsan*), especially toward wronged and persecuted women. Yet he

attacked Qasim Amin as the corrupter of Egyptian womanhood, and
asserted the intellectual inferiority of women to men.[81]

Contemporary critics have been at odds as to how they should categorize al-
Manfaluti as a writer. Some positively classify him as a translator, others make
him merely an adapter of Western fiction, [82] and still others regard him as a
translator with the special gift of rewriting a work in such a manner that the
new version became his own creation.[83] Some consider him primarily an
essayist and short story writer.[84] That al-Manfaluti as an essayist possessed an
exquisite and effective style is especially apparent in the three volumes of *al-
Nazarat* (1910-21). But he cannot properly be called a translator, for he
himself knew no European languages. He simply reworked the literal and probably unpolished translations made for him by friends and put them into his
own melancholy, sentimental style. Often he took extensive liberties with the
original to accommodate the theme to a Muslim background and to promote
his own didactic purposes. He could cut down an entire romance into a short
story, as with Dumas *fils' La dame aux camélias,* which he published as *al-
Dahiyya aw Mudhakkirat Margarit* (The Victim, or the Memoirs of
Marguerite). He condensed Chateaubriand's *Atala et René* and *Les Aventures
du ledernier Abencérage* into short stories, giving them the titles *al-Shuhada*
(The Martyrs) and *al-Dhikra* (Recollection), but indicated immediately
beneath their titles that they were translations.[85] From a literal translation
made for him by Muhammad Fu'ad Kamil he rewrote Alphonse Karr's *Sous
les tilleuls,* which he retitled *Magdulin aw Taht Zilal al-Zayzafun* (Madeleine
or Under the Shades of the Linden Trees). He also reworked an earlier version
of Edmond Rostand's *Cyrano de Bergerac,* gave it the title *al-Sha'ir aw Sirano
di Berjrak,* and published it in prose form at Cairo in 1921.[86] He took the
greatest liberty with his version of François Coppée's drama *Pour la couronne,*
reworking a previous translation made by Muhammad Abd al- Salam al-
Jundi. Al-Manfaluti's prose version, which he called *Fi Sabil al-Taj,* bears
deep traces of his highly rhetorical style.[87] He also adapted Bernardin de St.
Pierre's *Paul et Virginie,* publishing it under the title *al-Fadila* (Virtue) *aw
Paul wa Virginie* (Cairo, 1923).[88]

Al-Manfaluti's Arabic adaptations of Western fiction merit attention as
the works of a man of letters greatly influenced by Western ideas, which he
both admired and detracted. It is evident that his actual objective was to use
Western fictional techniques to project himself, his Islamic ideals, and the sentiments of his society. His adaptation of Coppée's *Pour la couronne* repeated-
ly subordinates the story to long and tedious orations in praise of patriotic
devotion to one's country and concern for one's fellows. In the second
chapter, the protagonist, Constantine, explains to his stepmother the necessity
of caring for women, and children, and those too weak to care for themselves.
Because of his didactic aim, al-Manfaluti often forgets about time, place, and
even the characters in order to confront his audience in the manner of a
religious preacher. His moralizing becomes repetitious, and the discerning

reader may find that it detracts from the main theme. The subject of the original French drama is essentially the attempt of the Balkan countries to throw off the Ottoman yoke, but its straightforward and vigorous French drama is weighted down by al-Manfaluti's tiresome moral exhortations. Moreover, he distorts the dialogue by interpolating Qur'anic verses, forgetting that the speaker to whom he assigns them is a Christian defending his country against the Muslim Turks.[89] As al-Manfaluti presents the matter, the chief issue is not the struggle of a vigorous nation for its freedom and independence, but the submissiveness of a defeated people blaming their tragic domination by their enemy on their arrogance, their confidence in themselves rather than God, and the contempt of the rich and strong among them for the poor and weak.[90] In many ways his attitude is curiously reminiscent of the early medieval Christian apologists, who made profane writers of the pre-Christian period unwilling and posthumous defenders of the Gospel. He was perhaps trying to do for Islam what St. Augustine had previously done for Christianity.

Al-Manfaluti's unique techniques are more clearly revealed by a comparison of his adaptation of St. Pierre's *Paul et Virginie* with that by Uthman Jalal. Jalal's objective was to Egyptianize this romance and give it a strong Muslim atmosphere, to make it more acceptable to a domestic audience of unsophisticated readers. Al-Manfaluti's adaptation, on the other hand, is written in a highly rhetorical and polished language and is intended for an élite group of readers, the graduates of Dar al-Ulum and similar schools established along Western lines since the time of the Khedive Isma'il.[91]

Nevertheless, al-Manfaluti was more successful than Jalal in choosing Western works which were suited to the tastes and sentiments of his audience. This fiction was produced by the romantic school in Europe and the Arab school in *al-Mahjar* (the Americas), whose Syrian members were influenced by Western romantic writers. Most of it dealt with such touching problems as ideal love and the plight of the poor and oppressed. These highly sentimental romances, together with his sentimental style, explain al-Manfaluti's infatuating appeal to the Arab reader's fundamentally romantic nature.

Al-Manfaluti's ideas and style were vehemently attacked by some of his contemporaries. Some of them found his writing affected and effeminate and his thoughts (if they credited him with any) quite superficial.[93] Others felt that he had distorted the original works and transformed them into essays because he had no genuine talent for writing fiction.[94] But at least one contemporary, Isa 'Ubayd, himself a pioneer in Arabic literature, does not blame al-Manfaluti for converting Karr's novel *Sous les tilleuls* into a fantastic piece of prose fiction, or for cruelly suppressing the personality of Stephen. With great respect for the man he calls "our greatest living writer," 'Ubayd defends al-Manfaluti's Arabicization of Karr's novel by asserting that he was subject to his Oriental temperament and highest ideals:

Do not his distortion of this romance and modification of the characters indicate that he was subject to his Oriental temperament, which motivated
him to portray human perfection and the highest ideals of immaculate
love? Furthermore, does not al-Manfaluti's choice of *Cyrano de Bergerac*
serve as proof enough that there is an inherent propensity in the Egyptian-
writer that motivates him to portray impeccable beauty and perfection
which are as far from reality as heaven is from earth.[95]

Regardless of the validity of these opinions, al-Manfaluti's wholly new
style captivated not only a large number of Arab readers, but even those
writers who were later to become his severest critics.[96] Young writers like Taha
Husayn and Ahmad Hasan al-Zayyat sat in the Abbasid porch of al-Azhar
Mosque, waiting for the newest issue of *al-Mu'ayyad* so that they could read
al-Manfaluti's articles, essays and stories. Al-Zayyat professes that he was
flabbergasted by al-Manfaluti's style, and he and his colleagues wished that
they might establish contact with this man "whom God has chosen to carry the
message of the newborn literature."[97]

More than that of anyone else, al-Zayyat's style in translating Western
fiction into Arabic bears the mark of al-Manfaluti's influence. Like al-
Manfaluti, he began his career in literature by absorbing the works of ancient
Arab writers and later fell under the influence of Western literature, which was
more viable, relevant, and universal than that of his native precursors.[98]

Born and raised in al-Daqahliyya in the Egyptian countryside, he reveals
the profound influence of Egyptian village life in works which are filled with
descriptions of the village and the sad lot of the wretched *fallah*. The four-
volume *Wahi al-Risala*, containing his essays and observations over twenty
years, to a great degree resembles al-Manfaluti's *Nazarat*, except that al-
Zayyat is less depressing and lachrymose. Yet every page of *Wahi al-Risala*
betrays his romanticism and his hopelessly unrealistic approach to
social, political, and moral problems of great magnitude.

Al-Zayyat studied law in France in the 1920's, and may have practiced
his profession upon returning to Egypt after receiving his degree in 1925. By
1930, however, he was in Baghdad, teaching Arabic literature at the Higher
Teachers' School.[99] There he established intimate relations with King Faysal I
as well as with Iraqi men of letters, including the famous poet Jamil Sidqi al-
Zahawi (d. 1936).[100] Three years later, however, this school was closed down,
and al-Zayyat returned to Cairo to embark on a long literary career which
began with the publication of his esteemed weekly *al-Risala*.

The anecdote he relates about the birth of this journal illustrates his
determination to carve for himself a place in the domain of Arabic literature.
One evening in November 1933, four months after his return from Baghdad,
al-Zayyat went to see his friend Taha Husayn, who had recently lost his chair
at the College of Arts in Fu'ad University. Al-Zayyat suggested the publication
of a literary weekly, but Husayn's response was discouraging. Such a

magazine, Husayn argued, would have little appeal in Egyptian society; the majority of the people were illiterate, and those who could read tended to prefer either European works or light, entertaining pieces written by domestic authors. Al-Zayyat, realizing the difficulties of his project, decided to go ahead with it anyway, and thus *al-Risala* was born. Until its disappearance in 1953, it served as a kind of "literary school," training and polishing the styles of formerly unknown writers. It became the mouthpiece of the Arab intelligentsia, who found in it a platform from which they could set forth their opinions. Its reputation reached the Western world, and many prominent Orientalists contributed articles to it.[101]

Unlike Tanius Abduh, al-Zayyat did not rely on translation for his living. He was a prominent litterateur with an exquisite and distinctive style, a prolific writer who produced nearly twenty books of his own, and his literary achievement in *Wahi al-Risala* was formally recognized when he received the State Prize in 1953.[102] While al-Zayyat, like al-Manfaluti, is a sentimental writer whose heart is particularly touched by poverty, his method of alleviating suffering does not extend beyond doling out some money in the form of alms or the Muslim poor tax. He believes it sufficient that tax monies should be collected from the wealthy and distributed to the poor. He sincerely feels that poverty can be combatted only through religion, which would create better relations among all members of the community and would force the rich to help the needy.[103]

More than for his essays or original works, however, al-Zayyat will be remembered for his translations of Goethe's *Werthers Leiden* (The Sorrows of Werther) and Alphonse Lamartine's *Raphael*. Drawing from the impeccable, highly polished language of the Qur'an, these will remain classics of Arabic literature.[104] The fact that al-Zayyat translated the *Sorrows of Werther* from French rather than the original German does not diminish the quality of his work; in Goethe's sentimental novella he found echoes of his own suffering in an early frustrated love affair, whose end pulled him back into the bitter world of reality. His Arabic version of Lamartine's *Raphael* was likewise motivated by his sentimental nature.

Both are considered as some of the best translations made from Western literature. Indeed, by the time I was introduced to them in 1938, they were commonly read by the students of secondary schools in Iraq, along with the adaptations of al-Manfaluti and the works of Gibran Kahlil Gibran.

For some time al-Zayyat felt the need for a systematic effort to translate Western literary and scientific masterpieces. In an open letter to the Minister of Education, Abd al-Razzaq al-Sanhuri, he proposed the establishment of a translation bureau independent of the Ministry, with the same status enjoyed by Egypt's institutions of higher learning, to be staffed by two hundred translators competent in at least three European languages. Its translation efforts would be selective and systematic, and its goal would be a complete translation of four hundred pages each day, so that any important new book published in Europe would soon be available in Arabic.[105]

Al-Zayyat stated unequivocally that modern Arabic writings were inadequate in both quality and expression, because the Arabs had repudiated their ancient literary tradition and were never able to keep pace with the rapid development of literature in the West. As a result, he argued, Arabic literature had neither enriched its past nor developed its present, but had merely become stagnant. Thus, the modern Arab readers could find no nourishment or satisfaction in either ancient or contemporary Arabic literature, particularly the latter, which was no match for the highly developed and sophisticated Western literature.[106]

To show the deficiency of Arabic writing in the present era, al-Zayyat pointed out that the most effective writer in Egypt could not find acceptable terms for new inventions or new ideas, as could his Western counterpart. And if the Egyptian Academy were to provide a comprehensive glossary with adequate translations of the common Western technical and literary terms, such a work would become hopelessly obsolete. Yet, he went on, the nation whose language is inadequate and whose writers cannot express themselves properly is half-dumb.[107] Scientific literature in Arabic, he complained, was very meager, consisting chiefly of adaptations which were likely to be of use only to beginners. The majority of the people who thirst for knowledge could find no edifying reading matter on scientific subjects. As long as such materials were not available to the public, the Arabic language and the Arab mind will remain within a medieval structure.[108]

Al-Zayyat conceded that the sources of contemporary scientific knowledge were European and American, and that the wide cultural gap between East and West could be bridged only through the sciences. The rapid expansion of knowledge which had enabled man to dominate the earth and the skies would always be unattainable for the Egyptians, he felt, unless they had it translated from the Western languages into their own. Neither schools nor great numbers of students would by themselves suffice to keep the nation abreast of modern scientific developments; the only answer was translation. Al-Zayyat emphatically concluded:

> If we translate into Arabic the scientific, artistic, and literary masterpieces of English, American, French, German, Russian, and Italian writers, these masterpieces will soon become part of our scientific and literary structure, which we shall cherish, preserve, and then add to, as did our ancestors, who translated the sciences of the Greeks, Indians, Jews, Syrians and Persians into their language.[109]

There is much to be said for the opinion that the only means of making Arabic literature viable and universal was through massive translation of Western literature. Al-Zayyat devoted most of his life to the advancement of Arabic literature and literary excellence both through original writings and through translations. He founded a periodical, *al-Riwaya*, devoted to the translation of Western stories, especially those of Guy de Maupassant, and the publication of Oriental short stories. The translations, generally preceded by a brief introduction, were remarkable for their precision and for the beauty of their language.[110]

Among the members of the "modern school" of translation, perhaps the most famous is Ibrahim Abd al-Qadir al-Mazini (d. 1949). He is considered by many of his contemporaries to have converted translation into a true literary art. His career was shaped by his sad childhood, his physical deformity, and the family troubles which gave him a deep-rooted inferiority complex he was never able to overcome.[111] His interest in translations from English was a natural outgrowth of his work in World War I, translating war dispatches and telegrams.[112] In the 1920's, al-Mazini contributed some translations of fiction to *al-Bayan*, a periodical with which he had been associated since 1907, and to such newspapers as *al-Akhbar*, *al-Ittihad*, *al-Siyasa*, and *al-Balagh*. He also translated several full-length works of Western literature, but has been criticized for being unconcerned about the artistic merits of the works he chose.[113] He translated Oscar Wilde's *Lord Arthur Saville's Crimes and Other Stories,* H. Rider Haggard's *Allan Quartermain*, and Richard Brinsley Sheridan's *School for Scandal*. Then he went on to John Galsworthy's *The Fugitive*, the Russian Artsibashev's *Sanine,* which he translated from an English version, entitling it *Ibn al-Tabi'a* (Son of Nature), and H. G. Wells' *The Time Machine.*[114]

In addition, he produced *Mukhtarat min al-Qisas al-Inqilizi* (Cairo, 1939), an anthology including English and American stories. In his introduction to this volume, al-Mazini explains that his sole purpose in choosing and translating particular works was to project the style of the writer, not the translator. He says that he adheres so strictly to the original that his translation may be considered literal, but admits that he has had to omit some phrases for lack of suitable Arabic equivalents. He uses some colloquial terms which may be incorrect but were found in Arabic lexicons and literary works. Finally, he states that he has not knowingly used incorrect phrases or terms, even though they may be in current use, except for two or three foreign terms which he presents in their original forms.[115]

Al-Mazini's stated purpose is borne out by the testimony of his lifelong friend and sometime co-author Abbas Mahmud al-'Aqqad. Al-'Aqqad says that he knows no one in Eastern or Western literature with a "translation genius" comparable to that of al-Mazini. He points out that al-Mazini translates prose in an elegant and rhetorical style like that of al-Jahiz or Khalid ibn Safwan, while to translate Western verse he uses the style of the Arab poets al-Buhturi and al-Sharif al-Raddi. Moreover, claims al-'Aqqad, he translates without losing so much as a letter of a word and without altering the sense of the original.[116] This claim is hardly credible: While al-Mazini is generally considered a first-rate translator, in many instances he appears quite careless. His version of Wells' *The Time Machine*, for example, omits many words and terms for which suitable Arabic equivalents are readily available. Moreover, he interpolates numerous terms on his own initiative and uses other words and phrases whose meanings do not correspond to the original. He also leaves some terms untranslated so as to preserve the consistency of his translation.[117]

More serious, however, is the charge of plagiarism against al-Mazini. In 1920 he translated Mikha'il Petrovich Artsibashev's *Sanine* from an English version made by Percy Pinkerton in 1915, and he afterwards incorporated parts of this work in his novel *Ibrahim al-Katib*, published in 1931. Some critics affirm that al-Mazini plagiarized parts of the Russian novel, while others contend merely that his protagonist, Ibrahim, has some traits in common with Sanine.[118] Al-Mazini defends himself by saying that he never intended to copy parts of the Russian novel, but that some of its scenes and incidents may have remained fixed in his mind when he wrote *Ibrahim al-Katib* a decade later—in short, that the similarity between the two works is sheer coincidence. But that he plagiarized Galsworthy's *The Fugitive*, which he published under the Arabic title *Gharizat al-Mar'a aw Bayt al-Ta'a,* was proved beyond doubt by Muhammad Ali Hammad in a series of articles published in *al-Balaqh* and later collected in a book titled *al-Mi'wal.* By comparing Galsworthy's text with that of al-Mazini, Hammad showed that al-Mazini's originality in this work consisted solely of changing the names into Arabic.[119] There is some truth also in the allegation that in writing his *Rihlat al-Hijaz* (al-Hijaz's Journey), al-Mazini was strongly influenced by Mark Twain's travel narrative *The Innocents Abroad.*[120] He also adapted parts of other works by Twain, among them *Tom Sawyer*, which became *al-Sighar wa al-Kibar*; *The Interview*, which he titled *al-Haqa'iq al-Bariza fi Hayati*; and *Adam's Diary*, which became *Muqtatafat min Mudhakkirat Hawwa Fi al-Janna.* These works were incorporated together with *Ba'd al-Khuruj min al-Janna* into his book *Sunduq al-Dunya* (Cairo, 1929).[121] Also published in this volume was his adaptation of Washington Irving's *Rip Van Winkle*, with the Arabic title *al-Ghurfa al-Mashura.*[122]

In the decade between 1920 and 1930, a group of translators was busy condensing novels and translating short stories, which they published either in journals like *al-Siyasa al-Usbu'iyya* or in anthologies *(mukhtarat).* Among these translators, working chiefly with French sources, were Muhammad Kamil Hajjaj, Aziz Abd Allah Salam, Faraj Gibran, Tawfiq Abd Allah, Muhammad Abd Allah Inan, and Kamil Gaylani.[123] Despite the fact that much of the attention of the translators was devoted to unsophisticated works of Western fiction, many qualified writers and men of letters made a sincere effort to put before the educated Arab reader artistic and substantial works. In the period between the two world wars Lajnat al-Ta'lif wa al-Tarjama wa al-Nashr endeavored to choose, translate and publish much worthwhile Western fiction. Besides the anthology of English and American stories made by al-

Mazini, this committee also published Hardy's *Tess of the d'Urbervilles,* translated by Fakhri Abu al-Su'ud; Goethe's *Hermann und Dorothea,* translated by Muhammad Awad Muhammad; and *Egmont*, translated by Muhammad Ibrahim al-Disuqi.[124] *Dar al-Katib al-Misri*, under the supervision of the celebrated Taha Husayn, was responsible for the publication of such works as Voltaire's *Zadig* and André Gide's *Oedipus and Theseus,* both of which were translated by Husayn himself; H. G. Wells' *The Food of the Gods*, done by Muhammad Badran; Aldous Huxley's *Brave New World*, translated by Mahmud Mahmud; Oscar Wilde's *The Picture of Dorian Gray* and *The Centerville Ghost,* both done by Louis 'Awad; François Mauriac's *The Mother*, translated by Abd al-Hamid Anbar, and *Vipers' Tangle*, by Nazih al-Hakim; Stendhal's *The Charterhouse of Parma*, by Abd al-Hamid al-Dawakhili; and Prosper Mérimée's *Colomba* by Muhammad Ghallab. The works of other Western authors, including Maurice Ries, Anton Chekhov, and Ivan Turgenev, were translated by such men as Muhammad Abd al-Hamid Anbar, Abd al-Hamid Abdin, Mahmud Tahir Lashin, Mahmud Abd al-Mun'im Murad, Abd al-Rahman Badawi, and Mahmud al-Shanity.[125]

The influence of these translations was certainly enormous. Indeed, there is hardly a writer in the modern Arab world who has not in some way or other been affected by Western fiction. Translations not only introduced the Arab writers of fiction to Western techniques and assisted in preparing many of them for their craft, but also changed the Arabic language by the many borrowed words which have become part of the Arabic vocabulary.[126] Through imitation and adaptation, and even through outright plagiarism, Arab writers learned their craft well enough to create domestic fiction. At the very least, the translations from Western authors provided entertainment for the reading public and shattered the traditional view that fiction was worthless and even detrimental to its readers. Not until the Arabs were disabused of this notion could prose fiction exist on a par with those literary genres which had traditionally enjoyed a dignified position in the Arabs' culture.

CHAPTER V

THE REVIVAL OF THE MAQAMA

Most of the Syrian émigrés in Egypt, especially after the Lebanese Massacre of 1860, were Christians with a fair degree of education and ambition. They were engaged in journalism, in various other kinds of writing, and in translating different types of Western fiction into Arabic. Some Egyptian writers welcomed these Syrians and appreciated their contributions, but many others thought of them as rivals seeking to control the literary field for whatever profits it might bring.

In fact, their translations from Western fiction were haphazard, hasty, and cheap productions.

Many Egyptian writers with a taste for classical Arabic considered these translations literary trash. Some even believed that they were intended to corrupt the morals of the young and to nourish dishonorable affections. Therefore, a few serious Egyptian writers began to revive and adapt an elegant medieval literary genre, the *maqama,* to criticize many aspects of their society. Their ideas and literary techniques were important to the development of modern Arabic fiction.

The earliest meaning of *maqama* is "an assembly" or "a place of meeting." The term was used in this sense by many pre-Islamic poets, such as Zuhayr ibn Abi Sulma, though one of them, Labid ibn Rabi'a, used it to signify the people who attended such an assembly. In the early Islamic era, *maqama* denoted the audience of the Caliph, in whose presence a witty person would deliver a speech or tell a tale, and it came also to refer to the tale told in the Caliph's presence. Later, it acquired the more general meaning of "a narration" or "an episode narrated by an eloquent individual." In this last sense, it is properly applied to the tales of Badi' al-Zaman al-Hamadhani and his followers.

Such a tale takes the form of a short narrative related by an imaginary *rawi* (narrator) who describes the adventures of a fictitious hero. The hero, a rogue and beggar, is generally endowed with the supreme gift for rhetorical speech. Indeed, the beauty of his language not only leaves his hearers spellbound, but forces them, almost involuntarily, to reach into their pockets and shower him with money. Always restless, this rogue goes from country to country and from town to town, using his power of eloquence to beg more and more. Each *maqama* focuses on a single event, which may either be drawn from experience or invented by the hero. Although its plot is usually connected with begging, the hero sometimes chooses to entertain his casual audience with another subject, such as poetry. He may roam into the realm of metaphysics, enchanting his listeners with tales about ghosts and the devil. Or he may assume the role of a preacher to remind the people of the true precepts of their religion and to inveigh against atheists and atheism. Badi' al-Zaman, for instance in *al-Maqama al-Maristaniyya,* supports the religious views of the Muslim Sunnites against the rationalist Mu'tazila, whom he criticizes bitterly. The central figure of the tale may even be an animal, as in *al-Maqama al-Asadiyya* (The Lion's Maqama), in which the same author provides a detailed description of the lion's life and character and enumerates his various names in the Arabic language. He also describes traveling and all the wonders and dangers associated with it. Similarly, in the interesting tale *al-Maqama al-Hamdaniyya,* named for Sayf al-Dawla al-Hamdani (d. 964), the founder of al-Hamdaniyya dynasty in Syria and Mosul, the hero Abu al-Fath al-Iskandari provides a copious description of the Arabian horse and shows his profound knowledge of the Arabic language. Still other *maqamas* elaborate the life in a particular city, such as Baghdad or Hulwan, as well as the character of its inhabitants.

Both in content and structure, the *maqama* is more limited in scope and theme than the modern short story. Basically, it is a dialogue between the narrator and the central figure, superbly framed in a highly rhetorical rhymed prose. There is no unified plot in the modern literary sense, and the aesthetic purpose is not primary. Its main objective is unmistakably didactic and rhetorical: to present to the Arab audience the quintessential beauty of their language. Thus, the tales are generally characterized by highly ornamental language, embellished with simile and metaphor. The narrative and its significance are of secondary importance.

Because of its loose and episodic structure, its lack of plot and description, and its dialogue form, the *maqama* can hardly be considered an antecedent of the modern short story. Properly polished and improved, it might have developed into a viable literary genre. But with form exalted over content, it remained stylized. Furthermore, Arabic society, which had been declining since medieval times and was conservative in religion, social, and literary matters, was unable to nurture the first-rate authors needed to develop this and other viable literary models.

Some recent Arab critics have sought to draw an analogy between the *maqama* and certain European literary types, particularly those of Spanish origin. Shawqi Dayf, for example, asserts that the *maqama* was introduced into Europe, along with other Arabic works, as a result of the intellectual interrelations between East and West in medieval times. He specifies that several of al-Hariri's *maqamas* were translated into Latin, German, and English. Dayf cautiously notes that the impact of the *maqama* upon European literature, unlike that of the *Thousand and One Nights,* is hard to trace because of its concentration on rhetorical style rather than narrative. Nevertheless, Dayf attempts to link the Spanish *novela picaresca* (rogue novel) with the *maqama*, largely on the basis of similarities between the Spanish picaro and the fictitious characters Abu al-Fath al-Iskandari of Badi' al-Zaman and Abu Zayd al-Saruji of al-Hariri.[1]

Another writer, Fakhri Abu al-Su'ud, believes that the *maqamas* of Badi' al-Zaman occupy a place in Arabic literature comparable to that held by the works of Addison and Steele in English literature. Abu al-Su'ud traces the parallel emergence of a fictional form characterized by social consciousness, close analysis of individual characters, skillful use of artistic devices, and unity of thought. This argument, however, rests on a weak analogy between the narrators of the *maqamas* and the invented personalities who populated the *Tatler* and the *Spectator*: Isaac Bickerstaff, Sir Roger de Coverley, Sir Andrew Freeport, and Will Honeycomb, along with a few female characters. Unlike the restless, ever-wandering heroes of the *maqamas*, these characters are static and stereotyped (except for Sir Roger) although endowed with some measure of individuality and humor. Abu al-Su'ud maintains, quite unrealistically, that had the *maqama* appeared in the eighth century, when Arabic literature was in its infancy, rather than in the tenth century, it would have been followed by developments which corresponded to those in English literature after the time of Addison and Steele, and would have led eventually to a full-fledged Arabic novel.[2]

In the modern period, the *maqama* was revived by writers throughout the Arab world, among them Ahmad al-Barbir (d. 1811), Niqula al-Turk (d. 1818), the priest Hannanya al-Munayyar (d. ca. 1850), Abu al-Thana al-Alusi (d. 1854), Nasif al-Yaziji (d. 1871), Ahmad Fairs al-Shidyaq (d. 1887), Ibrahim al-Ahdab (d. 1891), Muhammad al-Muwaylihi (d. 1930), Hafiz Ibrahim (d. 1932), and many others. Moreover, there were two distinct lines of development within this revival: while some writers, including the Lebanese al-Yaziji and al-Shidyaq, adhered tenaciously to the traditional form of the *maqama*, Egyptian writers, such as al-Muwaylihi and Hafiz Ibrahim, attempted to experiment with it.

Nasif al-Yaziji was, by virtue of his training and inclination, a perpetuator rather than a modifier of medieval Arabic literary models. Born at Kafr Shima in Lebanon to a Malkite Roman Catholic family, he learned the fundamentals of reading and writing at the local church school. In his youth he revealed a burning desire to master the Arabic language, which he deeply venerated. Probably because he considered Arabic sufficient for literary accomplishment, al-Yaziji never bothered to learn a European language, despite the fact that the Roman Catholic missionary schools of that time had made French popular in Lebanon.

His literary career started with poetry. One of his early poems, composed in praise of the Amir Bashir al-Shihabi (d. 1850), ruler of Lebanon, won the favor of the Amir, who attached the young poet to his court as his secretary.

After losing this position following the deposition of the Amir in 1840, al-Yaziji moved to Beirut and accepted several invitations to teach Arabic at various schools. He was also invited to revise the Arabic translation of the Holy Bible made by missionaries at the American Protestant College, later to become the American University of Beirut. In addition to teaching, he began writing on Arabic grammar, morphology, and rhetoric.

Al-Yaziji was capable not only of imitating the medieval belletrists who invented the *maqama,* but of actually surpassing them in the production of this complex literary form. His volume, *Majma' al-Bahrayn* (The Confluence of the Two Seas), contained sixty *maqamas,* ten more than the number composed by al-Hariri.

Nasif's *maqamas* seem keen imitations of al-Hariri's in both form and content. Like the medieval writers, he contrived two fictitious characters: Suhayl ibn Abbad, the narrator, and Maymun ibn Khuzam, the hero. Like al-Hariri, who always presented his hero Abu Zayd al-Saruji arguing with his wife, his disciple, or his associate, al-Yaziji often portrayed Maymun ibn Khuzam quarreling with his daughter Layla or his attendant Rajab. Furthermore, his hero, like al-Hariri's, was an eloquent scoundrel and beggar who used disreputable means to make a living. The secondary characters are also alike in sentiment, nature, and objectives. Finally, al-Yaziji's style is a highly rhetorical rhymed prose, embellished intermittently with lines of poetry. However, al-Hariri's natural and unpretentious rhymed prose flows more smoothly than the forced and involved imitation of al-Yaziji. The Lebanese writer even quotes the Qur'an so profusely that there can be no doubt that, although he was a Christian, his profound knowledge of sacred writings exceeded that of his Muslim predecessor. Essentially, he attempted to challenge, if not to surpass, al-Hariri's mastery of rhetoric.

Unfortunately, however, the *maqamas* of al-Yaziji are largely anachronistic, primarily because of their blindly imitative use of pre-Islamic and Islamic settings and themes. His hero travels between Mecca and al-Madina in the Hijaz, takes an excursion to al-Kufa, al-Basrah, Baghdad, and al-Anbar (an extinct town) in Iraq, or visits Alexandria, Cairo, and Dimyat in Egypt and Damascus in Syria. Al-Yaziji provides an elaborate description of the customs and way of life in each of these places, despite the fact that he never left his native Lebanon. He also provides detailed information about many aspects of pre-Islamic culture, such as food and its connection with Arab hospitality, the multifarious names and different characteristics of the Arabian horse, and the various types of Arab dwellings. He delves into astronomy to explain the names of the stars, the movements of the planets, and the different names of the nights, according to whether the moon is full, half, or new. He cites the names assigned to the sounds produced by the pen, the arrow, and the fire, and to those sounds related to laughing, chuckling, weeping, and snoring. And, of course, he does not fail to enumerate the endless names for the voices of many animals. In brief, he digresses into numerous realms of the knowledge which, despite his meticulous and most commendable scholarship, add nothing to the development of Arabic prose fiction.[4]

Moreover, the very nature of the *maqama* precluded its use as a contemporary form of imaginative literature. Its main purpose was to instruct the Arabs of medieval times in the subtleties of their language, and the adventures of its ever-restless, wandering hero were intended to render the didactic element more pleasant. Thus the element of romance in the *maqama* was of secondary importance. Indeed, if al-Yaziji is to be criticized for describing places he never saw, the same stricture must apply equally to al-Hariri, who very probably did not visit all the places he describes in his *maqamas*.[5] In fact, it is a mistake to expect al-Yaziji to have written according to modern Western fictional models when his prime purpose, as his introduction to *Majma' al-Bahrayn* implies, was purely conservative and didactic.[6]

A contemporary of al-Yaziji, Ahmad Faris al-Shidyaq, made a distinct step, however awkward, in the direction of the Western short story. Born and raised in Lebanon, and conversant with almost every branch of the Arabic language and Arabic literature, he was also conservative in style and literary outlook. Yet he had an advantage over al-Yaziji; his wide travels in the Mediterranean area and especially his contact with Europe had broadened his intellectual perspective and to some extent refined his style. The discerning reader can sense in his writing a creativeness and originality lacking in the work of al-Yaziji.[7]

In *Al-Saq 'ala al-Saq*, which is somewhat autobiographical, al-Shidyaq presents four *maqamas* written in the traditional rhymed-prose style and ornamented with bits of poetry. They are episodic in structure, and the narrative is rather longwinded at times. Following traditions al-Shidyaq invents a fictitious hero, al-Haris ibn Hitham, but the author himself, under the name al-Faryaq, serves as narrator. Furthermore, unlike the personages of the traditional *maqamas*, al-Shidyaq's characters are living creatures with a clear identity and some degree of independence. The plots and settings are contemporary, reflecting the spirit and sentiment of the communities in which he lived and worked.

The artistry of al-Shidyaq is most conspicuous in the work titled *Maqama Muqima*. The hero leaves home after a fight with his nagging wife, full of bitter feelings against all women. While wandering aimlessly, he meets a group of fourteen females whose physical charms win his attention and his admiration. His anger allayed, he feels himself again and even recites poetry in praise of their beauty. One of these women approaches al-Haris and informs him that he is not the only one of his kind among men. Then she recites to him a poem composed by her husband, and each of her companions in turn does the same. Enchanted by the ladies' recitations, al-Haris thinks so highly of their husbands that he wishes to make their acquaintance. He is told that they are at the seashore, and when he comes upon them, he discovers they have pitched a tent to protect themselves from the sun. Approaching, he enters in conversation with them about problems relating to women and marriage. Soon the quiet conversation turns into a heated but inconclusive argument, and al-Haris, impatient, leaves these men to seek answers to the problems elsewhere. Finally he meets al-Faryaq in the marketplace, carrying a shopping basket filled with dainty foods. Al-Haris asks him his opinion regarding women and marriage, and amid the hustle and bustle of an oriental marketplace, al-Faryaq recites a poem expressing his views on these matters.[8]

The social and human elements in this and other *maqamas* of al-Shidyaq are vigorously presented and the characters are witty and eloquent. Yet the absence of plot and the unrealistic portrayal of the characters' sentiments reveal the inadequacy of the form, however subtle the language might be, as a basis for new techniques of prose fiction. Indeed, the main interest of readers of *maqamas* of al-Shidyaq lies in the vividness of their poetry and the variety of amusing (though often trivial) details.

Medieval both in form and spirit, the *maqamas* of al-Yaziji did not set out to create an illusion of reality. Those of al-Shidyaq, by virtue of the relative independence of their characters, advanced only slightly in the direction of realism. But the romance *Hadith 'Isa ibn Hisham,* by Muhammad Ibrahim al-Muwaylihi,[9] is not only a modified form of the *maqama,* but also a genuine (though not quite successful) effort to create a new literary mode in the Western manner. A conservative by education and social upbringing, but liberal in thought, al-Muwaylihi must have found it quite difficult to produce a modernized fictional work which would not enrage the Muslim conservative element but would, at the same time, not dissatisfy the modernists. He therefore chose to present liberal ideas in the rigid form of the *maqama.*[10] The result was an interesting fictional narrative which was neither a medieval tale nor a full-fledged modern story.

Al-Muwaylihi was born at Cairo in 1858 to a conservative Muslim family, a number of whose members had achieved fame in literature, politics, and public life. His grandfather, the chief merchant of Cairo during the rule of Viceroy Muhammad Ali, established a silk industry in Egypt. His father, Ibrahim al-Muwaylihi, was the private secretary of the Khedive Isma'il Pasha and achieved prominence as a public servant, writer, and journalist. The young Muwaylihi was sent to the Kharanfash school, where he learned French. He was highly introverted, however, and shunned his schoolmates and showed little interest in his studies. Most of the time he did not even attend classes, but studied privately at home under the supervision of his father. At the age of fifteen he stopped going to school entirely. In the meantime, he attended lectures at al-Azhar, especially those delivered by the celebrated Muhammad Abduh, striving to perfect his knowledge of Arabic and of Muslim religious subjects. He also joined the informal assemblies of eminent philologists, grammarians,

Muslim jurists, and men of letters who called on his father.[11] He also established contact with the reformer Jamal al-Din al-Afghani, whose ideas strongly influenced him. His *Hadith* reveals that he had acquired a fair knowledge of many different aspects of Egyptian society.[12]

Al-Muwaylihi's cultural horizon was further broadened by his travels abroad, especially in Europe. After losing his position with the government because of his support of the revolution of Ahmad 'Urabi Pasha in 1882, he went to Italy, where he studied Italian and French under the direction of an Italian lawyer, once a neighbor and friend of his father. He remained in Europe for three years, traveling between Italy, France, and England. In France he became acquainted with Dumas *fils* and other leading writers and was involved in the literary activities of al-Afghani.[13] In 1885, he accompanied his father to London and then to Istanbul, where his father held an appointment as a member of the Supreme Educational Board. His stay at Istanbul afforded him an opportunity to read and to transcribe the newspaper *al-Muqattam*. Later he joined the government but resigned his post in 1895 to aid his father in publishing the newspaper *Misbah al-Sharq* (The Lamp of the East).[14]

It was in this newspaper that al-Muwaylihi published the first installments of *Hadith Isa ibn Hisham* between 1898 and 1900, when he left Egypt for Paris and London in the company of the Khedive Abbas Hilmi II. But he continued to publish in *Misbah al-Sharq* until its demise in 1903. He also contributed articles to other newspapers, although these did not attract as much public attention as his earlier work. His most important nonfiction is an interesting work titled *'Ilaj al-Nafs* (The Remedy of the Soul), a series of profound meditations about life and morality. It reflects the author's comprehensive reading of ancient and modern works, both Eastern and Western, as well as his life experience.

Of primary importance here is his fictional romance *Hadith 'Isa ibn Hisham* (The Narrative of 'Isa ibn Hisham), whose title character recalls the narrator of the *maqamas* of Badi' al-Zaman al-Hamadhani. In general, al-Muwaylihi restricts himself to the traditional rhymed prose of the *maqama*, but when he writes naturally, the result is a refreshingly smooth, free prose style. 'Isa ibn Hisham is not simply the narrator but also the central figure of the tale, and he frequently expresses the author's own attitudes. The *Hadith* attempts to diagnose and remedy the ills of Egyptian society, and to show the progress in the different sectors of Egyptian life since the era of Muhammad Ali.

Al-Muwaylihi begins the narrative with the traditional phrase "Haddathana 'Isa ibn Hisham" (Isa ibn Hisham related to us) which opened the *maqamas* of Badi' al-Zaman. 'Isa ibn Hisham recalls that he saw, as in a dream, a graveyard on a moonlit night. Touched by the tranquility of the night and the stillness of the graves, he became absorbed in profound thoughts about life and death, and especially about those who were lying in eternal rest and had been made equal by death. Only yesterday, he thought, there were, among these dead, great kings and rulers who controlled the destinies of their subjects, beautiful women who captivated and humbled men by their beauty, and many others who enjoyed the earthly vanity of pride, power, and prestige. Today they lie here, not only helpless, but sharing equally the same spot and the same destiny.

While deep in contemplation, he heard behind him a sudden, violent convulsion which shocked him terribly. Despite his fright, he turned around and, to his consternation, saw that one of the graves had cleft and a tall figure with an extraordinary but noble appearance had sprung from it. The sight of the resurrected figure snapped him out of his trance, and he found himself walking faster. But he heard the figure, who now seemed as real as a mortal being, calling to him to wait. He obeyed, he explains, to avoid the evil which might be inflicted upon him if he refused. The resurrected figure approached Isa and began talking to him, sometimes in Arabic and sometimes in Turkish.

With this incident the author initiates the lengthy dialogue between the two characters which runs throughout the book. Subsidiary characters are also introduced to explain a given situation or to illustrate some aspect of Egyptian society, as circumstances may require.

The resurrected character identifies himself as Ahmad Pasha al-Manikli, Minister of War under Muhammad Ali, and 'Isa identifies himself as a man of letters. When the Pasha asks to be led to his house, Isa answers that houses in Cairo are no longer identified by the names of their owners, but by a new system of numbers. The once prominent Minister is indignant and bewildered to discover not only that his house cannot be found, but that the entire city has changed. He is immediately faced with new situations, different people, and drastically changed social, cultural, judicial and administrative institutions. His inability to realize the changes brings him into conflict with both government and people. The series of predicaments which the Pasha encounters is obviously designed by the author to vindicate his criticism of Egyptian society. As one predicament leads to another, we are in each instance given a remarkably adroit portrayal of the Pasha's reaction to his new situation.[15]

The first problem arises from social and judicial institutions. On his way to search for his house, accompanied now by his guide Isa ibn Hisham, the resurrected Pasha pauses at the Citadel of Cairo to say a prayer over the tomb of his master Muhammad Ali. Immediately after leaving the Citadel, the two companions meet a donkey-driver whose slow-moving animal delays their progress. The donkey-driver, too, becomes impatient with the lazy beast. Craftily but jokingly, he invites the Pasha to mount the donkey since, he claims, the Pasha has for two hours blocked the way by walking right in front of him and his donkey. The Pasha feels insulted and retorts to this villain that he has not blocked the way, and that furthermore a man of his prominence would not so humble himself as to ride a braying donkey, when he had always had a thoroughbred stallion. As the argument continues, and the donkey-driver grows excited, he complains that while the Pasha was walking and talking with his companion, he beckoned as if he wished to hire the donkey. The donkey-driver insists that the Pasha must either hire his donkey or pay him on the spot for his delay. The Pasha obviously losing patience, pushes the donkey-driver aside and regrets that he has no weapon to kill him. Astonished by his companion's reluctance to rid himself of this nuisance, on the pretext that he cannot touch him because of the law, the Pasha decides to take the matter into his own hands. He begins beating the donkey-driver mercilessly, while the poor victim calls for aid from the police.[16]

Similar situations are used to explore the different institutions of Egyptian society and their methods of operation. The Pasha's quarrel with the donkey-driver leads him to the police, to the prosecutor, and to the attorney. In the Civil Court he is found guilty and sentenced to six months in prison, but the Court of Appeal dismisses his case and releases him. Despite his joy at his acquittal, he is disappointed to discover that he still must pay his attorney's fees. Where and how will he get the money to pay these fees? The lawyer becomes enraged and begins to lecture the humiliated Pasha on how, in the old days, he and his powerful colleagues among the aristocracy pilfered public money, oppressed the poor, the widows, and the orphans, and practiced every illegal method to amass wealth at the expense of the people.[17]

But the remorseless Pasha recalls that he had some property which he had retained during his lifetime as a *Waqf*, (religious endowment). While the Pasha is searching for his property, the author provides a detailed description of the uses and abuses of the *Waqf*.[18] The search for his descendants brings the Pasha to the sad discovery that the only surviving beneficiary, a young man, has squandered the income of the property through profligate living.

Next the Pasha seeks aid from three of his former colleagues, who are still living in apparent luxury, but the old men will not believe his story. Finally, when he sees that they have no more patience with him, he leaves. He notices that he has been followed by a businessman, who has evidently recognized him as his former master. Approaching the annoyed Pasha, the businessman recalls the kind favors which the Pasha did for him during his lifetime, and which brought him wealth and social prestige. He pulls out a purse and offers it to the Pasha in gratitude for his past favors. The desperate Pasha accepts the offer and asks his companion 'Isa ibn Hisham to take him immediately to the lawyer, so that he can pay his fees. But Isa advises him first to find a religious lawyer and claim his *Waqf*. Thus the author transfers the focus from the civil courts to the religious courts, which have jurisdiction over matters of this nature. Al-Muwaylihi never misses an opportunity to expose the maladministration and the chaotic conditions of the religious courts.[19]

From this point on, the narrative of Isa ibn Hisham becomes rather discursive and disjointed. Isa passes from one facet of Egyptian society to another, treating such topics as physicians and medicine and the plague with the confidence of one who has a thorough knowledge of his subject. He examines the worlds of sciences and literature, of business and agriculture, of politics and civil service, and describes in detail the social customs of his time, from Egyptian weddings to the functions of the *'Umda* (village headman), which he treats at length with evident charm. Finally, after an exhaustive portrayal of city and village life in Egypt, the author abruptly transports the reader to Europe, the setting of *The Second Journey,* which occupies the rest of the book.[20]

This shift is suggested on the spur of the moment by the Pasha, who seeks an explanation of the drastic changes which have occurred since his lifetime. Isa tells him that these, especially the lower standards of morality, have resulted from the invasion of Oriental societies by the West, and from the Orientals' blind imitation of the customs and behavior of Westerners.[21]

On this pretext, the scene abruptly changes to Paris. The author, through 'Isa ibn Hisham, shows marked astonishment at the crowded streets, the elegant shops, and the magnificent edifices of the city.[22] The Pasha is also astonished by what he sees and tries to compare Paris with ancient capitals such as Athens, Rome, and even Surra man Ra'a (Samarra), once the capital of the Abbasids. A subsidiary character, whom the author identifies as "a friend," is arbitarily introduced. The newcomer starts immediately to degrade French civilization and to accuse all Westerners of being arrogant especially the French, who he says believe their civilization superior to any other. To attain some objectivity in his judgment of European civilization, the author interjects another character, a learned old sage and Orientalist, who accompanies the Egyptian visitors on their tour of Paris and explains to them the good and the bad aspects of Western civilization.

The visitors stop first at the international exhibition sponsored by the French government, and then at an art gallery, where the author provides a description of some paintings. 'Isa ibn Hisham becomes upset when at the immaculate gallery he notices a filthy old man whom he characterizes as a "lump of dirt." Asking what this filthy creature is doing in such a beautiful place, he learns that the old man is a famous artist whose paintings are worth millions of francs. He marvels at the way Westerners respect their talented men. When the visitors are shown a lady posing in the nude for an artist, the Pasha, utterly shocked, condemns the sight as "debasement and vulgarity." But the old Orientalist interrupts to explain to him that what he has seen is generally accepted as beautiful art in Europe, both because of its Greek origin and because of its support by Christianity. On the other hand, the Orientalist remarks, Islam has forbidden this kind of art and has made it unpopular among Muslim nations.[23] The visitors' excursion subsequently takes them to a planetarium, an observatory, the Eiffel Tower, a night club with Egyptian dancers (whom the author condemns as disgraceful to Egypt's reputation), and carnivals in which some Egyptian customs are lampooned.[24]

When the journey to Paris is over, the Orientalist warns the visitors not to imitate Western civilization blindly, but to adopt what is good in it and reject the bad. With this advice, the narrative of Isa ibn Hisham comes to a close. The author halts it by stating simply that since there is nothing more to say, everyone should return to his country. He brings the travelers back to Egypt without giving the slightest hint to the destiny of the poor resurrected Pasha, who is left suspended in misery.

Of all the characters of the *Hadith*, that of the Pasha is the most interesting. As a supernatural phenomenon, he is in a unique position to explore the different changes in Egyptian society, unrestricted by any time element. This convenient device is cleverly used to pronounce the author's approval or disapproval of the changes in values and institutions in late nineteenth century Egypt.

From the beginning the Pasha appears as a fully developed character. He is intelligent, inquisitive and a keen observer of society. He even becomes vexed when he is denied the opportunity to quench his thirst for learning more about the new Egyptian society.[25]

Although he has returned to life at a time when the prevalent values are more or less in violent conflict with his own, he is not driven to return to his former state in order to escape the misery he experiences. He does sometimes complain, and even wishes he could return once more to the grave, but gradually he assumes a more positive attitude. He is capable of adapting himself to the new times, their values and institutions, and attempts to reestablish those ties which bound him to his former life. Although his former position as a minister of war does not exist any more, his children have died, his property—particularly his *Waqf*—is in ruins, and his grandson, who lives in dissipation, ridicules him and shuns him as a senile old man,[26] he does not despair. Nor does he condemn life as meaningless but strengthens his resolve to live on and understand his new life. He becomes more tolerant of the changes which he has witnessed, and reluctantly—even though they cause him pain—accepts some of them. Most important, he makes a very human attempt to reconcile his anachronistic values with those of the new Egyptian society.[27]

Perhaps the question the author is posing and attempting to answer through the device of the reborn Pasha is whether or not life itself is an abstract entity separate from the individual's lifetime and all the related phenomena that seemingly comprise it and bind man to it. Despite the fact that the Pasha's ties with his former life have all but disappeared and despite his reluctance to accept new values which contradict his own, he does not unequivocally demand to be returned to his former state. Life in any form seems to be much preferable to the oblivion and meaninglessness of the grave. But this is a questionable interpretation since the author does not give the poor Pasha a choice. He leaves his fate unresolved, apparently because al-Manikli's main role as an agent between the old and the new has been fulfilled.

Since the Pasha symbolizes the values of the old Egyptian society, his ongoing presence can only mean that those values have not completely faded away. Like a palimpsest, the spirit of the old society is still manifest in the person of the undying Pasha.

The *Hadith* uses the traditional rhymed prose style of the *maqama,* but with more vividness, simplicity, and smoothness. There is no attempt to emulate the style of the medieval belletrists. Rather the marked influence of traditional medieval Arabic style on his writing simply reflects the author's conservative sentiments. Like many writers of his time, al-Muwaylihi must have believed in the propriety and beauty of rhymed prose, despite its redundant and repetitive nature.

The dialogue of the *Hadith* is, however, more natural than the narrative portions and seems to be more effectual in expressing the ideas of the author. In general, the length or brevity of the dialogue depends upon the nature and magnitude of the situation to be treated. But in some parts of the *Hadith*, the dialogue is extended to cover issues not related to the main theme of the narrative, such as the chapter titled *al-Tibb wa al-Atibba* ("Medicine and Physicians").

Whereas the traditional *maqama* treats a single event, the *Hadith* is substantially wider in scope and comprehends a variety of characters, scenes, and settings. Although the characters may appear to move solely at the author's behest, one can detect in their actions the expression of extremely personal emotions, however stifled, as they react to one another or to a given situation. The author seeks, moreover, to ridicule with wit and wisdom various types of human behavior. But the comedy is generally grim and at times gives way to acrimonious sarcasm as it exposes man's foibles and his blind submission to his own whims. An excellent example in this regard is the Umda (village headman) who, by sheer folly, falls prey to a playboy panderer, a pretentious businessman, and a flirtatious dancing girl. Moreover, the author never misses an opportunity to examine the different aspects of Egyptian life, from food and eating habits to horses, from police and court procedures to the press. The author devotes eight chapters to describing the village headman (Umda) and other institutions of Egyptian society.[28] Focusing on the everyday world, the author admirably points out the follies of ordinary men and reveals hypocrisy, social chaos, and the exploitation of the masses in Egyptian society.

In scope and form, then, the *Hadith* is more flexible than the *maqama.* One modern critic, Ali al-Ra'i, regards it as a social satire intended to ridicule life in Egypt, comparing it with Cervantes' *Don Quixote.*[29] Cervantes, he says, presents a knight whose heart and mind are filled with dreams of past ages which refuse to die. So Don Quixote sets out, taking along a traveling companion, a horse, and a donkey, to search for truth and beauty, which have died in his world but still live in his heart. From the painful, yet humorous contrast between the world perceived by Don Quixote and that perceived by his society, Cervantes derives an extraordinarily brilliant criticism and moral lesson. In al-Muwaylihi's *Hadith*, a conspicuous contrast exists between the Pasha who has come back to life and the world around him, which has been drastically changed. Values which he thought were beautiful and eternal have been replaced by others of whose beauty and perpetuity he is most doubtful.[30]

Al-Ra'i also observes that from the conflicts in attitude between the resurrected Pasha and the people among whom he moves, al-Muwaylihi derives criticism of Egyptian society. Like Don Quixote, who sets out to search for the truth, the Pasha and his companion, 'Isa ibn Hisham set out on a quest for the spirit of Egypt. In their first journey, the author represents different aspects of Egyptian society; in the journey abroad, he attempts to assess the impact of European values on their society. From the author's criticism, al-Ra'i believes, we may realize that the "truth" these two companions hoped to find was a bourgeois Egypt. From the conflict of the Pasha and Isa ibn Hisham with such bourgeois characters as the lawyer and the physician, we may deduce that the author considers the bourgeoisie the most progressive of the social classes in Egypt.[31] Al-Muwaylihi may criticize the bourgeoisie at length and vigorously, but always constructively, for he desires to see it continue, despite its many faults. On the other hand, while 'Isa ibn Hisham decries the rigidly anti-progressive attitude of the Muslim jurists and the inflexibility of the Muslim religious courts, never does he advocate the abolition of these courts or the dismissal of the judges. Instead he suggests the reform of these courts and the establishment of civil courts to counterbalance them. In brief, the author expresses the hopes and expectations of the Egyptian middle class, which since the time of Muhammad Ali has seen in the various cultural, judicial, juristic, and political institutions impediments to its own progress. The *Hadith* shows in essence the struggle of this class to free itself from the Turkish aristocracy and from British imperialsim, and from the feudal system they had perpetuated. This struggle, of course, manifested itself in a series of conflicts which ultimately brought the middle class to power.[32]

Al-Ra'i concludes that on the whole we must consider the comparison between *Don Quixote* and *Hadith 'Isa ibn Hisham* valid, since each work centers about the conflict of an anachronistic protagonist with a modern culture, and in each encounter between old and new the bafflement of the protagonist serves to highlight not only the absurdity but also the pathos of the human condition. What gives *Don Quixote* its timelessness is repeated in a lower key in the *Hadith*; it is not so much the satire as the great humanity the author reveals by his deep compassion and tolerance in the face of man's folly. We cannot predict what the critical judgment of the *Hadith* may be in later generations, but we must recall that to Cervante's contemporaries, *Don Quixote* was little more than a comedy.[33]

Hadith 'Isa ibn Hisham is plainly episodic in structure; indeed, its events are so disjointed that they could be arranged in almost any order without serious damage to the continuity of the work. But the narrative and descriptive elements are merely a frame for the expository dialogue, which depicts the ills of Egyptian society and explains the impact of the West on that society. The moralizing which is its primary motive constantly reminds the reader that the importance of the *Hadith* lies in its meaning, not its story. Yet the discerning reader may observe that the author has sought to develop the central theme through a subtle, gradually intensified conflict of ideas rather than by a conventional plot. Thus, it may be argued, al-Muwaylihi left the Pasha's fate unresolved for the simple reason that he had already achieved the marvel and didactic purpose of his narration. Not only do the characters of the *Hadith* exist without a plot, but they are not seriously presented as complex human beings, and for this reason they have sometimes been regarded simply as stock figures to be manipulated by the author. In a real sense, al-Muwaylihi uses the Pasha to symbolize the old values of Egypt under Muhammad Ali, and Isa ibn Hisham to explain and evaluate the changes in these values resulting from Egypt's contact with European life and thought. Though he is a keen observer of the actions of his characters, the author never fully explains their nature or reveals their emotions and reactions to the surroundings and the behavior of other characters. Yet, crude and primitively handled as they may be, the characters of the *Hadith* have distinct personalities and are closely connected with the real world of the author. Some of them may seem static, and some may appear or disappear at random, yet many are lifelike characters who appear throughout the greater part of the romance. Among the latter group we may include the village headman, the dancing girl, and the playboy. Even the Pasha, perhaps the crudest of all the characters in the *Hadith*, is capable of development. At first arrogant, slow to understand, and intransigent in his refusal to accept the new values of Egyptian society, he becomes ultimately more tolerant of the changes in that society.[34]

Despite its episodic structure, the *Hadith* tells a complete story which begins with the resurrection of the Pasha and develops simultaneously with his personality. Because of its narrative quality and the relatively flexible nature of some of its characters, one may even venture to regard al-Muwaylihi's *Hadith* not only as a work which points up the palpable distinctions between the *maqama* and the novel, but in fact as an early form of the Egyptian novel.

While this conclusion may be appropriate, it is equally important to notice that in his effort to portray Egyptian life and institutions and the social characteristics of the people, al-Muwaylihi strove for an illusion of authenticity. This fact is evident from his attempt to cater to the conservative reading public, who disdained fiction, by stating in his introduction that the *Hadith* represents reality, not fiction. But despite his effort to minimize the fictional element of his romance, al-Muwaylihi never escaped the reproach of the conservative readers. According to Ali al-Ra'i, the famous Egyptian writer Tawfiq al-Hakim once related that some friends, concerned about the reputation of al-Muwaylihi's family, complained to al-Muwaylihi's father, "Your son has pursued a path the very thought of which was uncommendable."[35] This book stands as a milestone in the development of native prose fiction in Egypt. The very fact that al-Muwaylihi based his fiction upon contemporary life in Egypt and that his portrayal of this life as he knew it is remarkably accurate are in themselves a sufficient contribution. While the *Hadith* clearly cannot be considered a novel in the Western sense, it does contain the basic ingredients of that form. It is a step beyond Ali Mubarak's *'Alam al-Din,* which lacks not only vision but also the ingenious subtlety with which al-Muwaylihi satirizes Egyptian society. Whereas Ali Mubarak chose Europe alone as his setting, in order to instruct his countrymen in the virtues of the far superior European civilization, al-Muwaylihi concentrates on Egyptian life and society, treating Western civilization only as it bears upon his main subject.

The literary and cultural impact of *Hadith 'Isa ibn Hisham* upon Egyptian life was considerable, particularly after its inclusion by the Ministry of Education in the curriculum for Secondary Schools in 1927. As the Ministry stated:

> As the *Hadith 'Isa ibn Hisham* becomes reading matter for the pupils of the secondary schools, it will do them the greatest good, for it will attract them by the rhetorical style, sound expression, and exquisite wording with which it has treated the manifold questions of current interest among people. These qualities have been lacking in all the books written in earlier times. Moreover, it will broaden their faculties and accustom them to penetrating observations, powerful expression, and the handling of the different arguments on both sides of a given question.[36]

Another work of fiction which stands somewhat closer to the traditional *maqama* is *Layali Satih* (Satih's Nights), by the celebrated Egyptian poet Hafiz Ibrahim, whose portrayal of the hopes and sentiments of the common people gained him the epithet "The Poet of the Nile." He was also interested in prose and at one time he translated Victor Hugo's novel *Les Misérables* into Arabic.[37]

Layali Satih is constructed around two principal characters, a narrator and a second man similar to the resurrected Pasha in *Hadith Isa ibn Hisham.* The narrator is designated simply as Ahad Abna al-Nil (A Son of the Nile), and it is clear from the context of the work that he represents the author himself. The second character is Satih, a controversial ancient Arab with whom the narrator speaks about various political, social and literary matters relating to Egyptian society.

In the first of the seven nights which comprise *Layali Satih*[38] The anonymous narrator, feeling depressed, goes for a walk along the Nile to forget his cares. As he sits on the bank watching the majestic river, he notices a foul odor, apparently from a decayed corpse floating on the surface. He is outraged at the way people have desecrated the river and turned it into a graveyard. How long, he wonders, will the Nile bear this ignorant nation which has repaid its goodness and blessings with ingratitude? He decides to find another spot, but as he prepares to arise, he hears a voice praising the Merciful God. Drawing nearer, he hears, but cannot see, someone saying, "A miserable poet and man of letters, oppressed and dejected, came out to seek solace and diversion." The voice apparently refers to this Son of the Nile, no other than Hafiz himself, who has been attacked by jealous men for his Arabic translation of *Les Misérables*, on which he spent twelve months. Finally the voice (that of Satih) tells the Son of the Nile to go home and return to the same spot on the following night with a companion, so that they can resume their conversation.[39]

He keeps the appointment the next night even though he does not yet know the identity of the companion whom the voice mentioned. When he reaches the place, he sees a man of his acquaintance deep in thought. He may be the intended companion, but the Son of the Nile does not wish to interrupt his contemplation and whispers to himself that this great man would never be preoccupied with thoughts of anything other than the welfare of his country and his countrymen. He notices a boat passing on the river. On board are beautiful maidens, together with men of great wealth and prestige, drinking and indulging in pleasure. Suddenly the pensive man, raising his head and looking at the jocund company in the boat, begins to condemn their indecency. When he has finished, the Son of the Nile relates to him the events of the preceding night and finds that he too wishes a meeting with Satih.

As they near the place, the Son of the Nile hears the same cryptic voice hailing his companion as "the possessor of a new doctrine and new idea. He called on the people to discard the veil and free their women, but instead they discarded the veil of decency." Although the companion's name is not given, we know from Satih's words that he is Qasim Amin (d. 1908), the great Egyptian reformer and staunch advocate of the liberation of Eastern women. Satih assures Amin that his views on the liberation of woman will, within just fifty years, be proven correct. He also predicts that Western women will soon demand the liberation of their Eastern sisters. When the Son of the Nile begs the voice to reveal his identity, Satih promises to do so but asks the Son of the Nile to return to the same place the following night.[40]

The two companions leave the voice, which begins again to utter praises, and start home. On their way they meet two young men, one of whom asks his companion to name his chief ambition in life. The other replies that he wishes to become the president of the Mixed Courts—not, apparently to advance the cause of justice, but to gain a high salary and live comfortably. The first young man then says he wants to be like a certain student who entered the

Engineering School and has gained much respect. His teachers are English, and the lowest rank among them is paid thirty-five pieces of gold. If Caesar himself had wanted his son educated, the young man thinks, he could have desired no better training for him than that provided by the efforts of the Ministry of Education. With this thought, the events of the second night end.

When he returns to the same spot on the third night, the Son of the Nile sees an eminent Syrian man of letters sitting there in a pensive mood. After they exchange customary greetings, the Syrian says that he has been complaining to the river against the Egyptians, who, for no reason except that the Syrians are more industrious and active, have ostracized his countrymen. The Son of the Nile tries to console the man of letters and promises to present his complaint to Satih. When the Syrian, astonished, asks who Satih is, he is assured that he will presently see Satih himself. As they approach, Satih begins to praise Syria and Egypt as sisters whose mother is the Arabic tongue, and to defend those Syrians who immigrated to Egypt seeking a better living and greater freedom.[41] Specifically, he remarks on the achievement of the Christian Syrians in spreading the Arabic language, a task at which they have been far more successful than the missionaries who have attempted to spread Christianity. Moreover, he wonders whether, if the Syrian Muslims had taken as strong a role in the development of education as the Syrian Christians, there might not be among the Muslims men who would excel both in learning and in imparting their knowledge to others. Satih then cites some Syrian writers, both Muslim and Christian, who emigrated to Egypt and achieved fame and success. Among them are Abd al-Rahman al-Kawakibi (d. 1903), the author of *Umm al-Qura*, who he says fled from al-Sayyad (the hunter), most likely Abu al-Huda al-Sayyadi, Shaykh al-Islam, who was known for persecuting liberal thinkers and reformers: al-Shaykh Muhammad Rashid Rida, owner and publisher of *al-Manar* and the Syrian Christian Jurji Zaydan, author of *Ashhar Mashahir al-Islam* (more correctly, *Tarajim Mashahir al-Sharq, i.e.*, (Biographies of Famous Men of the Orient). Satih concludes that God has apparently destined the Muslims to live among the cattle, but has given the Christian the opportunity to become a man of action and knowledge. When the Syrian asks about the faults of his countrymen among the Egyptians, Satih criticizes them for monopolizing business and the press, and for competing with the Egyptians in making their living.[42] Having heard this judgment, the Son of the Nile inquires why the Syrian Christian community has so many eminent writers and journalists who have developed newspapers and periodicals like *al-Muqtataf, al-Diya, Da'irat al-Ma'arif, al-Hital,* and *al-Jami'a,* while the Syrian Muslim community in Egypt has produced only salesmen, brokers, horse trainers, and butchers. Satih attributes this difference to the Muslims' unwise decision to let his children attend the Christians' schools, where their opportunities for learning have been restricted. The Son of the Nile retorts that Egypt has thus far sent just one hundred and fifty students to a single Christian school in Beirut; Satih argues strongly, however, that the Egyptians have no need to send their sons to Beirut, but should establish their own college. With this remark the conversation is ended, and the Son of the Nile and his companion return home.[43]

When the Son of the Nile goes back to the same place on the fourth night, he sees a man weeping and wailing. The man laments that his brother, who was his sole refuge and support, has been stabbed to death by a foreigner residing in Egypt. The Son of the Nile consoles him and takes him to meet Satih. Seeing the bereft man, Satih begins condemning the concessions which have allowed foreign citizens to commit crimes against Egyptians and escape punishment under the protection of their governments. The Egyptians have no choice but to carry their dead and submit like slaves to this inequity. Satih bitterly criticizes "those who have occupied Egypt," (i.e., the British) to whom he attributes the dissension among the Egyptians and the perpetuation of the concessions which have weakened them and made them dependent upon foreigners.[44] The British, Satih says, are shrewd and treacherous; even if they are weak, they pretend to be strong and daring. They are like wine which seems powerless in the cup but grows strong once it goes to the head. He concludes by likening the fight for control of the East to a chess game played by two men, one Anglo-Saxon, the other French. It is evident to the careful observer that the winner will be whichever player can best avoid haste and rashness when temporization and caution are called for.[45]

When Satih finishes his remark, the two visitors leave, each going his own way. As he is returning home, the Son of the Nile hears two old men discussing the different types of happiness. One of them asserts that the happiest man is the shaykh who pretends to be religious and uses religion to make money. Even happier than this pretender, it is said, are the dead shaykhs whom gullible people believe to be men of God. Their remains are harbored in huge shrines, to which people flock to worship them and seek their blessing. The dialogue between the two old men describes other fortunate men. The list includes the legal guardians of orphans, who can appropriate their wards' money for their own use without being questioned, and administrators of religious endowments, who can make unrestricted use of the profits. Also happy are the crafty old women who fool gullible ladies of rank and then manipulate them to suit their own ends.

Leaving these men behind, the Son of the Nile hurries home to bed, but he cannot sleep because of the sad things he has encountered this day. Reaching for a copy of *al-Luzumiyyat,* by the blind poet Abu al-'Ala al-Ma'arri (d. 1058), he reads until morning, when at last sleep comes to him.[46]

On the next night the Son of the Nile, once more on his way to meet Satih, sees yet another man in despair. This man grieves because he cannot continue his studies at the state schools and has become a burden to his family. His efforts to find work have failed because he does not have a degree, and his desperate venture into journalism, as he explains, has caused his present misfortune. He established a weekly paper and did everything in his power to make it succeed, although his writing talent was severely limited. To his disappointment, however, the weekly was not successful, and after much reflection he ascribed its failure to the moral corruption of his nation. Wishing to combat this corruption, but feeling he was unqualified to do so effectively, he suddenly changed his policy and made his newspaper a wholly commercial affair. He published anything, even vilification, as long as he received payment for it. But he was indicted for libel, convicted, and fined, and soon he found himself without any means of subsistence. The Son of the Nile takes the man to Satih, who promptly rebukes him for having undertaken a task for which he was not qualified. In a long speech Satih explains the influence of the press on the public, quoting *Kalila wa Dimna* to prove that the journalist can "make the truth seem false and that which is false seem true." Therefore, he concludes, the press is not the right profession for this man; nor is he suited to use the methods of the journalists. Satih continues to discourse upon the advantages and disadvantages of weekly journals but offers no solution for the problems of the unfortunate man who has come to him.[47]

The Son of the Nile and his companion, taking leave of Satih, come to the palace of the Khedive Isma'il Pasha in al-Giza, which has been converted into a zoo. Here the narrator reprints a chapter of al-Muwayhili's *Hadith 'Isa ibn Hisham* describing this palace and the sad fate of the Khedive, who was deposed in 1879. From there the Son of the Nile goes to a club, where he notices three young men whose attire marks them as men of wealth and position. Soon becoming drunk, they begin to brag about the positions their fathers hold in the government or in the courts. One of them, jealous of another whose father holds a higher and more rewarding post than his own, makes no effort to conceal his feelings. At last the three young men leave the place, and the Son of the Nile returns home.

On the sixth night, again on his way to meet Satih, the narrator hears a friend reciting poetry and conceals himself to listen unobserved. When the friend has finished, the Son of the Nile emerges from his hiding place and asks who wrote the poem. The friend answers that it is his own work. The Son of the Nile then asks him why he does not offer such immaculate poetry to the public, as other poets do. However, the friend replies that he cannot do so because the market for poetry in Egypt is stagnant, and a poet cannot achieve popularity unless he finds favor with the press. He cites the case of Ahmad Shawqi (d. 1932) as an example of the press' ability to make the works of a poet popular. He declares that the press has assigned to Shawqi titles which the press in Constantinople would not have dared to give to the Sultan.[49] The Son of the Nile answers that his friend should not derogate the "Poet of the East" or underestimate his work. Shawqi, he says, is an excellent poet, but prolific, and such writers seldom avoid error. When his friend disagrees on this point, the Son of the Nile suggests that they consult Satih. Satih says that they have both been extreme in their evaluation of Shawqi: the Son of the Nile has praised him too highly, while his friend has criticized him too harshly. Satih attempts to defend Shawqi against the objections of the latter, who finds fault with his shallowness and his distortion of some of the works of the great Arab poet Abu al-Tayyib al-Mutanabbi (d. 965), whom Shawqi imitated. The debate continues, with each man citing examples from Shawqi's poetry to support his view, and finally Satih asserts the supremacy of Shawqi among Arab poets. Then he advises the poets to forget their rivalry and collaborate in revitalizing Arabic literature, and he praises the efforts of Jamal al-Din al-Afghani in this regard.

Satih goes on to assert that the language and literature of a nation reflect its vitality and progress. To illustrate the importance of language, he cites the example of Muhammad, the Prophet of Islam. Muhammad, he says, was sent by God at a time when the Arabic language was in its prime, but when the Arab nation had lost everything except her conscience and her tongue. He was able to communicate with the people in a language which touched the very conscience of the Arabs and, as it were, electrified their souls. Satih further calls on all men of concern to support what he calls the "state of literature," without which the Western nations could not have progressed. Contemplate their eminence, he argues, and you will find that their progress is due to the fact that their writers can influence the public by their ideas. They are assisted in this task by the fact that Westerners write in the same way they speak, and thus writers and poets are readily understood by the public. Satih then skillfully explains that the Arabs' difficulty in communicating with one another, and that of their writers in reaching the public at large, arises from the sharp distinctions between classical and colloquial Arabic. He cites the instance of an Arab orator familiar with European languages. When he addresses native speakers of those languages, the effectiveness of what he says is plain in their faces. But he can address an Egyptian audience from dawn till dusk and never be understood, even if he recites the Qur'an followed by the Gospels. The cause of this tragedy is that the Egyptians have two styles of language, one for writing and one for speaking, which differ sharply from each other. Writers thus cannot use the literary language in addressing people whose understanding is limited to colloquial Arabic. Satih declares that if concerned men of letters do not act to bridge the gap between the spoken and written languages, they will soon be writing the death notice of their tongue.[50]

On the seventh night the Son of the Nile, going as usual to seek Satih, meets a handsome young man who introduces himself in eloquent Arabic as Satih's son. The narrator asks to see Satih and is told to come to the same place the following day, when Satih will depart from this life. Apparently Satih, who is busy preparing for his departure, has sent his son to discuss his problems with the Son of the Nile.

Strolling along, they cross a bridge, and Satih's son breaks the silence by asking the Son of the Nile to take him to the Azbakiyya, where he imagines the Devil welcomes the people with a smile which conceals the destruction awaiting them. The Azbakiyya is full of night clubs, dancing halls and notorious places of vice. In one of the clubs they see a man whose ragged appearance and frail body reveal his miserable poverty. The Son of the Nile, recognizing him as old acquaintance, quite bitterly tells Satih's son that the man is a victim of the British policy in Egypt. Drawing the miserable man into a corner, the two companions listen as he tells them of his ordeal. He begins by criticizing the military law issued by Herbert Kitchener, the conqueror of Umm Darman, Governor of the Sudan, and destroyer of the tomb of the Mahdi. This harsh law revealed the full extent of the British discrimination against the Egyptian and Sudanese soldiers, which culminated in the ammunition incident (so called because the British military commander in the Sudan disarmed the native soldiers and forced them into rebellion). Furthermore, he explains, the British treated the native forces as inferior and punished the rebels with dismissal from the army and imprisonment. To substantiate his judgment of British policy in Egypt, the man reads from an article in the newspaper *al-Mu'ayyad* "al-Siyasa al-Da'ifa al-'Anifa" (The Weak Violent Policy). The article very strongly assails the policies pursued in Egypt by Lord Cromer, whom it portrays as an absolute ruler. So far-reaching were his powers that he would not trade positions with anyone in the British Cabinet, nor would he consent to represent his country as ambassador in the largest capitals of Europe. The article attacks Lord Cromer especially for his justification of the infamous Dinshaway tragedy, in which four Egyptian villagers were hanged by British authorities before the eyes of their own families, for having allegedly killed an English officer who had been hunting birds in the village of Dinshaway. Lord Cromer accused the Egyptians of religious fanaticism and xenophobia, and defended this action as an emergency measure taken to put down a potential rebellion of the lower class in Egypt.[51]

Leaving this unfortunate person to his misery, the two companions visit a dancing-hall, where they see a middle-aged woman dancing in a very debased manner. Here the author is critical of the places where Egyptian men waste their time and money. He becomes especially sad when he discovers that, though all of the dancers are Egyptians, their manager is a European. Moving on, the two companions come to the palace of a wealthy man who lives in luxury, but whose only talent is for accumulating still more wealth. Satih's son and the Son of the Nile discuss here whether the government should not legally control the wealth of misers as it does that of spendthrifts. Their conversation also includes an analysis of Egyptian society, particularly of the way the shrewd city dwellers snare the gullible villagers and take their money. Walking on, the two companions see a group of students running. The Son of the Nile, who understands that the British authorities encourage athletics and praises them for building up the students physically to achieve "a sound mind in a sound body," criticizes them for neglecting other aspects of education. Satih's son replies modestly that wealthy Egyptians too deserve blame for their negligence and indifference to such public concerns as the establishment of a college and the remuneration of writers.

The two men then come across a young man reciting poetry and recognize him as a pupil of the "Sage of Islam," Jamal al-Din al-Afghani. The pupil starts explaining al-Afghani's role in stimulating the Egyptians to achieve self-realization and take pride in their religious, political, literary, and social heritage. The discussion moves on to al-Afghani's political activities and the possible means of reforming Egyptian society, and all agree that the most effective way to achieve this goal is to establish an Egyptian university. Education is the ultimate remedy for Egypt, though religion and public morals should also be emphasized. While the Egyptians should harmonize their religious life with their secular life, they should in no way violate the interdictions of the Qur'an. A return to the quiet, warm, cohesive family life is needed if the Egyptians are to have a full and meaningful existence. Nightclubs and other places of vice have undermined the influence of the family. In the past, people gathered in family circles or with close friends to discuss and resolve their mutual problems. They felt like one family, sharing one another's sorrows and joys. Today, however, they spend most of their time in the clubs, isolated from others' concerns. Yet another remedy suggested for the ills of Egyptian society is more economical management of money and land, since most of Egypt's wealth is controlled by foreigners.[52]

At this point *Layali Satih* comes to an abrupt end. The reader can only guess about the characters' fate. In fact, the ending is so implausible that the author must surely have meant to continue his narrative beyond the seventh night.[53]

Like the *Hadith 'Isa ibn Hisham,* and *Layali Satih* of Hafiz serves both to convey criticism of different aspects of Egyptian society and to reproduce the traditional rhymed prose of the maqama. Satih reminds us to some extent of the resurrected Pasha, but, whereas al-Muwaylihi provided justification for the reappearance of the Pasha, Hafiz fails to account for the presence of Satih or even to identify him. Hafiz's romance lacks a continuous narrative and a carefully developed structure, and the characters are flat and static. Consequently, the *Layali* seems a series of essays criticizing various facets of Egyptian society. Thus it is far more limited in scope than the *Hadith 'Isa ibn Hisham.*[54] The fact that the narrator makes seven nocturnal excursions to see the soothsayer Satih at a specified place and ask his opinion on various matters has tremendously narrowed the range of the actions. The characters are merely spokesmen for the author, and the reader does not share their experiences. Furthermore, the plot is monotonous and tiresome.

Hafiz may have been seeking to imitate al-Muwaylihi's narrative, particularly in introducing casual characters to voice his own ideas. But he makes no attempt to express the problems of his society through the experiences of his characters. His description of the nightclubs and dancing halls of the Azbakiyya does not reveal the abuses connected with the lives of a woman dancer, a gullible village headman, and a shrewd city playboy. Furthermore, his treatment of the problems of his society lacks both system and purpose, and his presentation of these problems has little ingenuity or creativeness.

The problems which Hafiz discusses vary in their nature and dimensions. He advocates the removal of the veil and the extension of freedom and education for the Egyptian women. He reveals tolerance and understanding in defending the Syrian immigrants' competition with the Egyptians in the different spheres of activity. He vigorously attacks social and religious superstitions and ridicules the way people continue to revere religious imposters after their death. He assails the archaic system of marriages arranged by crafty, witchlike old women. His discussion of the Egyptian press centers upon the influence of the Syrian émigrés, the effect of commercialism, and the deterioration of journalism, which incompetents and charlatans have used as a means of making their living.

Hafiz also discusses the division of men of letters and poets into two groups, one supporting the right of Ahmad Shawqi to be called "The Prince of Poets," the other supporting himself. Although he praises Shawqi's poetry, he does not neglect an opportunity to present examples which show that not all his compositions were powerful and pleasant. Hafiz criticizes Shawqi indirectly by citing al-Asma'i's (d. 828) comment on Abu al-Atahiya (d. 825). "His poetry is like a King's court, containing earthenware and gold."[55] Generally, however, Hafiz remains impartial in this controversy, and ultimately he urges the opponents to forget their jealousies and unite.

This discussion of literature touches on one of the most critical and complex problems confronting the Arabs in Hafiz's time—namely, the Arabic language. The differences between classical and colloquial Arabic, he argues, have made it all but impossible for Arab writers and speakers to reach their audience, and this inability has been the cause of the tragic backwardness that has beset the Egyptians. Hafiz strongly criticizes the press for not attempting to bridge the gap in communications, while at the same time he defends the efforts of Jamal al-Din al-Afghani and his disciple Muhammad Abduh to stimulate the Egyptians to revive both their heritage and their language.

For the student of politics, perhaps the most striking feature of the *Layali* is the way the author presents the British occupation of Egypt and the numerous problems which he believed it had created. In fact, the *Layali* may even be regarded as a succinct historical portrayal of Anglo-Egyptian relations from 1882, when the British occupied Egypt, to the tragedy of Dinshaway in 1906.

Hafiz's vehement attacks against British policy in Egypt and the Sudan can be better understood if one realizes that he himself was affected by this policy. He had been an eyewitness to the expedition against the followers of the Mahdi in the Sudan, led by British military commanders and officers. After an unhappy career as an attorney, he decided to join the army in hopes that a government position afforded more stable income and greater security than the practice of law. He entered the military academy, became a second lieutenant upon graduation in 1891, and was promoted two years later to first lieutenant in the artillery.

But he did not enjoy his new position for long. In 1894 he was transferred to the police force, on which he served until October 1895. Shortly afterwards, he was placed on pension, and his meager allowance of four pounds per month was barely enough for subsistence. The next year, however, he was recalled as a recruitment officer with the Egyptian expedition led by the Sirdar Herbert Kitchener to reconquer the Sudan and put an end to the power of the Mahdi's followers, who had occupied that country.[56]

Hafiz does not confine his criticism to the way British authorities treated him and his colleagues in the Sudan, but recounts at some length their treatment of Egyptian army officers since the beginning of the occupation. The British, he says, maintained absolute control of the Egyptian army and gave native officers no opportunity for promotion. Moreover, they weakened the military schools' curricula and robbed them of competent instructors, lest they graduate efficient officers. Thus paralyzed, the military schools were reduced to turning out officers whose knowledge when they graduated was as poor as when they entered six months earlier. Consequently, the military schools soon became a refuge for incompetent and indolent students. Hafiz also discusses the discriminatory policies pursued by the British, which he saw as weakening still further the position of native officers in the army. Thus it is hardly surprising that he devotes a large part of his "seventh night" to criticizing this situation, and it is to illustrate this situation that he mentions the notorious "ammunition incident."

Another work related to the revival of the *maqama* is Muhammad Lutfi Jumu'a's *Layali al-Ruh al-Ha'ir* (The Nights of the Perplexed Spirit), which appeared in 1912. The imaginary dialogue between the author and the perplexed spirit of his late friend Mustafa, and the division of the book into fifteen nights recall the *Layali Satih* of Hafiz Ibrahim, and to a lesser extent the tale told of the resurrected Pasha in *Hadith 'Isa ibn Hisham*.[57]

Jumu'a's dedication of *Lavali* to the noble Egyptian young men reflects the author's didactic aims. Having lived among them and shared their ideas, doubts, and sentiments, he hopes they will find in his book solutions to the confusing problems besetting them, and be touched in their hearts by the cries of the "perplexed spirit."[58]

The first night of *Layali al-Ruh al-Ha'ir,* entitled "Ritha Sadiq" (The

Eulogy of a Friend), begins with the author's memory of an evening when, sitting on a stone of the great Pyramid, he was fascinated by the view of the sunset, the Nile, the buildings of Cairo, and al-Muqattam mountain in the backround. Finally darkness fell, bringing a deep silence interrupted only by the hooting of night owls. Behind the mountain lay the city of the dead, in which rested, among many others, the remains of his friend Mustafa. Only yesterday, he reflected, Mustafa was full of life, hope and determination, but alas! nothing is left of him today except dry bones. (This demonstration of man's weakness and the vanity of his existence recalls the beginning of *Hadith 'Isa ibn Hisham* at the cemetery). Walking to the cemetery outside Cairo, Jumu'a visited his friend's grave. Later, as he returned home, he fell deep into thought, contemplating the secrets of the universe and trying to find answers to the many problems which haunted his mind. He reviewed the history of mankind but found it could not provide an answer; it was only a drop in the vast ocean of existence. "And what is man, after all?" he asked. "He is nothing but a poor, miserable creature, lost in the eternal cosmos and shrouded by the sea of darkness, seeing nothing but darkness everywhere." While deep in thought, he heard a voice saying from the depths of the earth, "You who are searching for the truth and lost in the wilderness of doubt..." Startled by the voice, he managed to gather himself and inquire who had addressed him. "I am the perplexed spirit of your friend. I have come to answer your call," said the spirit. The two then engaged in a lengthy dialogue which lasted through the remaining nights.[59]

Among the different subjects discussed in the remaining nights of the narrative, the question of the qualities that make nations strong receives careful attention. Jumu'a mentions group solidarity, sound leadership, consideration of the public interest, and continuous progress and evolution. He decries the cultural decline in his country and criticizes the leaders who disappear in times of national crisis when they are needed most.[60] Then he goes on to discuss the decline of the East, which he naively attributes to the Easterners' disrespect, contempt, even hatred of their leaders. He calls on them to honor their great men if they aspire to regain their past glory.[61]

Then he divides the people into two categories, the exploiters and the exploited. This simplistic conception provides the basis for Jumu'a's view that many people who hide behind masks of feigned greatness, nobility, and knowledge are in fact charlatans who continue to survive solely by deceiving others. Even more naive is his definition of public opinion as the adherence by a large group of people to the ideas of an eloquent orator or able writer, even though he may have evil intentions or may seek only to increase his own power and fame.[62]

His obvious pessimism mingled with cynicism, the author dismisses morals, ethics, and virtues as nothing more than universal lies and fantasies, cunning devices invented by man in order to subdue his fellow men. The condition of men as either exploiters or exploited, he goes on, recalls the tale of Sinbad the sailor, who was once stranded on a desert island with a man who was blind and crippled. Out of sheer mercy, he offered to be this man's eyes and feet. So he walked about the island, carrying the man on his shoulders, so that he could pluck fruit from the trees and eat. But the cripple would not get off Sinbad's shoulders, lest he loses the source of his survival, and he gave his benefactor neither rest nor peace. Finally, however, Sinbad managed through a trick to free himself of his burden. In the same manner some people survive and even thrive by exploiting others, says Jumu'a, and such exploitation seems to be an accepted practice.[63]

Apart from the sixth, seventh, eleventh, and twelfth nights, which include rudimentary short stories, Jumu'a's work consists mostly of the author's reflections on life and death and various aspects of human existence. Like al-Muwaylihi, who made an excursion to Europe to better understand the impact of Western civilization of Egypt, Jumu'a transports his audience to Europe, more specifically to Lausanne. But he seems not so much interested in Western civilization as obsessed with the futility of life, which is symbolized by the visit to the cemetery in Lausanne related by the spirit of the author's friend. Because he had become disenchanted with Eastern cemeteries, says the spirit, he visited a Lausanne cemetery which resembled a beautiful park and went among the graves reading epitaphs. Here was the grave of a child named Charles who had died in 1900; there stood an unfenced grave marked by a marble musical instrument, revealing that the departed, Henri, had been a musician.

The spirit was then drawn to the English cemetery, which stood alone. In utter admiration of the English love for independence he exclaimed, "May God fight them! They love to be independent even when they are dead." But he criticized them mildly because "they deny independence to others in life." Seeing another English grave with the epitaph, "he lived and died free," he addressed these words to Freedom: "They [the English] praise your name even in death and love to be associated with you in the grave." His attitude toward the English in this regard is one of praise and admiration, despite the British occupation of his country.[64]

The account of the thirteenth night shifts from prose to what appears at first glance to be free verse. The names of poets like Verlaine and Whitman are mentioned. The contents are divided in two parts, *Basmat al-Rabi'* (The Smile of Spring) and *'Urush al-Jababira* (The Thrones of Mighty Men), separated by a short song titled *Ughniyat al-Nar* (The Song of Fire). These parts take the form of quatrains to which the author gives the title *Shi'r al-Arwah* (The Verse of the Spirits), creating the impression that they are poetry rather than prose. In fact, they are neither *Shi'r hurr* (free verse) nor *Shi'r manthur* (prose poetry), but simply prose. Arabic free verse, as the Iraqi poetess Nazik al-Mala'ika defines it, essentially uses the customary meters of Arabic poetry, but, instead of being limited to a single metrical foot, contains different feet and combines elements of different poetic meters.[65] Jumu'a's *Shi'r al-Arwah* does not satisfy this definition, and it would be equally incorrect to attempt to treat this portion of his work as *shi'r manthur,* as certain contemporary writers have done.[66] Indeed, the observation of one contemporary critic that "this is written in *shi'r manthur,* or prose poetry, in which there is neither meter nor rhyme,"[67] is very difficult to reconcile with the substantial body of opinion which holds that prose is wholly distinct from poetry.

From the point of view of fiction, the sixth, seventh, eleventh, and twelfth nights are of greatest interest. These contain short, episodic, plotless stories related by the perplexed spirit of the author's friend, who in some instances is apparently recounting experiences he had while on earth.

In the first story, "Narjis al-'Amya" (Narjis the Blind), the title character is a blind five-year-old orphan who lived with her poor but proud grandmother in a dingy room next door to the narrator. The old woman, reluctant to accept charity, chose to sell candy to the children in the district rather than beg. She was frequently seen carrying her grand-daughter on her shoulders; in her hand was a box filled with candy and toys, and she called in a faint voice for the children to buy her wares. The narrator relates that he saw Narjis and took pity on her. He tried to make her happy by taking her to the seashore, where they listened to the waves. Narjis anxiously asked what the waves and the sea were, and what they looked like. She also asked about ships and birds. She felt safer when she placed her head in his lap, he kissed her with great compassion and felt as if she had become his own. One day he told her a story which he had heard from an old woman, about a poor blind girl whom the son of the king saw and took to his palace and married after she had been healed by an Indian physician. Narjis, upon hearing the story, wished she could be cured by the same man.

Later, the narrator goes on, his family moved, and he left behind the poor blind girl, who had done nothing to deserve such misfortunes. One day, as he passed by a bridge, he heard a faint feminine voice chanting the Qur'an. Walking toward the place the voice came from, he saw an old woman in rags, sitting on the ground with two shabby-looking children. He recognized her as the poor, blind Narjis whom he had known as a child. But he felt helpless to relieve her misery, for now he belonged to the world of the spirit, and he appealed to his friend to aid her.[68]

This anecdote is clearly not a short story in the modern sense. Nor could the piece be classed, for example, as a social commentary. Many Western short stories avoid such a portrayal. The theme and style of the story reveal the influence of romanticism, which was strong in Egypt in the first quarter of this century, and whose chief exponent was Mustafa Lutfi al-Manfaluti.

This romantic influence is again revealed in the second story, "Sadiqi Ali" (My Friend Ali), whose title character, like the narrator, belongs now to the world of the spirit. Ali, the narrator proudly relates, was a black slave whose master, a physician, brought him to Egypt from the farthest part of Africa, whose inhabitants were mostly of Arab origin. Ali must have been a man of dignity and pride, not a common slave without social roots, for his father and relatives were businessmen and shipowners. But he was deceived by the physician, who enticed Ali to escape with him aboard an army ship and seek a better life in Egypt. On their arrival, the physician took care of Ali's up-bringing and education, treating him as one of the family. Ali studied chemistry and medicine, and helped his benefactor in his work.

But when Ali grew to manhood, the physician changed his attitude and would not allow him to associate with his daughter Zubayda. And when she came to marriageable age, her father shielded her from Ali and told him he could no longer see her. Having been in love with her since childhood, Ali obeyed the physician's order resignedly. He discovered that despite the generosity of his benefactor, he was only a slave, thought to be unworthy of marrying the free Zubayda. When he asked the physician to increase his pay, the latter reminded him that he should be grateful to him for what he had, and that he owed him his education and even his life. Ali had no choice but to leave the physician's home and try his fortune elsewhere.

But after moving to another town, he was stricken with tuberculosis, and Zubayda was given in marriage to someone else. Although gravely ill, he managed to leave his bed and go to the physician's home to censure him as the cause of his tragedy. In his fury he leapt at his one-time benefactor, but his weak body collapsed, and he cut his head so badly that he bled to death. Finally, in the world of the spirits, Ali met his beloved Zubayda, still as beautiful as when he had known her on earth. He also saw the spirit of her father, the physician, tormented by a Jinni's whip.[69]

These two stories draw their themes and characters from Egyptian life and society and may therefore be regarded as the most important portion of Jumu'a's book.[70] They are undoubtedly more typical of Egyptian sentiments than his other two stories, "al-Akhawat al-Thalath" ("The Three Sisters") and "al-Fakiha al-Muharrama" ("The Forbidden Fruit"), in which he abruptly transfers the reader to European settings to reveal some aspect of European life and society.

"Al-Akhawat al-Thalath" concerns three daughters born to an Italian father and a French mother. The first sister, with no apparent physical beauty, was practical and industrious. She visited Italy and lived in England for three years, during which time she married an Englishman. She soon came to the opinion that the English are doers rather than talkers, and this taught her to be practical. She controlled her husband and manipulated him "as the English play soccer," sometimes treating him like a child. She became the head of the family, while he became the hired hand. She was happily married.

The second sister, a pretty brunette, seemed more Sicilian, Neapolitan, or Venetian than French. She was secretive, almost enigmatic, capable of loving or hating with great vigor. She could have been Catherine de Medici or, had she been a man, Machiavelli. She was full of vindictiveness, but educated and well read. She was born to be a queen. The third sister, the plain and insignificant member of the family, received no attention from her mother. She did not remain with the family, but lived in other households, where she served as a maid. However, she had a magnificent character.[71]

The second story, "al-Fakiha al-Muharrama," relates some aspects of the life of the beautiful eighteen-year-old Renée, a brunette whom the narrator met in an Alpine village. She was a young woman with exquisite artistic taste. She was suspicious of men, however, because once she had loved a man who betrayed her. Once, when she was in church, her eyes met those of the priest during the sermon; after the service he followed her to the woods to express his love for her, but she spurned his suit. When they met for the last time, the priest asked her to stop hating men. She answered that she had no reason to hate men; after all, Adam did not hate Eve, though she was the one who had enticed him to eat of the forbidden fruit which cost him paradise.[72]

Layali al-Ruh al-Ha'ir is different from the traditional *maqama* in both structure and style. It is closer to *Layali Satih* than to *Hadith 'Isa ibn Hisham,* both because the perplexed spirit resembles Satih and because the narrative is divided into nights. Jumu'a's work belongs chiefly to the "romantic school," which was prevalent in the Arab countries in the late nineteenth and early twentieth centuries, and which drew heavily on Western models and ideas. But the opinion expressed by Ayyad, that the romantic themes of Jumu'a's four narratives treated in the *maqama* form freed Arabic prose fiction from the rigid formalism of that genre, is hardly convincing. It seems even less plausible to assert that plot, which in the *maqama* followed a single pattern, has in these narratives been freed from any pattern and thus come closer to the pattern of the Western short story.[73] What Ayyad has apparently missed is that like the traditional *maqama*, these stories are simply chains of unconnected incidents which do not form a unified plot. Their style is not so rigid as the rhymed prose of the *maqama,* however, and the aesthetic subjects with which they deal are more sophisticated, although less empirical, than those of the *maqama.* Jumu'a's work unmistakenly reflects the great resolution of the intelligentsia in Egypt to prevent their Islamic heritage from being overcome by the invading Western ideas which were already making their impact on Eastern societies.

CHAPTER VI

SALIM AL—BUSTANI AND THE BEGINNING OF MODERN ARABIC FICTION

In the two decades following the death of Marun Naqqash in 1855, most writers of fiction in Syria were providing the public and private theaters with dramas whose themes were drawn from Arab history or from Western works which they knew in translation. All of these plays were designed to suit the social customs, taste, and moral views of a conservative Oriental society. When theatrical activities were transferred to Egypt, the development of the drama in Syria lagged. In fact, the theater had been a novelty, more a curosity than a genuine reflection of Syrian cultural life.

Prose fiction received more attention, largely because of the press. In 1858, Khalil al-Khuri (d. 1907) established his weekly *Hadiqat al-Akhbar,* Al-Khuri devoted a portion of this periodical to original prose fiction and translations. He published serially his story "Wai Idhan Lastu bi Ifranji" ("Shame, I am not then a 'European' "), which Tarrazi describes as "a moralistic book written in the manner of a story, in which the author incorporated a careful criticism of morals and customs with subtle observations on al-Mutanabbi and Lamartine."[1] The effect of this romance on the public is hard to determine, but it must surely have set the precedent for later writers' use of the popular magazines in advancing their techniques and ideas.

The most notable magazine promoting Arabic fiction was *al-Jinan,* established by the celebrated Butrus al-Bustani (d. 1883) in Beirut in January 1870. Its scope included not only literary but also social and political matters. Its popularity, which to no small degree stemmed from the name and fame of its founder, helped to attract contributions from many renowned writers. One of them was al-Bustani's son, Salim, whose voluminous output of stories of varying length marked the beginning of modern Arabic prose fiction. Salim's background and literary talents equipped him to undertake at an early age the publication and edition of several periodicals, including *al-Jinan, al-Janna,* and *al-Junayna.*[2]

Born at Abayya, Lebanon, in 1848, Salim was fortunate in being raised in a home filled with learning.[3] Also, he was privileged to study the Arabic language and literature under the eminent master of those fields, Nasif al-Yaziji, and he mastered Turkish, French, and English as well. In 1862 Salim succeeded his father as the translator for the American Consulate in Beirut. With seemingly inexhaustible energy, he undertook formidable assignments, ranging from editing several periodicals to teaching English at *al-Madrasa al-*

Wataniva (The National School), established by his father at Beirut. He also assisted his father in writing his Arabic encyclopedia and participated in the myriad activities of *al-Jam'iyya al-'Ilmiyya al-Suriyya* (The Syrian Scientific Society), of which he was vice-president. He contributed numerous articles to his journals and wrote the editorials for *al-Jinan* under the heading *Jumla Siyasiyya* (Political Commentary).

But Salim al-Bustani was best known for his purely literary activity. He was in fact rather unique in the Arab literary world. Most of the writers we have examined so far were more or less isolated cases. There is no apparent continuation or relationship among them. This separateness was compounded by their relative isolation in the Arabic world. For the most part unsophisticated, they labored alone, never really known and appreciated and almost immediately forgotten.

Salim al-Bustani, however, was caught up in the whirlwind of the new and heightened intellectual and social consciousness of the late nineteenth century that engulfed, and had its effect upon, all but the most isolated outposts of civilization. Although he was well acquainted with the West and appreciated many of its progressive aspects, he remained devoted to Arabic civilization. Accordingly, he epitomized two unique but different qualities: Arabic traditionalism and Western liberalism. On the one hand, he loved and wished to preserve those unique customs which were the foundations of the moral and ethical fiber of the Arabs. On the other, he was acutely aware of, and influenced by, the contemporary currents of rationalism, empiricism, and liberalism emanating from the West, and was therefore anxious to acquaint his Arab countrymen with, and have them adopt the most liberating and humanizing approaches, ideas, and usages of the socially and scientifically advanced West. Thus he assumed the self-appointed role of critic and educator, utilizing as his main theme the necessity to participate in *Ruh al-'Asr*—that is, the spirit of liberality and human progress emanating from the West. Only if one understands the underlying educative purpose of his whole life's work, his sense of Western humanism, can one really appreciate, indeed truly understand, the importance and place of his writings.

Furthermore, one can establish a definite link between the prolific and innovative al-Bustani and later writers. Indeed, he may be rightfully considered the true father of the Arab short story and novel, including historical fiction. And if one peruses the lists of subscribers which al-Bustani appended at the end of his popular journal *al-Jinan,* one can quite justifiably conclude, because of their position and importance, that his ideas must have reached some fairly influential circles.

As for his purely fictional activities, between 1870 and his death in 1884 al-Bustani composed and translated numerous pieces of prose fiction, and wrote three plays. His stories range from short didactic pieces of only a few pages to historical novels of considerable length. Despite this productivity, however, the themes and structure of much of his fiction are, on the surface at least, generally limited in scope. Love and marriage, and all the moral lessons pertaining to them are his favorite subjects, even in some of his historical short stories. Furthermore, his stories are crammed with so many facts and incidents, all within a short space, that they often lack coherence and sometimes tend in their undistributed impact to confuse the reader. For the most part, also, al-Bustani's plots are monotonous and repetitive. Commonly, they depict the rivalry of young men who hope to marry the same girl and the intrigue, deceit, and violence which surround these rivalries. On a deeper plane, however, the works of al-Bustani stand as a testimony to his "Western conscience" and his concern for the freedom and dignity of his own countrymen. It is significant that he was the first Arabic writer to transmit some of his characters beyond the Mediterranean to Europe, using Italy as a setting.[4]

The tone and narrative technique of his stories are, at times, reminiscent of the *Thousand and One Nights.* For example, several young men are in rivalry for the hand of Asma in the novel which bears her name, but only one of them, Karim al-Baghdadi, wins at the end.[5] This plot is repeated in *Bint al-'Asr* and *Fatina.*[6] The situations in other stories by al-Bustani, such as *Salma* and *Samiya,* are similarly simplistic.[7] A typical *Thousand and One Nights* technique which al-Bustani employs in the introduction of an experienced and cunning woman employed to help achieve the amorous goals of a young suitor.

All of al-Bustani's characters are fully developed symbols of vice or virtue. Primarily occupied with their own love affairs and/or intrigues, they are completely oblivious of their surroundings, and other people are only incidental to their lives. Typically bourgeois, they enjoy the amenities of life and appreciate their middle class status. The male figures are mostly businessmen and merchants with a fair degree of education, although some of them use their mental keenness to achieve sinister goals, which invariably include the elimination of a rival for the love of a beautiful and virtuous young woman.

The names of his heroines—Rima, Asma, Fatina, Salma and Samiya—are stereotypical. They are all highly educated young women, indeed surprisingly so, given the lack of opportunity for a woman to gain a decent education in nineteenth century Syria. They are always virtuous, beautiful, balanced and bright. But those who are not heroines for instance, sisters, servants, and girlfriends—are, for the most part, uneducated, superficial, or frivolous. They are, in short, unvirtuous.[8]

This dichotomy between virtue and vice is manifested even more strongly among the male characters. In *Bint al-'Asr,* Majid epitomizes all the good qualities that a hero should have: humility, refinement and intelligence. His unworthy rivals are, on the other hand, evil, arrogant and deceitful. They plot to compromise Majid in a shoddy financial transaction in order to make him lose his money and therefore lose Rima, the virtuous and beautiful heroine.[9] In his adversity, Majid, being of firm and noble character, never loses his faith in people. Neither does he condemn the villains, but rather ends up by judging man as a noble creature although, at times, he himself shows signs of avarice and envy.[10]

The opposite poles of virtue and vice are also reflected in men's attitudes toward their jobs and family. In the novel *Asma,* for instance, Nadir, the heroine's father is a rich but humble merchant who never boasts of his position or wealth. Furthermore, he always puts his family ahead of his work. His friend, Sadir, is just the opposite: he brags about his wealth and, because he puts his work ahead of his family, his neglected children grow up to be weak and ill-bred.[11] Another character, Karim al-Baghdadi, is an educated and virtuous gentleman who believes that wealth alone cannot make men better. More important is the development of those essential spiritual qualities which elevate man from an elemental baseness to a truly refined human being. His opposite is Badi, Asma's brother, an arrogant braggart who believes himself to be better than other people in every respect.[12] He is so evil and envious that he even conspires to kill Karim in order to prevent Asma from marrying him.[13] But whereas Majid faces his predicament with patience and forebearance, never losing his faith in the human race, Karim, a man of like quality and faced by s similar situation, loses his confidence in the human justice represented by the Ottoman court.

Al-Bustani appears to share this view since he shows a great deal of sympathy for his character's ordeal. Interjecting himself into their narrative, as was his usual practice, the author indicates that the reader should sympathize with Karim, sharing his tears and sadness.[14] Of course, al-Bustani could never have criticized Ottoman justice openly without exposing himself to the punishment of the authorities and without jeopardizing his whole career. He condemns Badi's attempt to kill Karim and observes that there is no limit to the savagery of man, although he gives the appearance of being civilized. He believes that only an enlightened education makes man truly civilized and prevents him from attempting such atrocities.[15]

Al-Bustani's attitude reflects a certain eighteenth-century enthusiasm about the healing balm of education. In the bloody crucible of two world wars, and the continuing agony of the twentieth century, such overt optimism about education—although natural under the circumstances—betrays a certain naiveté. It is symptomatic of the social and cultural ethos in al-Bustani's time.

In *Fatina,* Murad is portrayed as an envious cheat and intriguer, although a man of considerable means.[16] His friend Sabir is a further example of meanness and vice, who would do anything in order to harm people. Sabir is the instrument of the hero's woe, in an intrigue which appears in almost every story with numbing repetition: he lures him to a brothel to besmirch his name, thereby preventing him from marrying Fatina.[17] This scheme is little different from the stock characters of al-Bustani's other works, whose crimes are as multiple as their vices.

More important than this simple moral dichotomy of good and evil, however, is al-Bustani's attempt to represent the spirit of his time, including the effect of the cultural changes which had taken place in the Arab East as a result of the invasion of the thought and culture of the Western world. He was the first Arab writer to use the term *Ruh al-'Asr,* literally "The Spirit of the Agem" and he applied it to the writing of fiction. Because of his deep understanding of Western thought, al-Bustani could have found no better translation for the German term *Zeitgeist* than *Ruh al-'Asr.*[18]

He used it to identify those collective forces which reflect the most progressive and most enlightening, edifying, and humanizing aspects of contemporary civilization no matter from what country or continent they spring. When a society violates these principles, for whatever reason, then it is said that the Ruh—spirit—of the nation is opposite to *Ruh al-'Asr*—The Spirit of the Age.[19]

Al-Bustani believed that his own society was opposed to the *Ruh al-'Asr* as he observed and interpreted its operation in Europe. He described those principles which best characterize its essence as equality, freedom, and religious toleration. More specifically and adamantly, he emphasized the freedom of the individual and the necessity to bring about a consciousness of his political rights.[20] In this context, obviously, al-Bustani was influenced by the West and, most especially, those principles of the French Revolution, which he believed characterized France the "wet-nurse" of *Ruh al-'Asr.*[21]

But *Ruh al-'Asr* as al-Bustani views it, is more than these principles alone. It is a combination of historical customs, traditions, institutions, and activities, including religion, which characterize a truly civilized society. But those elements that constitute the spirit of a certain age in a certain place, are in effect its *Weltanschauungen,* of another age and another place. What was common in the past, for example, may not be suitable for the changed aspect of contemporary times in mid-nineteenth-century Syria; therefore, it is necessary, according to al-Bustani, for the individual and society to conform to the *Ruh al-'Asr* as it currently appears in every age. In fact, al-Bustani believes it inexcusable to cling tenaciously and irrationally to outworn traditions and customs which obviate progress, since they do not correspond with the spirit and exigencies of the new age.[22]

It is evident that al-Bustani's conception of *Ruh al-'Asr,* expressed among other things, the idea of the liberation of one's self from outworn tradition, customs, and laws which are prejudicial to the freedom, dignity, and progress of man. Much of Syrian life was based upon narrow provincialism, state despotism, infantile religious bigotry, and gross restrictions upon individual freedom. These, al-Bustani affirmed, are out of step with the true spirit of the age, the *Zeitgeist* of human freedom and dignity emanating from the West, and should be rejected because they militate against the progress of Syria as well as other Eastern societies. Progress, he believed, would be promoted by the liberal influx of the imperatives of the spirit of the times into a hitherto stagnant society, his own, which was out of harmony with edifying ideas and thought. In other words, *Ruh al-'Asr* recognized no national boundaries or artificial restrictions. It leaped over and squeezed under the arbitrary boundaries of state and society, encompassing in its ontological thrust all peoples and all countries. Obviously, the *Zeitgeist* of freedom, equality, liberty, parliamentary government, and religious liberty, etc., was much stronger and more apparent in the Western world at the time of al-Bustani. Nevertheless, he believed that its force was so strong and its imperatives so noble that if Arab society did not conform to its spirit, it would be out of harmony with the true and noble history of humanity.

And his own society was in fact beginning to change because of the sudden invasion of European concepts, values, customs, and style. But al-Bustani was disappointed because most of these changes were, as yet, based upon a mere superficial assimilation and veneer. Dancing, for instance, and the acceptance of European "party dresses" was just one example of European society that al-Bustani himself disliked. Al-Bustani remarked that such customs should be rejected by his fellow Arabs because they were not useful.[23]

Since the concepts, values, and customs of the West were vastly different from the Eastern ones, al-Bustani thought it necessary to explain them to his countrymen so that they would adopt those that were the best while maintaining their own individuality. Thus, the purpose of his novels *Asma* and *Bint al-'Asr,* literally "Daughter of the Age," was to explain certain customs and practices which were different than, or incompatible with, the cultural approach of his countrymen.

The adoption of different customs, practices, and ideas usually takes place at a time when a country is trying to adapt itself to the customs of other people who have preceded them in cultural progress.[24] *Bint al-Asr* deals nicely with both situations. However, al-Bustani also inserts a word of caution: rather than the wholesale assimilation of external forces emanating from a more culturally progressive society, he counselled the exercise of judgment and prudence in adjusting one's self to the invasion of foreign concepts and values. Above all, he did not want to see his society completely transform itself into a Western society, but only to adopt those ideas and adapt those practices which conform to the essence of the *Ruh al-'Asr,* reflecting the universal exigencies of human freedom, dignity, and equality. He believes strongly in retaining those unique historical commitments to custom and tradition that allow for a unique individuality and that distinguish one society from another. He preferred to see an ontological unity in diversity characterized by the mutual sharing of the *Zeitgeist* rather than a oneness of complete conformity.

The protagonist in *Bint al-'Asr,* unlike other girls of her age, is very beautiful. But she is also educated, enlightened, and modest. Thus, Rima possesses those physical and mental qualities which al-Bustani apparently considered requisite for a model woman. Although in externalities she is, perhaps, not very different from other young women of her age, she is perspicacious enough to realize that the times are changing and that her country must change with them. But she is careful not to adopt those meaningless European practices which have invaded her country and which outrageously conflict with established traditions. In other words, Rima represents, in her attitude and actions, the correct approach to an adaptation to the *Ruh al-'Asr*: selective and prudent assimilation of the good practices and ideas of the West.

Furthermore, nothing could exemplify the meaningful connotations of *Ruh al-'Asr* better than the diverse attitudes of Rima and her sister Jamila. While the heroine is an open-minded and intelligent young woman who approaches life in a rational manner, her sister is frivolous and superficial. Above all, whereas Rima ignores European dancing because it lacks any redeeming value, Jamila adores it and criticizes her sister's failure to understand "civilized manners" and the requisites of the *'Asr* (age).[25] Indeed, when Rima rebukes her sister for her frivolity and superficiality, Jamila retorts that she is not in need of her advice because it is she, not her sister, who is "in step with the times." Of course, she is mistaking superficial activities for true freedom, but she tries to live and behave the way she sees fit, ignoring all the values of her society.[26]

Rima epitomizes the rational approach, which differentiates between the essential and non-essential. She does not wish to overthrow everything, nor does she wish to be completely "free." She accepts and conforms to those unique spiritual attitudes and good customs of her country. She does not want to displace, but built upon that which is good in the old familiar. Hers is the voice of reason which understands the necessity of using the past in a rational way, of evolving slowly but surely with the *Zeitgeist* while maintaining one's essential character through the retention of those individual traits of custom of life that marks a people as historically and spiritually different.

It is not clothes, dancing, smoking or drinking that brings one into conformity with the spirit of age, but the slow and steady inculcation of those universally valid ideas and values that mark the late nineteenth century but stand for the most important imperatives of the human spirit: freedom, the dignity of the individual, equality, and tolerance. These are the qualities that the Arab East lacked and that al-Bustani would like to see his countrymen attain through an open-minded, educated approach to the essential spirit of the age. Anis, one of the young men who is struggling to win Rima's hand in marriage, represents the bad example of a young man who has been corrupted by the detrimental influence of European civilization. In an existential sense, the author meant to portray in *Bint al-'Asr* that particular period in the nineteenth century when Syrian society was experiencing the brunt of Western influence. The transition in manners, customs, and values had thrust it into conflict. As he states:

> These things are taking place at a time whose meaning, like the uncertain
> light of dawn, is as yet unclear. Therefore, the minds of many people, too,
> are not clear. Even strangers (Europeans) are in the dark, like the natives.
> This state of affairs indicates that the country is suffering under the burden
> of a cultural situation whose values are in an uncertain state of transition.[27]

Another work, *Fatina,* demonstrates this transition of values.[28] Like Rima, Fatina symbolizes *Ruh al-'Asr.* She is educated and enlightened. She values learning and right thought more than money, sumptuous clothes, or external appearance. Above all, she is aware of the transitional tension in her society as the result of the invasion of European civilization. Moreover, she is prudent enough, unlike most of her friends, not to imitate the superficial European customs without appreciating her own native customs.[29]

Al-Bustani realized that the rejection of established customs and the adoption of new foreign ones is not an easy task. The problem, as he sees it, is that the conflict between two rival traditions creates a most unsettling crisis of conscience and peace of mind. The problem becomes even more acute when the foreign customs are completely unsuitable to those who adopt them.[30]

Indeed, young al-Bustani himself was often confused about the confrontation of European manners and values with those of his own society. In his attempt to reconcile the values of his society with those of Europe, he found himself genuinely perplexed and uncertain. To him, what constituted "genuine" civilization were not superficial graces or external appearances, or material acquisitions such as beautiful homes, clothes, and carriages, but those human qualities which marked, on an individual basis, a mind as charitable as it is sound and, on a collective basis, a society free from sophisticated ideas and corrupting principles.[31]

This mental attitude of al-Bustani is reflected in his protagonist Asma, who, like her creator, is deeply perplexed over the conflict of her own values with those of Europe. Should she follow her friends who have aped the "counterfeit" aspects of a foreign civilization into her being? In order to find a solution to her mental predicament she seeks enlightenment through reading and learning. Thus, she finally finds peace of mind through knowledge and finally marries Karim al-Baghdadi, who understands the true meaning of civilization which, based upon certain important values, transforms men into decent human beings.[32]

The impact of Western civilization on Syria and other Arab countries may have first been deeply felt by intellectuals like al-Bustani, but the abundant tensions of the conflict are still present in Arab societies. Indeed, the con-

tinuing impress of the mores and manners of the West has created one of the
most crucial problems of the twentieth-century Middle East. Nations are still
seeking, without much success, to maintain their cultural integrity while
somehow reconciling it with Western values which reflect a history and
culture, in most cases, entirely antithetical to their own. They recognize that
the momentum of progress lies with the West, but that raises the difficulty.
They want to adopt those trends of modernization which have swept over the
world from the West but, at the same time, are loathe to make—because of
their traditions and history—the full and free commitment that is necessary.
Thus, caught in the throws of an eternally frozen antithetical tension, the syn-
thesis which implies compromise and promises progress lies forever uncon-
summated.

It is not surprising to find that al-Bustani criticizes European customs
and, most of all, his own countrymen for imitating the most worthless and unsuitable of them. But he himself is never very explicit and clear about just what
it is that he wishes his fellow Arabs to assimilate. One can only infer that it is
those ideas and activities that will not "corrupt" Arab society but will, at the
same time, put that society in step with the spirit of the age.

Of course, a rather subtle psychological element entered into and compounded the whole problem. The invading European way of life had created a
sense of inferiority in Arab society. In fact, this was so strong that the collective notion arose that everything European was good while all that was Eastern
was inferior. This belief became so deeply imbedded in the Eastern mind that
until this day there is a rather widespread belief that in almost every way the
West is far superior to the East.

The behavior of al-Bustani's characters reflects this attitude. Nabiha,
one of his female characters in his novel *Asma,* for example, prefers Western
clothes not because they are suitable for the weather of her country, but
because she believes wearing them will somehow elevate her to a more exalted
status. She goes to the extreme of determining to marry a European husband
even if he is poor. Indeed, she believes that being a European means being—without exception—highly cultured, civilized, and moral.[33]

If Nabiha goes to extremes, her mother is even more drawn to imitating
everything Western. She thinks that by mimicking European manners she will
automatically become a better and more respected woman—in effect, a European woman. Her attitude is unequivocally expressed in her response to her
son-in-law when he ridicules the European clothes she had made for herself:

> How unfortunate I am. My son-in-law has ridiculed me while I thought he
> would consider me a European woman in every respect. I mingle with men,
> appear unveiled in public, wear European dress and communicate in a
> European language, but still I am told that I am far from being one of
> them.[34]

Another female character, Badi'a, especially likes European men's manners and their behavior toward women, such as the concept of "ladies first." But, having little real education, she appreciates these external forms of European manners without understanding the reasons behind them. Al-Bustani believed he did understand, and he interjects himself in the narrative to state that one of the reasons European men always give their wives deference is because their women are more fragile and, therefore, require more care and attention by men. But more important, he continues, with sly insight, European men behave gallantly toward their women in unimportant matters in order to make it easier for them to subjugate them in more essential things. Badi'a could not, of course, understand these things.[35]

Asma recognizes that the European surpassed the Easterners in many respects, particularly in social progress. But she believes that it is wrong to prefer one nation to another and that individuals should be judged according to their relative merits regardless of their racial or ethnic origin.[36] At this point al-Bustani—true to his usual approach—injects his own ideas and declares Nabiha not only wrong but considers her indiscriminate preference for European manners as a demonstration of an unwarranted feeling of inferiority.[37]

The most predominant situations in al-Bustani's stories revolve around love between a young man and a young woman. This typically involves the latter's freedom to marry a man of her own choice, and the conflict between such freedom and parental authority. The freedom which the heroines exercise in their relations with young men and their mature understanding of love is particularly striking because al-Bustani was writing in the 1870's. Indeed, they seem to act completely against the established modes of behavior and traditional mores of society. The question is, therefore, why did he depict such unrealistic situations? The only answer can be that he was influenced by the role of the heroine and her relation with her lover as portrayed in Western literature. It must be noted, however, that this freedom never leads to, or even implies illicit relations. Al-Bustani is a conservative and a moralist, and his characters reflect many of his own ideas of what love and courtship should mean.

The lovers meet in their homes and in sight of their families. They are either engaged or about to be engaged. It is during the period of engagement that the couple can test each other regarding their likes and dislikes, their ideas and inclinations before deciding to take the serious step of marriage. For this reason, Asma's father, an enlightened man, allows his son Jalil to meet alone with Badi'a, and his daughter Asma to meet alone with Karim al-Baghdadi and other young men at his home. He ridicules those parents who prevented their children, even if engaged, from meeting with each other before the marriage. He believes that the meeting of the couple, especially if they are serious, is healthy, and aids the couple to know each other better. This, in turn, will help obviate problems which might arise after their marriage. He even allows the couple to determine the time and mode of entertainment; but the meeting should be at home.[38]

To a modern Western reader such a relationship appears natural and commonplace, but in nineteenth-century Syria even this degree of freedom between an unmarried young man and woman would be considered not only serious but incredible. Again, this rather puzzling superimposition of Western love upon Eastern characters must be understood in the light of, and operative under, his main philosophical and literary theme: *Ruh al-'Asr*. Certainly al-Bustani believed that the social progress which includes courting and marriage customs in the West was part of and reflective of the liberating force of the *Zeitgeist*. The brutal social customs and stagnant traditions he wanted to liberate his own society from were epitomized in the total subservence of young people in relation to marriage and love to the whims of their elders. Here we can find the difference between important and nonimportant aspects of *Ruh al-'Asr*—almost, indeed, its essence. This was truly a theme that he could get his teeth into. It consistently conforms to his essential idea of *Ruh al-'Asr* as a metaphysical force in terms of its moral imperatives of liberty, freedom, equality, and justice. Thus, his emphasis upon the theme of love and marriage between a young man and a young woman and what it should be is merely one aspect of the greater macrocosm of the *Zeitgeist*.

Al-Bustani portrays his protagonists, particularly Asma, not as teen-age girls—which they in fact are—but as mature women with consummate wisdom and reasoning power. Asma has read about love and acquired a fair knowledge about the ecstacy awaiting the meeting of two lovers. She discusses intellectual topics and is knowledgeable about a variety of disciplines. We are told nothing about the kind of books she read and in what language, however. Certainly they were not in Arabic since in the 1870's the Arabic press in Syria was in its infancy, Arabic literary materials were rare, and translation from Western literature into Arabic was even more meager.

Al-Bustani habitually portrays his female characters as paragons of knowledge, maturity, and resourcefulness despite their young age, because he has more than the realistic portrayal of a young girl's manner or intelligence in mind.[39] The heroines serve to express many of his ideas about the edifying results of the conformity of one's being to high standards of intelligence, common sense, and decency—the essence of *Ruh al-'Asr*.

As an idealistic young woman, Asma believes that love is not an accidental but an essential aspect of life. She craves the experience through which she will be transported to an emotional realm beyond human experience. But the love she craves in her idealized fantasies is immaculate and pure,[49] the noble emotion which transforms man into a decent human being. "It makes the miser generous and the lisper eloquent."[41] She rejects the actions of Helen of Troy who deserted her husband to join her lover, arguing that if love motivated people to do what is dishonorable and infamous, it would be shameful to fall in love.[42] Love, then, as Asma—or, to be precise, as al-

Bustani himself—sees it, is not a sensual relationship, but that indomitable force through which the short and often melancholy existence of man is redeemed. It is the path of selflessness and dedication; a participation in the life of the spirit and, therefore, in the existence of God, who is pure love.[43] Al-Bustani constantly emphasizes the spiritual beauty, the strength and the nexus of love. He seems almost the knight errant reincarnated in the guise of a nineteenth-century Christian Arab. Because he believed in that spiritual beauty which united in a metaphysical chain the love of man, woman, and God, he felt that, in essence, love is based on spiritual not physical beauty. In conformity to his whole approach, he maintained that man should not allow his reason to be controlled by his more passionate and primitive proclivities—such perhaps, that he saw as all-too-dominant in the relationships of his own Arab contemporaries and, therefore, not in conformity with one of the most noble impulses of *Ruh al-'Asr*—love.[44]

This is the love that is pre-requisite for marriage, without which it becomes a nightmare. While Asma likes and respects Badi', she really does not love him because he does not fulfill her own expectations of love based upon a, perhaps overtly, idealized goodness and nobility. But Asma is fortunate to have an enlightened father who champions marriage based upon love. In this regard she is more fortunate than al-Bustani's other female protagonists. Their problem, for the most part, is one of the pull between the old and the new, between parental selection and the daughter's freedom of choice.

In *Fatina,* for instance, the conflict between the heroine's free will and parental authority is acute. Her parents want her to marry Murad because of his wealth and social status. But Fatina is in love with Fu'ad, who is of noble character but less rich than Murad. She insists that hearts are not a commodity available to the highest bidder.[45] But her parents do not share this attitude and think her unrealistic. Torn between her own concept of individual freedom and filial obedience, Fatina becomes confused and is unable at last to distinguish between the many facets and demands of reality. She even goes so far as to deny that the whole world is real.[46] Finally, realizing that it is futile to oppose her parents' will, Fatina fatalistically submits, fully cognizant of the fact that marrying a man she does not love is to enter a living death. But, of course, the story does have a happy ending, for al-Bustani predictably adopts the last minute device of reprieve and rescue through the uncovering of Murad's deceits and intrigues. Like the other villains in al-Bustani's stories, Murad stands for the forces of reaction and unreason.

In depicting one of the intrigues designed by Murad to eliminate Fu'ad and marry Fatina, al-Bustani uses Italy as a setting and the "Mafia" as its executors. Of course, he had to be careful of the censor's ban, and this device enabled him neatly to expound certain points through foreign characters and foreign settings. For instance, a socialist bandit chieftain is the voice and conscience of al-Bustani himself who seems to have been strongly influenced by the socialist thought of the West. Murad's involvement with the chieftain comes about when Fatina's health deteriorates as a result of the conflict between will and authority over the question of her marriage. Italy is suggested as a place for rest and recuperation and her father accompanies her there. To Fatina's delight Fu'ad is asked to come along. But her happiness is marred when Murad decides to join the group. The company stays in a quiet, middle-sized town only a short distance from the main highway and not far from an Italian seaport.

Murad arranges to have Fu'ad abducted, and he is brought to the lair of the bandit chieftain. The bandit leader rules over his followers like an absolute monarch with unchallenged authority, though he has come to power through the election of the members under him.[47] This democratic idea, awkward as it is, is necessary because it serves to expound al-Bustani's democratic and egalitarian principles. Angered by the insinuations of Murad, the bandit chieftain instructs him in "right thinking." While people consider taking money from the rich as robbery, he and his followers regard it as restitution of what is rightfully theirs. God has made money and property for the benefit and enjoyment of all people, he explains. It is wrong that only a few should have all the wealth and property at the expense of the happiness of the majority of the people.

It is not only the rich that are criticized, however. The government and its officials are no different, for they extort money and exploit people in the same way. Therefore, the leader informs Murad, he and his followers decided to obtain what was rightfully theirs without harming anybody—except, of course that they take the money and possessions of the rich and the rulers, "which are also ours." To explain his principles regarding the distribution of wealth further, the chieftain argues that the wealth acquired by individuals through accidents of birth is unjust. "Why should people starve," he asks, "because they are born to poor parents?" "Why should," he asserts, "a man inherit a million from his father while the other has nothing to cover his body? Is this not an injustice and a corruption of divine justice? Therefore, you see us here abide by the rules of religion and justice. We truly shun evil."[48]

Finally, the leader startles Murad by accusing him of acting unjustly against his friend. For this he, himself, must pay a large sum of money before being released.[49] Having announced his terms to Murad, the leader then calls Fu'ad and attempts to convince him in turn, of the soundness and humanness of his principles. When Fu'ad attempts to defend Murad, the leader rebukes him for being a simpleton who cannot understand that it is Murad who had connived with him and his men to have him killed.[50] Wherever men are willing to be deceived, al-Bustani seems to be saying, there are always those who will deceive them and exploit them.

Neither Murad nor Fu'ad accept the leader's argument in defense of the principles which guide him and his band. Murad is so frightened that he says nothing, but the innocent Fu'ad is bolder.[51] If the band is defending a just cause, he points out, they should go out and preach their principles to the public rather than resort to illegal practices. The leader retorts that habit has so bound people and controlled their minds that nothing can change them. As for the few who are in a position to help, greed and self-interest have obviated any action on their part. It is, therefore, imperative to resort to force and clandestine activity to take the excess money in society and distribute it to the poor.[52]

Al-Bustani seems rather hard-headed in his belief that it is very difficult to reform people—especially the rich and the powerful. Although the plot against Fu'ad boomerangs, and both men are soon released, Murad continues his intrigues to eliminate Fu'ad and take Fatina for himself. Eventually, however, his plots are unsuccessful, and after Fatina and Fu'ad are married, Murad sinks more deeply into vice and finally dies—the wages of sin.[53] Love and individual freedom at last triumph over irrational convention, parental authority, and evil ways!

The highly romantic and, to the Western reader, somewhat simplistic themes of free will versus parental authority and marriage based on love and nobility of character versus wealth and social status are more predominant in *Samiya* than in *Fatina* or *Asma*. That novel also expresses a plea for religious freedom and an end to bigotry. It examines socialism and its implications as al-Bustani understood them. First and foremost, however, it argues in defense of the rights of women and the dignity of the individual.

Samiya's parents, of course, have no understanding of what constitutes the happiness or freedom of their daughter. The clash of old and new values is, of course, the West. Samiya's parents want her to marry Wasif for his wealth, while she refuses on the ground that riches are peripheral and that nothing is more essential than the decent and intelligent qualities in the man she wants to marry.[54] She tells her parents that if they try to force her to marry someone against her will, she would prefer to stay single all her life. They accuse her of being inexperienced, unrealistic, and unaware of the hardships of life. This argument reflects the attitude of nineteenth-century Middle Easterners who, almost without exception, married for security.[55] In fact, such an attitude still prevails in many Middle Eastern societies.

To criticize such practices and champion human dignity and freedom, al-Bustani, as we have seen, endows his young women protagonists with a strong will. Samiya is no exception. She is determined to assert freedom as a conscious and free individual. Such heroines exposed readers to the tyranny of one of the most ugly practices as they related not only to women, but to the dignity and the freedom of all individuals.

In this respect, al-Bustani was following in the footsteps of his father, for the celebrated Butrus al-Bustani was one of the first Middle Easterners to raise his voice in defense of women's liberation and education.[56] However, his son's zealous championing of individual freedom, particularly that of a young woman against patriarchal authority, may have exaggerated the freedom of action and thought possible in his time. But al-Bustani's purpose was not accurate portrayal of the behavior of Syrian or Eastern characters and their societies. He tried to show the impact of European manners, habits of thought, and social doctrines upon middle nineteenth-century Syria and the slowly changing societal patterns that resulted. Some of these changes were too slow in relation to the more edifying and necessary developments he believed necessary. This is made evident in the attitude of parents toward their daughters whose desire for Western freedom led to clashes with their authority, often with melancholy consequences.

There is little detail about time and place in al-Bustani's works. Even the names of the characters, although Arabic, are not typical of any particular country. Whether al-Bustani based his characters on real Syrian models is a matter of conjecture. However, by presenting them in universal terms, he was able to criticize those traditions, practices, and beliefs he considered harmful to individual freedom and social progress without arousing the indignation of either the omnipresent censors or his largely conservative public.

Nowhere does al-Bustani show parents pressuring their sons to marry a particular girl. This may seem unimportant on the surface, but it reflects the unique position of the male in Middle Eastern societies. The social and moral values which applied to women did not necessarily apply to men. Samiya's brother Zahir, for example, is a gambler, conniver, and playboy, but al-Bustani seems to take his faults for granted. By demonstrating that his young men characters had greater freedom than that given to young women he was, in fact, showing, whether he meant to or not, the supremacy of the male in Eastern society. This was especially apparent in social matters such as the right to choose a wife. His major interest was in ameliorating the handicapped freedom of the woman. Nevertheless, some of his Eastern readers may have found *Samiya* an appealing statement of the male ethos.

Samiya also champions religious freedom and denounces bigotry. Through the vivacious character Sida, who appears too mature for her age, al-Bustani affirms religious tolerance and calls for respect of all faiths. Sida expresses al-Bustani's belief that religion should never be a source of hatred and discord among citizens of the same country.[57] That position, in turn, reflects the religious attitude of the family in which he was raised. His father, a Maronite Catholic, was a convert to Protestantism. In spite of his advocacy of tolerance, however, al-Bustani does not accept those who profess unbelief. He believes that religion is necessary for civilization and that man cannot with impunity ignore it.[58] Moreover, he regards faith as a source of consolation and hope, motivating man to constantly improve his life.[59]

The most interesting and unusual aspect of *Samiya* is that in this novel al-Bustani treats al-Ishtirakiyya (socialism) for the first time. When one considers that this young Arab writer attempted to deal with the doctrine of socialism in one of his novels in the 1880's, at a time when socialism was still in its infancy in Europe, and when the majority of the Arab reading public had not heard of this ideology or its implications, his achievement both as a writer and as an intellectual informed about many things that escaped the attention of the Arab world is apparent.

The opening chapter establishes that young Fa'iz is deeply in love with Samiya although she does not return this love. He is a radical socialist determined to use any means to eliminate his rivals, Wasif and Fu'ad, for the love of Samiya.[60] His extremist methods in quest of this end, born of his commitment to revolutionary ideas, include force, extortion, and violence. If al-Bustani does not sympathize with him, it is because he had a deep distaste for such an imprudent and impious revolutionary. Al-Bustani equates socialism with nihilism, for which term he coined the word, *Ibahiyya*, a term which is in use to this day in the Arab world.[61]

In order to promote his aims Fa'iz establishes a clandestine society whose members swear, under oath, to uphold the principles of socialism and obey, even at the cost of their own lives, their leader. Fa'iz's ideology can be epitomized in two words—universal equality. According to his simplistic principles, all people are members of the human family and, therefore, no one of them should possess more than the others. It is not an abstract goal that Fa'iz advocates, however, but concrete equality on the economic, political, social and cultural levels. He and his followers, fifteen in number, meet once a week in his home, and, after some entertainment, he speaks to them about his beliefs. He contrasts their righteousness with the corrupt exploited people:

> Brethren, you are the pillars of equality, the germ of true principles, the pride of the age and the foundation of true success in a country in which the darkness of ignorance prevails. Here tyrants have control and the oppressors have plundered property and money and left the people and their children in misery and want. They have increased their wealth at the expense of the poor and helpless through cruel measures. In the world of equality there is no dominion, privilege, bravery, wealth or noble birth. Dominion is public and skill, knowledge, bravery and wealth are common. No man has the right to claim the possession of parts of them to the exclusion of others. How can we recognize the rich man's ownership and wealth if he acquired them through sheer luck or coincidence? And why should man be privileged because of his birth because he was born amongst people whose ignorance made them incapable of understanding that others were no more noble than themselves? All privileged things are acquired through coincidence, luck or as a gift of nature.[62]

This espousal and promulgation of egalitarianism is very extreme. Fa'iz even professes a belief in complete and uniform psychological and physiological equality. He places equality in wealth, social status, and opportunity on the same plane with equality in mental and natural ability. Fame and fortune are gained through sheer coincidence or circumstances.

In Fa'iz's view, nature alone is the source of all things and to nature they shall return. Therefore, nature alone is worthy of the praise and gratitude of men whose minds have been freed from ignorance and bias and who, in turn, should devote their energies to freeing society from unjust and unegalitarian practices. These practices were perpetuated by men for their self interest and ambition. The result has been that the few came to possess what in fact belongs to the many and in the process they have dominated the many.[63]

Fa'iz, or perhaps al-Bustani himself, seems to embrace a rather anachronistic and thoroughly confused view of the role of nature. No doubt the meaning he attached to it was learned from his reading of Enlightenment literature, but his understanding of the term was more naive and less rational. Nature is the "source of all things;" nature alone is worthy of "praise and worship;" all cleverness is a "gift of nature;" all distinctions are "due to nature." But if all men are equal through nature and by nature, how then is it possible to say in the next breath that it is nature that makes us unequal? Or further, that men are not better through their own merit and abilities but because nature has endowed them with distinct and different qualities and abilities? These are examples of the many instances whereby al-Bustani's interest in the doctrines, ideas, and thoughts of the West outstripped his mental ability to grasp them. The insular cocoon of geography, thought, and centuries had done its work.

Fa'iz and his followers maintain that much of the source of evil in society springs from false teachers and leaders who have corrupted its natural order. They have controlled peoples' minds by their false doctrines, usurped their rights, extorted their wealth and the sources of their livelihood. And since these usurpers will never give up their possessions and privileges of their own will, force is the only means left to overpower them and achieve equality.[64] It is left up to the socialists, the "mighty men," as Fa'iz calls them, to destroy the present world order, including the unresponsive and corrupt government, and to build a foundation for a new order.[65]

Fa'iz maintains that the majority of the people are not satisfied with the present order or with their lot. But because of fear, selfish interest, laziness, or ignorance, they do not join the socialist's ranks to achieve their goals. He sees ignorance as the greatest impediment to progress. The state of ignorance has been perpetuated by those in power through the use of money, force, and religion to control the masses and prevent them from obtaining their rights.

Furthermore, Fa'iz and his socialist group, true to the extremist revolutionary principles that they espouse, are atheists. They do not believe in God, resurrection, eternal punishment, and reward. Their secular eschatology is based on a vague egalitarianism reminiscent of the dictatorship of the proletariat. They reject the teachings of Prophets and consider religion as humbug. Commensurate with their atheism, Fa'iz and his group are materialists, a unique and rather mystical Eastern twist, that they are an inseparable part of all that exists.

Injecting his own ideas into the texture of the narrative, al-Bustani condemns socialism and the methods adopted by Fa'iz to achieve universal equality. He describes Fa'iz and his followers as extremists, nihilists, and anarchists. He even condones killing them or putting them in prison in order to rid society of their evil. In more than one place he strives to refute socialism and its principles as manifested by the extremism of Fa'iz and his group. Men like Fa'iz agitate the common people to do things contrary to order, things which involve grave dangers and which are, most of all, contrary to the moderation called for by conformity to *Ruh al-'Asr*.

Al-Bustani has an inherent, deep-seated distrust of the masses. He believes they are a dangerous force, since they are easily led because of the instinctive greed and an inclination toward hatred and jealousy of those who surpass them in any way. It is education, not revolution, that will bring about true reform. Al-Bustani believes that equality under the law is possible, but absolute equality—which Fa'iz calls for—is not and can never be a practical possibility. While affirming the belief that equality in property and money is not possible, he does believe that the state should guarantee work for the people and grant social benefits—which until recently, have been established in the Middle East—such as compensation for sickness and unemployment. But these measures were to be brought about through legislation, education, and enlightenment, not revolution.[66]

Fa'iz appears as a confused young man with an erratic passion for his convictions. At one time he seems as a staunch socialist, a man of conviction; at another, mean and petty. Moreover, he tries to use socialism as a device to justify the elimination of his rivals in love.[67] Even though he succeeds in having his chief rival, Fu'ad, killed by his followers, he loses Samiya in the end and spends many years in jail.[68] His behavior and his fate demonstrate that it is not only the deprivation of man's property or livelihood but also less material and more enduring elements, such as unrequited love, that can drive man to the extreme of sacrificing his convictions. At one point, Fa'iz even assures Samiya that he has forsworn his socialistic convictions and that she alone is the idol of his worship.[69]

Wasif is no less a compromiser. At the outset he is portrayed as an advocate of socialism, praising equality and believing in the communal ownership of property. But when he becomes rich, his attachment to socialism weakens and his lust for revenge against his rivals for Samiya's love becomes intensified. Believing that socialism means that everything should be shared in common is not the same as believing that he would or could tolerate sharing his love for Samiya with other men.[70]

Although al-Bustani's sources on socialism are not known, it is clear from his editorials in *al-Jinan* that he must have been following its development in Europe. One of them mentions the Second Communist International and emphasizes the point that more moderate reformers—with whom he could more comfortably identify—were trying to ensure social and economic justice through legislation rather than extreme revolutionary measures.[71]

There is no doubt that al-Bustani detested the extreme and violent revolutionary doctrines preached by certain followers of socialist ideology. He was not against socialism *per se* but rather against the wrenching up and destroying—in the name of abstract principles—the concrete traditions, values, and ways of life that, among all the abuses and wrongs, were good. He denounced the peripheral extremes associated with socialism, nihilism, and anarchism. As he believed his own country to be out of touch with the edifying main winds of the Western *Zeitgeist,* so he believed that these offshoots were cancerous growths disrupting and imperiling the momentum of moderation that hitherto characterized the essential strength of *Ruh al-'Asr.* With this in mind, al-Bustani tried to show the spread of the good and bad effects of socialism on the political, social, and economic planes in European countries in the 1880's.[72]

For the first time in all Arab literature, *Samiya* deals, in fictional terms, with mature social and political questions rather than the more superficial romantic themes and *Arabian Nights* triangles. It attempts to portray the virtues and vices of socialism both as a Western doctrine and as a possible palliative to the social and economic ills of Arab society. While al-Bustani himself cannot be styled as a socialist, it is, nevertheless, through his socialist protagonist—a fully realized and interesting character—that he vehemently attacks the unjust, unegalitarian, and unintelligent ways of much of his society.

How was he able to do this, considering the censorship exercised by the Ottoman authorities? While no satisfactory answer is forthcoming we can advance the tentative hypothesis that it was only because he prefaced this work (as well as others) by telling his readers that the characters, places, and incidents were not to be interpreted as taking place at any particular time and place, but were universal. This may have satisfied the Ottoman censor.[73]

Most of al-Bustani's works, but most evidently *Samiya*, offer an important warning to his society. If it does not change its ways so as to better conform to the liberal and moderating winds of the scientific and democratic *Zeitgeist* blowing from the West; if it does not implement an open social system whereby refreshing and revitalizing ideas can be let in and aired, then it is asking for trouble from extremists like Fa'iz. Al-Bustani is basically in agreement with egalitarian principles but is ardently against extremist violence. His approach is moralistic, idealistic, and didactic.

Al-Bustani may be regarded as one of the pioneer writers of fiction to derive his themes from Arab history. Prominent among his stories is *Zenobia* which, as the title suggests, treats the affairs of the queen of Palmyra. The little kingdom of Palmyra was conquered by the Roman Emperor Aurelian in

273 A.D. Zenobia and her daughter Julia were captured and taken to Rome. The story concentrates on the conquest of Egypt, the love affair between Julia and a Roman prince, and Zenobia's ill-fated war with the Romans. The author's purpose was to inculcate moral virtues rather than to reconstruct a faithful picture of the Palmyran society. He admits that he was concerned with reconstructing the past by providing his reader with a few historical facts. He also admits that he refrained from incorporating depressing events of Zenobia's suppression by the Romans in order not to sadden his readers.[74]

In *Zenobia*, al-Bustani interrupts the narrative to criticize indirectly the customs and morals as well as the actions of Ottoman governors and civil servants. He exaggerates the traits of Zenobia whom he presents as a model of beauty, courage, and political sagacity. Zenobia's two sons and her other daughter Livia whom he mentions at the beginning of the story, play hardly any role as the narrative progresses. His characters are pale and flat and never develop as events progress. Generally, they are al-Bustani's mouthpieces, voicing his own principles and values. The only part of the story which stimulates the reader's anxiety over the outcome is the love of the Roman prince Pisa for Julia, even though they belong to two hostile camps.[75]

His second historical story, *Budur*, is set about 750 A.D., during the period when the Umayyads lost their power to the Abbasids. Budur (Full Moons) is the daughter of an Umayyad prince who, among other princes, was killed by the Abbasid Caliph, Abu al-Abbas al-Saffah (d. 754). The story centers on Budur's love for her cousin, an Umayyad prince. Abd al-Rahman ibn Mu'awiyah ibn Hisham ibn Abd al-Malik, who later established an Umayyad dynasty in Spain. Budur hurries to explain to him the Abbasid conspiracy against the Umayyad house and urges him to leave immediately because his life is in danger. Appreciating her advice, Abd al-Rahman and three companions flee to Egypt. In the meantime, Budur, her mother, and the rest of the Umayyad women are arrested by the soldiers of the Abbasid caliph. News of Budur's beauty and intelligence reaches the caliph who becomes anxious to meet her. When he meets her in a palace which he has made ready for her and her mother in al-Sham (Damascus), he becomes infatuated by her beauty and asks her to marry him. She does not give him a definite answer but leaves him uncertain. He even urges Budur's mother to convince her daughter to accept him as her husband but meets with no success. Annoyed by the caliph's insistence, Budur manages to escape with the assistance of the maid and eunuch. When the news of Budur's escape reaches the caliph, he becomes infuriated and orders Budur's mother thrown in jail. Budur hides in a village, disguised as the prince Sadiq. She captures the hearts of the good villagers by her wonderful manners and the gifts she lavishes upon them. Her true identity is soon discovered, however, and she is arrested and returned to jail.

In the meantime, Abd al-Rahman seeks refuge with some bedouin tribes and meets Sa'd, Budur's messenger, who hands him a letter from his beloved.

To escape arrest by his Abbasid pursuers, Abd al-Rahman travels to Egypt where he spends two years in wandering. Then he goes to North Africa and becomes the guest of a tribal chief, Wanus, nicknamed Abu Qurra. But the soldiers of Ibn Habib, the governor of Barqa, chase him, and finally he finds a refuge with his cousins in Zanata in North Africa. The Zanatis receive him with alacrity, and after a short time he becomes a chief among them. When internal strife arises among the Arab tribes who settled in Spain in the time of the Arab governor Yusuf ibn Abd al-Rahman al-Fihri, an influential Arab Wuhayb ibn Dahir, suggests to prominent Arabs that they establish a government in Spain and invite Abd al-Rahman to become their ruler. The suggestion is accepted and Abd al-Rahman arrives in Spain, defeats al-Fihri, and establishes an Umayyad state in Spain.

In the meantime, Budur is able to escape from prison, and on learning that Abd al-Rahman is in North Africa, she decides to find him. She rents a ship, but she and her companions are attacked by pirates who capture the ship. The pirates' leader sends Budur and her mother to his city beyond the Pyrenees and uses Budur's attendants to work on his farms. The pirates' leader falls in love with Budur and hires a tutor to teach her Spanish and the tenets of Christianity. Budur coaxes the pirates' leader to believe that she is in love with him, but in reality she is trying to find the right moment to escape. Finally, she manages to escape through the efforts of her Spanish tutor who in turn, falls madly in love with her. Budur escapes with her mother, her tutor, and her attendants, but barely misses falling into the hands of the pirates' leader, who has sent a company of men to chase her. Of all the people who were with Budur, only her mother, her eunuch, and Sa's and herself are safe. Budur arrives in North Africa and learns at Zanata that Abd al-Rahman is in Spain about to be crowned king. After suffering many incredible vicissitudes and falling once again in the hands of pirates, Budur and those with her reach Spain, and she is crowned as queen at the same time.[76]

The story abounds with adventures, battles, and shipwrecks, interspersed with moral preachment and exhortations which indicate the author's didactic purpose. The author digresses to advocate the education of women, to praise the benefit of learning, and to inveigh, though cautiously, against the Ottoman rulers and their corrupt administration. In some places he refers to the present to discuss affairs in his own time. Although he is careful in presenting the historical facts connected with the story, he makes the obvious mistake of calling Abd al-Rahman and Budur "king" and "queen," while in reality, Abd al-Rahman was an emir (prince) and never even assumed the title of caliph.

Al-Bustani's *al-Hiyam fi Futuh al-Sham* (Love During the Conquest of Syria) derives its theme, as the title suggests, from the Arab conquest of Syria in 632-6 A.D. The story centers on two romances, the one taking place at the Byzantine camp, the other in the Arab camp. Julian, a Byzantine commander, is in love with Augusta, daughter of a Byzantine official. But when they are engaged and ready to marry, Julian is called to fight against the Arabs. Augusta accompanies her fiancé to the battlefront and tries to spy on the Muslims' camp, pretending to be mute. She is arrested by the Muslims but manages to escape with Julian's help. Then she loses track of Julian and returns to Damascus, broken-hearted and despairing to finding him. Apparently, Julian has been wounded and is under treatment. Augusta goes to Antioch to enter a convent after she has given up hope of seeing Julian again. Julian finds out that she is in Antioch, repairs to that city, and convinces her to marry him. The two lovers then go to Constantinople and are united in marriage.

Meanwhile, in the Arab camp, another love affair is going on. Salim, the son of a Yemenite prince and Arab hero, is in love with Salma, daughter of another Yemenite prince. Salma joins her prince in the battlefield and is captured and sent to Aleppo to be thrown in jail. When the Arabs finally conquer Syria, Salma is released and marries her prince.[77] Nothing is new in this story, which like others by the same author abounds with similar and often repeated themes. Commenting on this story, Muhammad Yusuf Najm states that al-Bustani indirectly and shrewdly underplayed the Arab conquest of Syria. Najm complains that al-Bustani attributes the victory of the Arabs to the weakness and division of the Byzantines, not to the religious valour and fervor of the believers of Islam. Thus, he portrays the love, sincerity, and will to sacrifice of Salim and Salma in a manner which makes us admire them less than we do Julian and Augusta.[78] Historical evidence, however, seems to be partly on the side of al-Bustani. The Byzantine persecution of the Syrian co-religionists, who believe in the "one incarnate nature of the God-Logos," and who are erroneously called "monophysites," was a decisive factor in opening the gates of Syria to the invading Arabs and their final victory. The Syrian Christians also believe that the Arab conquest of Syria was a divine punishment inflicted upon the Byzantines by God for persecuting the Syrians.[79]

The last historical story by the author is *Hadhir wa Layla*, whose theme is taken from the notorious war between the two tribes of Bakr and Taghlib known as Harb al-Basus. The story centers on the love between Hadhir, a Taghlibite, and Layla, daughter of a notable Bakrite named Ramih. During the war Layla saves the wounded Hadhir from a Bakrite woman who is about to kill him, then cleans and dresses his wounds. Although he is an enemy, she loves him at the first sight. Naturally, she is afraid of her father, who, according to Arab custom, will prevent her marriage if he knows that she is in love with Hadhir. In spite of the enmity between the two tribes, Layla finally obtains her father's approval to marry Hadhir, and love triumphs.[80]

Al-Bustani believed that the function of fiction is to reform and regenerate society by portraying the operative efficacy of correct principles in terms of characters and situations.[81] As a corollary, bad qualities are to be exposed through the actions of bad characters. In his novel *al-Hiyam fi Jinan al-Sham* he states:

It is imperative that we should expose our faults as well as those of others through the writing of novels and reveal the good and bad through the portrayal of the characters whose actions we are presently narrating.[82]

He further defends "moralistic" novels as a means to implant proper principles in the readers and show them, in a perceptive way, the rewards of right thinking. He believes that the critical novels which he calls "al-Riwayat al Tankitiyya," that is, works which expose bad qualities through fictitious characters, are "the most effective means to reform."[83]

Because he is a moralist, his characters always receive their punishment or reward according to their deeds. No one of them escapes justice, whether human or divine. Behind this there is a moral lesson pointing to a fault of the character of society or of the family which inevitably brings about misfortune and misery for one or the other.

For all this, al-Bustani's novels as well as some of his short stories, are saturated with a great deal of sentimentalism and sensibility. The characters, both male and female often fall apart under their misfortune and break into tears. They faint, grieve, and constantly complain. They are extremely serious and seldom laugh or express joyfulness. To them, love or falling in love is a matter which requires thorough study and time, an attitude prevalent in Middle Eastern societies to this day. They are mere devices used by the author to further his own ideas in relation to decency and virtue or his criticism and condemnation of immorality and vice.

Al-Bustani's style is episodic and lacks warmth. But it is free from the time-honored "saj'" (rhyme prose).[84] The narrative tone is similar to that of the *Arabian Nights;* indeed, the author used many phrases and situations akin to those found in the *Nights*. Although he strove to create a modern genre, he was unable to break from the rather sterile tradition of Arabic fiction. Furthermore, his style tends to be journalistic, naive, and technically unsophisticated. Al-Bustani never uses dialogue in his fiction, despite the fact that he had written several plays. His characters, like those of the *Nights*, are presented at the outset as fully developed personalities whose attitudes and traits are rigidly set and forever formulated. They are exemplars of either virtue, endurance, beauty, and nobility, or wickedness and villainy. While the historical novels and stories are packed with facts, the reader cannot re-experience the social and human feelings, aspirations, and motives which inspired men to live, feel, think, and act as they did in the past. The characters remain mere stock figures, superimposed upon historical narrative.

Al-Bustani's novels abound with improbabilities and implausible situations. In many of them the central theme and moral exhortations are freely interspersed. The author frequently digresses to unrelated subjects, halting the action while he dwells on long discussions of social topics. This projection of the writer into the texture of the narrative may be artistically indefensible, but it was the only method al-Bustani could practically use to convey his opinions to his readers. Furthermore, the monotonous narrative and the repetition of identical events and situations renders the reading of al-Bustani's novels tedious and sometimes boring.

Nevertheless, al-Bustani's contribution to modern Arabic fiction cannot be ignored. He was the first Arab writer who attempted to write a novel in the modern sense and to incorporate in his art a semblance of originality. He is a unique figure who stands in the middle of the road between the traditional Arab tale and the modern novel. Furthermore, al-Bustani is the first Arab writer to show more than a passing interest in, and knowledge of, things happening in the world beyond the Mediterranean, most especially in Europe. He incorporated for the first time not only Western themes and a Western style but real events and real people that were really happening in a real world beyond his own country—a country which, at this time was trying to come to grips, albeit, rather slowly and perhaps reluctantly, with the real world. Thus, while his main themes and didactic endeavors are germane to the Arab world, he does not hesitate to use a European setting to speak of European ideology—socialism—or to convey to his readers that the West can and must be learned from. It is the West which avoids encasing in a sanctimonious aura many traditions, customs, and practices which their more rational and scientific approach would never tolerate.

Most of all, al-Bustani was the first Arab in the nineteenth century to have a real understanding of the instructional possibilities of the novel. A strong point in his favor is that he did not feel compelled to strive for an illusion of complete authenticity, contrary to the demands of his contemporaries. In fact, he emphasized the fictitiousness of some of his novels to demonstrate that he was using fiction as a vehicle for a worthy purpose. Despite the many artistic and technical handicaps which prevented him from creating the first "pure and artistic novel," al-Bustani can be rightfully considered the father of the modern Arabic prose fiction.

CHAPTER VII

FROM AL-BUSTANI TO JURJI ZAYDAN:

FRANCIS MARRASH AND NU'MAN AL-QASATLI

Between 1870, which marks the birth of modern Arabic prose fiction through the writings of Salim al-Bustani, and 1891, when another celebrated Syrian writer Jurji Zaydan (d. 1914), published his historical novel *al-Mumluk al-Sharid*, no other Arab writer appeared who could measure up to the status of these two. If al-Bustani was first to lay the foundation of the Arab novel in 1870, as well as the Arab historical novel in 1871, in his novel *Zenobia*, it was Zaydan who later popularized Arab history in fictional form.

The scope of Zaydan's historical novels is broader than that of al-Bustani's. While the three historical novels of al-Bustani, *Zenobia, Budur, al-Hiyam fi Futuh al-Sham,* and the historical short story *Hadhir wa Layla,* treat only certain events in Arab history, the twenty-two historical novels of Zaydan cover much of the spectrum of Arab and Islamic history from the sixth century to the first decade of the present century.

Between these two pioneers of Arabic fiction stand several other writers who were not as gifted, prolific, or versatile. One of them, Francis Marrash of Aleppo died prematurely in 1873, at the age of 37. His literary background is somewhat similar to that of al-Bustani. He was born in Aleppo in 1836 to a family whose literary achievements were no less prominent than that of the Yazijis or the Bustanis.[1] His brother, Abd Allah (d. 1899), and his sister Maryana (d. 1919), were both prominent in the writing of prose and poetry.[2]

Marrash, at first, studied the Arabic language and its literature privately. He also received private tutoring in medicine for four years under an English physician and practiced medicine for a year.[3] Then, in 1866, he went to Paris to continue his formal education. Weak health and failing sight forced him to suspend his studies, however, and in less than a year he returned to his native Aleppo totally blind. But this loss was compensated for by a keen mind and gifted pen—both of which were amply demonstrated by his multiple writings, covering diverse literary and scientific subjects. He also wrote poetry as well as an account of his journey to Paris. Furthermore, he contributed many articles on various subjects to popular periodicals, including, most importantly, al-Bustani's *al-Jinan.*

The first significant work of fiction that Marrash wrote was *Ghabat al-Haqq* (The Forest of Truth), which he began in 1862 and published three years later in Aleppo.[4] Chronologically, *Ghabat al-Haqq* precedes the writings of al-

Bustani and, properly speaking, it is not a novel but an allegory. But it does contain certain novelistic elements, and, of course, it is fiction. The other work by Marrash, *Durr al-Sadaf fi Ghara'ib al-Sudaf* (literally Pearl Shells in Relating Strange Coincidences), published in Beirut in 1872, is a social romance bearing a great similarity to al-Bustani's work in this genre.

Ghabat al-Haqq reflects Marrash's belief in the liberating principles of equality and freedom. It portrays the conflict between man's freedom and the many restrictions placed upon it by an arbitrary social system. This conflict, as the author sees it, does not involve abstract principles but is concrete, affecting man's daily existence as well as the institutions of his society. The basic concept echoes the idea of the Caliph 'Umar ibn al-Khattab (d. 644) and of Rousseau, that man was born free but everywhere is in chains. From the cradle to the grave, man is subject to an infinite variety of repressions. This state of bondage is, however, of man's own making and constitutes, in the mind of Marrash, an insult to God, who intended man to be free.

Ghabat al-Haqq presents the utopian world of the author. There are three kingdoms: the kingdom of freedom, the kingdom of bondage, and the kingdom of spiritual freedom. The first, an ideal state as the author sees it, is the "true" kingdom of civilization, where man has attained the highest human goal—happiness. The king and queen of this kingdom symbolize freedom and wisdom, its army is called the army of civilization, and its chief minister is the minister of love and peace.[5]

This ideal state is in constant war with the kingdom or state of bondage, which is based on despotism and denies individual freedom. Such warfare is inevitable because the two states stand for antithetical and irreconcilable concepts: freedom of the individual and force. In the final showdown between these two states, the king and army of bondage are defeated, and he and seven of his commanders are taken captives to the state of Freedom to be tried. The description of the commanders of the army of the kingdom of bondage reveal their true natures. They exemplify ignorance, arrogance, envy, miserliness, malevolence, calumny, falsehood, and treachery. In contrast, the commanders of the army of the kindgom of freedom stand for knowledge, humbleness, contentedness, generosity, truthfulness, and tolerance.[6] The leaders of the state of bondage are tried and found guilty of causing all the trouble in the world, most of all disturbing the peace of civil society. It is resolved that they should be placed under the charge of the State of Civilization to be taught and trained in the noble ideals of life. If they refuse to learn, banishment would be their fate. Civilization and barbarism cannot live side by side.

Of course, this solution to the ills of the state of barbarism is idealistic and impractical, but it reflects Marrash's social philosophy. His primary belief was that men can achieve the highest degree of civilization through education. With knowledge man becomes better, more civilized, and is able to gain freedom, which is found only within the limits of the laws, responsibilities and restraints of civilization. Marrash was amazingly restrained in his ideas about the operative conditions of freedom. The liberty he speaks of is not the kind to be found in the utopian visions of many thinkers of the modern world; it implies responsibility, restraint, not as mere abstractions but as realities that find their true meaning within the social structure of organization, duties, and laws.

Marrash seems to have recognized the great danger is advocating the immediate and unqualified re-ification of an abstract and often liberal terminology. The freedom of the individual is important to Marrash, and society as a civilized entity cannot exist without the fecundation of this freedom, but freedom as an abstract ideal can, if abused, become enslavement or shibboleth. Freedom is an historical concept, and it is attendant upon and operative only in those societies which have matured historically through the development of law, the organization of responsive institutions, and the acquisition of a mass consciousness of civilized responsibility and restraint. In the ambience of true civilization, freedom is a moral imperative and cannot be denied.[7]

Marrash also develops a philosophy of history which is rather interesting for a time when speculative excursions into the genesis and development of society were entirely absent. His ethos was not only for the most part ahistorical, but it was a world entirely content to believe in the present without any relation to the past except that past idealized in literature. Marrash maintains that the family is the origin of society. It develops into a tribe, which multiplies into a society when a strong chief assumes power by force. The society, builds a city, where the strongest chief becomes a ruler. In the meantime, other families and tribes go through the same process. The city states become engaged in wars and one of them expands its realm at the expense of others. In this manner, empires are created.[8] It is with the aid of laws and organization that civilizations are primordially created.

Marrash does not engage in an overtly idealistic approach to history. He has a sane grasp of the realities of war and dominance and the part these two factors have played in the evolution of society and civilization. While he does not condone the dolorous spectacle of the bloodletting and cruelty of the past, he does recognize it as a primordial factor—even if one to be lamented—in the almost necessary growth of society and civilization.

This philosophy of history contains the kernel, perhaps even the inspiration of Marrash's literary productivity. Most of his works are mildly polemical statements about the need to advance knowledge, whether in the scientific, legal or social-economic realm. The more civilized a society, the more advanced, humane, and intelligent its treatment of its problem. Historically, society advances from underdeveloped to more developed state. And one may assume that this progress would be enhanced through the enlarged and accelerated inculcation of ideas and educated consciousness into a more or less moribund society, a society that would be, of course, Marrash's own.

The third kingdom in *Ghabat al-Haqq* (The Forest of Truth) is the spiritual kingdom, or the Church. Marrash believes that the existence of the secular realm is imperative. But so is that of the spiritual state. He denounces the allegations that the church has been propagating untruths in order to deceive and control gullible people. He maintains that the church has always taught those principles which bring fulfillment and happiness. The church is the guardian of morality and brings its followers together in universal fellowship. The existence of the church is, therefore, necessary for the existence of the state; they complement each other.[9] Marrash believes that the destruction of the church means the end of the state of civilization. Furthermore, his strong Christian belief manifests itself in his positive attitude that the destruction of the church is impossible because the Lord has promised that "the gates of hell cannot prevail against her."[10]

The basis of *Ghabat al-Haqq* springs from Marrash's deep conviction in God as source and author of freedom. His *Shahadat al-Tabi'a fi Wujud Allah wa Al-Shari'a* (Nature's proof of the Existence of God and the Divine Law), is a strong testimony to this conviction.[11] But such allegories which portray the paradox of human existence, the conflict between good and evil, while insisting upon the freedom of man were not completely unknown in ancient Arabic writings.[12]

Ghabat al-Haqq has no hero, no visible character, not even a portrayal of particular surroundings and personages. The characters are materializations of virtues and vices. But they demonstrate the author's dream of a better and more progressive society—a society where people live in collective harmony and individual dignity without discrimination or prejudice. Such enlightenment would exemplify the triumph of man's most noble proclivities and accomplishments.

Marrash realized, however, that his utopian world was completely inapposite to the political, social, and cultural conditions in his own country. There were no freedoms of any kind under the Ottomans, no viable political institutions, and no cultural progress. He saw nothing but desolation beyond the beautiful dreamlike society in the *Ghabat al-Haqq*.

In desperation he asked himself how the wilderness of man could bloom once again after an infertility of a thousand years. The answer is disappointing; His Majesty, the Sultan Abd al-Aziz has turned his attention toward Syria and, there is "no doubt that reform and prosperity will soon come to her."[13] It may seem surprising that Marrash, who glorifies freedom and attacks every form of human bondage, should praise the very symbol of despotism, the Ottoman Sultan, and expect prosperity for his country through his effort. He may have feared the chastisement of the Ottoman censor and Ottoman authorities and tried to escape both by undue praise of the Sultan. What seems more plausible, however, is that Marrash was an idealist removed from the reality of an external world by blindness and ill health. And in his idealism and zeal he perhaps believed in the distinctions he had already made between the pathway to real truth and the entangling disappointment of false prophets and premature hopes.

Marrash's style is lucid, at times even elegant, and certainly less florid than the embellished prose of most of his contemporaries. Most important, he knew how to use effective dialogue, and in this sense, he surpasses Salim al-Bustani who hardly used it. The dialogue between two slave brothers, Yaqut and Murjan who met by chance on the Galata bridge in Istanbul is an example:

> "Greetings, friend."
> "Greetings to you."
> After looking at him carefully I felt something like an electric shock running through my body.
> I asked him.
> "What is your name?"
> "Murjan." I felt more compassion for him.
> "How did you leave the country?"
> "Kidnapped."
> "Were you kidnapped alone or with others?"
> "A band of Egyptians kidnapped my brother with me after they killed our mother who tried to protect us."
> I had no doubt that this slave was my brother. My eyes were filled with tears of joy and my heart throbbed with compassion but I attempted to control my emotions in order to obtain more information from him and further inquired:
> "What is your brother's name?"
> "Yaqut and he is older than me."
> I held his hand and told him "follow me in order to see your brother."
> I took him to my residence and told him, "I am your brother Yaqut."
> We embraced and wept. I told him my story and asked him to tell me his.[14]

The work of fiction by Marrash, *Durr al-Sadaf fi Ghara'ib al-Sudaf* (Pearl Shells in Relating Strange Coincidences), published in Beirut in 1872,[15] is inferior to *Ghabat al-Haqq* in the expression of ideas and itensity of ideals and human compassion. Nor does it treat a complex human issue. As this title suggests, it narrates a series of events brought about by strange coincidences, one of the oldest of all literary devices. The narrator, depressed by the saddening news of the defeat of France—whose culture he knew and admired—by the Germans, seeks solace in a deserted place outside the city. Here he meets an old friend who tells him not only his personal love story, but also another story told him by a friend. In substance, then, *Durr al-Sadaf* contains two unrelated stories told by a friend to the narrator who in turn transmits them as told to him. There is nothing about the characters or the theme to excite the imagination. In every aspect it is inferior to the work of Salim al-Bustani, and

one is tempted to conclude that Marrash, who was a contributor to *al-Jinan*
had, in essence, followed closely in this romance—in the footsteps of al-
Bustani.

Durr al-Sadaf is effusively moralistic, exhorting the reader to learn the
noble traits of perseverance, fortitude, and pursuit of knowledge and not to
judge people by their appearance. The author reiterates many of his ideas concerning human compassion, respect, and love of mankind.

Measured by the standards of learning in his time, Marrash was a highly
educated man. He saw the evils of his society and attacked them where they
were worst. And a romance was perhaps the most effective and least abrasive
of all devices to communicate his ideas to his countrymen without provoking
the wrath of backward civil authorities. Yet his technique conforms with the
familiar techniques of Arabic fiction, which, still in its infancy, leaned heavily
on models of antiquity. It fell short of the much more advanced handling of
characters, plot, and locale in Western literature.

Marrash's characters are drawn from the middle class, but they are
singularly devoid of color and life. Diligent, industrious, and sober, they show
no signs of being as vicious and intriguing as some of al-Bustani's characters.
However, Marrash does cast a shadow of suspicion on the behavior of
Su'da—one of the main characters in *Durr al-Sadaf*—toward her private
tutor. This by no means denigrates a decent young woman; the novelty in her
behavior is her ability to love two persons simultaneously. Otherwise, there is
nothing exciting about her. Like the rest of the characters, she serves as a
mouthpiece voicing the author's criticism of different social behaviors of his
time. This theme was used again almost seven decades later in *Ibrahim al-
Katib* (1931) by Ibrahim Abd al-Qadir al-Mazini, although in reverse manner.

Like most of al-Bustani's romances, the outcome of *Durr al-Sadaf* is the
sudden and unexpected meeting of the lovers and their ultimate happy union in
marriage. Yet other factors in part compensate for the shortcomings of this
romance. Marrash's protest against stagnant traditions and practices may appear commonplace today but were, in his own time, most daring. As with al-
Bustani, it required tremendous courage to voice criticism of customs and
authority at a time when it could cause loss of career, individual freedom, and,
sometimes, one's own life.

Marrash's ironic title *Ghabat al-Haqq* reflects his philosophy of history.
He understands that the pathway to truth, which is the prerogative of a
historically mature society, is covered over with the brambles and tangles of in-
experience, superstition, dominance, warfare, cruelty—in short, all those
handicaps to a truly civil society.

Once man has pushed through the shadows and tangled undergrowth of
the forest of human passion and ignorance, truth can be found by those who
truly seek it and the nature of freedom can be understood. Freedom is difficult
to acquire and it becomes increasingly fructified in a society through history as

that society brings to bear productive laws on enlarged civil consciousness and enlightened institutions. These imply a society capable of restraint, responsibility, and responsiveness.

Less well known than either al-Bustani or Francis Marrash is Nu'man Abduh al-Qasatli of Damascus. Between 1880 and 1882 he contributed a number of romances to al-Bustani's periodical *al-Jinan,* but then he seems to have sunk into complete oblivion until his death in 1920. The circumstances that caused this silence remain unknown. His small fictional output reveals a remarkable writing talent at any early age, despite al-Qasatli's apology that he was not qualified to write fiction.[16]

Born in Damascus in 1854, al-Qasatli was six years old when Syria was inflicted with the notorious Druzes' massacre of the Christians in 1860. He relates that he was saved from death by hiding in an old oven. Soon after 1860 his family left for Damascus to seek freedom and fortune in a more peaceful place.[17] Dividing his time between Beirut and Damascus, where he came into contact with educated circles, al-Qasatli showed his talent early. He was hardly twenty-two years old when he wrote the history of Damascus as well as another book entitled *Mir'at Suriyya wa Filastin* (The Mirror of Syria and Palestine), of which there are no copies extant. Later he visited Sinai and Egypt and was greatly attracted to the "natural" life of the bedouins. This left a visible stamp on his writing of fiction.[18]

Al-Qasatli was twenty-six when he submitted his first romance, *al-Fatat al-Amina wa Ummuha* (The Faithful Young Woman and Her Mother), to be serialized in *al-Jinan* in 1880.[19] Amina, the heroine, is the embodiment of faithfulness in its purest form. She is determined to preserve her love for the hero, Thabit, against the rest of her family. But she is the victim of an impudent, selfish, and cruel mother who does not hesitate to insult her daughter in public or private. Amina falls ill but recovers when Thabit pays her a visit and determines to marry her, even though he has no sufficient material means to support her. To prevent this, Amina's family has her thrown into a dark prison, chained, and subjected to harsh physical punishment and humiliation. When her sister Da'c protests against her mother's ruthlessness, she meets the same fate as Amina. Finally Thabit's friend, Khalil, intercedes with the mother, who relents and admits the great wrong she has done her daughters. Moved by a sense of remorse and awakened parental compassion, she releases her daughters and admits that she has been the victim of imprudent social customs.

In essence, this romance is a protest against the cruel social tradition which denied young women freedom to marry for love. The basic theme is the female right of choice versus a social and familial authority which was considered inviolable in nineteenth century Middle Eastern society, and is still dominant in many areas.

Amina's virtue lies in her fidelity to the man she loves. She is totally his and marrying someone else would be a violation of a sacred trust. But Amina is an example for every man and woman fighting against harmful practices and obsolete traditions. In her prison she declares to her sister that, "My death would be a great lesson to the country's young men and women."[20] What gives Amina more importance than her counterparts in al-Bustani's stories, is her awareness of her role as an opponent of deleterious social customs and the embodiment of a moral lesson. Thabit is equally aware of his role as a champion and symbol of freedom and social progress against the archaic prohibitions precluding two lovers from uniting in happiness. By remaining loyal to Amina to the end, he is attempting to break down the walls of social prescription. He, too, believes that his death will serve as a message of love and inspiration for future generations.[21]

Riwayat Anis is another social romance but on a wider canvas.[22] Its two distinct plots are superficially joined together by the fact that their principal characters are relatives. More important, the principal characters in both fall in love, suffer deeply, and, through that suffering, find final redemption and reward.

Anis is an orphan whose father died when he was five years old, leaving him in the care of his mother, Fadila, and a testator, Wakid. He receives an education and becomes a successful businessman. When Anis falls in love with a young woman Anisa, Nur, the daughter of the merchant with whom Anis worked at the beginning of his career, who is in love with him, tries to separate them. She causes great suffering by her many intrigues, but finally Anis marries Anisa. In the meantime, Fahima, Anis's cousin, falls in love with a young man, Adib, but the wicked Shakir, the antagonist, tries to separate the lovers in order to marry Fahima himself. His intrigues against Adib also cause great tribulation, but finally Adib and Fahima crown their long suffering by marriage.

Fahima, a vivacious and educated young woman, refuses to marry Shakir because of his vices. In order to force their daughter to marry the husband they chose for her, Fahima's parents beat and whip her and tell her that her death is better than their dishonor stemming from her disobedience.[23] Of course, like al-Bustani, al-Qasatli defends the freedom of young women to marry husbands of their choice; indeed, he tenaciously defends the individual's freedom as sacred.[24]

But, even though he defends man's freedom, al-Qasatli seems convinced that man is imperfect and has a tendency toward evil. He maintains that evil exists co-eternally with the world. In fact, one of his characters, Adib, explains to his beloved that the true source of their misery and misfortune is man's inherent wickedness.[25] Nevertheless, like al-Bustani, he criticizes those traditions and practices which he considers impediments to the progress of the East. He lauds the West for its ability to reject harmful customs while adopting mores which are beneficial to mass society.[26]

Al-Qasatli's characters are not much different from those of al-Bustani. They are typically middle class, well-educated, and conscious of the importance of their education and social status. They are fully developed personalities from the beginning and exemplify either vice or virtue. Thus La'im and Talib are villains who connive to prevent Anis from marrying Anisa. On the other hand, Adib and Anis are virtuous, chivalrous, and decent characters. But unlike al-Bustani's bourgeois characters who are aloof from their surroundings and oblivious to the people around them, some of al-Qasatli's characters have a consciousness of responsibility to the lower classes. One of these is Fadila, Anis's mother, a woman of some education, who thought that she should try to educate the "uncouth and ill behaved" children of the village where she was spending the summer.[27]

Al-Qasatli also advocates political freedom, condemns the tyranny of arbitrary government, and calls for the establishment of democratic parliamentarian governments.[28] Considering the despotic rule of the Ottoman Sultan Abd al-Hamid II, this was a daring and audacious advocacy which could have cost al-Qasatli his career, if not his life. But, as in the case of al-Bustani, it got by the inefficiency and ignorance of the Ottoman censor, who perhaps did not bother to read fiction.[29]

All in all, Marrash and al-Qasatli, while both gifted individuals, did not really contribute significantly to the rise of Arabic fiction. For the most part they dealt with the themes, utilized the characterization, and promoted reforms in much the same way as al-Bustani. After al-Bustani's death until the appearance of Jurji Zaydan's first work of fiction in 1891, there was in fact, a hiatus of fictional creativity. Al-Bustani stands as the solitary beacon in the rather sterile landscape of literature at this time. Marrash and al-Qasatli are secondary candles whose light of creativity is lost in the more glowing accomplishments of al-Bustani. We are speaking in relative terms, of course, since measured against the sophisticated literary criteria in the West, al-Bustani would not be considered a great writer of fiction.

He was, however, representative of a time during which certain of the Arab intelligentsia were attempting to promote a unique Arab consciousness. And they did this in the best way they could, given the limitations of their numbers and the limited scope of their freedom. It is a testimony to the restrictions of this movement that only Marrash and al-Qasatli tried to emulate al-Bustani and only they achieved anywhere near the importance of al-Bustani. And al-Bustani's achievement itself, in the content of the Western world, was very modest.

It was with the appearance of the eminent writer Jurji Zaydan (d. 1914) that the Arab novel, and in particular the historical novel, was brought to fruition.

CHAPTER VIII
JURJI ZAYDAN

The appearance of what can be considered the first Arab novel by Salim al-Bustani, however clumsy, was still an admirable literary achievement and a necessary if modest beginning for its further development. Inspired by and deriving his theme and characters from the *Arabian Nights*, al-Bustani may have indirectly alerted future Arab writers to the significance of utilizing fiction as a vehicle for popularizing history. When Jurji Zaydan embarked upon his prolific novel-writing career less than a decade after the death of al-Bustani, his primary objective was the popularizing of the Arab historical novel.

Unlike al-Bustani, Zaydan was born in Beirut in 1861 to a poor Christian family with no special literary interests. His father ran a small restaurant in Beirut and, being illiterate, he relied completely on young Zaydan to keep his accounts. He also cooked for the customers.[1] But Zaydan's ambition and inclination lay beyond the routine and unrewarding life of the restaurant and its customers. After completing his elementary schooling, Zaydan enrolled in the Syrian Protestant College (the present American University of Beirut) in 1881 to study medicine.[2] When the dismissal of a faculty member, Dr. Louis, caused a rift between teachers and students because of his lecturing on Darwin and Darwinism, Zaydan decided to go to Egypt to continue his studies.[3] Instead of studying medicine, however, Zaydan turned to journalism and soon became the editor of *al-Zaman,* a small newspaper. In 1884, as war correspondent and interpreter he joined the British expedition to the Sudan to rescue General Gordon. Afterwards he was decorated for his participation and the courage he demonstrated during the campaign. Because of his journalistic experience and his first hand participation with Gordon in the making of history, his interest in history was heightened and he now determined to research, write about, and popularize the long neglected part of the Islamic world. Therefore, in 1886, with the intention of researching material for his contemplated works on Arab history, he visited London and spent most of his time at the British Museum's Library. There he consulted ancient Arabic manuscripts which resulted in the writing of his monumental historical works: *Tarikh al-Tamaddun al-Islami* (History of Islamic Civilization). After that (from 1891 until his death in 1914), Zaydan devoted his time writing on a vast range of literary topics and cultural subjects, including 23 novels—all of which except one, entitled, *Jihad al-Muhibbin* (Lovers' Struggle), treats of subjects drawn from Arab or Islamic history.[4] This output was encyclopedic and he stands as the most productive and versatile Arab writer of modern times. His periodical, *al-Hilal,* which he founded in Egypt in 1892 became an unofficial school and important source of inspiration for young writers, poets, historians and *littérateurs* of every stripe and age.[5]

Perhaps Zaydan had no intention at the beginning, of re-evoking and disseminating so much Arab and Islamic history through the medium of fiction, but when his first historical novel *al-Mamluk al-Sharid* (The Escaping Mamluk), appeared in 1891 and was well received, some of his friends suggested that he write a series of novels about the whole history of Islam.[6] Accordingly, in 1892-1893 he produced two more novels *Asir al-Mutamahdi* (The Captive of the Mahdi Pretender), treating of the Mahdi's rebellion in the Sudan and *Istibdad al-Mamalik* (Despotism of the Mamluks), dealing with the despotic rule of the Mamluks in Egypt in the first half of the nineteenth century. Beginning in 1895 he began a series of historical novels about Islamic history in general. They began with *Armanusa al-Misriyya* (Egyptian Armanusa), which dealt with the Arab conquest of Egypt in 640 and ended in 1913-1914 with the novel *Shajarat al-Durr* which portrays the events leading to the ascent to the throne in the thirteenth century of Shajarat al-Durr, wife of the Ayyubid Sultan, al-Malik al-Salih. Zaydan's historical novels did not attempt to deal with the history of Islam in chronological order, nor did they attempt to deal with the whole of Islamic past.[7]

Zaydan's purpose was to popularize Islamic history through the medium of fiction "as a means of arousing the desire of the public to read history and read it abundantly,"[8] and, of course, he meant Arabic history. To achieve this purpose Zaydan saw fiction as subservient to history, and not vice-versa, a mistake he accused Western writers of.[9] These writers, he claimed subjected history to the fictional narrative so that the reader was misled into believing that the fictional events were real. It seems entirely palpable that he misinterpreted the aims of Western writers whose objective was not so much to portray real history but to use historical background, including real people, to more fully realize the aims of their craft, the most important of which was to entertain.

His main concern on the other hand, was to relate history as it really was within the context of the novel form. He asserted that the historical facts he related in his novels could be relied upon as authentic sources of history as in a history book.[10] Zaydan does not identify those Western writers whom he believed to have "subordinated" history to fiction, he may have meant among others, Sir Walter Scott and Alexandre Dumas, *père*.[11] While Scott and Dumas used historical events only as a frame for the novel and took liberty in relating these events to achieve their novelistic ends, Zaydan, on the contrary, emphasized true historical events because his main objective was to teach history to the public.[12]

The method he pursued in the writing of almost all his novels was similar. Because he serialized his novels in his periodical *al-Hilal*, Zaydan usually used the summer months (when the periodical was not published) to write a novel and prepare it for the fall. He began by first choosing the historical topic of the novel and reading all the relative sources until a skeleton outline based on historical fact was developed. He then concocted a romance, usually a love story, chose fictitious characters, and began writing. He followed this method with all his novels except *Armanusa al-Misriyya,* which he first completed in 1895.

Because his basic task was to faithfully portray the past, Zaydan, very concerned with historical fact, even went as far as documenting his sources. He also began each novel with a chapter explaining the historical events relative to the work. In many cases his characters relate historical events extracted from Islamic sources and referred to in footnotes.[13] In Chapters XIX to XXI of his novel, *al-Hajjaj Ibn Yusuf,* he refers ten times to *Kitab al-Aghani* (Book of Songs).[14] Often, he provided in separate introductory chapters a thorough historical and geographical description of the city in the country in which the event took place.[15] In his novel *Fath al-Andalus* (the Conquest of Spain), he provides beforehand a full description of that country together with its capital, Toledo; while in another novel, *al-Inqilab al-'Uthmani* (The Ottoman Coup d'Etat), not only does he describe Salonika (Thessalonike), the headquarters of the Young Turks, but also the city of Constantinople (where the Young Turks went).[16]

Thus his novels consist of two aspects: history and romance—with the latter always integrated into actual historical events. In all of *Fatat Ghasan* (The Young Woman of Ghassan), for instance, the major theme is the Islamic conquest of Syria which was predominantly a Christian country and the contrast between the conditions of Christianity and Islam in the beginning of the seventh century. The characters are relegated to being a vehicle for what the author deemed most important: depicting the then condition of Christianity in Syria and the rise of nascent Islam as a dominant force.

It is the story of the love between Hammad and Hind that is used to depict historical events. Hammad follows the movements of the Muslim armies in search of an elusive, exclusive earring that he must give to Hind as dowry in exchange for her hand. In quest of this prize he visits Mecca, meets with Christians, Muslims, and pagans, and in the company of the Arab armies he witnesses the Arab conquest of Jerusalem and Damascus. In brief, the novel demonstrates the collapse of an historical era in Syria which preceded the rise of Islam and its beginning rule.

In *Armanusa al Misriyya* (Egyptian Armanusa), where Zaydan portrays the Arab conquest of Egypt in 640 A.D. He used the love affair between Armanusa, daughter of al-Muqawqis, governor of Egypt, and Arcadius, son of the Byzantine army commander, as a means to portray the historical narrative. The Byzantine Emperor, Heraclius (d. 641), however, also desired to marry Armanusa and had already asked her father to send her to his imperial palace in Constantinople. Loving Arcadius and not wanting to marry Heraclius she joined the Arab army on its way to invade Egypt. Its commander, Amr Ibn al-As, offered her protection and his friendship until he conquered Alexandria. In Alexandria she miraculously meets Arcadius, and the two marry after Alexandria fell into the hands of the Arabs.[17]

In *Ghadat Karbala* (The Young Lady of Karbala), the author portrays the murder of al-Husayn, grandson of the Prophet Muhammad by the Umayyad authorities in Karbala, Iraq, and the religious and political impact of this murder. The romance again portrays the circumstances surrounding a particular historical event. The central character, Abd al-Rahman, loves his cousin Salma but the problem is the Umayyad Caliph, Yazid, son of Mu'awiya who also covets Salma. After many adventures Salma arrives in the city of al-Kufa where she witnesses the killing of al-Husayn, whose head was cut off and sent to the Caliph in Damascus. At the end, the Caliph Yazid goes to Houran, where he dies. Salma then finds Abd al-Rahman and the two travel to Mecca where they marry and live ever after.[18]

In *Abu Muslim al-Khurasani*, the main theme is the accession of the Abbasids to power in 750 through the support of the Persians in Khurasan. The love story pivots around Jullinar, daughter of a Persian leader and Abu Muslim, who was instrumental in overthrowing the Umayyads and bringing the Abbasids to power. The romance, however, does not culminate in the marriage of the two lovers but their separation. Jullinar loved Abu Muslim, who did not return her love but rather used her to further his political ambitions. Thoroughly ruthless, when Abu Muslim discovers that Jullinar's father has betrayed the Abbasid cause, he has him assasinated. Jullinar escapes to Syria where she learns that the Abbasid Caliph Abu Ja'far al-Mansur distrusts Abu Muslim and has ordered him killed. She hurries to Baghdad, witnesses the beheading of Abu Muslim and then enters a convent.[19]

In *Abd al-Rahman al-Nasir,* the historical theme deals with the rule of the Umayyad Caliph, Abd al-Rahman al-Nasir, in Spain, while the love interest involves A'ida and Sa'id.[20] In *al-Amin wa al-Ma'mun,* the author portrays the struggle for power between the Arabs and the Persians in the persons of the two brothers, the sons of the Abbasid Caliph, Harun al-Rashid. It ends with the killing of the Amin and the ascendance of al-Ma'mun to power, while the romance concentrates on the relationship between Maymuna, daughter of Ja'far al-Barmaki, confidante of Harun al-Rashid and Bahzad, grandson of Abu Muslim al-Khurasani who becomes involved in the conflict between the two royal brothers. Like the love affair in Zaydan's other novels, this one between Maymuna and Bahzad ends in marriage.[21] The same pattern is followed in the novels of Zaydan dealing with the recent Middle East past. Of these novels we may mention *Asir al-Mutamahdi* (The Captive of the Mahdi Pretender), *al-Mamluk al-Sharid* (The Escaping Mamluk), and *al-Inqilab al-'Uthmani* (The Ottoman Coup d'Etat).

As mentioned above, since Zaydan's primary objective was to popularize history, his plots and characters were subservient to the historical events he attempted to popularize. In many instances, therefore, the plots are weak and the characters unnatural, with fate and coincidence playing a large role in the tying together of historical events. For example, in *al-Mamluk al-Sharid* (The Escaping Mamluk) the "coincidences" pile up as when Gharib suddenly meets his father and neither recognizes the other; or his chance meeting with his brother, Salim, in the city of 'Akka (Acre); or when one of the characters, Sulayman, turns out to be no other than the escaping Mamluk himself.[22] In a similar view, *al-Hajjaj Ibn Yusuf,* who was the governor of Iraq under the Umayyads, Layla al-Ukhayliyya seemingly appears out of thin air in al-Hajjaj's camp to rescue him.[23] In *Fatat Ghassan* (The Young Woman of Ghassan), Hind meets coincidentally with Hammad in a convent[24] and in *Adhra Quraysh* (The Maiden of the Quraysh), Muhammad appears out of nowhere and rescues Asma.[25] Such coincidental meetings might, perhaps, be more meaningful in a fairy tale or in a detective story but are terribly contrived in these historical novels.

While Zaydan excites our curiosity by introducing at the beginning of most of his novels a puzzling secret, or "mystery," the excitement fades as our attention becomes focused on the sequence of historical events, as Zaydan seems to forget about the "mystery." When the reader reaches that point in the novel when Zaydan finally revives or unravels the "mystery," usually toward the end, it is diluted and out of place. It does not involve our imaginative sympathy as it would have if the whole plot focused on the "mystery" and its solution. Every now and then Zaydan might remind the reader of the "mystery" before the climax, but he does so rather haphazardly and without compelling the reader's avid interest.

This is shown for instance, in Zaydan's novel, *Asir al-Mutamahdi* (The Captive of the Mahdi Pretender). The story opens in Cairo, Egypt, in 1878. Ibrahim, an employee of the British Consulate, and his wife, Su'da, are nervous because of a secret connected with a certain box in their possession. Ibrahim shows his wife the box but refuses to divulge the secret of the box or the circumstances associated with it despite his wife's pleas.[26] The focus of the novel then shifts to Shafiq, Ibrahim's son, his rescue of a beautiful young lady Fadwa, how they fall in love, how Shafiq's friend Aziz, an indolent and spoiled wealthy young man tries to destroy that love in order to marry Fadwa himself. We also learn along the way that Shafiq uses Fadwa's father, a greedy man, and Dalila, a cunning old woman to achieve his aim. A little after this in the narrative we see Ibrahim open the box because of his wife's insistence that he should open it. In the box, Ibrahim's wife, Su'da, sees a piece of hair stained with dried blood. She pleads with her husband to tell her the secret of the hairpiece but he refuses.[27] In the meantime, the story is interrupted several times by Zaydan to relate the history of the rebellion of Ahmad Ibn Muhammad of Dongola, who claimed to be the expected Mahdi, against the Anglo-Egyptian authorities. The military campaign, commanded by Hicks Pasha against the Mahdi and his followers known as the Darawish (Dervishes), led to the total annihilation of Hicks's forces, and the subsequent delegation of General Gordon to the Sudan and his murder by the followers of the Mahdi in the city of Khartum. He continues to interpolate historical events until the very end when we have almost forgotten about the box.

When he finally does divulge the secret of the hair it is most disappointing. We anticipate that Ibrahim is the one who would reveal the secret. But the secret is revealed through a letter sent by Fadwa's mother in Egypt, to her husband who is vacationing with their daughter, Fadwa, in Lebanon. Although the letter is not signed, we discover from the contents of the letter that Ibrahim had written it to his wife Su'da.[28] Zaydan does not tell us how and why Fadwa's mother possessed the letter which Ibrahim addressed to his wife. We also have no idea why Zaydan chose to reveal the secret of the bloodstained hair piece through an anonymous letter and not through Ibrahim (after he found out that his sister was Fadwa's mother and that Fadwa was his niece, another "twist"). The convolution of the plot and the strained attempt to impart fictional intrigue are frustrating and deny the reader any real literary satisfaction.

All in all, however, the nature of Zaydan's characters fit in perfectly with his purpose to teach history. His fictitious characters are particularly suited to fulfill this purpose. They are not deeply rooted in life and we know nothing about their skills and professions nor are we given insight into how they feel or what they think about the people, society or the institutions of their time. They seem only to be Zaydan's means to relate the historical narrative. They are fixed characters and often portrayed as models of vice or virtue. As such, they resemble the characters of Salim al-Bustani.

Zaydan usually introduces his character with a description of his/her qualities which does not require a profound effort on the part of the ordinary reader to guess the outcome—good or bad—which will result from these generalities. This obviates the possibility of any character development and the normal unfolding of a personality.[29] Thus, upon reading *Seventeenth Ramadan,* the reader discovers from the first few pages that Qatam, daughter of Shihna, son of 'Adi, from the tribe of Rabab, is a young woman whose beauty has become the daily talk of the people of the city of Karbala. The reader soon discovers, however, that she was bent on revenge because her father and brother were killed in the battle of the Nahrawan fought between Ali and Mu'awiya.[30] There is also the character of Lubab who, we are informed, is a cunning old woman whom Qatam employs to execute her plan for avenging her father and brother. This incarnation of evil is typical of the stereotypes that Zaydan constantly depicts, i.e., she is hunch backed and limps but manages to move more swiftly than her old age might allow; her cheeks are wrinkled, her toothless mouth is sunk in her face and her weary eyes ooze with discharged mucous.[31] We know that she is up to no good! In the meantime, young Sa'id whom Lubaba employs to carry out her plan of assassinating the Caliph Ali is portrayed as a handsome and naive young man but not so naive that he lacks personal vanity. It is this vanity that Qatam shrewdly plays upon so as to extract from him a pledge to assassinate the Caliph Ali in exchange for Qatam's hand. The gullible but vain Sa'id did not realize that Qatam loathed him.[32]

In *al-Abbasa Ukht al-Rashid* (The Abbasa Sister of al-Rashid), Zaydan has the story begin with a description by the poet Abu al-Atahiya (d. 825), of the much discussed and highly controversial love affair and secret marriage between the Abbasa, sister of the Caliph, Harun al-Rashid, and the Caliph's minister, Ja'far al-Barmaki of the famous Barmaki (Barmecide) family. Zaydan also provides an in-depth historical biography of Abu al-'Atahiya himself. He tells the reader among other things that Abu al-'Atahiya was known for his stinginess and for using his poetry as a means to make money through praising prominent people. But mostly he dwells upon Abu al-Atahiya's close connection with the court of the Caliph, al-Rashid.[33] Al-Abbasa and Ja'far, we found out, were in love with each other, but al-Abbasa's brother the Caliph, Harun al-Rashid, was too fond of his sister and could not bring himself to let her leave the palace in order to marry Ja'far. Thus, he arranged a marriage contract between his sister and Ja'far which allowed them to see each other, but only in his presence, while denying them the opportunity to live together or consummate their marriage. Despite, the jealous Caliph's wishes however, al-Abbasa and Ja'far secretly had two sons as a result of their marriage.

On the day the events of our story unfold, Abu al-'Atahiya happened to spend the evening at the home of Phinehas, a Jewish slave trader who provided slave girls to the Caliph's court as well as to rich men in Baghdad. While there, Abu al-'Atahiya sees a man and a woman carry two young boys into one of the rooms in Phinehas's house. Nosey and alert to any opportunity for ill-gotten gain Abu 'Atahiya peeped through the key hole and saw a beautiful woman whom, with the two boys lying in her lap, he recognized as al-Abbasa, sister of the Caliph. He surmised immediately that they were her sons and that in order to avoid her brother's wrath she met secretly with them in the house of Phinehas. Having discovered what he believed to be proof of the defiance of her brother's will, Abu al-'Atahiya, who was greedy, intended to blackmail al-Abbasa and Ja'far,[34] and he does, but in the end al-Rashid finds out anyway, and true to character, not only beheads Ja'far but kills his two sons. Al-Abbasa managed to escape.[35]

Occasionally Zaydan exaggerates, and endows his characters with extraordinary qualities. Perhaps the most unbelievable of all Zaydan's characters is

Gharib in the novel *al-Mamluk al-Sharid* (The Escaping Mamluk). Gharib, we learn, was only eight years old when he accompanied the Amir Bashir al-Shihabi (d. 1850) whom he thought to be his father (he was not), to Egypt in 1821. Zaydan states that he looked and acted as if he were at least fifteen[36] and portrays the eight year old as tall, mature, intelligent, and serene with the benefit at such a tender age of an excellent education from his private tutor, Butrus Karama (d. 1851), secretary to the Amir Bashir. Also, he would have us believe that at this age, he was an excellent horseman and fencer.[37] While in Egypt this wondrous young boy never ceased writing to his mother, describing his journey to Egypt.[38] In brief, if we follow Zaydan's description, Gharib possessed all the qualities of an exemplary young man despite the fact that he was only eight years old.[39]

In *al-Amin wa al-Ma'mun*, Zaynab, daughter of al-Ma'mun, and her slave girl, Dananir, are likewise portrayed by Zaydan as possessing rare qualities. Although Zaynab was only twelve years old, she like her father, was intelligent, strong-willed and independent-minded.[40] She attended the private councils of her grandfather, the Caliph Harun al-Rashid, in the company of her grandmother, Zubayda.[41] Often she entered into dialogue with her slave girl, Dananir about astronomy, celestial bodies, and signs of the zodiac.[42] Dananir is even more extraordinary. She was raised in the home of Yahya al-Barmaki where she developed interest in intellectual matters. Zaydan tells us that when Yahya decided to have Ptolemy's book *al-Magest* translated into Arabic, Dananir met with the translators and discussed astronomy with them. Although Zaydan knows that few books of astronomy and medicine have been translated into Arabic at this time (eighth-century) he attempts to justify Dananir's knowledge of sciences, especially astronomy and medicine, by having us believe that she heard them discussed in the home of Yahya al-Barmaki.[43] Dananir was not a typical slave girl looking after a prince. Everytime she took him to the palace garden to play, she brought astronomical diagrams or medical problems to ponder over and teach to the prince. As a consequence, when al-Ma'mun came of age, we are told, he had developed a strong inclincation toward learning and he became not only a rationalist Mu'tazilite but a patron of learning and sponsor of translations from the Greek.[44] Of course, Islamic history relates the talents of extraordinary women but in the case of Dananir her intellectual sophistication is much exaggerated by Zaydan. Some critics have pointed out these and other weaknesses in Zaydan's historical novels.[45] But the point is that Zaydan was not really an historian in a strict sense but a writer of historical romance. His characters were essentially instructive, as he intended them to be.[46] He was a writer of fiction capable of telling an entertaining story which had a great deal of historical truth to it. Herein lies the key to Zaydan's continuing popularity—he was not a great novelist but an entertaining teller of historical tales. He had no antecedent novels or tradition to build upon except the old Arabian tales and the simple stories of Salim al-Bustani, despite the fact, however, that Zaydan succeeded in producing historical romances, whose technical proficiency, including plot, were much more polished and sophisticated than those of al-Bustani or any other Arab writer before him. Therefore, while Zaydan may not be considered a great novelist, he revolutionized the Arab novel and paved the way for future novelists whether inspired by historical themes or not.

In his historical novels Zaydan did not follow strict canons of historiographical practices in his attempt to reproduce the past; rather, he wished to recall some of its more salient and entertaining, if not important aspects, in an attempt to reach a popular audience and inform them of their hitherto unknown past. This is why Zaydan's novels attempt to recall general historical events rather than to minutely reconstruct and profoundly analyze. Thus Zaydan portrayed most of his fictitious characters as simple and fixed—being merely the more or less passive instruments for the unfolding of an already determined general historical sequence. In many cases he was compelled to create fictitious characters and tie them in somehow with the real ones in order to lend the novel necessary excitement and adventure. He could not do this with real historical characters.

Accordingly, in the novel, *al-Inqilab al-'Uthmani* (The Ottoman Coup d'Etat), which brought the Young Turks to power in 1908, the plot is based not only on the aforementioned "coincidence" approach but the detective-like maneuvers of the fictitious characters.[47] Sirin, a young lady, is in love with Ramiz, a revolutionary, who attacks the Sultan's despotism. But Sadiq, an opportunist who comes from an influential Turkish family is also in love with Sirin and connives with Sirin's father, to destroy the love between Sirin and Ramiz so that he might marry Sirin. After many intrigues which take us in and out of the Sultan's palace and the company of Young Turks, Sirin finally marries Ramiz. As for Sadiq, he is killed in the Coup of 1908.[48]

In his novels dealing with ancient Arab and Islamic historical themes, Zaydan's characters reflect his own understanding of those themes as they are recorded by Arab historians. For this reason it is difficult to judge Zaydan's novels unless we understand that his passion for history was his motivating force. Zaydan's history is made alive not through the actions of his characters but through the sequence of historical events these characters relate at the behest of their creator. This is invariably true of the characters in any of his novels whether they are Hammad in *Fatat Ghassan* (The Young Woman of Ghassan), the queen, Shajarat al-Durr, in the novels which bears the same name, Qatam in *Seventeenth Ramadan* or Florenda in *Fath al-Andalus* (The Conquest of Spain). No major events which influenced the march of Islam to the station of a world power provoke excitement or curiosity. Thus, the pitched battle of Badr between the Prophet of Islam and his enemies, the tribe of the Quraysh, the decisive battle of the Yarmuk which laid Syria open to the Arabs, or the battle which opened the gates of Spain to the Muslim armies, are disappointingly lifeless related as they are by characters who parrot an account of them in rote high school manner. In addition the cause and effect relationship of these great events is entirely ignored. Zaydan may be justified, since his purpose, after all, was to make the fictitious subservient to history and to pay the price of sacrificing literary artistry for historical factualism. He was especially handicapped when the facts dealing with a certain historical era or event were few. Furthermore, Zaydan is no master of style. His journalistic approach obviated a more colorful description and delivery.[49] He was writing after all, for relatively unsophisticated Arab readers hopelessly severed from their past history by long cultural stagnation.

He was careful, however, to reflect in all his works the moral outlook and social viewpoint of contemporary Arab society. Zaydan himself was highly moralistic and viewed love as a pure and sacred thing which has inevitably to end in marriage. The lovers in Zaydan's novels meet each other and speak of love, but they never touch, hug, or kiss—this is the line drawn between pure love and cheap love.

Zaydan's characters in *Jihad al-Muhibbin* display the normal strengths of unblemished lovers but no sooner does the anxious reader get there than he encounters disappointment. This is most conspicuous in his novel *'Arus Farghana* (The Bride of Farghana) which deals with the affairs of the Abbasid state in the time of the Caliph al-Mu'tasim (d. 842), and the ambition of the Persians to restore their state, lost since the Arab conquest of their country in the first half of the seventh century.[50] Young Jehan, the beauty of the city of Farghana and daughter of Tahmasp, a Persian leader, was in love with Dirgham, chief guard of the Caliph, al-Mu'tasim. As the story unfolds with the description of Jehan's manners, dress, and most of all, her enthralling beauty, our curiosity is provoked when we learn that Jehan is soon to meet her lover whom she has not seen for a long time since he was on duty in Iraq. When the great moment arrives, we see Jehan enter a room and Dirgham stands to greet her with outstretched hands; Jehan immediately releases her hand and sits on a separate chair facing her lover. A dialogue then begins during which Jehan asks Dirgham to forgive her for calling him her love. Dirgham answers that, to the contrary, now that she has called him "love," he finds the courage to call her "love," too. At these words Jehan bows her head in exquisite shyness, and Dirgham becomes even more enthralled "embracing her with his eyes where he could not embrace her with his arms."[51] The movement is solemn and the lovers' talk is solemn, again. In another novel, *Asir al-Mutamahdi* (The Captive of the Mahdi Pretender), he describes the lover's meeting thus; "they were careful not to touch the dress of each other in great respect for purity and chastity."[52]

This is the pinnacle of romantic love as Zaydan envisaged it, pure, lofty and sacred. It is a romance based on the avowed devotion of lovers and their anticipation of eventual marriage.

Jihad al-Muhibbin (Lovers' Struggle) which appeared in 1893 is Zaydan's only non-historical novel. Zaydan intended it to show the agony of love.[53] The locale is Egypt, but the characters are Syrian émigrés with whom Zaydan could feel more at home and with whom he could more easily identify. In most aspects this novel is little different from the historical novels of Zaydan except that its theme is not historical. It contains his "eternal plot," that is, love between two young people and the machinations of unscrupulous men to frustrate it, ending with the triumph of good over evil and the lovers' union.[54] Zaydan appears, however to have freed himself from the restricted frame of reference attendant upon his historical novels by the creation of more rounded and believable characters. Muhammad Yusuf Najm has recognized the fact that, "in this novel Zaydan presents his characters in their normal life which is a step forward in the writing of a realistic novel."[55] The novel itself is really not too successful, but it does show that he is capable of creating believable characters.

In *Jihad al-Muhibbin* while Salim, the main character, appears to be tense, emotional and, at times, compulsive, Habib appears to be a calm, devoted, selfless friend who sacrifices time and effort to insure Salim's happiness. There is also Salma, his "girlfriend," who understands Salim's fears and tries to help him. Then there is Dawud the Alexandrian businessman casting a shadow on Salma's moral behavior because he is jealous of Salim.[56] There is also the wicked and cunning woman, Warda, who uses the greedy Dawud and her subservient maid Sa'ida to trap Salim into marrying her beautiful daughter.[57] Amidst this miscellany of characters stands Salim's mother, a naive and simple old lady who is manipulated by the crafty Warda.

Zaydan's characters in *Jihad al-Muhibbin,* display the normal strengths and weaknesses of man, his problems and pleasure, stopping short of being really different in this work by the inclusion of the same lover's triangle as in all his works and the strict preservation of the sanctity and purity of love as Zaydan understood it. Nonetheless, the "affair" between Salim and Salma was, in itself, a revolutionary social phenomenon in a conservative country like Egypt.[58] It would be difficult to find any Egyptian writing in the year 1887, who would give his characters such a degree of social freedom as Zaydan in *Jihad al-Muhibbin*. We should remember also that Zaydan came from Lebanon, a country which was influenced by Western concepts of freedom and where there was a heightened degree of social consciousness particularly in the defense of women, going back to men like Butrus al-Bustani who as early as 1849 wrote social criticism which helped result in the fact that women in Lebanon enjoyed more freedom than in any other Middle Eastern country. Zaydan was influenced by this but he was equally aware that he was in Egypt, not Lebanon, and therefore, chose all of his characters from Syrian émigrés in order not to outrage the conservatives in Egypt who could not understand or tolerate liberalized attitudes towards women. Abd al-Muhsin Taha Badr is correct when he states that in his early period (1887), Jurji Zaydan was not able to use Egyptian names (characters) in a free social situation involving men and women.[59] This is also why the characters in *Jihad al-Muhibbin* appear detached from the Egyptian society and bereft of a clear sense of time and place. Apart from a cursory allusion to the pyramids or other places like Cairo and Alexandria, Zaydan's characters reveal nothing about the country of their adoption.

Zaydan, a man of various talents, was historian, philologist, essayist, linguist, biographer, sociologist, and novelist. He even wrote on natural history. His output was tremendous,[60] and our admiration for this remarkable man increases when we consider the fact that except for a very brief period of study at the Syrian Protestant College (the present American University of Beirut), he was self taught. In the field of Islamic history he did what no other writer before or since has done. His five volumes of *Tarikh al-Tamaddun al-Islami* (History of Islamic Civilization) which appeared for the first time in 1902 remain a classic. He also for the first time accomplished the popularization of Islamic history through the medium of fiction. It was a momentous step only a man of Zaydan's intellectual caliber could have accomplished. His greatness does not solely rest on his writing of historical novels, although his influence on succeeding Arab writers was great. Zaydan may not have been a great Arab novelist nor a great Arab historian, but he did revolutionize the writing of Islamic history for the first time giving it a valid existential relevance. In short, it was alive and meaningful.

Unfortunately, his detractors, mostly extremist Muslims, have judged him more as a professional historian than as a popularizer of history. While others admired his histories and historical novels, some Muslim apologists thought in the words of Muhammad Yusuf Najm that "it was too much for a Christian to impinge on the field of Islamic History."[62] Furthermore, they accused him of prejudice against and distortion of Islamic history.[63] Perhaps the severest criticism of Zaydan's historical writing was leveled by the Shaykh Amin Ibn Hasan al-Madani who wrote a book entitled *Nabsh al-Hadhayan min Tarikh Jurji Zaydan,* Bombay 1307 A.H./1889 A.D., (Exposing the Ravings in the History of Jurji Zaydan). In response, Zaydan wrote a refutation of al-Madani's allegations entitled *Radd Rannan 'ala Nabsh al-Hadhayan* (Resounding Refutation of Nabsh al-Hadhayan), published in 1891. According to the celebrated Orientalist Ignaz Kratschkowsky, most of al-Madani's criticism dwells upon the trivial.[64]

In undertaking the tremendous task of writing Islamic history, Zaydan must have found himself in a very difficult situation. The fact that he was a Christian was sufficient to discredit him *a priori* in the eyes of many Muslims as a biased writer. It is ironic that while some Muslims accused Zaydan for not having fully presented the excellences of the Arabs and Islam in his writings, some of his Christian compatriots condemned him for having exaggerated the excellence of the Arabs and Islam. They even considered him an apostate.[65]

Regardless of the opinions of his detractors, Zaydan occupies a prominent place in the history of the Arab novel. He should be studied and judged not as a "scientific" historian, but as a popularizer of Islamic history who did his homework well. He endeavored to present the past to the modern Arab reader in a vivid and entertaining quasi-fictional manner. This explains his appeal to many readers. The eminent Egyptian writer Taha Husayn (d. 1973) expresses his own fascination with Zaydan's novels. He states that when he was young he read Zaydan's works and became infatuated with them to the point that they distracted him from his study at the Azhar Mosque (the present Azhar University).[66]

Abd al-Muhsin Taha Badr cites several later novelists who relied upon the stylistic devices and writing methods of Zaydan, including the Qa'imma-qam Nasib Bey's *Khafaya Misr* (The Secrets of Egypt), Farah Anton's is *Urushalim al-Jadida aw Fath Bayt al-Maqdis* (New Jerusalem or the Conquest of the Holy City of Jerusalem) and Abd al-Halim al-'Askaris' *Su'ad,* as well as several other anonymous writers. At the same time, Mahmud Hamid Shawkat also shows that several other prominent historical novelists, such as Muhammad Farid Abu Hadid, Ibrahim Ramzi, and Ali al-Jarim were also influenced by Zaydan.[67]

Even today Zaydan's works are immensely popular, appealing to a wide spectrum of Arab readers. His novels have an international appeal as well, having been translated into both Western and Oriental languages.

EPILOGUE

After Zaydan, who symbolized the end result of the slow and not always steady evolution of Arabic fiction during the nineteenth century, the rate of production and the quality of the work accelerated appreciably. The Industrial Revolution had begun to slowly penetrate into the Near East with the beginning of all that it had brought in its wake earlier in the century in the West. A middle class, reasonably literate, and moderately wealthy began to emerge. The mandate system which came out of the Versailles Conference also meant, at least for a while, the presence and influence of Europeans. The world of the twentieth century was shrinking; the Middle East was no longer, at least to Europeans, some exotic, far-away place mentioned in the history of the Crusades, or at times whispered about, with perhaps more than a touch of self-righteous indulgence, concerning the Sultan's harem, and the general profligacy of his court.

The twentieth century was impinging with a vengeance upon the Middle East—so much so that more was accomplished in the area of Arab fiction since 1920 than during the whole of the nineteenth century until that time. As a matter of fact, Arabic literature, following a general cultural decline begun in late medieval times, reached its nadir in the nineteenth century. This century was truly a difficult time for the Moslem Middle East. Illiteracy was widespread, the economy was stagnant, based as it was on primitive agriculture, and censorship and religious proscription were facts of life.

The one institution of higher learning in the Middle East was one founded by American Protestant Missionaries, the Syrian Protestant College (1866; the present American University of Beirut). No similar institution was to exist until the turn of the century. This uninspiring state of affairs was compounded and perpetuated by the despotic rule of the Mamluks, under whom illiteracy deepened and the last and only refuge of learning was the famous al-Azhar Mosque. Furthermore, the hostility of the Azharite 'Ulama (learned men) towards the study of the humanities and the liberal arts, together with the lack of an enlightened or educated middle class, retarded the development of viable modes of Arab fiction.

Yet, there was some literary activity, as this book has been devoted to showing. What, then, can be concluded about the nature and worth of the works of those we have been discussing and those that came after them? Veritable cultural beacons dimly lighten a darkened social and intellectual world, their work being characterized in a general way as naive and unsophisticated, although it is at times, very charming and quite entertaining.

This was true of the drama as well as other literary forms. Inspired by and, for the most part, molded upon the example of the West, its audiences were, at any rate, very limited in number. The establishment by the Khedive Isma'il of *Masrah al-Komedi* (Théatre de la Comédie) in 1869 was less a response to public demand than a manifestation of his Westernizing policy. The first popular Egyptian stage was established in 1870 by Ya'qub Sanu (d. 1912), an Egyptian Jew whom the Khedive once considered the Molière of Egypt, but who later fell into disfavor and was compelled to leave the country. Sanu's works portrayed many details of Egyptian society and, given fuller support, might well have provided a substantial foundation for native drama.

The bulk of modern fiction writers were either native Egyptians who were much influenced by men like al-Bustani and Francis Marrash, or they were Syrians who emigrated to Egypt, where the climate was more conducive to literary freedom, especially after 1882, when the British protected it by law. Even earlier, the immigration of Syrian men of letters and journalists after the Lebanese massacre of 1860 injected life into a moribund state of literary affairs in Egypt. Most of these émigrés, curiously enough, were Christians, who by and large were better acquainted with European culture and literature than the conservative climate of Egypt would allow its own subjects (which situation was more or less true throughout the Middle East in general). While some, like Jurji Zaydan, tried to recreate the glorious Arabic past in historical novels, the majority was engaged in translating European novels into the native idiom. This latter effort met with bitter opposition from conservative spokesmen who condemned the translations as frivolous and immoral. In the meantime, some writers used a medieval literary form, the *maqama,* as a vehicle for the writing of fiction.

Thus Arabic fiction developed in direct relationship to the influx of Western influences. Where it was paramount, Egypt, the advance of modern Arabic fiction went apace. It was part of a natural evolutionary process, much later than in the West, but inevitable in any case and dealing on its own terms with the problems of time and place, most of which difficulties had to do with a changing society under the impact of Western ideas and influences.

By the turn of the century, Arabic writers, most probably Egyptian, were trying to produce native fiction patterned after Western models, but with domestic themes and settings. Unable to free themselves from conservative attitudes, however, they assailed the deleterious influence of Western civilization upon their own cultural tradition. Typical of their works is *al-Hal wa al-Ma'al* (The Present and the Future), by Ahmad Hafiz 'Awad, which appeared in 1905.[1] The story concerns a young Egyptian lady, Asma, whose relationships with other people reveal the evils of Western influence: she dares to read French novels, and she defies traditional Egyptian morals by greeting young men openly.

However naive and inartistic these romances may appear, they did help to establish the foundation of modern Arabic fiction. Yet the writers of fiction in the first decade of the twentieth century adhered to social themes and moral preachment and defended their social institutions, particularly marriage, against what they imagined to be the debasement threatened by Western fiction, already widely available in translation. These writers felt love to be essentially connected with marriage, and believed it must therefore be wholly pure. If lovers were characters in a romance, it was necessary to idealize their relationship and to represent them as innocent. Sensual love, on the other hand, must invariably be portrayed as wicked.

The adherence to moral themes and preachment reflects also the inclination of the Egyptian public towards this type of approach. Perhaps the most important works of this nature are *al-Fata al-Rifi* (The Country Youth), published in 1902, and *al-Fatat al-Rifiyya* (The Country Maiden), published three years later, both by Mahmud Khayrat. Unfortunately, Khayrat has been all but ignored by literary critics, who have almost unanimously acclaimed *Zaynab,* by Muhammad Husayn Haykal (d. 1956), which appeared anonymously in 1912, as the first full-fledged Egyptian novel.[3] Considered apart from Khayrat's observations on the low state of Arab fiction, his didacticism, and the interpolations in the text, *al-Fata al-Rifi* should be regarded as an authentic Egyptian novel. Here for the first time we find a purely Egyptian romance with native themes, characters, and settings. Mustafa, a poor peasant, falls in love with a peasant girl, Fatima, but is sent to fight in the Sudan during the Mahdi's rebellion. In his absence, Fatima's family arranges her engagement to another man, and when Mustafa returns home, he disposes of his adversaries and marries his Fatima. Though lacking in technical dexterity and sophisticated language, *al-Fata al-Rifi* tells a straightforward, compassionate story and depicts accurately the life of the Egyptian peasant.

Indeed, with some slight alteration of the outcome, the plot of *Zaynab* is almost identical with that of *al-Fata al-Rifi,* and the similarity seems more than accidental. In the later work Hamid, a well-to-do young man, falls in love with Zaynab, a pretty peasant girl, but she spurns his suit because of their class difference. She herself loves Ibrahim, who is of her own class, but marries another man. Hamid finds solace in a fleeting affair with his cousin 'Aziza and flirts with other women. Yet he cannot put aside his love for Zaynab, and when she again rejects him, he is driven to despair which becomes more acute when 'Aziza marries. Zaynab, torn between her love for Ibrahim and her obligations toward her husband, lives in constant agony. When Ibrahim is drafted to fight in the Sudan, she can no longer repress her emotions; growing steadily weaker, she contracts tuberculosis and dies, finally acknowledging her love for Ibrahim.[4] *Zaynab* is more artistic and polished than *al-Fata al-Rifi* though at times it seems digressive. But its theme is not new, and the esteem in which it has been held by Egyptian critics is exaggerated.

In the period between the two world wars, Arabic fiction underwent substantial changes both in its themes and in its techniques. There were strong nationalistic feelings and the desire for political independence accompanied by a concomitant cultural upheaval which affected many facets of Egyptian society. This was essentially so in Egypt. Touched by the surging new spirit, young writers labored seriously to create indigenous fiction which would reflect distinctively Egyptian characteristics. While they sought their themes in Egyptian life and society, they had to acknowledge the superiority of Western techniques to such traditional Arab literary forms as the *maqama*.[5] They tended to portray their society as realistically as possible, regarding the romantic outlook of their predecessors as outmoded. Among the pioneers of the new realism were 'Isa 'Ubayd, Mahmud Timur, and Tahir Lashin.

In Isa Ubayd's *Thurayya* (1922), the central figure is not the vivacious *Thurayya,* but Wadi' Na'um, an eccentric and neurotic young man who has struggled since childhood to overcome adversities. Honest and hard working, yet shy and introverted, he falls in love with *Thurayya,* who is attractive and well educated. But she is ambitious and intends to marry for wealth and prestige; so she rejects Wadi' and renounces her Christian faith to marry Ahmad Bey, a wealthy Muslim Turk. She is denounced by her family for this action, but Wadi' is firm in his love for her and cherishes that dream that someday she will return to him. Hoping to win *Thurayya's* affection by becoming rich, Wadi' opens a large shop in Cairo; unfortunately, we never learn whether he achieves his dream. *Thurayya* is generally episodic in structure and offers only a superficial portrait of Egyptian society. The characters are drawn from the Syrian immigrant community, not from the whole range of Egyptian society, and are merely superimposed on what the author considered an authentic background; in fact, they are so generalized that they might well be assigned to any society. At the same time, however, 'Ubayd's thorough psychological analysis of Wadi' and the greater independence and mobility of his characters represent distinct advancements over the fictional techniques of his predecessors.

Mahmud Timur, one of the most prolific Arabic writers in modern times, is acclaimed today as the master of the short story and has also written plays and novels.[6] Like 'Ubayd, he had little success in projecting a realistic view of Egyptian life, due to his naive concept of realism as merely the use of Egyptian names and places in conjunction with native manners, traditions, and settings.[7] Thus, Timur's *Rajab Effendi* (1928) presents only a superficial analysis of Egyptian society, and we are shown mere stereotyped characters against an unchanging and unrealistic background. Indeed, had the author not stated in the introduction that his was "a modern Egyptian story with a simple theme drawn from ordinary life in which I have attempted to analyze the sentiment of some middle and lower classes," the reader would have had to guess whether the story was truly Egyptian. Like 'Ubayd's Wadi', Timur's hero Rajab is an eccentric, introverted bachelor, but extremely religious, who falls under the influence of an Armenian, al-Haj Ahmad Halajyan, who claims to be a spiritualist. Rajab grows obsessed with the idea of communicating with his parents, who died in his childhood, but recognizes that Halajyan is only a charlatan. In an outburst of rage, he strangles Halajyan and is committed to an asylum for the rest of his days. From the very outset, Rajab's character is fixed by the author, and he is given no opportunity to develop. Timur skillfully analyzes the conflict between Rajab's religious motivation and his recognition of Halajyan's true nature, although this conflict does not arise from Rajab's behavior but is plainly forced by the author.[8] Although Timur draws his characters from the lower and middle classes, his aristocratic Turkish background makes it clear that his interest in these people sprung from curiousity rather than genuine sympathy.

Timur's second novel, *al-Atlal* (Ruins), which appeared in 1934, focuses on the Turkish aristocracy rather than the lower and middle classes. Sami, an orphaned aristocrat living with his married brothers, proposes to marry Fathiyya, a poor young lady who is pregnant with his child, but his brother prevents the marriage. Driven to mental instability by his separation from Fathiyya, Sami seeks solace in the company of prostitutes and falls in with wicked companions. Bent on revenge, he enters into an affair with Tahani, his brother's wife, and plans to kill his brother. The brother, discovering their illicit relationship, hates his wife but feels remorse for the harm he has done to Sami; soon afterwards, he dies. Sami searches for Fathiyya, only to learn that she had died, and determines to have a happy and honorable life with his son.[9] While *al-Atlal* treats such matters as sadism and illicit sexual relationships more fully than previous works of Egyptian fiction, it frequently seems digressive and does not provide sufficient justification for the sadistic actions of the hero. Moreover, Timur seems to have created a sequence of situations revealing the behavioral pattern of an eccentric character to demonstrate his capacity for understanding human sentiments, but with little regard for plot structure.

Tahir Lashin, however, was apparently better fitted than 'Ubayd and Timur, both by his background and by his occupation, to portray Egyptian society realistically. Born of a wholly Egyptianized family, Lashin came in contact with middle-class city dwellers and small businessmen in his work as a city planning engineer, and he familiarized himself with the concerns of ordinary men by frequently visiting the Muslim religious courts.[10] His *Hawwa bila Adam* (Eve without Adam), published in 1934, admirably treats the predicament of the educated middle-class in Egyptian society. Hawwa, the daughter of a poor family determines to better her fortunes through education, but is denied a scholarship which goes to an aristocratic and wealthy girl. Convinced that social status and prestige are more powerful than intellectual qualification, she decides to assert herself by becoming active in community life. She soon establishes cordial relations with members of the aristocracy and falls deeply in love with the son of a pasha. Though he admires her talents, he never thinks of marrying her, and when he finally marries within his own class, Hawwa, unable to overcome her grief, commits suicide. Lashin's novel presents faithfully the inability of a proud, brilliant young woman to bridge the gap between two irreconcilable worlds. The story is well constructed and builds logically toward a climax; Hawwa herself is a dynamic character, with lofty social ideas, whose behavior is characteristic of her environment. But Lashin exaggerates the sympathy of the aristocratic characters for the heroine, for it is clear that the Egyptian aristocracy lived, at least until the revolution of 1952, with little regard for the poorer classes. Moreover, he is less successful in drawing secondary characters, and, despite its literary charm, Hawwa seems episodic and follows the style of other novels written during the same period.

While these men sought an Egyptian identity through their fiction, other writers, more fully masters of the Arabic language and its rhetoric, were beginning to use fiction to analyze social and psychological themes. Among them were Taha Husayn, Abbas Mahmud al-'Aqqad, Tawfiq al-Hakim, and Ibrahim Abd al-Qadir al-Mazini. Close contemporaries, all of them except al-Mazini were raised in rural communities where they experienced poverty and witnessed the social backwardness of the Egyptian peasant life. All, moreover, were influenced greatly by European thought and culture and were thus made conscious of the deprivation inherent in Egyptian life. The conflict between the traditional society in which they were raised and the brighter future of which they dreamed is manifested in their writings.

Typical of the new trend in fiction is Taha Husayn's *al-Ayyam* (The Stream of Days), an autobiographical novel which appeared in two volumes in 1929 after special publication. Using a third-person narrative, Husayn portrays in an original and exquisite style the hardships of his early childhood and adolescence, his primitive schooling, and the tragedies which befell his family. Most authentic and realistic, however, is his vivid and detailed description of life and learning at the al-Azhar mosque, a surviving monument of the Fatimid era.[11] Husayn's bitter criticism of the follies and injustices of his society was probably a reaction to the hostility aroused by his book *Fi al-Shi'r al-Jahili* (On Pre-Islamic Poetry). Unable to refute openly the accusation of fanatics that he was a blasphemer, he used fiction to state his liberal views. The epistolary *Adib* (Man of Letters) may well be considered a continuation of *al-Ayyam,* as it, too, is largely autobiographical.

While these works may or may not be accepted as novels, Husayn's other works *Du'a al-Karawan* (The Call of the Plover) and *Shajarat al-Bu's* (The Tree of Misery), unmistakably are. In the first of these works, an engineer rapes a Bedouin girl, and by tribal custom her uncle kills her to clear the family name. Ironically, the victim's sister, trying to defend the family's honor by taking revenge on the engineer, falls in love with him and marries him. Though the work may be sentimental, it has amazingly cohesive structure, unity of theme and depth of characterization. *Shajarat al-Bu's* which should more properly be titled *al-Ajyal* (The Generations), exhibits the conflict between the established religious practice of polygamy and the changing trend of modern Egyptian society. A pious young man marries an ugly girl whom, according to social customs, he has never seen before the wedding. Dissatisfied with this marriage, he takes another wife, thus straining his already weak financial position to the point of bankruptcy. But instead of seeking a logical solution to his problems, he attributes them to the influence of unseen factors. And when he dies, his widows lament their bad luck, not acknowledging that their misery has resulted from their husband's foolish behavior and abuse of Islamic institutions.[12]

Between 1931 and 1944, Ibrahim Abd al-Qadir al-Mazini (d. 1949) produced several novels in which he tried to apply social analysis to love and marital relations.[13] He sought to show that the unemancipated status of the Arab-Muslim women as portrayed in fiction did not have to be modeled after concepts which governed Western novels.[14] But al-Mazini oversimplified the moral and social issues in his *Ibrahim al-Katib* (1931), and the Muslim woman appears in that work as an ineffectual personality. The novel concerns itself with the feasibility of loving several women simultaneously and with the complex problems that arise from such a situation. Structurally, it consists of three distinct sketches of the title character and accounts of his affairs with three women. Ibrahim is a restless, confused, and frustrated individual who attempts to overcome his feeling of inferiority and his disappointment with life by searching for love. Critics familiar with al-Mazini's background of physical deformity, lack of parental affection, and poverty, which resulted from his elder brother squandering the family's fortune, have seen in *Ibrahim al-Katib* a truthful picture of the author's own life and psychological tensions.[15] The author concentrates on the actions of his hero, giving only fragmentary exposure to the other characters, and the resultant tenuous relationship of the hero with his environment seems to contradict the author's advocacy of a domestic novel emanating from and representing Egyptian life and society.[16] *Ibrahim al-Katib* is characterized, however, by skillful portrayal of the central figures and by a certain grandeur of vision. Its graceful style and beautiful descriptions cannot be diminished by the fact that, as al-Mazini admitted, the novel was inspired in great part by the *Son of Nature*, written by the Russian novelist, Artsibashev.[17] On the whole, it marks a progressive step toward a more sophisticated Arab novel.

While Husayn and al-Mazini strove to create a domestic novel through autobiography and social analysis, yet another writer, Tawfiq al-Hakim, also Egyptian, was making remarkable progress mastering the art of fiction. During his secondary education in Cairo, he developed a liking for art and music, and he also discovered his inclination for literature. Tawfiq started his literary career in the early 1920s by writing plays for the stage, and despite their im-maturity, they revealed the talent which would later make him a master of fic-tion. Having gone to Paris in 1924, purportedly to study law, he divided his time among literature, music, and the stage, burning with desire to master whatever Western civilization had to offer. Undiscouraged by failures, he con-tinued to write in the hope of portraying the Egyptian national aspirations and the struggle which led to the revolt of 1919. Reportedly he tried to write his *'Awdat al-Ruh* (The Return of the Spirit) in French before writing it in Arabic; its two volumes appeared in 1933.[18]

On the surface, *'Awdat al-Ruh* depicts the loves, joys, and sorrows of a middle-class family—a young student, his three uncles, and his spinster aunt —living in Cairo. The intense degree of harmony which characterizes their life is not unusual, but their wholly communal existence is remarkable, although at times it seems contrived and overdrawn. They share the same circumstances, the same emotions, and the same misfortunes. The men of the family fall in love with a neighbor girl, but she rejects them all. Together they join the revolt of 1919, and together they suffer imprisonment and disease. Al-Hakim leads the reader to believe that his primary purpose is to portray accurately the life of an ordinary family. But the forward behavior of the neighbor girl, Samiya, who seeks to allure the men with her physical charms, is thoroughly unreal-istic, and the family's apparent ignorance of the leader of the revolt is unbelievable.

Perhaps al-Hakim chose the family to symbolize the history of Egypt and its people since Pharaonic times. In the preface he produces a quotation from the *Book of the Dead* which relates the legend of Isis and Osiris. As Isis gathered the pieces of Osiris's body, restored life to it, and finally gave him eternal life, Samiya brings together the members of the family to compete for her love.[19] Although they fail to win the favor of the idol they worship, this failure unites them in their suffering and inspires them to give themselves for the greatest idol, Egypt, by joining the revolution.[20] To the author, the history of Egypt from Pharaonic times to the present is continuous, and the peasants are the descendants of once glorious ancestors. Their simple, oppressed life conceals their dynamic spirit and their inherited greatness and determination. Like their ancestors, they work and suffer together, and their primitive life is not an object of disdain, but a source of pride and dignity. Once these people find the idol which reflects their hopes and ideals, they will perform miracles. Egypt, which has slumbered for generations, waited to be aroused by her son (Sa'd Zaghlul, the great nationalist leader), a peasant like herself.

Like the works of Husayn and al-Mazini, *'Awdat al-Ruh* is largely autobiographical, but its fictional elements are so elaborately interwoven with its factual fabric as to make it a superb example of fertile imagination and ex-quisite taste. Its characters are earnest, understanding, and unselfish, con-scious of their existence and their ideals, and stern and unyielding in the face of adversity. But their participation in the revolt of 1919 is presented not as the consequence of the gradual development of their political views but as a sudden and impetuous action.[21] Al-Hakim's assumption that Egypt has preserved its old indomitable and immutable spirit misinterprets the reality of Egyptian society. Even more disturbing is the tenuous connection between the realistic and symbolic aspects of the novel. "The symbolic aspect," Haqqi comments, "seems majestic and is supported both by a dynasty of gods and by the *Book of the Dead,* while the realistic aspect contains childish narratives and events marked by ostentation, sham, and inconsistencies."[22] Moreover, al-Hakim received such bitter criticism for using colloquial Arabic in the dialogue—most surprisingly from al-Mazini, that he was compelled to withdraw his novel from circulation.[23] Still, he may be considered the first Egyptian writer to create a genuinely artistic and sophisticated novel. His later efforts, however, did not match the imagination, technical dexterity, and highly skilled characterization of *'Awdat al-Ruh.*

Abbas Mahumad al-'Aqqad's *Sarah* (1938) deviates sharply from the social analysis which marks much Egyptian fiction of his time. Al-'Aqqad is concerned not with his characters' moral and political principles, but with their emotional relationships and their reactions to sensual and physical intimacies. His heroine is a beautiful, warm, licentious female, ruled by her instincts rather than her mind, possessed of the supreme gift of femininity, yet so completely an abstraction that her name is not even mentioned until nearly sixty pages have gone by.[24] In brief, she is the same immortal Eve who throughout generations has learned to love, lie, and intrigue to conquer men.[25] The subject of the novel is the renewed relationship of Sarah and Humam, who were lovers in their youth; but this relationship is dominated by suspicion with the result that the characters lack freedom of action. *Sarah,* then, remains a series of disjointed sketches which do not develop into a coherent, plausible novel.[26] While its greatest merit is its analysis of woman's nature and the conflict between her reason and feminine instinct, Ali al-Ra'i seems correct in observing that the author's exaggerated portrayal of Sarah as a cheap, lustful woman has destroyed her image as a shrewd, spirited, intelligent woman capable of loving and worthy of being loved in return.[27]

Together with the growth of realism in Arabic fiction came an increased emphasis on society as a whole rather than on individual characters. This new trend reached its highest degree of sophistication in the works of Najib Mahfuz, who was greatly influenced by Taha Husayn. Educated at the Egyptian University, he began writing short stories and then turned to historical romances, but his excellence is made most evident in his non-historical novels. In Mahfuz's works the environment is not merely given an individual identity, but treated as a living reality; indeed, because it is slow to change, it becomes the dominant factor in the characters' behavior. Thus their lives begin, develop, and move toward a climax in logical sequence and with full dimensions.[28]

Mahfuz's *Khan al-Khalili* (1946) apparently focuses upon the love of two brothers for the same young girl, but in fact the author is as much concerned with the quarter of Cairo in which they live as with its inhabitants. The novel provides a true picture of the lives, hopes, and frustrations of middle-class Egyptians in the early years of World War II. *Zuqaq al-Midaqq* (Al-Midaqq Alley), published in 1947, is perhaps the most realistic of Mahfuz's novels, depicting the inhabitants of the Midaqq alley in all their poverty and ignorance. These people appear and disappear at intervals in the drama of life, while the alley remains eternally unchanged, always ready to serve as the stage for the actions of the occupants. Two less successful novels appeared during the next two years, and for seven years afterwards Mahfuz produced no new works.

But at last, in 1956, Mahfuz published *Bayn al-Qasrayn,* which was followed the next year by *Qasr al-Shawq* and *al-Sukkariyya.* Because the three novels relate the life story of three generations of the same family, they came to be known as the *Thulathiyya* (Trilogy). The *Thulathiyya* marks the high point in the development of artistically sophisticated Arabic fiction because of its cohesive structure, coordination of characterization, and connection of the behavior of its characters with their environment. Although the trilogy has been dismissed as a disjointed work lacking a central figure, its major character is in fact the Egyptian society of the period between 1917 and 1944. *Bayn al-Qasrayn* deals with the family of al-Sayyid Ahmad Abd al-Jawad, a conservative middle-class businessman, and covers the period from 1917 to 1919. Much of the focus is on Abd al-Jawad's tight control over the actions of the other members of the family and on the sharp differences between two of his sons, Yasin and Fahmi. Mahfuz also illustrates the varying effects upon the family of the national aspirations for independence, which culminated in the revolution of 1919. The events of the second novel, *Qasr al-Shawq,* cover the years from 1924 to 1927, and Abd al-Jawad evinces far more tolerance in his dealings with the members of his family. Fate is less kind, however, for Yasin is again unhappy in marriage, and Abd al-Jawad's daughter, A'isha, loses her husband and two of her children by typhoid. *Al-Sukkariyya,* the third novel, sees the deaths of Abd al-Jawad and his wife and the rise of the third generation. The activities of these younger characters reflect the diversity of Egypt itself in the middle of the twentieth century: one grandson holds fast to the traditional Muslim religious ideals, while his brother is attracted to Communism; Yasin's son, Radwan, repulsed by his father's life of marriages and divorces, devotes himself to a distinguished career in politics; A'isha's daughter, Na'ima, in obedience to her grandfather's authority, remains at home and receives no formal education. As the story of each character is brought to a logical conclusion, one is aware of the influence time has exerted both on the family of Abd al-Jawad and on the environment which conditions their actions. Thus, the *Thulathiyya* stands as a unique work in Egyptian fiction, one whose wide scope and universal values puts it on an equal level with universally acclaimed works of fiction.[29]

So the history of the growth of modern fiction in Egypt is, in large measure, an accelerated version of the development of modern fiction in the Western world. As the West has made its influence felt in the politics and economy of the Arab world, so has it affected Arabic fiction. Today, it is clear that the Egyptian novelists of the past fifty years have learned their craft well, and that they are capable of developing that larger vision which enables literature to transcend the limitations of time and place.

NOTES
CHAPTER I: HISTORICAL BEGINNINGS: EGYPT

1. For the life of 'Umar ibn Shabba al-Numayri and the description of his collection of tales, see Jurji Zaydan, *Tarikh Adab al-Lugha al-Arabiyya* (Cairo, 1911-1914), II, pp. 194 and 291.

2. *Maqama* (literally an assembly or seance) is in essence a romance whose events concern a shrewd, learned, and rhetorical hero who moves from place to place seeking adventure. It is retold by a *rawi* (narrator), who always meets with the hero, relates his adventures, and memorizes his composition. Its style is basically a *saj* (rhymed prose), which, although rigid and lifeless, yet is highly rhetorical. The theme in the *maqama* is secondary and always sacrificed for the florid style. See C. Brockelmann's *Geschichte der arabischen Literatur,* II, (Weimar, 1898-1902), 94 and his article "Makama" in the *Encyclopedia of Islam*. See also R.A. Nicholson, *A Literary History of the Arabs* (London, 1907), pp. 328-336.

3. In Part III of his *Studies on the Civilization of Islam* (Boston, 1962), Sir Hamilton A.R. Gibb has very admirably traced the development of modern Arabic literature in Syria and Egypt in the nineteenth century and has shown the influence of Westernization on this literature. Of particular interest is his systematic study of the factors which prevented the creation of indigenous prose works of entertainment in the Western style.

4. The hostility of these 'Ulama to the hummanities was even manifested in their opposition to the printing of the Qur'an in the time of Muhammad Ali. This problem of printing the Qur'an remained unsolved for nearly forty years. See Ibrahim Abduh, *al-Waqa'i al-Misriyya* 1828-1942 (Cairo, 1942), p. 7.

5. See Abd al-Rahman al-Jabarti, *'Aja'ib al-Athar fi al-Tarajim wa al-Akhbar* (Bulaq, 1297 A.H./A.D. 1879).

6. See Muhammad Rif'at, *Tarikh Misr al-Siyasi,* II, (Cairo, 1929), 118.

7. See Abd al-Rahman al-Rafi'i, *Tarikh al-Haraka al-Qawmiyya wa Nizam al-Hukm fi Misr,* 4th ed. (Cairo, 1955), Chapter I, passim.

8. See al-Jabarti, Chapter III. Al-Jabarti was an eyewitness to the French occupation of Egypt under Napoleon Bonaparte in 1798. His description of the behavior of the French shows clearly the reaction of a conservative Muslim to Western ideas.

9. Al-Shaykh Muhammad al-Mahdi al-Misri was born a Copt, but later embraced Islam. He became the rector of al-Azhar in 1812, and the French appointed him a member of the Diwan (Council) established by Napoleon. Al-Mahdi wrote many tales, similar to the *Thousand and One Nights*, which were compiled in a volume entitled *Tuhfat al-Mustayqiz al-Anis fi Nuzhat al-Mustan'im al Na'is*. See Zaydan, IV, 232. Another writer gives the title as *Tuhfat al-Mustayqiz al-Anis fi Nuzhat al-Mustanm wa al-Na'is*. Jacques Tajir, *Harakat al-Tarjama fi Misr Khilal al-Qarn al-Tasi' 'Ashr* (Cairo, 1946), p. 11.

10. In 1835 Marcel translated into French in three volumes Muhammad al-Mahdi's *Tuhfat al-Mustanim,* under the title *Contes du Cheikh El Mohde: Traduites de l'arabe d'après le manuscrit original.* In the introduction to this translation, Marcel refers to the close friendship between himself and al-Shaykh al-Mahdi and the manner in which he came to know about this manuscript. One day he asked al-Mahdi about a copy of the *Thousand and One Nights.* On the next day, al-Mahdi took a manuscript containing tales similar to those of the *Thousand and One Nights* to Marcel and presented it to him as a gift. Marcel remarks that the manuscript was in the handwriting of al-Shaykh al-Mahdi and adds, "I believe that he is the author, although he did not admit this." See Tajir, p. 11, and Clement Huart, *A History of Arabic Literature* (Beirut, 1966), pp. 425-426. For further information on J.J. Marcel, see A.M.B. "Marcel, Jean Joseph," *la Grande Encyclopédie Française* XXIII, 23, R.G. Canivet, *L'Imprimerie de l'Expédition d'Égypte, Les Journaux et les Procès-Verbaux de l'Institut, 1798-1801.* 5ème série, III (Alexandrie, 1909), 5-20 passim; F. Charles-Roux, *Bonaparte Gouverneur d'Égypte* (Paris, 1936), pp. 138-140; Ibrahim Abduh, *Tarikh al-Tiba'a wa al-Sihafa fi Misr Khilal al-Hamla al-Faransiyya* (Cairo, 1949), and Salaheddine Boustany, *The Press During the French Expedition 1798-1801* (n.p., 1954), pp. 7-15.

11. See Marcel, Translation of *Tuhfat al-Mustanim* entitled *Contes du Cheikh El-Mohde, Ibid.*

12. *Ibid.*

13. For the different schools established by Muhammad Ali, their operation and number of students see Zaydan, IV, 31-34; Ali Mubarak, *al-Khitat al-Tawfiqiyya,* XV (Bulaq, 1304 A.H./1886-8 A.D.), 53-55, and Abd al-Rahman al-Rafi'i, *'Asr Muhammad Ali,* (Cairo, 1951), pp. 380-392, 441, and 446-478. Perhaps the most thorough treatment of Egyptian schools both public and private in the nineteenth century is J. Heyworth-Dunne's *An Introduction to the History of Education in Modern Egypt* 2nd ed. (London, 1968). For Muhammad Ali's educational missions to Europe see Rifa'a Rifi' al-Tahtawi, *Takhlis al-Ibriz ila Talkhis Paris* (Cairo, 1905), p. 26; Ahmad Izzat Abd al-Karim, *Tarikh al-Ta'lim fi 'Asr Muhammed Ali* (Cairo, 1938), pp. 90-91 quoting Douin, *Une Mission Militaire de Meh, Ali,* 40 (de Boyer à Jomard, 20 mai, 1825); and Jamal al-Din al-Shayyal, *Tarikh al-Tarjama wa al-Haraka al-Thaqafiyya fi 'Asr Muhammad Ali* (Cairo, 1951), pp. 11-14 and al-Amir Umar Toson, *al-Ba'that al Ilmiyya fi Ahd Muhammad Ali* (Alexandria, 1934).

14. See Ali Mubarak, *al-Khitat al-Tawfiqiyya, Ibid.,* XV, 54; Abd al-Karim, pp. 328-341; by the same author, *Tarikh al-Ta'lim fi 'Asr Abbas wa Sa'id 1848-1863* (Cairo, 1946), pp. 58-61; and al-Shayyal, 38-44.

15. See al-Tahtawi, *Takhlis al-Ibriz fi Talkhis Paris* (Bulaq, 1834). The edition of 1905 comprises 263 medium-sized pages and is entitled *Kitab Takhlis al-Ibriz ila Talkhis Paris,* or *al-Diwan al-Nafis bi Iwan Paris, Being the Journey of the Distinguished Learned Man Rifa'a Bey Badawi Rafi al-Tahtawi, may God have mercy upon his soul.* Amen. Published through the effort of Mustafa Fahmi the bookseller, near al-Azhar in the year 1323 A.H./A.D. 1905.

16. See Albert Hourani, *Arabic Thought in the Liberal Age* 1798-1939 (Oxford University Press, 1970), pp. 67-84.

17. See Louis Awad, *al-Mu'aththirat al-Ajnabiyya fi al-Adab al-Arabi al-Hadith* (Cairo, 1962), Part I, *Qadiyyat al-Mar'a*, pp. 7-9.

18. See Rifa'a Rafi' al-Tahtawi, *Mawaqi' al-Aflak fi Waqa'i Tilimik* (Beirut, p. 451, 1867). *Télémaque* was later adapted for the stage by a Lebanese writer, Sa'd Allah al-Bustani, and was performed for the first time in July, 1869. See As'ad Daghir, Fann al-Tamthil fi Khilal Qarn:, *al-Mashriq*, XLII (1948).

19 See Abd al-Rahman al-Rafi'i, 'Asr Muhammad Ali (Cairo, 1951), Abd al-Karim, p. 58 and Jamal al-Din al-Shayyal, *Rifa'a Rafi' al-Tahtawi* (Cairo, 1958), pp. 39-40.

20. Al-Tahtawi's intention to express his grievance through allegory is evident from his introduction to *Mawaqi' al-Aflak*, p. 3.

21. See Izzat Abd al-Karim, *Tarikh al-Ta'im fi Misr: 'Asr Isma'il* (Cairo, 1945).

22. See Shafiq Ghirbal's introduction to Abd al-Karim, *Ibid*.

23. See Zaydan, IV, 32.

24. See Abd al-Rahman al-Rafi'i, *'Asr Isma'il* (Cairo, 1948), 1, 1-22 and Abd al-Karim, *Tarikh al-Ta'lim fi 'Asr Abbas wa Sa'id* 1848-1863, pp. 5-6. For a defense of the policies of Abbas I, see Toson, pp. 416-418.

25. Abd al-Muhsin Taha Badr, *Tatawwur al-Riwaya al-Arabiyya al-Haditha fi Misr 1870-1938* (Cairo, 1963), p. 26.

26. For the life and educational activities of Ali Mubarak, see *al-Khitat al-Tawfiqiyya*, IX passim; Zaydan, IV, 290 and Louis Cheikho, *al-Adab al-Arabiyya fi al-Qarn al-Tasi' 'Ashr* (Beirut, 1926), p. 11, p. 97, and al-Rafi'i, *Ibid.*, p. 1, pp. 207-241. 207-41.

27. Ali Mubarak, *'Alam al-Din*, 3 vols. (Cairo, 1888).

28. That the main purpose of Mubarak in writing this romance was didactic is evident from his introduction to *'Alam al-Din*, pp. 6-7.

29. *Ibid.*, II, 82-132.

30. *Ibid*.

31. *Ibid.*, II, 30-38.

32. Zaydan, IV, 33-36 and 44-45.

33. Muhammad 'Uthman Jalal ibn Yusuf al-Hasani al-Dana'i, born in 1829, enrolled in the School of Languages in al-Azbakiyya and later joined the staff of the Translation Bureau. He became a minister under the Khedive Tawfiq, and was appointed a judge in the Egyptian Court of Appeals and a judge in the Mixed Courts until his retirement in 1895. He died on January 16, 1898. See Cheikho, II, 100-101; Ali Mubarak, *al-Khitat al-Tawfiqiyya*, XVII, 111-118; Alyan Sarkis, *Mu'jam al Matbu'at al-Arabiyya wa al-Mu'arraba*, II, 1306-1307, (Cairo, 1928); Zaydan, IV, p. 245; and Tajir, pp. 103-104.

34. Muhammad Yusuf Najm has recently published the full texts of the five comedies of Molière which Jalal translated from the French, together with Jalal's only original play, *al-Khaddamin wa al-Mukhaddimin*. These Molière comedies are *Tartuffe, ou l'Imposteur* (al-Shaykh Matluf); *Les Femmes Savantes* (al-Nisa al-Alimat); *L'Ecole des Maris* (Madrasat al-Azwaj); *L'École des Femmes* (Madrasat al-Nisa); and *Les Fâcheux* (al-Thuqala). See Muhammad Yusuf Najm, *al-Masrah al-Arabi: Dirasat wa Nusus-Muhammad Uthman Jalal* (Beirut, 1964).

35. To realize the extent to which Jalal adapted the French text to suit the taste of his Egyptian audience, compare the following exchange from his translation of *Tar-*

tuffe, Act IV, Scene I, with the French text:

Matluf: Those who have known or heard of me will never believe that I have covetousness of inheritance. Whether little or plenty, there was a day when money delighted or attracted me, and if I accepted a gift from his father, it is because of wisdom unknown to you. I am afraid that this money will fall into the hands of unscrupulous men who will spend it on debauchery or fall into wicked hands. As for me, I will only spend this money in a lawful manner, and instead of drinking wine I shall drink pure water. I will also give to the poor, help the righteous and fulfill all the needs of the Muslims.

Tartuffe: Ceux qui me connoitront n'auront pas la pensée.

Que ce soit un effet d'une ama interéssée.

Tous les biens de ce mond ont pour moi pou d'appas;

De leur éclat trompeur je ne m'éblouit pas;

Et, si je me résous à receivoir du père

Cette donation qu'il a voulu me faire,

Ce n'est, à dire vrai, que parce que je crains

Que tout ce bien ne tombe en de méchantes mains;

Qu'il ne trouve des gens qui, l'ayant en partage,

En fassent dans le monde un criminel usage,

Et ne s'en servent pas, ainsi que j'ai dessein,

Pour la gloire du Ciel et le bien du prochain.

For an elaborate study of Molière's plays which Jalal adapted see Muhammad Yusuf Najm, *al-Masrahiyya fi al-Adab al-Arabi al-Hadith* (Beirut, 1967), pp. 273-288. The Arabic text of *al-Shaykh Matluf* is in Najm, *al-Masrah al-Arabi*, pp. 9-92. For further opinion on whether Jalal's work was a faithful translation from the French or mere adaptation, see Louis 'Awad, *Dirasat fi Adabina al-Hadith* (Cairo, 1961), pp. 144-51.

36. Muhammad 'Uthman Jalal, *al-'Uyun al-Yawaqiz fi al-Amthal wa al-Hikam wa al-Mawa'iz* (Bulaq, 1313 A.H./A.D. 1895), the introduction, p. 2. This introduction is reproduced in Mahmud Hamid Shawkat, *al-fann al-Qisasi fi al-Adab al-Misri al-Hadith* 1800-1956 (Cairo, 1956), pp. 72-73.

37. On this point see Mahmud Hamid Shawkat, *Ibid.*, p. 42.

38. The texts he adapted not only reflected aspects of French society at that time, but also revealed the domestic troubles, frustrations, and passions of the authors. This particular quality is especially notable in the case of Molière, and when Jalal's version of *L'École des Femmes (Madrasat al-Nisa)* was performed twice in February and March, 1895, on the stage of Sulayman al-Qirdahi in Alexandria, it met with widespread popular objection for its treatment of problems thought to be irrelevant to Egyptian society at that time. See *al-Masrah al-Arabi: Muhammad 'Uthman Jalal,* ed. Muhammad Yusuf Najm (Beirut, 1964), p. 2 of the introduction.

39. The Khedive Isma'il supported morally and financially those papers which promoted his ideas as well as the interests of Egypt to the Ottoman government such as *al-Jawa'ib* founded by Ahmad Faris al-Shidyaq, and *Wadi al-Nil*, by Abd Allah Abu al-Su'ud. On the other hand, he suspended and even persecuted the publishers of papers that opposed his policies, such as *Nuzhat al-Afkar,* jointly published by Ibrahim al-Muwaylihi and Muhammad 'Uthman Jalal, and *Abu Naz-*

zara, by Ya'qub Sanu, whom the Khedive expelled from Egypt. See Tarrazi, *Tarikh al-Sihafa al-Arabiyya* I (Beirut, 1913), 61-69 and 78, and II, 254, 283-284.

40. For al-Afghani's ideas and their impact on Egyptian society see Nikki R. Kiddie, *"Sayyid Jamal ad-Din al-Afghani:* A Case of Posthumous Charisma?" in *Philosophers and Kings: Studies in Leadership,* ed. Dankwart A. Rustow (New York, 1970, pp. 148-179, and by the same author *Sayyid Jamal ad-Dinal-Afghani: A Political Biography* (University of California Press, Berkeley, 1970). See also *al-A'mal al-Kamila li Jamal al-Din al-Afghani,* ed. Muhammad Imara (Cairo, 1968), Albert Hourani, *Ibid.,* entire Chapter 5. Muhammad Pasha al-Makhzumi, *Khatirat Jamal al-Din al-Afghani al-Husayni* (Beirut, 1931); Abd al-Qadir al-Maghribi, *Jamal al-Din al-Afghani* (Cairo, 1948); Eli Kedourie, *Afghani and Abduh: An Essay on Religious Unbelief and Political Activism* (London, 1966); and Charles Adam, *Islam and Modernism in Egypt* (Oxford U. Press 1933), Chapter I.

41. See Kiddie "Sayyid Jamal al-Din al-Afghani," *Ibid.,* p. 170; Muhammad Rashid Rida, *Tarikh al-Ustadh al-Imam al-Shaykh Muhammad Abduh,* I (Cairo, 1350 A.H./A.D. 1931), 42-53; and Cheikho, *Tarikh al-Adab al-Arabiyya fi al-Rub al-Awwal min al-Qarn al-Ishrin* (Beirut, 1926), p. 9. See also the treatise titled *Jamal al-Din al-Afghani* by the Imam al-Sayyid Muhsin al-Amin (n.d., n.p.); Zaydan, *Tarajim Mashahir al-Sharq,* II, (Cairo, 1902-1903), 55; Tarrazi, *Tarikh al-Sihafa al-Arabiyya,* II, 293-299; and Ahmad Amin, *Zu'ama al-Islah* (Cairo, 1965), pp. 59-120. See Kiddie, "Sayyid Jamal al-Din al-Afghani, etc.," *Ibid.,* p. 170.

42. Hafiz Ibrahim, *Layali Satih,* ed. Abd al-Rahman Sidqi (Cairo, 1964), p. 39.

43. See sources above in footnote 41. See Muhammad Abduh's introduction to al-Afghani's treatise entitled *al-Radd 'ala al-Dahriyyin,* 4th ed. (Cairo, 1333 A.H.), p. 15, and Muhammad Pasha al-Makhzumi, *Khatirat Jamal al-Din al-Afghani al-Husayni* (Beirut, Sadir press, 1931, p. 67, and J. M. Ahmad, *The Intellectual Origins of Egyptian Nationalism* (Oxford University Press, 1960), p. 16.

44. See J. M. Ahmad, *Ibid.*

45. Al-Shaykh Muhammad Abduh, "al-Kutub al-'Ilmiyya wa Ghayruha," *al-Ahram* (May, 1881). For the life and thought of Muhammad Abduh, see Muhammad Rashid Rida, *Ibid;* Hourani, Chapter 6; Charles Adams, *Islam and Modernism in Egypt* (Oxford U. Press, 1933), entire Chapter VIII; Osman Amin, *Muhammad Abduh,* translated by C. Wendell, (American Council of Learned Societies, Washington, 1953); Eli Keddourie, *Afghani and Abduh: An Essay on Religious Unbelief and Political Activism* (London, 1966).

46. See sources in the previous footnote.

47. See Zaydan, IV, 243-244.

48. See Abd al-Muhsin Taha Badr, *Tatawwur al-Riwaya al-Arabiyya al-Haditha fi Misr 1870-1938,* (Cairo, 1963), p. 37.

49. See Zaydan, IV, pp. 19-20.

50. See Ahmad Fathi Zaghluls' introduction to his Arabic translation of Demolins' *A quotitient la superiorité des Anglo-Saxons* (Sirr Taqaddum al-Ingiliz al-Saksuniyyin); (Cairo, 1899), p. 92, and Cheikho, *Tarikh Adab al-Lugha al-Arabiyya fi al-Rub' al-Awwal min al-Qarn al-Ishrin,* p. 92.

51. Badr, *Ibid.,* pp. 37-38, and 41-42.

52. Muhammad Abd al-Muttalib and Abd al-Mu'ti Mar'i, *Hayat Muhalhil aw Harb al-Basus* (Cairo, 1911), p. 3.

53. See Zaydan, IV, 230.

Another pioneer writer and novelist, the Palestinian Khalil Ibrahim Baydas (d. 1949), praises the novel and considers it an effective means of promoting culture and morals as well as a delightful source of entertainment. He encourages the translation of Western fiction into Arabic and makes it clear that he had intended to promote fiction in his periodical *al-Nafa'is*. See his introduction to the first issue of *al-Nafa'is* (October, 1908) and his introduction to his anthology of short stories entitled *Masarih al-Adhhan* (Cairo, 1924), pp. 13-14.

54. See Ahmad Hasan al-Zayyat's editorial in al-Risala, No. 183 (1937).

55. Zaydan, IV, 44-45, and Badr, pp. 41-2.

CHAPTER II: THE RISE OF THE ARAB DRAMA IN SYRIA AND EGYPT

1. See Tawfiq al-Hakim's *introduction to his al-Malik Odib* (King Oedipus), (Cairo, 1949), pp. 10-11; Muhammad Mandur, *Masrahiyyat Shawqi* (Cairo, 1954), pp. 3-12; and by the same author, *al-Masrah,* (Cairo, 1963), pp. 17-19. But a native European post-classical drama developed from the Catholic Mass, without apparent connection with Greek or Roman drama.

2. See Aristotle's *Poetics,* trans, into Arabic by Abu Bishr Matta ibn Yunus in Abd al-Rahman Badawi, *Fann al-Shi'r* (Cairo, 1953), pp. 95-96.

3. See Sa'id Taqi al-Din's play, *Lawla al-Muhami,* (If It Were Not for the Attorney), (Beirut, 1924), the introduction; Edward Hunayn's discussion of the reasons which prevented the rise of the Arabic drama in *al-Mashriq* (1930), XXXII, 563, and by the same author *Shawqi 'ala al-Masrah* (Shawqi on the Stage), (Beirut, 1936), the introduction. A contemporary critic states that Hunayn's judgment is improvised and mostly based on the biased deductions of Father Henri Lammens. See Hashim Yaghi, *al-Naqd al-Adabi al-Hadith fi Lubnan* II (Cairo, 1968), 157. See also Tawfiq al-Hakim's introduction to his work *al-Malik Odib* (King Oedipus), *Ibid.*, pp. 10-11; Muhammad Mandur, *Masrahiyyat Shawqi, Ibid.*, pp. 3-12; and by the same author, *al-Masrah, Ibid.*, pp. 17-19. Of particular interest is Georg Jacob's *Geschichte des Schattentheaters* (Berlin, 1907), p. 93.

4. See Izz al-Din Isma'il, *Qadaya al-Insan fi al-Adab al-Masrahi al-Mu'asir* (Cairo, n.d.), pp. 49-50. Isma'il's opinions have been attacked on the ground that he is influenced by Western writers who have glorified the creativity of the Arian intellect and its supremacy over other intellects. This Arian intellectual supremacy, these critics maintain, has created an inferiority complex in modern Arab writers like Isma'il, who cannot more believe that the ancient Arabs were creative people. These critics argue that if this is true, how could then these same ancient Arabs create highly polished and perfected types of poetry? Al-Hifni believes that customs and traditions, not biological deficiency or lack of creativity, prevented the ancient Arabs from composing the drama. See Abd al-Mun'im al-Hifni, "Al-Ruh al-Arabi fi al-Adab wa al-Fann," *Adab* (Beirut, 1963), No. 7, pp. 68-72. Still another contemporary Arab writer attributes the Arabs' ignorance of the drama to the attitude of the Christian church in the sixth century A.D. 'Umar states that the Greek drama was considered by the church as a pagan literature which should be suppressed. He argues that if this particular genre were available to the translators of the early Abbasid period they would have translated it into Arabic. See Mustafa Ali 'Umar, *al-Waqi'yya fi al-Masrah al-Misri* (Alexandria, 1968), p. 112.

5. The study of the Arab shadow plays of Ibn Daniyal has interested both Eastern and Western writers. Pioneer Western writings on the shadow-play in Georg Jacob, *Zur Geschichte des Schattenspiels* (Keleti Szemle, i. (Budapest, 1900), pp.

233-236; *Drei arab. Schattenspiele aus dem 13. Jahrhundert* (ib. ii (1902), 76; *Das Schattentheater in seiner Wanderung vom Morgenland zum Abendland* (Berlin, 1901), *Textbroben aus dem Escorial-Codex des Muhammad ibn Daniyal* (Erlangen, 1902), and *Geschichte des Schattentheaters,* already cited. Also of interest is Th. Menzel, "Khayal-i-Zill," *The Encyclopedia of Islam,* II (London, 1927), 934-935. See also, Jacob Landau, *Studies in the Arab Theater and Cinema* (Philadelphia, 1958), pp. 9-47, footnotes 32 and 33. Eastern writings include Ibrahim Hamada, *Khayal al-Zill wa Tamthiliyyat Ibn Daniyal* (Cairo, 1963), in which the author produces the text of the plays with the history and analytical study of these plays, and Jurji Zaydan, *Tarikh Adab al-Lugha al-Arabiyya,* IV (Cairo, 1913), 111-121.

6. Landau, *Ibid.,* and Hamada, pp. 62-76. Edward William Lane states that "the puppet show of 'Kara-gyooz' has been introduced into Egypt by Turks, in whose language the puppets are made to speak." But he goes on to say that these puppet shows were meant to amuse the Turks residing in Cairo and did not appeal to the natives who do not understand Turkish. However, Hamada has demonstrated that this theory is incorrect. See Edward William Lane, *An Account of the Manners and Customs of the Modern Egyptians* (London, 1895), pp. 396-397; Hamada, pp. 62-76.

7. For a short account of the shadow play in Syria and North Africa see Landau, pp. 33-45.

8. See M. C. Niebuhr, *Travels Through Arabia and Other Countries in the East.* Trans. Robert Heron I (Edinburgh, 1792), pp. 143-144.

9. Lane, p. 395.

10. For a full description of this play see Lane, pp. 395-396.

11. Jonquiere (C. De la) *l'Expédition d'Égypte,* II, (1798-1801), (Paris, 1899), 382.

12. Abd al-Rahman al-Jabarti, *'Aja'ib al-Athar fi al-Tarajim wa al-Akhbar,* 111, 139.

13. Zaydan, *Ibid.,* IV, pp. 152-153.

14. *Ibid.*

15. Gérard De Nerval, *Voyage en Orient,* I (Paris, 1867), 109-111. See also the English translation of this work made by Conrad Elphinstone under the title *The Women of Cairo,* I (London, 1929), 88-91.

16. A. Regnault, *Voyage en Orient; Grèce, Turquie, Égypte* (Paris, 1855), p. 438.

17. Louis Gardey, *Voyage du Sultan Abd-ul-Aziz de Stanbul au Cairo* (Paris, 1865), p. 103.

18. Dr. Staquez, *l'Égypte, la Basse Nubi, et le Sinai,* p. 63, quoted by Muhammad Yusuf Najm, *al-Masrahiyya fi al-Adab al-Arabi al-Hadith 1847-1914* (Beirut, 1967), pp. 19-25.

19. See Nevill Barbour, "The Arabic Theatre in Egypt," *Bulletin of the School of Oriental Studies* (London, 1935-1937), p. 173.

20. About the life and activity of Marun Naqqash see *Arzat Lubnan* (Beirut, 1869) compiled by Marun's brother, Niqula Naqqash. This volume contains Marun's three dramas *al-Bakhil, Abu al-Hasan al-Muqhaffal aw Harun al-Rashid,* and *al-Salit al-Hasud.* It also contains an introduction, a short biography of Marun, and his views about the theater. It is appended by poems composed by Marun and other poems in his eulogy. The three dramas by Marun are partially annotated by the compiler. What is peculiar, however, is that the title page ascribed the whole

work to Marun himself. It states"Arzat Lubnan composed by the able, learned and eminent Man of Letters, the late Marun Naqqash." See Louis Cheikho, *al-Adab al-Arabiyya fi al-Qarn al-Tasi 'Ashr,* I (Beirut, 1924), 106-109; Zaydan, *Tarikh Adab al-Lugha al-Arabiyya,* IV, 154-157; Zaki Tulaymat, "Nahdat al-Tamthil fi al-Sharq al-Arabi," *al-Hilal* (April, 1939), p. 144; and by the same author "Kayfa Dakhala al-Tamthil Bilad al-Sharq," *al-Kitab* (February, 1945), p. 582; Barbour, *Ibid.,* pp. 174-175; Fu'ad Afram al-Bustani, "Awwal Masrahiyya bi al-Lugha al-Arabiyya," *al-Shira'* (1948), No. 1 and No. 3; Najm, *al-Masrahiyya fi al-Adab al-Arabi al-Hadith,* pp. 31-40; and by the same author his edition of Naqqash's dramas in *Marun Naqqash: Dirasat wa Nusus* (Beirut, 1961).

21. See *Arzat Lubnan,* p. 388 and Najm, *al-Masrahiyya fi al-Adab al-Arabi al-Hadith,* pp. 33-35.

22. According to Zaydan, *Ibid,* IV, 153 and 250-251, the drama *al-Bakhil* was staged before the beginning of the literary renaissance in Beirut and ten years prior to the establishment of Arabic newspapers in Syria. The guests Naqqash invited to the performance at his home included foreign consuls and the dignitaries of Beirut. Soon news of this drama spread, and it was even written about in the European press. (There was no press in Syria at the time). *Al Bakhil* was reprinted through the efforts of Nasim Murad and Shukri al-Khuri and published in Sao Paulo, Brazil in 1916. See Yusuf As'ad Daghir, "Fann al-Tamthil fi Khilal Qarn," *al-Mashriq,* XLII (1948), 446.

23. *Arzat Lubnan,* pp. 11 and 388; Zaydan, *Ibid.,* IV, 154; Barbour, *Ibid.,* p. 174; and Najm, *Ibid.,* pp. 35-38.

24. *Arzat Lubnan,* p. 6; Zaydan, *Ibid.,* IV, 154.

25. Salim al-Naqqash, "Fawa'id al-Riwayat aw al-Tiyatrat," *al-Jinan,* (1875), p. 521.

26. *Arzat Lubnan,* p. 389.

27. *Arzat Lubnan,* p. 6.

28. Zaydan, IV, p. 154.

29. Najm, Ibid., pp. 416-417. Compare Molière's *L'Avare,* Act I, Scene 2 with *al-Bakhil,* Act I, Scene 5.

30. Molière's *L'Avare* deals with the petty attitudes of a miser who is extremely avaricious. But no matter how ugly and deformed, this miser, like other men, is a human being. He loves to be flattered beyond belief. He wants to marry a young, pretty girl—provided his marriage brings him financial gain, because money is his chief love. His love of money even tempts him to sacrifice the happiness of his own children if it collides with his own. While he vies with his son to wed the same pretty young lady for pure selfish interest, he denies his daughter the right to marry the man she loves. He would rather have her marry an old but wealthy friend of his.

31. *Arzat Lubnan,* p. 90.

32. *Ibid.,* and Jacob M. Landau, *Studies in the Arab Theater and Cinema* (Philadelphia, 1958), pp. 57-58.

33. *Arzat Lubnan, Ibid.,* p. 16.

34. For example, when Hind discovers that her father has determined to marry her to the miser and deformed Qarrad she laments her bad luck and cruel traditions which were the cause of her misfortune by singing a highly sentimental verse which must have excited the emotion of the audience. *Al-Bakhil,* Act II, Scene 1.

35. *Ibid.*, pp. 25-26. For the index of melodies see *Ibid.*, pp. 93-107. Two of these melodies are based on popular French songs. One of them is based on the song "Malbrough s'en va t'en guerre." Both are still known in Lebanon. The Arabic version of the second one is probably "Mabruk Safar 'ala al-Harb," "Mabruk went to War."

36. *Ibid.*, pp. 26-27.

37. See Najm, *al-Masrah al-Arabi: Dirasat wa Nusus-Marun Naqqash*, p. 23.

38. *Arzat Lubnan*, p. 110.

39. See Landau, pp. 58-59, and Najm, *al-Masrahiyya fi al-Adab al-Arabi al-Hadith*, p. 369.

40. *Arzat Lubnan*, p. 324. In another place Niqula Naqqash makes the following observation, "This romance is unique in this art. It is one of the most beautiful of all his [Marun] compositions," *Ibid.*, p. 389. Yusuf As'ad Daghir states without justification that Naqqash's *al-Salit al-Hasud* is a condensation of one of Molière's plays. See Yusuf As'ad Daghir, "Fann al-Tamthil fi Khilal Qarn," *al-Mashriq*, XLII (1948), 457.

41. The author could have ended his drama with the marriage of Rachel to Ishaq al-Qudsi. But for no demonstrable reason he engages Sim'an and the rest of the cast in unnecessary intrigues. Thus, his finale becomes flat and inept.

42. For the sake of analogy we may present here these similar dialogues in both *al-Salit al-Hasud* and in *Le Bourgeois Gentilhomme*. *Al-Salit al-Hasud*, Act I, Scene 4:

    Abu Isa: You may know my beloved that prose is not verse. It is the speech commonly used by the public. What is prose, therefore, is not verse and what is verse is not prose.

    Jirjis: I have learned and understood its meaning now. So, if I tell my servant to hand me my turban and help me wear my slippers I would then be using prose...I am almost thirty years old now and had no idea that I have been speaking in prose all that time.

    Le Bourgeois Gentilhomme, Act II, Scene 4:

    Maître de Philosophie. Par la raison, Monsieur, qu'il n'y a pour s'exprimer que la prose, ou les vers.

    M. Jourdain. Il n'ya que la prose ou les vers?

    M. de Phil. Non, Monsieur: tout ce qui n'est point prose est vers; et tout ce que n'est point vers est prose.

    M. Jourdain. Et comme l' on parle qu'est-ce que c'est donc que cela?

    M. de Phil. De la prose.

    M. Jourdain. Quoi? guand je dis: "Nicole, apportez-moi mes pantoufles, et me donnez mon bonnet de nuit," c'est de la prose?

    M. de Phil. Oui, Monsieur.

    M. Jourdain. Par ma foi! il y a plus de quarante ans que je dis de la prose mans que j'en susse rien, et je vous suis le plus oblige du monde de m'avoir apprise cela.

43. *Les Précieuses Ridicules,* Act I, Scene 9, and *al-Salit al-Hasud,* Act II, Scenes 7, 8 and 9.

44. *Al-Salit al-Hasud,* Act III, Scene 4 in *Arzat Lubnan,* p. 389.

45. *Arzat Lubnan*, p. 324.

46. David Urquhart, *The Lebanon (Mount Souria): History and a Diary* II (London, 1860), 178-181, and Najm, *al-Masrahiyya fi al-Adab al-Arabi al-Hadith,* pp. 35-38.

47. Zaydan, *Tarikh Adab al-Lugha al-Arabiyya,* IV, 154, and Najm, *Ibid.,* p. 52. The title page of al-Bustani's Arabic version reads thus: *Riwayat Tilimak Ta'lif* (Composed by) *al-Mu'allim* (Master) *Sa'd Allah Effendi al-Bustani* (Cairo, n.d.). Also it includes July, 1869, as the date of its performance.

48. Of the plays performed on the stage of al-Sharfa Monastery we may cite *Adam wa Hawwa* (Adam and Eve) in 1886, written by a clergyman; *Yusuf al-Hasan ibn Ya'qub* (Joseph the Fair, Son of Jacob) in 1869, written by Rev. Stephen al-Shamali; *Malik Faris* (A Horseman King), translated from the Italian by Rev. Yusuf Mi'mar Bashi and performed on February 27, 1884; *Ihsan al-Insan* (The Charity of Man), written by Rev. Mikha'il Dallal, and *al-Fatat al-Kharsa* (The Dumb Girl) by the same author. See Yusuf As'ad Daghir, "Fann al-Tamthil fi Khilal Qarn," *al-Mashriq,* XLII (1948), 434 and 438; XLIII (1949) 272 and 296; and Najm, *Ibid.,* pp. 51-2.

49. The Jewish school of Zaki Cohen usually performed a play at the beginning and one at the end of each academic year. Of the plays performed by this school we may cite *Intisar al-Fadila aw Hadithat al-Ibna al-Isra'iliyya* (The Triumph of Virtue or the Incident of the Israeli Girl), composed by Salim Cohen and performed in 1894 and 1895. Najm, *Ibid.,* pp. 52-3 quoting Niqula Fayyad, *Dhikrayat Adabiyya,* being one of a series of lectures delivered at al-Nadwa al-Lubnaniyya (The Lebanese Club). See also the number of *al-Ahram,* newspaper cited by Najm in this regard. Najm, *Ibid.*

50. Most if not all of the plays performed by the Jesuit College were of a religious nature since the main objective of the college was religious. The following are some of the plays (whose titles are given in English); *The Sentence Herod Passed Over His Two Sons, The Martyrdom of St. George, Zedekiah, David and Jonathan.* Other plays whose themes were drawn from Arab history, include *Wafa al-Khansa* (The Faithfulness of the Poetess al-Khansa) *Shuhada Najran* (The Martyrs of Najran), *Ibn al-Samaw'al* (The Son of) *al-Samaw'al, al-Muhalhil, Nakbat al-Baramika* (The Calamity of the Barmecides) *Ikhwan al-Khansa* (The Brothers of the Poetess al-Khansa), *Abdalonim the King of Sidon.* It is interesting that Rev. Cheikho provides this information to show that the Christian Catholic schools restored acting to its dignified position after it had been abused by others. After crediting Marun Naqqash with the introduction of the theater to Beirut, Cheikho, who always judged aesthetic literature from a somewhat narrow religious view, remarks that acting was abused by public stages where many immoral plays were performed. The results were harmful. Cheikho, *al-Adab al-Arabiyya,* II, 70.

51. Tarrazi, *Tarikh al-Sihafa al-Arabiyya,* II, 69; Cheikho, *al-Adab al-Arabiyya,* II, p. 127; and Najm, p. 31. This society was established in 1847 and was officially recognized by the Ottoman government in 1868. It contained 150 members, mostly from Beirut. Some of them came from Hims, Damascus, as well as from Constantinople. One of its members was Salim al-Bustani whose dramas were performed by the society.

52. Zaydan, IV, p. 82.

53. Tannus al-Jirr, *al-Shabb al-Jahil al-Sikkir* (The Foolish and Drunken Young Man), Najm, pp. 57 and 397-399. It was performed in Beirut in 1863 and published in B'abda, Lebanon, in 1900.

54. Zaydan says that he saw this play himself in Beirut in 1878. Zaydan, IV, 157. Khalil al-Yaziji, *al-Muru'a wa al-Wafa* (Chivalry and Fidelity), (Beirut, 1884). Al-Yaziji adapted this verse drama from an original romance entitled *al-Nu'man wa Hanzala* written by Khalil al-Khuri, already mentioned. This drama was translated into French by Michel Sursuq. See Yusuf As'ad Daghir, *Masadir al-Dirasa al-Adabiyya* II (Beirut, 1956), 346.

55. Zaydan, IV, 157.

56. The translated text of *Andromache* is to be found in *al-Durar*, which is a selection of the works of Adib Ishaq, compiled by his brother, 'Awni Ishaq, and published in Beirut in 1909. *Al-Durar*, pp. 533-573. Another undated version which may be earlier than this one carries the title *Andromache A Tragedy in Five Acts by the Renowned Poet, Writer and Orator Izzatlu Adib Bey Ishaq.*

57. Tarrazi, *al-Sihafa al-Arabiyya*,1, 137.

58. Of al-Ahdab's plays we may mention *Alexandre of Macedon, The Sword and the Pen, al-Mu'tamid ibn Abbad, Riwayat al-Wazir Abi al-Walid ibn Zaydun. Tuhfat al-Rushdiyya fi 'Ulum al-Arabiyya* and others. Rashid Pasha was so pleased with al-Ahdab's work that he asked him to perform his play *Alexander of Macedon* in Damascus. See Tarrazi, II, 103-104. The most comprehensive collection of original and translated dramas is Yusuf As'ad Daghir, "Fann al-Tamthil fi Khilal Qarn," *al-Mashriq* XLII (1948), 434, and XLIII (1949), 118 and 296.

59. Tarrazi, II, 122.

60. *Arzat Lubnan*, p. 3.

61. *Ibid.*, p. 5.

62. Shakir al-Khuri, *Majma' al Masarrat* (Beirut, 1908), p. 445.

63. *Arzat Lubnan*, p. 5.

64. Muhammad Yusuf Najm published five dramas by Salim Naqqash with an introduction. Najm complains that he has been unable to discover the originals from which Naqqash adapted his dramas. See Muhammad Yusuf Najm, *al-Masrah al-Arabi: Dirasat wa Nusus—Salim al-Naqqash* (Beirut, 1964). The dramas which this anthology contains are *Aida,* composed by August Marriette Pasha and scored by Verdi; *May,* an adaptation of Corneille's *Horace;* and *al-Kadhub,* an adaptation of Molière's *Le Menteur.* Naqqash adapted this drama specifically to suit Lebanese audiences, which perhaps was the reason it was not well received when it was performed in Egypt. Other dramas are *al-Zalum* (The Tyrant) and *Ghara'ib al-Sudaf* (The Strangeness of Coincidences). The first one sometimes appeared under the Arabic title *Hifz al-Widad* and the second one under the title *Salim wa Asma.*

65. Zaydan, IV, 287 and Cheikho, *al-Adab al-Arabiyya fi al-Qarn al-Tasi' 'Ashr,* II, 153.

66. *Ibid.*

67. Salim al-Bustani, "al-Riwayat al-Khedaywiyya al-Tashkhisiyya," *al-Jinan* (Beirut, 1875), pp. 694-696. Al-Bustani himself had probably seen the performance of this drama. He is incorrect in stating that it was composed by Salim Naqqash.

68. *Ibid.*

69. *Al-Jinan* (1875), p. 521, and Najm, *al-Masrahiyya fi al-Adab al-Arabi al-Hadith*, p. 94.

70. Al-Jinan, *Ibid.*, p. 422, and Najm, p. 95.

71. On December 16, 1876 *al-Ahram* announced the arrival of Salim Naqqash's troupe in Alexandria and its forthcoming performance of Marun's drama *Abu al-Hasan al-Mughaffal* on Saturday, December 23, 1876 at 8:30 p.m. at the Zizinya theater. See a summary of *al-Ahram's* announcement in Najm, *al-Masrahiyya fi al-Adab al-Arabi al-Hadith*, pp. 96-97.

72. From French fiction Ishaq translated *Andromache* by Racine, *Charlemagne* whose author is not known to us, and *La Belle Parisienne* by Contesse Dash. See 'Awni Ishaq, *al-Durar* (Beirut, 1909), pp. 5-15; Tarrazi, I, 134-135 and II, 105-109 and 150, 257-258; Zaydan *Tarikh Adab al-Lugha al-Arabiyya*, IV, 274-275; and by the same author *Tarajim Mashahir al-Sharq* II (Beirut, Dar al-Hayst) 3rd., 94-100.

73. Tarrazi, II, 107, and Yusuf As'ad Daghir, "Fann al-Tamthil fi Khilal Qarn," *al-Mashriq* XLII (1948), 449.

74. According to Zaydan, Salim Naqqash and Adib Ishaq left the troupe and devoted their effort to journalism in 1878. Zaydan, *Tarikh Adab al-Lugha al-Arabiyya*, IV, 155 and Rashid Rida, *Tarikh al-Ustadh al-Imam al-Shaykh Muhammad Abduh*, l, 45; Barbour, *Ibid.*, p. 174 and Najm, pp. 100-101.

75. The full Arabic title of this drama is *May Trajidiyya Dhat Thalathat Fusul Ta'lif Salim Khalil Naqqash al-Maruni* (May Tragedy in Three Acts composed by Salim Khalil Naqqash the Maronite and finished on January 2, 1868), (Beirut, the College's Press, 1875). Considering the date of publication and Naqqash's statement that he had "composed it" eight years ago, he must have finished its adaptation into Arabic in 1867 not 1878.

76. *Al-Durar,* p. 559, and Najm, p. 215.

77. Zaydan, IV, 154 and *al-Ahram* (September 28, 1877), and by Najm, *Ibid.*, p. 103 and p. 106, footnote l.

78. Zaydan, IV, 155, and Barbour, *Ibid.*, p. 175. Najm refers to *al-Tijara* (March 31, 1879) claiming that Yusuf Khayyat and his troupe did not leave Egypt as Zaydan states but were still performing on the Zizinya theater. He speculates that Khayyat and his troupe might have remained in hiding somewhere in Alexandria. Najm, *al-Masrahiyya fi al-Adab al-Arabi al-Hadith*, p. 104.

79. Zaydan, IV, 155, and Najm, pp. 107-115. Generally, the plays performed by al-Qirdahi were either adaptations of foreign plays or were reconstructions of past Arab history.

80. Kamil al-Khal'i, *al-Musiqi al-Sharqi,* (Damascus, 1948) and Adham al-Jundi "al-'Abqariyya al-Shamikha: Abu Khalil al-Qabbani," *al-Fayha* (Damascus, July 12, 1952) quoted by Najm, pp. 61-62.

81. Muhammad Kurd Ali, *Khitat al-Sham* VI, (Damascus, 1925), 111-112 and 143-144; Tarrazi.

82. Muhammad Kurd Ali, *Ibid.,* IV, 111.

83. Najm, *Al-Masrahiyya fi al-Adab al-Arabi al-Hadith,* pp. 62-65.

84. *Ibid.*, p. 65.

85. See Najm, *al-Masrah al-Arabi: Dirasat wa Nusus—al-Shaykh Ahmad Abu Khalil al-Qabbani* (Beirut, 1963), the introduction, p. 3.

86. *Ibid.*, pp. 355-400.

87. Shakir Mustafa, *Muhadarat an al-Qissa fi Suriyya hatta al-Harb al-'Alamiyya al-Thaniya* (Cairo, 1958), p. 190. Al-Qabbani, as Najm suggests, might have read some Western dramas translated into Turkish. Najm, *al-Masrahiyya fi al-Adab al-Arabi al-Hadith,* p. 64.

88. See al-Khal'i, *Ibid.;* al-Gaylani, *Ibid.,* p. 65; and Mustafa, pp. 189-90. Mustafa rejects Muhammad Kurd Ali's statement that al-Qabbani staged *Nakir al-Jamil* in 1865 during the term of the governor Subhi Pasha on the ground that Subhi Pasha became governor of Syria in 1871.

89. It is reported that Midhat Pasha allowed Iskandar Farah, who was an employee of the Damascus Customs, to attend to his duty one hour a day only in order to devote the rest of the time to the training of actors. He also gave Farah twenty thousand piasters to purchase costumes and other materials for the stage. See Qustandi Rizq, *Tarikh al-Musiqa al-Sharqiyya* II, (Cairo, n.d.), 171; Najm, pp. 66-68 and 125-133; Mustafa, pp. 191-192; Barbour, p. 176; and Landau, p. 69.

90. During the Friday prayer, which Sultan Abd al-Hamid performed with great pageant and pomp, al-Ghabra popped out of the masses to admonish the Sultan with ardent zeal against the "hellish heresy which has jeopardized the creed of the Muslims."

> Help, O Commander of the Faithful, immorality and
> debauchery have spread in al-Sham (Syria), Women's honor
> has been shattered, virtue has died, morality has been buried,
> and women have mingled with men.

See Rizq, *Ibid.,* and Najm, pp. 67-68.

91. Barbour, p. 176, footnote 2. For the folk song ridiculing al-Qabbani and accusing him of corrupting the morals of young men and women, see al-Gaylani, *Ibid.,* and Najm, p. 70.

92. Anwar al-Jundi, *A'lam al-Adab wa al-Fann* (Damascus, 1954), pp. 252-254, and al-Gaylani, *Ibid.,* p. 50, who states that al-Qabbani took along with him few members of his troupe which seems less likely. Mustafa, p. 193 states that al-Qabbani's troupe consisted of fifty actors. See Najm's comment on this point. Najm, pp. 115 and 123.

93. Barbour, p. 176, and Najm, p. 126.

94. Mustafa, p. 194.

95. *Ibid.*

96. For al-Qabbani's activity in Egypt and his vicissitudes, see Najm and all the other sources which he has quoted in this connection. Najm, *Ibid.*

97. Muhammad Yusuf Najm, (ed.), *al-Masrah al-Arabi: Dirasat wa Nusus—al-Shaykh Ahmad Abu Khalil al-Qabbani* (Beirut, 1963). In the summer of 1970 I met with Dr. Muhammad Yusuf Najm in Beirut and he told me that he has discovered more dramas by al-Qabbani and that he hopes to make them available through a future publication. But he refused to show me the texts of these dramas.

98. This drama is produced by Najm in his edition of al-Qabbani's anthology, pp. 231-300.

99. See the unpublished dissertation (Cairo University, 1957) by Latifa al-Zayyat, "Harakat al-Tarjama al-Adabiyya min al-Ingiliziyya ila al-Arabiyya fi Misr fi al-Fatra ma bayn 1882-1925 wa mada Irtibatuha bi Sihafat hadhihi al-Fatra," pp. 63 and 101 and Badr, *Tatawwur al-Riwaya al-Arabiyya al-Haditha,* pp. 133-136.

100. Al-Qabbani omitted two scenes from Act IV, and added eight scenes to Act II, three scenes to Act III and two scenes to Act V. Najm, *al-Masrahiyya fi al-Adab al-Arabi,* p. 212.

101. *Ibid.,* p. 213.

102. Najm, p. 214; Zaki Tulaymat, "Kayfa Dakhala al-Tamthil Bilad al-Sharq," *al-Kitab* (February, 1946), No. 4, p. 586; and Mustafa, p. 201.

103. Al-Qabbani, *Riwayat Harun al-Rashid ma' al-Amir Ghanim ibn Ayyub wa Qut al-Qulub,* Act I, ed. Najm, pp. 3-8.

104. See Act III of this drama in *al-Masrah al-Arabi: Dirasat wa Nusus-al-Shaykh Ahmad Abu Khalil al-Qabbani,* ed. Muhammad Yusuf Najm, *Ibid.,* (Beirut, 1963), pp. 212-219.

105. See particularly Acts II and IV in which 'Antara feels jealous when he learns that Mas'ud, the King of Yaman, has pretended that he is in love with 'Abla, and 'Antara threatens to retaliate against him. *Ibid.,* pp. 204-212, 219-229, particularly pp. 210 and 222.

106. For the text of *Riwayat Harun al-Rashid ma' Uns al-Jalis* in five acts, and of *Riwayat al-Amir Mahmud Najl Shah al-'Ajam* see *Ibid.,* pp. 33-85 and 89-127 respectively. For a short account of al-Qabbani's dramas studied here, see Mustafa, pp. 196-202.

107. These plays are *Riwayat 'Afifa* in five acts, revised and set to music by Kamil al-Kha'i, *Ibid.,* pp. 129-137. Najm believes that it is an adaptation of a Western play entitled *Geneviève.* The other two dramas are *Riwayat Hiyal al-Nisa al-Mashhura bi Lucia* (Drama of the Craftiness of Women known as Lucia), in four acts, pp. 301-50 and *Nakir al-Jamil* (The Ungrateful), in four acts, *Ibid.,* pp. 351-400.

108. Najm, *Ibid.*

109. Zaki Tulaymat, "Kayfa Dakhala al-Tamthil Bilad al-Sharq," *al-Kitab* I (February, 1946), No. 4, 585-586, and Najm's introduction to al-Qabbani's anthology.

110. See for example, the play, *Harun al-Rashid ma' Uns al-Jalis,* in Najm, *Ibid.,* pp. 37-85 in which the author divides the acts into ajza (parts) rather than scenes. In *Riwayat Mahmud Najl Shah al-'Ajam,* he uses the term *manazir* (Scenes), while in *Lubab al-Gharam aw al-Malik Mitridat* he uses another term *waqi'a* (event). Still in his play *Harun al-Rashid ma al-Amir Ghanim ibn Ayyub wa Qut al-Qulub* he uses only acts without subdividing them into scenes.

111. See the indexes in Muhammad Yusuf Najm, *al-Masrahiyya fi al-Adab al-Arabi Al-Hadith,* pp. 474-504 and the date of their performance as well as the number of times they were performed.

CHAPTER III: YA'QUB SANU AND THE RISE OF THE ARAB DRAMA IN EGYPT

1. Sanu (Tsanu) is a Hebrew name meaning "modest." Anwar Luqa, "Masrah Ya'qub Sanu," *al-Majalla* (Cairo, March 15, 1961), pp. 51-52, peculiarly writes the name in Arabic as Sanua, with a fatha vowel on the S, silent n, and another fatha vowel on the letter ayn. For Sanu's life and works, see Irene L. Gendzier, *The Practical Visions of Ya'qub Sanu* (Cambridge: Harvard University Press, 1966).

2. Ibrahim Abduh, *Abu Nazzara Imam al-Sihafa al-Fukahiyya al-Musawwara wa Za'im al-Masrah fi Misr* (Cairo, 1953), p. 18. Abduh, like Luqa, claims to have seen Sanu's memoirs, but merely paraphrases them in his book instead of translating them into Arabic with comments. Gendzier, p. 154, notes 34 and 35, says this autobiographical essay "has, to my knowledge, not been published or reprinted." But her references to this document strongly suggest that it is identical with a lecture published by Sanu in *Ma Vie en Vers et mon Théatre en Prose* Montgeron, 1912), cited by Luqa, p. 53. (Cf. also notes 8 and 56 below). In 1955 Abduh published another book about Sanu, *al-Suhufi al-Tha'ir* (The Rebellious Journalist), which may seem to the uninformed reader to be an entirely separate study. In fact, the two books are largely identical; the later book has a shorter introduction and omits a list of Sanu's journals and publications, but includes facsimiles of the journals. Subsequent references in these notes will be to the earlier volume. volume.

3. This writer recalls that while practicing law in Mosul, Iraq, he met a Muslim whose name was Matti, a typical Christian name in that country, not used at all by Muslims. On being asked why he had a Christian name, the man replied that his mother, having lost many children in infancy, was advised to go to the monastery of al-Shaykh Matti (St. Matthew's Monastery) near Mosul to seek divine aid. She went and vowed that if she bore a male child who survived, she was to call him Matti. Evidently her request was answered, and the son, though Muslim, bore the name of the celebrated Syrian saint. Thus, Muhammad Yusuf Najm's opinion that the story reported by Abduh is "one of the many nonsensical anecdotes related by Abu Naddara" appears untenable. The story is not nonsense, so much as it is a matter of faith. See Najm, *al-Masrahiyya fi al-Adab al-Arabi al-Hadith* 1847-1914 (Beirut, 1967), p. 92, n. 3. Abd al-Hamid Ghunaym, *Sanu Ra'id al-Masrah al-Misri* (Cairo, 1966), p. 22 suggests that Sanu may have used this anecdote to win the Muslims' sympathy in a country where the Jews were a minority.

4. Philip Tarrazi, *Tarikh al-Sihafa al-Arabiyya* II (Beirut, 1913), 283.

5. Jacob M. Landau, "Abu Naddara, an Egyptian-Jewish Nationalist," *The Journal of Jewish Studies,* III, No. 1 (1952), 33-34.

6. "An Arabic Punch," *The Saturday Review of Politics, Literature, Sciences and Arts,* XLII (July 26, 1879), 112.

7. In his "memoires" Sanu gives 1863 as the date of his first employment at this school. Jacques Chelley, who based his study *Le Molière Égyptien* primarily on Sanu's memoirs and first published it in *Abu Nazzara Zarqa* in August, 1906, fixes the date at 1868. John Ninet, in "The Origin of the National Party in Egypt," *The Nineteenth-Century,* XIII (January-June, 1883), places the date at 1872, which seems most unlikely. Sanu mentions his association with the Polytechnic School in the tenth chapter of "The Vision of Abu Naddara," in Paul De Baignières, ed., *L'Égypte Satirique* (Paris, 1886), p. 96, but gives no date.

8. Tarrazi, II, 283.

9. *Ibid.* Abduh also relates this anecdote, claiming he found it at Paris in a manuscript in Sanu's handwriting, containing fifteen issues of the journal *Abu Nazzara.* These are the same issues which appeared in Egypt and were destroyed on the orders of the Khedive Isma'il. Further, he states emphatically that he knows of no place in the world where one may locate any numbers of this periodical. Tarrazi says he is indebted to Sanu, who sent him the only extant collection of his journals, with many other publications. Tarrazi based his brief sketch of Sanu's career on the journals and other information he received from Sanu. See Abduh, pp. 43-47, and Tarrazi, I, 39.

10. Abduh, p. 24.

11. *Ibid.*

12. De Baignières published forty-eight of these cartoons, with both Arabic and French captions, in a section of his book *Album d'Abou Naddara.*

13. *The Saturday Review,* p. 112.

14. De Baignières, p. 11.

15. De Baignières, p. 12.

16. He makes this point clear through some of the characters in his comedy *Mulyir Misr wa ma Yuqasihi* (The Egyptian Molière and What he Suffers,) particularly in I.ii. A new edition of this play was published by Najm in *al-Masrah al-Arabi; Dirasat wa Nusus—Ya'qub Sanu* (Beirut, 1963), pp. 190-222.

17. Luqa, p. 60, conjectures that the title of this operetta is *Lu'bat Rastur wa Shaykh al-Balad wa al-Qawwas,* basing his idea on *Mulyir Misr wa ma Yuqasihi,* I.ii. But in the same play Habib, apparently referring to the same operetta, says to Hunayn (II.v.), "...why do you deny the blessing we received that evening when we performed at Qasr al-Nil, when James Sanu was honored by the title 'the Egyptian Molière,' and when the comedy *al-Qawwas wa Shaykh al-Balad wa Rastur* received the admiration of our Khedive Isma'il? The hundred pounds which Sanu was awarded by the Khedive he distributed among us."

18. According to Abduh, p. 27, the Khedive gave Sanu the title "the Egyptian Molière" after the performance of *Anisa ala al-Muda* and *Ghandur Misr* (cf. note 18 above; Najm, p. 219; Luqa, p. 55). Other writers referred to Sanu as "the Egyptian Beaumarchais." See *The Saturday Review,* p. 112, and De Baignières. p. 14.

19. Najm, *al-Masrahiyya,* pp. 432-33.

20. Abduh, pp. 27-28.

21. *Ibid.*

22. Abduh, p. 28.

23. Ghunaym, pp. 51-52, presents an abridged text with comments for this one-act

comedy, titled *Muhawara bayn Ali Effendi wa Mr. Bull fi Qahwat al-Bursa bi Misr al-Qahira,* (A Dialogue between Ali Effendi and Mr. Bull in the Stock Market Coffee shop in Cairo). We should note that Sanu pointedly refers to the city as Misr al-Qahira in order to distinguish it from "Misr," the name Egyptians give to their country.

24. The text of this dialogue, included in Najm, *al-Masrah al-Arabi* pp. 75-76, contains nothing to substantiate Gendzier's view (p. 37) that "the caricatured Englishman...was ridiculed for his criticism of the use of the colloquial Egyptian language."

25. Tarrazi, II, 284.

26. Ya'qub Sanu, *Mulyir Misr wa ma Yuqasihi* in Najm, *al-Masrah al-Arabi,* pp. 209-210.

27. *Ibid.,* pp. 200-201.

28. Jacob Landau, *Studies in the Arab Theater and Cinema* (Philadelphia, 1958), p. 66.

29. De Baignières, p. 14; Najm, *al-Masrahiyya,* p. 91; Ghunaym, pp. 96-97. Najm rightly argues that Sanu exaggerates his achievements both in his autobiography and in *Mulyir Misr wa ma Yuqasihi,* in which he relates his success and frustration in the theater. In his introduction to this play, Sanu merely refers to Isma'il as his best friend, making no mention of the closing of his stage. See Najm's introduction to *al-Masrah al-Arabi,* p. 2.

30. Abduh, p. 33.

31. According to Tarrazi, II, 283, both societies were founded in 1874. De Baignières, pp. 14-15, mentions the same two groups, but says *Muhibbi al-'Ilm* was established in 1875.

32. Abduh, p. 35.

33. Abduh, p. 34; De Baignières, p. 15; Gendzier, pp. 42-43.

34. Abduh, p. 35.

35. Tarrazi, II, 283.

36. Abduh, pp. 38-39.

37. *Ibid.,* pp. 35-37.

38. *Ibid.,* pp. 35-37.

39. *Ibid.,* pp. 39-40.

40. *Ibid.,* p. 40.

41. De Baignières, p. 15; Tarrazi, II, 284; Abduh, pp. 41-55. There is some doubt concerning the circulation of this journal. See Gendzier, p. 64.

42. Abduh, pp. 46-47.

43. *Ibid.,* p. 51.

44. *Ibid.,* p. 54

45. Tarrazi, II, 284.

46. De Baignières, p. 14.

47. Abduh, p. 57. Tarrazi, II, 284, does not make clear whether Sanu was deported from Egypt by order of the Italian consul, but simply says the Khedive asked the Italian consul to issue such an order, after which Sanu departed to Alexandria and then sailed to Europe.

48. *Ibid.,* p. 57

49. *Ibid.,* p. 58. Khayri Pasha was evidently Sanu's friend. See also *Mulyir Misr wa ma Yuqasihi,* in Najm, *al-Masrah,* p. 221.

50. Abduh, pp. 59-60. According to *The Saturday Review,* p. 112, Sanu resided in Paris at 65 Rue de Provence.

51. Abduh, pp. 61-62. Tarrazi, II, 284, briefly mentions Isma'il's appearance at the wharf and Sanu's prediction that the Khedive would be banished within a year, but his description of the events of that day is not as full or as dramatic as Sanu's own account.

52. The French journalists' report on Sanu is reproduced by De Baignierès, pp. 13, 15.

53. De Baignierès, pp. 15-16. Sanu's self-praise is enunciated in *Mulyir Misr,* I.2, when Istephan says "Regarding our uncle James, let him be content with the praise he receives in Eastern and Western journals. Learned men testify that he is unique." This praise is substantially repeated in the same play, II.1. Najm says in the Introduction to *al-Masrah al-Arabi* that his studies have led him to believe that Sanu gave European reporters exaggerated reports about himself, being under no duress or fear of criticism. Anwar Luqa, p. 53, states that one should not believe all that Sanu said about himself in a lecture delivered in 1902 at *La Coopération des Ideés,* later published in a pamphlet titled *Ma Vie en Vers et mon Théatre en Prose* (Montgeron, 1912), pp. 9-16. Luqa believes that Sanu published this lecture in hopes of reviving his forgotten fame by relating the account of his struggles and achievements, and that his recollections of his younger days may have been colored by his imagination, since his memory was failing.

54. Among these journals we may note *Rihlat Abu Nazzara Zarqa* (The Man with the Blue Glasses), *al-Nazzarat al-Misriyya* (The Egyptian Glasses), *Abu Saffara* (The Flutist), *Abu Zammara* (The Clarinettist), *al-Hawi* (The Snake Charmer), *Abu Nazzara Lisan Hal al-Umma al-Misriyya* (The Man with the Glasses, Voice of the Egyptian Nation), *Abu Nazzara Zarqa Lisan Hal al-Umma al-Misriyya al-Hurra* (The Man with the Blue Glasses, Voice of the Free Egyptian Nation). The issue of *Abu Nazzara Zarqa* which appeared on January 19, 1883, was probably the most interesting of all Sanu's journals for its analysis of many important aspects of Egypt's history, and especially of the Khedive Tawfiq's collaboration with the British and his subservience to them. In a very touching poem Sanu rather satirically exposes the Khedive's connivance with the British. He devotes no less than two full pages to a bitter criticism of British policy not only in Egypt but in other countries, especially India. He also uses a large part of this journal to relate the history and development of the Mahdi's revolt in the Sudan. Sanu's other journals include *al-Watani al-Misri* (The Egyptian Patriot), *Abu Nazzara: Misr li al-Misriyyin* (The Man with the Glasses, Egypt for the Egyptians), *al-Tawaddud* (Friendly Relations), *al-Munsif* (The Just One), and *al-'Alam al-Islami* (The Muslim World). He also published another journal, written in eight languages, both Eastern and Western, and entitled *al-Tharthara al-Misriyya* (The Egyptian Chatterbox), or in French *Le Bavard Égyptien.* See Abduh, passim, and Tarrazi, II, 254 and 284. An interesting account of Sanu's activity in Paris is in De Baignierès, pp. 9-21, based on the reports of several European journalists.

55. Tarrazi, II, 285.

56. For an account of Sanu's activities at Paris and the honors and decorations he received from various heads of state, see Abduh, De Baignierès, and Tarrazi, whose works have been cited previously.

57. Cf. note 2 above.
58. Luqa, "Masrah Ya'qub Sanu," *al-Majalla*, pp. 51-71. Luqa may be correct in observing that the Egyptian writers who recorded the history of the ruling family under the monarchy in Egypt, either out of hypocrisy or from fear of retribution, were careful to exclude Sanu from their writings, as Isma'il had banished him from Egypt.
59. Najm, *al-Masrahiyya,* describes his contact with Anwar Luqa.
60. Abd al-Hamid Ghunaym, *Sanu Ra'id al-Masrah al-Misri,* cited in previous notes.
61. Abduh, p. 24. The one-act comedy, entitled *Il marito infedele,* was published at Cairo in 1876. *Fatima,* a three-act play of unknown date, is probably the one performed in 1868-70 and may also have been translated into French. See Abduh, p. 214.
62. Gendzier, p. 40, mentions *al-Salasil al-Muhattama* which she erroneously renders as "The Unconnected Essays."
63. *Ibid.*
64. Abduh, p. 27.
65. In his introduction to Sanu's dramas, Najm explains the various difficulties in their text, and even provides a list of the terms whose spelling differs from conventional Arabic orthography. At the end of the text (pp. 225-33), he also explains the meanings of the French and Italian terms which abound in Sanu's dramas.
66. Najm, *al-Masrah al-Arabi,* Introduction.
67. Sanu, *Mulyir Misr wa ma Yuqasihi,* I.ii, in Najm, *al-Masrah al-Arabi,* pp. 199-200.
68. *Ibid.,* p. 201.
69. Ghunaym, p. 48.
70. Abduh, p. 25.
71. *Ibid.,* p. 30.
72. De Baignières, pp. 7-8; al-Sayyid Hasan Id. *Tatawwur al-Naqd al-Masrahi fi Misr* (Cairo, 1965), pp. 69-70.
73. For these and other nicknames, see Abduh, *passim;* Ghunaym, pp. 50-53.
74. Ghunaym, p. 50.
75. This comedy appeared in *Abu Nazzara Zarqa,* No. 4, 14th Rabi' al-Awwal, 1295 A.H. quoted in Abduh, pp. 46-50/1878 A.D.
76. *Abu Nazzara Zarqa,* No. 5, Wednesday, 21st Rabi' al-Awwal, 1295, A.H./1878. Abduh rightly observes that in the first five issues of this journal, Sanu criticized conditions in Egypt, particularly the exaction of taxes from the peasants by oppresive methods, but avoided antagonizing the Khedive Isma'il. In his short autobiography, however, Sanu clearly states that the success of his journals encouraged him to "remove the mask from my face and courageously attack the Khedive Isma'il, who looted his own subjects by imposing numerous taxes and duties, which broke their backs." See Abduh, p. 54.
77. Ghunaym, pp. 62-68.
    Ibid., pp. 69-74.
79. *Ibid.,* pp. 53-61.
80. *Ibid.,* pp. 74-78.
81. *Ibid.,* p. 78.

82. Abduh, p. 24, mentions *al-Bint al-'Asriyya, Ghandur Misr, Rastur wa Shaykh al-Balad wa al-Qawwas, Zubayda,* and *al-Watan wa al-Hurriya.* Abduh, p. 177, says Sanu published another play, *Suqut Nubar* (The Fall of Nubar, depicting the downfall of the Khedive Isma'il's Prime Minister), in *Abu Nazzara Zarqa,* No. 4, July 14, 1877. For the titles of other dramas, see De Baignières, pp. 7-8, and Gendzier, p. 39.

83. This operetta is summarized in Luqa, pp. 59, 60, and Ghunaym, pp. 104-106.

84. Ghunaym, p. 106.

85. *Ibid.,* pp. 109-111.

86. Sanu refers here to the Alabama Arbitration of Claims.

87. *Bursat Misr.,* Act II, Scene VII, Najm, pp. 31-33; Luqa, p. 68.

88. *Al-'Alil,* Act II, Scene X, in Najm, pp. 70-71; Ghunaym, pp. 133-141; Luqa pp. 63-65 and Gendzier, p. 39.

89. *Abu Rida al-Barbari wa Ka'b al-Khayr,* in Najm, pp. 81-106; Ghunaym, pp. 141-147; Luqa, pp. 63-65.

90. This is a short drama, containing one act and seven scenes.

91. *Al-Darratan,* in Najm, pp. 157-188; Ghunaym, pp. 157-165.

92. Luqa, p. 62. This drama contains one act and thirteen scenes.

93. *Al-Sadaqa,* in Najm, pp. 109-134; Ghunaym, pp. 147-157.

94. *Al-Amira al-Iskandaraniyya,* in Najm, pp. 137-171; Ghunaym, pp. 152-157. According to Luqa, p. 67, quoting Jules Barier, *L'Aristocratica Allesandrina* (Cairo 1875), Sanu also translated this drama into Italian.

95. *Mulyir Misr wa ma Yuqasihi,* Act I, Scene II, in Najm, p. 200; Luqa pp. 68-70.

96. *Mulyir Misr,* Act I, Scene II, Najm, p. 201; Luqa, p. 70.

97. Najm, *al-Masrahiyya fi al-Adab al-Arabi al-Hadith,* p. 433.

98. See *al-Amira al-Iskandaraniyya,* Act I, in Najm, pp. 139-156.

99. *Ibid.;* Luqa, p. 67; Ghunaym, p. 157.

100. Ghunaym, pp. 190-191.

101. *Bursat Misr,* Act I, Scene VI, in Najm, p. 12.

102. *Al-'Alil,* Act I, Scene V.

103. See the lively argument between the two rival wives in *al-Darratan,* Scene V, and Luqa, pp. 61-62.

104. *Al-Darratan,* Scene V.

105. De Baignières, pp. 6-7, quotes *The Saturday Review* twice. The first quotation is allegedly from the issue of July 26, 1879; no specific date or number is cited for the second. The issue dated July 26, 1879, contains an article titled "An Arab Punch" (p. 112), but this article on Sanu has nothing to do with the quotations by De Baignières. Najm, in *al-Masrahiyya,* p. 79, produces a long quotation, purportedly from *The Saturday Review* of July 26, 1876 (sic), which has no connection whatever with the article "An Arab Punch." Najm, evidently, has reproduced De Baignières' second quotation, and other writers have followed Najm without paying adequate attention to the source of his evidence. See al-Sayyid Hasan Id *Tatawwur al-Naqd al-Masrahi fi Misr,* pp. 77-80; Ghunaym, pp. 163-165; also Abduh, p. 32.

106. *Ibid.,* pp. 31-32; Ghunaym, pp. 114-115; Luqa, p. 61.

107. Abduh, p. 32; Ghunaym, pp. 112-114.

108. Abduh, p. 32.

CHAPTER IV: THE TRANSLATION OF WESTERN FICTION

1. Faruq Khurshid, *Fi al-Riwaya al-Arabiyya; 'Asr al-Tajmi'* (Alexandria, n.d.), pp. 5-19. Khurshid apparently uses *riwaya* to mean merely "a narrative," not specifically the modern novel or short story. Arab writers who first become acquainted with the Western novel in the nineteenth century had no term which could appropriately convey the meaning of "novel" and therefore applied to this genre the term *riwaya* (derived from the verb, rawa "to tell," and properly designating any romance) or *qisas* ("stories"). Others solved their problem by Arabicizing the term commonly used by Westerners, calling the translations of Western prose fiction *romaniyat*.

2. Khurshid, p. 95.

3. Mahmud Timur, *Muhadarat fi al-Qisas fi Adab al-Arab Madihi wa Hadiruhu* (Cairo, 1958), pp. 1-25.

4. Timur, p. 26; Mikha'il Nu'ayma, Ibrahim al-'Arid, Mahmud Timur, and Jibra'il Jabbur, *Fi al-Adab al-Arabi al-Hadith* (Beirut, 1954), p. 22.

5. Yahya Haqqi, *Fajr al-Qissa al-Misriyya* (Cairo, n.d.), p. 18.

6. Haqqi, pp. 17-20.

7. Mikha'il Nu'ayma, *al-Ghirbal*, 7th ed. (Beirut, 1964), p. 126.

8. See Sa'id al-Bustani's introduction to *Dhat al-Khidr* (Beirut, 1884), pp. 4-5, and Mahmud Khayrat's introduction to *al-Fatat al-Rifiyya* (Cairo, Musamarat al Sha'b, 1905), pp. 3-7, Cf. also Henri Pérès, *Le roman, le conte et la nouvelle dans la littérature arabe moderne, I, Bibliographie des Ouvrages originaux, in Annales de l'Institut Oriental d'Alger,* III (1937), and by the same author, *Littérature Arabe Moderne: Grands Courants—Bibliographie* (Algiers, 1940); Latifa al-Zayyat, "Harakat al-Tarjama al-Adabiyya min al-Ingiliziyya ila al-Arabiyya fi Misr fi al-Fatra ma bayn 1882-1925 wa Mada Irtibatuha bi Sihafat hadhihi al-Fatra" (unpublished dissertation, Cairo University, 1957), pp. 86-181.

9. Hamilton A. R. Gibb, *Studies on the Civilization of Islam* (Boston, 1962), p. 287

10. By Syria we mean here greater Syria, which included Syria proper, Lebanon, Jordan, and Palestine. After World War I, these countries, except Palestine, assumed their present geographical and political boundaries.

11. The Maronites, through the financial and educational assistance of the Vatican, were forerunners in establishing schools. The oldest Maronite school was founded in 1584 by Pope Gregory; other schools were later established in the Lebanese villages of Ihden, Supher, and Qarqasha. The Maronites also set up small schools in their monasteries, which were commonly known as *untush* (a Greek term meaning a place of refuge for strangers or a place of retreat); See Bulus Jwun, in *al-Mashriq*, II (1899), 1134-5, including Untush 'Ajaltun (1751), Untush Jubayl

(1761), Untush Zahla (1769), and Untush Dayr al-Qamar (1782). Among the oldest schools were those at Ajaltun and Wadi Shahrur, both established in 1751. Among the most famous Maronite institutions is 'Ayn Warqa School, originally the Monastery of St. Antonius, but converted into a school in 1789 by the Maronite Patriarch Yusuf Istefan. It should be remembered that all these schools were basically religious, although they also offered instruction in elementary sciences, logic, and rhetoric. See Jurji Zaydan, *Tarikh Adab al-Lugha al-Arabiyya,* IV, 46-47.

12. Constantine François Chasseboeuf, Comte de Volney, *Voyrage en Syrie et en Égypte, Pendant les Années 1783, 1784, et 1785,* II (Paris, 1787), passim.

13. See Louis Cheikho, "Tarikh Fann al-Tiba'a fi al-Mashriq," *al-Mashriq,* III (1900), 360-361, Jurji Zaydan, IV, pp. 14-15 and 54-55, and de Nerval, *Voyage en Orient,* I, (Paris, 1867), 304, and the English translation of this work by Conrad Elphinstone, *The Women of Cairo* II (London, 1929), 223.

14. See Bachatly, *Un Membre Orient;* Bulus Qara'ali, *al-Suriyyun fi Misr* (The Syrians in Egypt), I (Cairo, 1928), 20 and 76; Yusuf Alyan Sarkis, *Mu'jam al-Matbu'at al-Arabiyya wa al-Mu'arraba,* II, (Cairo, 1928), 895-896; Jamal al-Din al-Shayyal, *Tarikh al-Tarajama fi Misr fi Ahd al-Hamla al-Faransiyya* (The History of Translation in Egypt during the French Campaign); also by the same author, "Kayfa wa Mata 'Arafat Misr Kitab al-Amir li Machiavelli," *al-Katib al-Misri,* IV, No. 13 (October, 1946), 107-116; and al-Khuri Constantine al-Pasha; "Tarajamat al-Ab Rafa'il Zakhur," *al-Majalla al-Patriarchiyya* (1932), pp. 486-488, 561-564. Zakhur also compiled an Italian-Arabic dictionary published at Bulaq in 1238 A.H./1822 A.D.

15. Al-Shayyal, *Tarikh al-Tarjama wa al-Haraka,* etc., p. 81.

16. 'Anhuri translated seven French medical books into Arabic versions which were revised by two prominent Muslim learned men, Muhammad 'Umran al-Harawi and Ahmad Hasan al-Rashidi. The date of his death is unknown, but is probably about the middle of the last century. See 'Isa Iskandar al-Ma'luf, *Dawani al-Qutuf fi Tarikh Bani al-Ma'luf* (B'abda, Lebanon, 1907-08), p. 257, n. 1; Louis Cheikho, *al-Adab al-Arabiyya fi al-Qarn al-Tasi' 'Ashr,* II, p. 123; Zaydan, *Tarikh Adab al-Lugha,* p. 190; Zaydan, *Tarajim Mashahir al-Sharq fi al-Qarn al-Tasi 'Ashr,* II (Cairo, 1902-03), p. 20; Al-Khuri Mikha'il Burayk al-Dimashqi, *Tarikh al-Sham* 1720-1782, ed., al-Khuri Constantine al-Pasha (Harisa, St. Paul Press, 1930), p. 115; al-Shayyal, *Tarikh al-Tarjama wa al-Haraka,* pp. 83-87; Sarkis, *Mu'jam al-Matbu'at,* II, 1389-1390. For the rest of this translation see al-Shayyal pp. 87-88.

17. Al-Shayyal, p. 81.

18. Sarkis, I, p. 558.

19. See Zaydan, IV, pp. 46-54, and by the same author, *Mudhakkirat Jurji Zaydan,* ed., Salah al-Din al-Munajjid (Beirut, 1968), pp. 27-28 and 65-97.

20. Philip Tarrazi, *Tarikh al-Sihafa al-Arabiyya,* I (Beirut, 1913), p. 68. Another translation by al-Shalfun himself was published serially in *al-Najah,* Beirut, 1871-1872.

21. Among those stories we may mention *Edward and Sylva,* translated from Italian by Sa'd Allah al-Bustani, which appeared in *al-Jinan* (1870), pp. 109-112; *Al-Amir al-Faris wa Imra'atuhu Isabella* (The Knight Prince and his wife Isabella),

translated from French by al-Khawaja Philip Ni'mat Allah Khuri, in *al-Jinan* (1870), pp. 211-3; *Rajul dhu Imra'atayn* (A Man with Two Wives), adapted from French by Jurji Effendi Jibra' il Balit al-Halabi, in *al-Jinan* (1871), pp. 132-40; and *Yusuf wa Zawjatuhu Maryam* (Joseph and his Wife Mary) adapted from French by al-Khawaja Constantine Qitta, in *al-Jinan* (1871), pp. 366-367 and 404-07, and supposedly written by al-Sit Adeleid al-Bustani, was probably an adaptation from the French, although no mention of this is made. Between 1875 and 1878, Salim al-Bustani published in *al-Jinan* sixteen translations of Western fiction. Since he does not indicate the sources of these stories, it is quite difficult to identify their authors. Although most of these were apparently translated from French, the titles of some reveal their English origin. The Arabic titles, somewhat freely translated, are as follows: (1875) *al-Gharam wa al-Ikhtira'* (Love and Invention); *al-Sawa'iq* (Thunderbolts); *al-Hub al-Da'im* (Eternal Love); *Madha Ra'at Miss Darington* (What Did Miss Darington See?); *al-Sa'd fi al- Nahs* (Good Luck from Misfortune); *Jurjinya* (Georgina); (1867) *Hulm al-Musawwir* (A Photographer's Dream); *Summ al-Afa'i* (Vipers' Venom); *Sirr al-Hub* (The Secret of Love); *Hila Gharamiyya* (Love Trick); *Hikayat al-Gharam* (The Story of Love); *Zawjat John Carver* (John Carver's Wife); (1877) *Khatun 'ala al-Muda* (A Fashionable Lady); *La Tansani* (Forget Me Not); *Qumriya* (Turtledove); (1878) *Qissa Ghariba* (A Strange Story). In 1884-85, *al-Jinan* serialized a translation of Le Sage's *Gil Blas* made by Jamil Mikha'il Mudawwar.

22. In addition to Pérès's bibliography and al-Zayyat's dissertation, cf. Muhammad Yusuf Najm, *al-Qissa fi al-Adab al-Arabi al-Hadith* (Beirut, 1961), pp. 6-21.

23. Other translations and adaptations of *Télémaque* were made, including an unpublished version by Habib al-Yaziji (d. 1870), of which brief mention is made in *al-Jinan* (1871), p. 194; Jurji Shahin Atiyya, *Waqa' i Tilimak* (Beirut, 1885); Sa'd Allah al-Bustani, *Riwayat Tilimak* (Cairo, n.d.); and Wadi' al-Khuri, *Riwayat Tilimak* (Beirut, 1912), a verse adaptation. Cf. Sarkis, II, 1340; Pérès, p. 297.

24. Zaydan, IV, 276; al-Zayyat, p. 206; Ibrahim Abduh, *Tatawwur al-Sihafa al-Misriyya* (Cairo, 1945); and by the same author *Jaridat al-Ahram* (Cairo, 1951).

25. *Al-Diya,* established by Ibrahim al-Yazji in 1898, published about 120 translations of Western short stories until its suppression in 1906. Muhammad Unsi, editor of *Rawdat al-Akhbar,* was greatly interested in French fiction. He usually serialized a translated story from the French at the end of his newspaper. The first translated work of fiction from the French which appeared in this newspaper was *Gil Blas* by Le Sage (d. 1747). See Abd al-Latif Hamza, *Adab al-Maqala al-Suhufiyya,* Part 1, 2nd ed., (Cairo, 1958), pp. 176-182.

26. J. C. Hurewitz, *Diplomacy in the Near and Middle East,* I (Princeton, New Jersey, 1956), 24.

27. Abd al-Muhsin Taha Badr, *Tatawwur al-Riwaya al-Arabiyya al-Haditha fi Misr 1870-1938* (Cairo, 1963), p. 126.

28. The Earl of Cromer, *Modern Egypt,* II (New York, 1908), 536.

29. For a thorough treatment of the condition of the press particularly in Syria and Egypt in the nineteenth century see Tarrazi, *Tarikh al-Sihafa al-Arabiyya;* Abduh, *Jaridat al-Ahram;* and by the same author *Tatawwur al-Sihafa al-Misriyya 1789-1951* (Cairo, 1951); Martin Hartman, *The Arabic Press of Egypt* (London, 1899); Abd al-Latif Hamza, *Adab al-Maqala al-Suhufiyya,* 6 vols., and Shams al-

Din al-Rifaʻi, *Tarikh al-Sihafa al-Suriyya,* 2 vols., (Cairo, 1969). For an Egyptian point of view regarding Cromer's press policy see Sami Aziz, *al-Sihafa al-Misriyya wa Mawqifuha min al-Ihtilal al-Ingilizi* (Cairo, 1968).

30. Abduh, *Jaridat al-Ahram,* p. 330.

31. Abd al-Rahman al-Rafiʻi, *Mustafa Kamil Baʻith al-Haraka al-Wataniyya,* 4th ed., (Cairo, 1962), p. 145.

32. Zaydan, IV, 60; Cheikho, *al-Adab al-Arabiyya,* II, 191.

33. Tarrazi, II, 126, al-Zayyat, p. 176.

34. Al-Zayyat, pp. 125-164. See also *al-Muqattam,* January-April, 1890.

35. Mikha'il Nuʻayma, *Abʻad min Moscow wa min Washington* (Beirut, 1957), pp. 58-64; and by the same author, *Sabʻun; Hikayat ʻUmr al-Marhala al-Ula* (Beirut, 1959), p. 75. See also I. Y. Kratschkowsky *Among Arabic Manuscripts* (Leiden, 1953), pp. 54-61.

36. Nuʻayma, *Ibid.,* and *Sabʻun,* pp. 120-155.

37. Nuʻayma, *Ibid.,* pp. 63-64.

38. Nasir al-Din al-Asad, *Muhadarat an Khalil Baydas Ra'id al-Qissa al-Haditha fi Filastin* (Cairo, 1963), p. 21.

39. Nuʻayma, *Sabʻun,* p. 75, and *Abʻad min Moscow,* pp. 59 and 61.

40. Al-Asad, pp. 21-22.

41. Al-Asad, *Ibid.,* pp. 29-30 and Yusuf Asʻad Daghir, *Masadir al-Dirasa al-Adabiyya* II (Beirut, 1956), 213.

42. For Baydas' translation of Russian fiction see al-Asad, pp. 34-38.

43. Al-Asad, *Ibid.,* pp. 34-37; Abd al-Rahman Yaghi, *Hayat al-Adab al-Filastini al-Hadith hatta al-Nakba,* pp. 325-331. This work which is basic for the study of Arabic literature in Palestine is still in manuscript form. See also Hashim Yaghi, *al-Qissa al-Qasira fi Filastin wa al-Urdun* 1850-1965 (Cairo, 1966), p. 162.

44. This translation appeared serially in *al-Nafa'is al-Asriyya* Vol. III (1911).

45. Al-Asad, pp. 59-61 and Muhammad Yunus al-Saʻidi, "Tolstoy," *al-Aqlam* (Baghdad, November, 1969), pp. 76-78.

46. Al-Saʻidi, *Ibid.,* and Badr p. 131.

47. *Ibid.,* and I. Y. Kratschkowsky *al-Mukhtarat,* III, (Moscow, 1956), 330.

48. For the works of French fiction translated into Arabic, see Peres, *Le roman, le conte et la nouvelle dans la littérature arabe moderne,* III, (1937), and Sarkis, *Muʻjam al-Matbuʻat,* passim.

49. Sarkis, I, 1108, says this translation was published in 1870 by Wadi al-Nil Press. Pérès, p. 295, gives 1871 as the date of its publication.

50. Pérès, p. 295. A second translation of *The Three Musketeers,* by ʻUmar Abd al-Aziz Amin, was published in two volumes at Cairo in 1928.

51. A novel by Dumas *père* and Gaboriau was translated into Arabic by Salih Jawdat with the title *al-Yad al-Athima wa al-Silah al-Khafi* (Cairo, 1906). Another novel, *Le Capitaine Richard,* by Dumas *père* and Schlegel was translated by Nasib Mashʻalani with the title *al-Qaʻidan* (Cairo, 1906). See Pérès, pp. 295-297.

   Of Jules Verne's stories, we may cite *Voyage en ballon,* which Yusuf Sarkis translated and published as *al-Rihla al-Jawwiya fi al-Markaba al-Hawa'iyya* (Beirut, 1875); *Voyage au centre de la terre,* translated by Iskandar Ammun under the title *al-Rihla al-ʻIlmiyya fi Qalb al-Kura al-Ardiyya* (Alexandria, 1885); *Le tour du monde en 80 jours,* translated by Yusuf Asaf, and published as *al-Tawaf Hawl*

~ *al-Ard fi Thamanin Yawm* (Cairo, 1889); and *Voyage au pole nord,* translated by Tawfiq Bubariya ibn Yusuf Bey under the title *al-Rihla al-Shitwiyya fi al-Jihat al-Thaljiyya* (Cairo, 1894). Chateaubriand's *Les Aventures du dernier Abencérage* was translated into Arabic by Ahmad al-Faghun and was published under the title *al-Jawhar al-Wahhaj al-Manfusi fi Ghara'ib ibn Siraj al-Andalusi* (Algiers, 1864); another translation of this romance by al-Amir Shakib Arslan, who appended to it a short history of the Banu Siraj, was published as *Riwayat Akhir bani Siraj* (Alexandria, 1897; Cairo, 1924). Pierre Zaccone's *La vengeance* was adapted by Adib Ishaq and Salim Naqqash and published as *al-Intiqam* (Alexandria, 1880). *La Belle Parisienne,* by Comtesse Dash, was also adapted by Adib Ishaq and published in Cairo (n.d.). Eugene Sue's *Mathilde,* translated by Sami Qusayri, was published in two volumes (Beirut, 1885). See Pérès, pp. 292, 294, 307.

53. Pérès, pp. 290-309, provides an extensive bibliography of the works of French fiction translated after 1900, including both authors and others whose names are known only to a few students of French literature.

54. See Muhammad Yusuf Najm, *al-Masrahiyya fi al-Adab al Arabi al-Hadith 1847-1914* (Beirut, 1967), pp. 183, 222-256. Shaw's *Caesar and Cleopatra* was translated by Ibrahim Ramzi and published in 1914. Voltaire's *Mérope,* translated by Muhammad Iffat under the title *Tasliyat al-Qulub fi Mayrub* and was staged in January, 1889. Cf. Najm, p. 188, quoting *al-Ahram* (January 10, 1889), No. 3339.

55. Mahmud Hamid Shawkat, *al-Fann al-Qisasi fi al-Adab al-Misri al-Hadith* (Cairo, 1956), p. 127; al-Zayyat, p. 178.

56. Other monthly and bi-monthly publications which offered to their readers translations of fiction were *al-Bustan al-Zahir* (Cairo, 1907), *al-Fukahat al-Asriyya* (Cairo, 1908), founded by Abd Allah Ghazala al-Halabi; *Silsilat al-Riwayat al-'Uthmaniyya* (Tanta, 1908) by Jurji Dahhan; *Hadiqat al-Riwayat* (Cairo, 1909), founded by Sharikat Nashr al-Riwayat; *al-Rawi* (Beirut, 1909), by Tanius Abduh; *al-Riwayat al-Jadida* (Cairo, 1910), by Niqual Rizq Allah; *al-Samir* (Alexandria, 1911), by Kaiser Shumayyil; *al-Riwayat al-Kubra* (Cairo, 1914), by Murad al-Husayni; *al-Musamarat* (Cairo, 1921); *al-Nadim al-Riwa'i* (Cairo, 1922); *al-Samir al-Musawwar* (Cairo, 1921); and *al-Riwaya* (Cairo, 1937). See Pérès, pp. 269-70; al-Zayyat, p. 178; and Najm, *al-Qissa fi al-Adab,* p. 12.

57. Pérès, p. 270. This writer recalls that his sixth-grade Arabic teacher forbade the reading of such works of fiction, especially those published in the *Musamarat al-Jayb* series, on the grounds that they were of no literary value. Moreover, translated fiction of this work was so popular among the elementary school students in Mosul, Iraq, that many of them possessed substantial collections of these books. Indeed, this writer and other pupils in 1937 sent to Cairo for two boxes full of detective and mystery stories which they divided by lot.

58. See the Introduction of Anton Bey al-Jumayyil to the anthology *Diwan Tanius Abduh* (Cairo, 1925).

59. Pérès, p. 270.

60. Al-Zayyat, p. 173.

61. The first volume of this work by Hajjaj (Haggag, as he writes the name) is undated and bears the French title *Choix de poèmes lyriques et prose d'auteurs français avec leurs biographies,* while the second volume, dated 1922, is indicated to be a translation: *Traduction de quelques chef-d'ouevres des littératures française, allemande, italienne, et anglaise.*

62. Al-Zayyat, pp. 171-172.

63. *Ibid.*

64. Al-Zayyat, p. 101. 'Awad also translated a French novel entitled *al-Intiqam* (Vengeance), published in the Arabic version in 1905, without giving either the name of the author or the original title. Pérès, p. 309, lists the work as anonymous.

65. Badr, p. 133.

66. Pérès, pp. 309-311. See also Abdel-Aziz Abd al-Mequid, *The Modern Arabic Short Story* (Cairo, n.d.), pp. 97-98.

67. *Al-Hilal,* quoted by al-Zayyat, p. 63. We have found titles of several translated novels whose authors are not identified, published by al-Fawa'id Press in Beirut. They include Khalil Effendi Badawi's translations of *Riwayat Shaytan al-Mal* (1891), *Riwayat al-Fatat al-Siberiyya* (1892), and *Riwayat Khatf al-Ibnatayn* (1896), and Amin Effendi al-Halabi's translations of *Riwayat Mir'at al-Shahama* (1894), *Riwayat Jaza al-Ghadir* (1895), and *Riwayat al-Faqid al-Mawjud* (1895). See Louis Cheikho, "Tarikh Fann al-Tiba'a fi al-Mashriq," *al-Mashriq,* IV (1901), p. 323.

68. Salim Sarkis, *Majallat Sarkis* (1910), quoted by Anwar al-Jundi, p. 15, and al-Mequid, p. 98, n. 3.

69. Karam Milhim Karam, *Manahil al-Adab al-Arabi,* XVII, pp. 67-68, quoted by Najm, *al-Qissa fi al-Adab,* pp. 22-23. Anton al-Jumayyil states in his introduction to the Diwan of Tanius Abduh that Abduh produced no less than seven hundred translations and adaptations of fiction which became widely circulated, and adds, "No wonder that one finds the poor and the excellent among the output of a man whose books are counted by the hundreds."

70. See, for example, Muhammad Badran's translation of Wells' *The Food of the Gods,* entitled *Ta'am al-Aliha* (Cairo, 1947).

71. Al-Jundi, p. 49.

72. Al-Bayan greatly encouraged the translation of Western fiction into Arabic, and both al-Siba'i and his colleague Abbas Hafiz became engaged in translating novels and short stories, which they offered regularly to its readers. So strong was this periodical's concern with fiction that in 1914 it began to call itself a journal of fiction, as well as history and literature. According to Sayyid Hamid al-Nassaj, *Tatawwur Fann al-Qissa al-Qasira fi Misr* 1910-1933; (The Development of the Modern Short Story in Egypt, 1910-1933, Cairo, 1968), pp. 56-60, it emphasized the publication of Western fiction in translation to such an extent that not one "short story by an Egyptian writer appeared in it until its suspension in 1919."

73. See the article by al-Siba'i's son Yusuf, a contemporary Egyptian novelist, in *al-Jumhuriyya,* August 4, 1956. Al-Siba'i translated works by Chekhov, Dostoevsky, Pushkin, Gorski, Balzac, de Maupassant, France, Shakespeare, Byron, Dickens, Carlyle, Fitzgerald, Herbert Spencer, Wilkie Collins, and Irving. See Muhammad al-Siba'i, *Qisas Rusiyya* (Russian Stories) in *Iqra* Series. See also al-Jundi, pp. 47-57, and al-Nassaj, pp. 55-58. I am partially indebted for this information to Yusuf al-Siba'i, who graciously provided me with several biographies of Egyptian writers, including that of his father.

74. See al-Mazini's introduction, titled *al-Ustadh al-Siba'i wa Adabuhu,* to al-Siba'i's book *al-Suwar* (Cairo, 1946).

75. For a short account of al-Manfaluti's temperament and style see Gibb, pp. 258-268, though this source says little concerning al-Manfaluti's adaptations of Western fiction. Also of interest is Nevill Barbour, "Al-Manfaluti—An Egyptian Essayist," in *Islamic Culture*, VII (1933), 490-492. Barbour draws his information from al-Manfaluti's son, Hasan, the Egyptian writer Shafiq Ghirbal, and other sources. He mentions al-Manfaluti's contradictions and the vehement criticism of his writings by al-'Aqqad and Taha Husayn. Included in an appendix in the same journal is an English translation of several essays by al-Manfaluti. See also C. Brockelmann, *Geschichte der arabischen Literatur*, Supplement III (Leiden, 1942), 197-202.

76. Mustafa Lutfi al-Manfaluti, *al-Nazarat*, 11th ed., I (Cairo, 1954). Introduction, 9; Ahmad Hasan al-Zayyat, *Wahi al-Risala*, 7th ed., I (Cairo, 1962), 385-390, discusses al-Manfaluti's life, upbringing, and literary achievement.

77. *Al-Nazarat*, I, 5-8; Ahmad Hasan al-Zayyat, 1, 389.

78. Al-Zayyat, I, 389; Shawqi Dayf, *al-Adab al-Arabi al-Mu'asir fi Misr* (Cairo, 1961), p. 228.

79. *Al-Diwan fi al-Adab wa al-Naqd* (Cairo, 1921), particularly Chapter 11. See also Abbas Mahmud al-'Aqqad, *Muraja'at fi al-Adab wa al-Funun* (Cairo, 1925), pp. 170-84, and Barbour, pp. 490-92.

80. See al-Manufaluti's essays *al-Inithar* (Suicide) and *'Ala Firash al-Mawt* (On the Deathbed) in *Al-Nazarat*, Volume I; in each work the principal character ends his own life.

81. Gibb, pp. 264-5; al-Manfaluti, *al-Nazarat*, I, passim. In his essay *al-Madaniyya al-Gharbiyya* (Western Civilization) al-Manufaluti emphatically but unjustifiably says, "Each step that the Egyptian takes toward the West will bring him to his end, to an abyss where he will be buried until doomsday. The Egyptian, weak and submissive as he is, when he approaches Western civilization, becomes like a sieve which holds the bran and lets the flour out. Or he will be like a wine-filter which holds the residue and siphons the wine. He should flee from Western civilization as the healthy person flees from the patient who is stricken with scabies." Shukri Ayyad, p. 105, rightly comments that if this Egyptian is so weak and submissive that he cannot take from Western civilization what benefits him and reject what is harmful to him, it is truer still that he should be unable to reject this civilization, which has entered his gates. See Shukri Muhammad Ayyad, *al-Qissa al-Qasira fi Misr: Dirasa fi Ta'sil Fann Adabi*, (Cairo, 1968), p. 105.

82. Shawkat, pp. 80, 1, makes al-Manfaluti a *mutarjim*, i.e., a translator, by which he probably means "an adapter." Shawqi Dayf, p. 229, correctly considers al-Manfaluti an adapter.

83. Badr, pp. 179-80.

84. 'Ayyad, pp. 105-18, studies al-Manfaluti as an essayist and short story writer. Abbas Khidr, *al-Qissa al-Qasira fi Misr mundhu Nash'atiha hatta Sanat 1930* (Cairo, 1966), pp.55, 62-66, likewise studies al-Manfaluti as a short story writer.

85. Al-Manfaluti, *al-Dahiyya aw Mudhakkirat Margarit*, in *al-Abarat* (Cairo, 1956), pp. 159-208; *al-Shudada*, pp. 22-49; and *al-Dhikra*, pp. 71-93. Directly beneath the Arabic titles of these short romances appears the term *mutarjama* (translated). See also Pérès, p. 292, on further translations and adaptations of these works.

86. Pérès, p. 306. According to Yusuf As'ad Daghir, "Fann al-Tamthil fi Khilal Qarn," *al-Mashriq,* XLII (1948), 127, a translation of this play made by Muhammad Abd al-Salam al-Jundi was published in Egypt in 1921. According to Pérès, p. 293, n. 1, an Arabic verse translation by Halim Dammus appeared at Beirut in 1925.

87. Al-Manfaluti, *Fi Sabil al-Taj* (Cairo, 1920); Pérès, p. 293.

88. Pérès, p. 291. For details of al-Manfaluti's manipulation of the original French work, see E. Saussey, "Une Adaptation Arabe de *Paul et Virginie,*" *Bulletin d'Etudes Orientales,* I (1931), 49-80.

89. See Constantine's speeches in *Fi Sabil al-Taj,* pp. 30-31, in which he uses Qur'anic verses. See also Badr, p. 183.

90. *Fi Sabil al-Taj,* pp. 30-31.

91. Shawkat, p. 81.

92. Shawkat, p. 81; Dayf, p. 229.

93. See the criticism of al-Manfaluti by al-Aqqad and al-Mazini in *al-Diwan fi al-Adab wa al-Naqd.*

94. Dayf, p. 229. In *al-Ahram,* July 19, 1921, Hasan al-Sharif says that al-Manfaluti's work is neither an Arabicization, translation, adaptation, nor a composition, but simply a distortion of the original. He goes on to say that it does not conform with the accepted principles of translation.

95. 'Isa 'Ubayd's introduction to *Ihsan Hanim Majmu'at Qisas Misriyya 'Asriyya* (Anthology of Contemporary Egyptian Stories) 2nd ed. (Cairo, 1964). For a glimpse of 'Isa 'Ubayd's role in the development of modern Arabic fiction, see this writer's article "The Growth of Modern Arabic Fiction," *Critique: Studies in Modern Fiction,* XI (1968), No. 1, pp. 8-9.

96. A controversy arose between Mansur Fahmi and Taha Husayn over al-Manfaluti's adaptation of *Cyrano de Bergerac.* Fahmi admired al-Manfaluti's effort and described his adaptation as useful, because it presented to Arab readers a masterpiece of Western literature. Although al-Manfaluti did not produce the original exactly, Fahmi argued, he succeeded in presenting in a clear Arabic style a reasonable likeness of it; indeed, his presentation of some parts of this romance was impeccable. In defending al-Manfaluti, Fahmi contended that it would be better to have some slight notion of a new work of literature known only in translation than to avoid this literature altogether. Taha Husayn criticized al-Manfaluti's conversion of Rostand's drama from verse to prose. Furthermore, said Husayn, al-Manfaluti did not work from the original but from someone else's translation. He questioned whether it was worthwhile to have a deficient and distorted translation, or to argue that such a work is better than no translation at all. See al-Jundi, p. 60.

97. Ahmad Hasan al-Zayyat, *Wahi al-Risala,* I, 386-7, throws some light on the reason Husayn attacked al-Manfaluti. He relates that when al-Manfaluti's articles in *al-Mu'ayyad* were compiled and published in *al-Nazarat,* the nationalist writer Abd al-'Aziz Shawish, who succeeded Mustafa Kamil as editor of *al-Liwa,* criticized al-Manfaluti severely in an article entitled "Tabaqat al-Kuttab" (The Categories of Writers.) Al-Zayyat believes Shawish composed this article at the behest of the nationalist leader Sa'd Zaghlul. Taha Husayn, who had relations with Shawish, was then apparently instigated by Zaghlul to criticize al-Manfaluti's

work. Al-Zayyat says Husayn wrote more than thirty articles vigorously attacking al-Manfaluti, so that his own relations with al-Manfaluti and those of his colleagues were permanently ruined. Husayn confirms al-Zayyat's observations in his recently published memoirs, *Mudhakkirat Taha Husayn* (Beirut, 1967), pp. 36-38, saying that Shawish instigates him to write his fiery articles criticizing al-Manfaluti and *al-Nazarat*.

98. Muhammad Husayn Haykal, *Thawrat al-Adab* (Cairo, 1965), pp. 24-34, 211-19, makes some interesting observations on the influence of Western literature on both al-Manfaluti and Ahmad Hasan al-Zayyat.

99. See Al-Zayyat, *Wahi al-Risala,* IV, 154, in which he mentions that he went to Baghdad in 1930.

100. Al-Zayyat, *Wahi al-Risala,* I, 45-48 and 355-358.

101. Al-Zayyat, *Wahi al-Risala,* IV, 72-75.

102. Ni'mat Fu'ad, "Sahib al-Risala Yahtajib," *al-Ahram,* January 21, 1968, p. 13. Al-Zayyat, *Wahi al-Risala,* IV, 102-106, gives the reasons for which he suspended publication of *al-Risala.*

103. Al-Zayyat, *Wahi al-Risala,* II, 1-4, 11-13, 98-114 and 328-333.

104. Al-Zayyat, "Limadha Tarjamtu Alam Werther," in *Wahi al-Risala,* I, 44, defends his use of Qur'anic language in translating *Werthers Leiden,* in response to query by the Iraqi writer and journalist Rafa'il Butti. A much less popular translation of the same was made earlier by Izz al-Arab Ali under the title *Ahzan Werther* and appeared serially in the newspaper *al-Jarida* in 1914. See Hamza, *Adab al-Maqala al-Suhufiyya: Ahmad Lutfi al-Sayyid* (Cairo: 1954), p. 174.

105. Al-Zayyat's letter to the Minister of Education appeared in *al-Risala* in April, 1945, and was followed by an article on the same subject in June, 1945; both are published in *Wahi al-Risala,* III, 38-46. Al-Zayyat reiterates some of his proposals in *Wahi al-Risala,* IV, 299-307.

106. Al-Zayyat, *Wahi al-Risala,* III, 38-39 and IV, 301-303.

107. Al-Zayyat, *Ibid.,* III, 39.

108. Al-Zayyat, *Ibid.,* III, 40 and IV, 301-303.

109. Al-Zayyat, *Ibid.,* IV, 301, complains that in 1953 only fifty-four Western books were translated into Arabic in Egypt, and most of these were badly done. See also Muhyi al-Din Muhammad, "Risala min al-Qahira," *Adab,* I (1962), 128-132.

110. For titles of the stories of de Maupassant translated and published in *al-Risala* and other periodicals and anthologies, see Pérès, pp. 303-304, and Shawkat, *al-Fann al-Qisasi,* p. 131.

111. The most detailed sources of information on al-Mazini are his autobiography *Qissat Hayat* (Cairo, 1961) and Ni'mat Ahmad Fu'ad, *Adab al-Mazini* (Cairo, 1954).

112. Al-Jundi, *Tatawwur al-Tarjama fi al-Adab al-Arabi al-Mu'asir,* p. 63.

113. Badr, p. 341.

114. Badr, p. 341; Fu'ad, pp. 180-187.

115. Al-Mazini, Introduction to *Mukhtarat min al-Qisas al-Ingilizi.*

116. Al-Jundi, p. 65.

117. Fu'ad, pp. 179-188, in a chapter titled "al Mazini al-Mutarjim," critically studies this aspect of al-Mazini's career, showing both the excellence and the shortcomings of his translations. The author also provides specific comparative samples to

illustrate al-Mazini's alteration of the original text.

118. Gibb, p. 303, especially n. 205; Fu'ad, pp. 189-90.
119. Fu'ad, pp. 187-8.
120. Al-Nasr, pp. 259-66.
121. Al-Mazini, *Sunduq al-Dunya* (Cairo, 1929), includes *al-Sighar wa al-Kibar,* pp. 30-38; *al-Haqa'iq al-Bariza fi Hayati,* pp. 75-86; and *Muqtatafat min Mudhak-kirat Hawwa,* pp. 92-112. See also Pérès, pp. 324-5.
122. Al-Mazini, *Sunduq al-Dunya,* pp. 311-20; Pérès, p. 325.
123. 'Aziz Abd Allah Salama, *Mukhtarat* (Selections; Cairo, 1926) and Faraj Gibran, *Qisas an Jama'a min Mashahir Kuttab al-Gharb* (Stories by a Group of Famous Western Writers; Cairo, 1927) include some works of Alphonse Daudet, Maxim Gorky, Anatole France, Marcel Prevost, and other anonymous writers. See also Tawfiq Abd Allah, *al-Qisas al-'Asriyya* (Modern Stories; Cairo, n.d.), Muhammad Abd Allah Inan, *Qisas Ijtima'iyya wa Namadhij min Adab al-Gharb* (Social Stories and Examples from Western Literature; Cairo, 1932); Pérès, pp. 290-307, *passim,* and Kamil Gaylani *Rawa'i' min Qisas al-Gharb.*
124. Shawkat, p. 130.
125. *Ibid.*
126. See Charles 'Issawi, "European Loan-Words in Contemporary Arabic Writing: A Case Study in Modernization," *Middle East Studies* (Spring, 1967), pp. 110-133.

CHAPTER V: THE REVIVAL OF THE MAQAMA

1. Shawqi Dayf, *al-Maqama* (Cairo, 1964), pp. 10-11. This work presents a concise yet very interesting study of the origin, theme, and style of the maqama.
2. Fakhri Abu al-Su'ud, "Al-Qissa fi af-Adabayn al-Arabi wa al-Ingilizi," *al Risala* (1937), No. 198, pp. 653-654; Muhammad Yusuf Najm, *al-Qissa fi al-Adab al-Arabi al-Hadith* (Beirut, 1961), pp. 223-225. Obviously Abu al Su'ud ignores the complete disparity between the circumstances in which the maqama arose and those in which Addison and Steele developed the fictionalized essay. During the late seventeenth and early eighteenth centuries, England offered a substantial and growing body of readers who were delighted by the presentation of factual accounts in an exciting, imaginative manner. Journalism came in this period to be a potent force in the development of new modes and new tastes in literature, as is evident from the popularity of Sir Roger L'Estrange's *Observateur* (1679), John Dunton's *Athenian Gazette* (1690), Pierre Motteux's *Gentleman's Journal* (1692), Ned Ward's monthly *London Spy* (1968), and Daniel Defoe's newspaper *The Review* (1704-1713). Furthermore, the rising commerical class, with more and more leisure time available, formed an indispensable reading public for English writers. These two elements, the ready audience and the means of reaching it, were lacking in Arab society even at the height of its cultural development in the tenth century.
3. Al-Yaziji humbly states in *Majma' al-Bahrayn* (Beirut, n.d.), p. 3, that he is only an intruder in the realm of the great belletrists. Although he considered his output of no great worth, his motivation for writing the maqamas was his desire to produce something new.
4. For discussion of the maqamas of Nasif al-Yaziji, see Dayf, pp. 83-109; Henri Pérès, *Les premiers manifestations de la renaissance littéraire arabe en Orient au XIX siècle; Nasif al-Yazigi et Faris as-Sidyaq*, *Annales de l'Institut d'Etudes Orientales de la Faculté des Lettres d'Alger*, 1, (1934-5), 233-56. The earliest biography of Nasif al-Yaziji is by Salim Effendi Dhiyab in *al-Jinan* (1871), pp. 150-7, 190-6, and is based on the author's friendship and association with al-Yaziji. For comprehensive studies of al-Yaziji's life and works, see Fu'ad Afram al-Bustani, "Nasif al-Yaziji," *al-Mashriq* (1928), pp. 834-843, 923-939, and Ignaz Kratschkowsky, "Al-Yazidji," *The Encyclopedia of Islam* (1934) IV, 1170-1171.
5. Al-Bustani, "Shadharat fi al-Nahda al-Adabiyya: Nasif al-Yaziji wa Faris al-Shidyaq," *al-Mashriq* (1936), pp. 443-447; Ra'if Khuri,: Yaqdat al-Wa'i al-Arabi fi Maqamat al- Yaziji," *al-Makshuf*, Nos. 426 and 427, quoted by Najim, p. 332; Dayf, pp. 83-109; Najim, pp. 223-225.
6. Al-Yaziji, *Majma' al-Bahrayn*, introduction, p. 3.
7. Ahmad Faris al-Shidyaq, *al-Saq 'ala al-Saq fi ma huwa al-Faryaq*, 2 vols. (Cairo, 1855). Al-Faryaq is a compound name denoting the full name of the author. For

statements on the influence of French writers on al-Shidyaq, see Pérès, pp. 250-2.

8. One should not be misled by the exaggerated view of Henri Pérès, who zealously attempts to attribute al-Shidyaq's ideas, creativeness, and lively style solely to his contact with European life and thought. He leads the reader to believe that in his monumental work *Al-Saq 'ala al-Saq fi ma huwa al-Faryaq* (literally Leg upon Leg in explaining who is al-Faryaq, i.e., the author himself), Faris al-Shidyaq was greatly influenced by French writers, particularly Rabelais. In this regard Fu'ad Afram al-Bustani, a contemporary writer and critic, observes:

> It would have been more appropriate if Pérès had been less precipitate in attributing whatever beauties are contained in *al-Saq 'ala al-Saq* to Western sources, such as the author's remark to his wife, "Let us now come back to the question of farewell," which Pérès connected with Panurge's famous saying, "Retournons à nos moutons," while the difference between the two sayings and their circumstances is obvious. Pérès should have been less outspoken in his evaluation of *al-Saq 'ala al-Saq*, an imaginative style, but still lacking many of the characteristics of Western story writing. See al-Bustani, "Shadharat," *al-Mashriq* (1936), pp. 446-447.

9. Muhammad al-Muwaylihi, *Hadith 'Isa ibn Hisham aw Fatra min al-Zaman,* 4th ed. (Cairo, 1964), with an introduction by Ali Adham.

10. Ali Adham, Introduction to *Hadith Isa ibn Hisham;* Ali al-Ra'i, *Dirasat fi al-Riwaya al-Misriyya* (Cairo, 1964), p. 20. The contemporary writer Abbas Khidr, *al-Qissa al-Qasira fi Misr Mundhu Nash'atiha hatta Sanat* 1930 (Cairo, 1966), p. 51, indicates that al-Muwaylihi wanted to introduce "the art of the story as it is known in the West today into modern Arabic literature, but did not do so. Instead, he searched for an Arab literary form to suit his purpose, and found that the Maqama was most suitable."

11. Adham, *Ibid.;* Abd al-'Aziz al-Bishri, *al-Mukhtar* I (Cairo, 1959), 236-252. According to Abd al-Latif Hamza, *Adab al-Maqala al-Suhufiyya,* III (Cairo, 1959), 32, the young Muwaylihi's burning desire to learn motivated him to seek knowledge from an apothecary who lived next door to his father.

12. Adham, *Ibid.*

13. The influence of Western culture on al-Muwaylihi is most apparent in his literary criticism, particularly of poetry. See Abbas Mahmud al-'Aqqad, *Rijal Araftuhum* (Cairo, 1963), pp. 76-88, and al-Muwaylihi's Introduction to the *Diwan* (Anthology) of Hafiz Ibrahim (Cairo, 1901-3). On al-Muwaylihi as a critic, see Hilmi Ali Marzuq, *Tatawwur al-Naqd wa al-Tafkir al-Adabi al-Hadith fi Misr* (Cairo, 1966), pp. 201-23.

14. According to al-Bishri, I, 241, *al-Misbah* opened an entirely new vista in Arabic literature and by itself constituted a new school of refined literature in Egypt.

15. Al-Muwaylihi, pp. 1-6.

16. *Ibid.,* pp. 7-13.

17. *Ibid.,* pp. 51-7.

18. *Ibid.,* pp. 57-61.

19. *Ibid.,* pp. 61-98.

20. *Ibid.,* pp. 289-351.

21. *Ibid.*, pp. 284-5.
22. For a description of the crowds and shops in Paris see al-Muwaylihi, *Ibid.*, p. 290.
23. *Ibid.*, pp. 312-7.
24. *Ibid.*, pp. 332-3.
25. *Ibid.*, p. 162.
26. *Ibid.*, pp. 16, 55-60 and 125.
27. *Ibid.*, p. 185.
28. *Ibid.*, pp. 185-285. See also Mahmud Hamid Shawkat, *al-Fann al-Qisasi fi al-Adab al-Misri al-Hadith* (Cairo, 1956), pp. 46-47, and 'Ayyad, pp. 72-73.
29. See al-Ra'i, p. 19; 'Ayyad, p. 70. This judgment is not shared by Ghali Shukri, who in *Thawrat al-Fikr fi Adabina al-Hadith,* (Cairo, 1965), pp. 186-88, states that al-Ra'i was very anxious to demonstrate similarities between Arabic literary works and the great classics of the West, in order to give the former more prestige. Another view is presented by 'Ayyad, p. 70, who states that in his *Hadith* al-Muwaylihi reflected the state of Egyptian capitalism, which began showing its impact in the time of the Khedive Isma'il, and which supported the Urabi revolution but later was overwhelmed by foreign capital during the British occupation.
30. Al-Ra'i, *Ibid.*, p. 19.
31. *Ibid.*
32. *Ibid.*
33. *Ibid.*
34. Cf. Mahmud Timur, *Fann al-Qisas* (Cairo, 1948), p. 37, and *Nushu al-Qissa wa Tatawwuruha* (Cairo, 1936), pp. 46-7; 'Umar al-Disuqi, *Muhadarat an Nash'at al-Nathr al-Hadith wa Tatawwuruhu* (Cairo, 1962), pp. 137-8. Abd al-Muhsin Taha Badr, *Tatawwur al-Riwaya al-Arabiyya al-Haditha fi Misr* (Cairo, 1963), p. 37. According to 'Ayyad, pp. 73-4, since al-Muwaylihi's purpose was to expose and criticize social problems in Egypt, he chose to voice his opinions through several different characters rather than a single character. Thus his characters should not be faulted for lacking coordination of action or unity of values.
35. See al-Ra'i, p. 10.
36. Al-Disuqi, p. 138.
37. This translation, generally poor, reflected Hafiz's inadequate grasp of the French language.
38. Hafiz Ibrahim, *Layali Satih,* ed. with introduction by Abd al-Rahman Sidqi (Cairo, 1964); later references are to this text. *Layali Satih* first appeared in 1906; another edition worth noting is that of Muhammad Kamil Jumu'a (Cairo, 1959).
39. Ibrahim, pp. 1-4.
40. *Ibid.*, pp. 4-9.
41. See Lord Cromer, *Modern Egypt* (New York, 1908), II, 213-217; *al-Hilal,* I (1906-1907), 265; and Marzuq, pp. 38-51.
42. For a justification of this allegation see Lord Cromer, II, 214.
43. Ibrahim, pp. 9-13.
44. For the extra-territorial privileges which foreign nationals enjoyed in Egypt and the British attitude toward these privileges, see Cromer, II, 254-259, 426-442 and Muhammad 'Awad Muhammad, *al-Isti'mar wa al-Madhahib al-Isti'mariyya* 3rd ed. (Cairo, 1961), pp. 54-56.

45. Ibrahim, p. 16.
46. *Ibid.*, pp. 17-9.
47. *Ibid.*, pp. 19-23.
48. The reproduction of a chapter from al-Muwaylihi's *Hadith* is not an indication that Hafiz consciously imitated al-Muwaylihi, but rather evidence that he was influenced by some of al-Muwaylihi's ideas. Cf. note 56 below, and Muhammad Kamil Jumu'a, *Hafiz Ibrahim ma lahu wa ma 'Alayhi* (Cairo, 1960), pp. 323-32.
49. In recognition of Shawqi's superb poetic talent and the defense in his poetry of Eastern, especially Arab and Islamic attributes, poets from all over the Arab world assembled in Cairo in 1927 to confer upon him the title "The Prince of Poets." A very interesting study of various aspects of the lives and poetry of Hafiz and Shawqi is Taha Husayn, *Hafiz wa Shawqi* (Cairo, 1966).
50. Ibrahim, pp. 40-2, and Nafusa Zakariyya Sa'id *Tarikh al-Da'wa ila al-'Amiyya wa Atharuha fi Misr* (Cairo, 1964), present the views of those Egyptian writers who advocated the widespread use of colloquial Egyptian instead of classical Arabic as the literary language. Interestingly, some Arab writers who teach the Arabic language and culture in the United States hold an entirely opposite view. Khalil Semaan, for example, complains that Western Orientalists and some Arab writers consider the Arabic language difficult to teach and learn, largely because of alleged differences between its spoken and written forms. This distorted view, he explains, is but one of many held by Orientalists, particularly those concerned with the study of the Arabs' language and culture, about the Arab East, which they often associate with the desert, camels, and tents. See Khalil Semaan, " 'Ala Hamish Da'wa al-Su'uba fi Ta'allum al-Arabiyya," *Majallat Majma' al-Lugha al-Arabiyya bi Dimashq*, XLII (October, 1967), p. 795.
51. For a criticism of Lord Cromer's policies, particularly his educational policy in Egypt, see Umar al-Disugi, *Fi al-Adab al-Hadith*, I (Beirut, 1967), 449-454 and II, 10-50, and Ali Yusuf in *al-Mu'ayyad*, May 7, 1907. A more detailed analysis of Lord Cromer's different policies is found in Afaf Lutfi al-Sayyid, *Egypt and Cromer: A Study in Anglo-Egyptian Relations* (New York, 1969).
52. In this chapter Hafiz seems to come closest to al-Muwaylihi's *Hadith* in his moral preachment and his condemnation of immoral practices.
53. Badr, p. 70.
54. Fu'ad Dawwara, *Fi al-Riwaya al-Misriyya* (Cairo, 1968), p. 7, notes that although the *Hadith* and *Layali Satih* share some common characteristics, the widely different moods of their authors are reflected in the manner of their writing. While a touch of delight and cheerfulness pervades al-Muwaylihi's *Hadith* even when he sternly criticizes the foibles of his society, Hafiz appears gloomy and extremely pessimistic in his work. The difference in the two authors' moods, Dawwara feels, may be attributed to the conditions under which they lived and worked. Mahmud Timur, *Malamih wa Ghudun* (Cairo, 1950), p. 215, expresses the opinion that al-Muwaylihi, by presenting more mature characters and depicting interesting situations, moved farther from the old, traditional maqama toward a sophisticated story resembling modern Western prose fiction, while Hafiz adhered to the maqama's principles and emphasized the didactic aspect of his work rather than its artistic qualities. Also of interest is 'Ayyad's chapter on *Layali Satih*, pp. 80-89.
55. Ibrahim, p. 34.

56. See Sidqi's introduction to *Layali Satih,* pp. 67-70.

57. Muhammad Lutfi Jumu'a, *Layali al-Ruh al-Ha'ir* (Cairo, 1912) pp. 4-11; Ayyad, p. 92.

58. But while Jumu'a shows a deep concern over the problems facing Egyptian youth, the intelligent reader who anxiously awaits their solution puts the book aside with resentment and disappointment when he finds his expectations have not been met. He will be absolutely appalled, after finishing the account of the third night, to learn that the author blames the decline of the East on the simplistic premise that Easterners do not respect or appreciate their great men. This oversimplification of complex issues, however, should not detract from Jumu'a's importance among the intelligentsia in Egypt in the first quarter of this century. Jumu'a, *Layali al-Ruh al-Ha'ir,* pp. 22-28.

59. Jumu'a, *Layali al-Ruh al-Ha'ir,* pp. 4-11.

60. *Ibid.,* pp. 12-21.

61. *Ibid.,* pp. 22-28.

62. *Ibid.,* pp. 29-35.

63. *Ibid.,* pp. 36-41.

64. *Ibid.,* pp. 41-43.

65. For the controversial origin of the Arabic free verse see Nazik al-Mala'ika, *Qadaya al-Shi'r al-Mu'asir* (Beirut, 1962); Cheikho, *Adab al-Lugha al-Arabiyya fi al-Rub al-Awwal min al-Qarn al-'Ishrin,* pp. 6, 7 and 40-43; 'Umar al-Disuqi, *Fi al-Adab al-Hadith,* II, 225-237; Anis al-Khuri al-Maqdisi, *al-Ittijahat al-Adabiyya fi al-Alam al-Arabi al-Hadith,* (Baghdad, 1967), pp. 235-290.

66. Ayyad, p. 92.

67. See footnote 65. Of interest are Jamil Sa'id, *Nazarat fi al-Tayyarat al-Adabiyya al-Haditha fi al-Iraq* (Cairo, 1954), pp. 95-99, and *al-Adab al-Arabi al-Mu'asir,* minutes of the conference on Arabic literature which met in Rome in October, 1961, p. 171-191. A more detailed study in Jalil Kamal al-Din, *al-Shi'r al-Arabi al-Hadith wa Ruh al-'Asr* (Beirut, 1964).

68. *Ibid., Layali al-Ruh al-Ha'ir,* pp. 42-50.

69. *Ibid.,* pp. 51-56.

70. Ayyad, p. 89.

71. Jumu'a, pp. 88-97.

72. *Ibid.,* pp. 98-104.

73. 'Ayyad, p. 99.

CHAPTER VI: SALIM AL-BUSTANI AND THE BEGINNING OF MODERN ARABIC FICTION

1. Viscount Philip de Tarrazi, *Tarikh al-Sihafa al-Arabiyya,* I (Beirut, 1913), 103.
2. *Al-Jinan,* established by al-Mu'allim (Master) Butrus al-Bustani, was a political, scientific, literary, and historical magazine. The motto printed on its first page, "The Country's love is of faith," shows the beginnings of national sentiment in Syria. It was probably the first Arabic periodical to adopt a motto, and others followed its precedent. *Al-Jinan* was very popular in the Arab countries and attracted such eminent writers as Shibly Shumayyil, who contributed many articles on modern sciences; Ibrahim al-Yaziji, Sulayman al-Bustani, who translated Homer's *Iliad* into Arabic; Bishop Anton Qandalaft; Cornelius Van Dyke, the pioneer American missionary; Iskandar Abkarius; Marquis Musa de Fraige; al-Shaykh Nawfal Nawfal; Adib Ishaq; Ibrahim Sarkis; Francis Marrash; Shakir Shuqayr; Jamil Mudawwar; Jurji Yeni; As'ad Tirad; Nu'man Abduh al-Qasatli; and many others.
3. For the life and works of Salim al-Bustani, see Tarrazi, II, 68-70; Cheikho, *al-Adab al-Arabiyya fi al-Qarn al-Tasi 'Ashr,* II, 127-28; Yusuf Alyan Sarkis, *Mu'jam al-Matbu'at al-Arabiyya wa al-Mu'arraba,* I (Cairo, 1928), 559; and Muhammad Yusuf Najm, *al-Qissa fi al-Adab al-Arabi al-Hadith* (Beirut, 1961), pp. 31-65, 140-156, and 236-243.
4. See *al-Jinan* (1877), p. 393.
5. *Asma* appeared serially in *al-Jinan* in 1873.
6. *Fatina* appeared serially in *al-Jinan* in 1877.
7. *Salma* was serialized in *al-Jinan* in 1878 and 1879 and *Samiya* in 1882, 1883, and 1884.
8. See for example *Asma, Ibid.,* p. 284.
9. *Bint al-'Asr, al-Jinan* (1875), p. 143.
10. *Ibid.,* p. 318.
11. *Asma,* p. 35.
12. *Ibid.,* pp. 68-69.
13. *Ibid.,* pp. 214-215.
14. *Ibid.,* p. 317.
15. *Ibid.,* p. 430.
16. *Fatina, al-Jinan* (1877), p. 66.
17. *Ibid.,* pp. 70 and 102.
18. Al-Bustani wrote an article entitled "Ruh al-'Asr" (The Spirit of the Age), in the July issue of *al-Jinan* (1870), pp. 285-288. See also Leon Zolondek, "Socio-Political View of Salim al-Bustani" (1848-1884), *Middle Eastern Studies* 2 (1965-1966), p. 144, and Salih J. Altoma, "Ruh al-'Asr wa Salim al-Bustani," *al-*

Adab (October, 1970), pp. 44-46.

19. *Ibid.* of interest is al-Bustani's article entitled *al-Ams* (Yesterday) is *al-Jinan* (1870), pp. 641-48 in which he explains that the components of common ethnic origin, language, religion and historical background, for which he uses the term "al'Usba al-Jinsiyya," are against *Ruh al-'Asr*, because they are particular and cannot be achieved without the exclusion of certain peoples.

20. See al-Bustani's editorial which he commonly called "Jumla Siyasiyya" (Political Commentary) in *al-Jinan* (1873), p. 362. His association of equality, justice, and religious tolerance with *Ruh al-'Asr* is evident in many of his editorials, articles, and novels. For example, see his article "al-Dawla al-'Aliyya," *al-Jinan* (June, 1870), p. 354 and his editorial in *al-Jinan,* (August, 1872), pp. 505-506.

21. *Al-Jinan* (1872), p. 650. In his editorial in *al-Jinan* (March, 1873), p. 145, al-Bustani discusses the effect of the principles of the French Revolution on the regimes of Europe, especially those which were overthrown because of the Kings' insistence on preserving their own rights in opposition to *ruh hadha al-'Asr* (the spirit of this age), by which he means the age of the freedom of man. For further elaboration on this subject see his editorials in *al-Jinan* (1873), p. 685 and (1877), p. 3.

22. See al-Bustani's article "al-Insaf," *in al-Jinan* (1870), pp. 369-371.

23. *Bint al-'Asr, al-Jinan* (1875), pp. 67-68.

24. *Asma, al-Jinan* (1873), p. 826.

25. *Ibid.*, p. 68.

26. *Ibid.*, pp. 31-32.

27. *Ibid.*, pp. 39-40 and 141. It is evident that al-Bustani was fully aware of the social, economic, and cultural transition of his society not only in his writing of fiction but in his articles, too. In his article entitled "al-Tawfir al-Siyasi wa Tahsin Ahwal al-Umma" (Political Economy and the Improvement of the Conditions of the Nation) published in *al-Jinan* (1875), al-Bustani, after discussing the economic decline in Syria, shifts from economics to sociology and discussed the inability of the Syrian society to accept new and unfamiliar forms and customs such as permitting women to sit in the assemblies of men before they could learn how to discuss subjects other than engagements, marriages, clothes, and cosmetics. See *al-Jinan,* (1875), p. 204.

28. *Fatina* appeared serially in *al-Jinan* in 1877.

29. *Ibid.*, pp. 68-69.

30. *Ibid.*, p. 33.

31. *Asma*, p. 32.

32. *Asma*, p. 67.

33. *Ibid.*, pp. 249, 537-538, and 608-610. Of interest is Nabiha's conversation with a certain European man about the East and West and that both of them have their own good and bad aspects, p. 610.

34. *Ibid.*, p. 642. In his editorial "Jumla Ababiyya," al-Bustani states that it is not shameful to adopt European customs. What is shameful is to adopt ugly European customs just because they are European. *See al-Jinan* (January 15, 1874), pp. 38-39.

35. *Ibid.*, p. 211.

36. *Ibid.*, pp. 608-610.

37. *Ibid.*, p. 249.

38. *Ibid.*, p. 140.

39. Beside Asma, see for example, Samiya who although eighteen years old, speaks like a sage who has profound knowledge of her society and is aware of the responsibilities of the individual as well as those of the society. Consider also Sida who enters with Fu'ad into intellectual, philosophical, and religious conversation which demonstrates her to be a near prodigy. See *Asma,* p. 33, and *Samiya* pp. 477, 703, and 729.

40. *Asma,* p. 33.

41. *Ibid.,* p. 104.

42. *Ibid.,* p. 66.

43. *Ibid.*

44. *Samiya,* p. 731.

45. *Fatina,* p. 105.

46. *Ibid.,* pp. 107, 214 and 284-285.

47. *Ibid.,* p. 393. Al-Bustani states that the reader would like to know the details about this incident. This incident took place in Italy in which of late, there were many robbers who attacked passengers and travelers. Some of them live in underground caves and obey their ruler who is their chief as well as their judge. He further states that they are generous and magnanimous.

48. *Ibid.,* p. 428.

49. *Ibid.*

50. *Ibid.,* pp. 430-431.

51. *Ibid.,* pp. 429-431.

52. *Ibid.,* p. 756.

53. *Ibid.*

54. *Samiya, al-Jinan* (1882), pp. 538-539.

55. *Ibid.,* p. 539.

56. See the text of Butrus al-Bustani's speech advocating women's education, delivered at the meeting of the Syrian Society on January 14, 1849 in *al-Jinan* (1882), pp. 207-214.

57. *Samiya, al-Jinan* (1882), p. 729.

58. See the long dialogue between Sida and Fu'ad in *Ibid.,* pp. 702-703.

59. See Sida's conversation with Fa'iz in *Samiya, al-Jinan* (1883) p. 621.

60. *Ibid., al-Jinan* (1882), pp. 411-412. Al-Bustani is probably the first Arab writer to have used the term *Ishtirakiyya* as the translation of socialism. This term has become part of the Arab political vocabulary until this day.

61. *Samiya, al-Jinan* (1883), pp. 286 and 350.

62. *Ibid.,* p. 524.

63. *Ibid.*

64. *Ibid.,* p. 525. There is a rather close parallel between the ideas that al-Bustani has his so-called socialist spokesmen espouse and those of the philosophers. Socialist doctrine is not based upon "natural law," but it is an ideology founded upon a particular view of history and society.

65. *Ibid.,* p. 526.

66. *Ibid.,* pp. 350-351 and 526-527. Al-Bustani believes that equality in rights is desirable, but those who belive in equality in mental and physical powers are mere dreamers. Equality is, furthermore, not possible in the possession of wealth. He states that the inequality in livelihood is the one which requires reform. This

reform should be achieved through laws and statutes not violence, plunder, and killing. He seems to advocate a moderate kind of socialism. He states that legislation should be enacted to enable every person to have a sufficient living by doing work commensurate with his ability. Furthermore, legislation should guarantee adequate compensation for the poor, the disabled, and the sick, p. 526.

67. *Samiya* in *al-Jinan* (1882), pp. 410-411 and 507.

68. *Ibid., al-Jinan* (1884), p. 127.

69. *Ibid., al-Jinan* (1882), p. 569.

70. *Ibid.,* p. 508.

71. *Al-Jinan* (March 1, 1873), p. 145. In this editorial, al-Bustani wishes that Europeans would put a stop to the extremists, not the socialists, because their violent expectation of the millenium is detrimental to the moderate social reformers who call on countries of the world to enact laws to insure more social and economic justice.

72. *Samiya, al-Jinan* (1882), p. 415.

73. *Ibid.,* p. 507. As an example of the length to which the censor would go in restricting the freedom of writers and critics in handling a theme inimicable to their tastes, we have only to look at an incident which happened in 1906. In this year, Niqula Haddad published a novel entitled *Hawwa al-Jadida aw Yvonne Monar* (The New Eve or Yvonne Monar), in which he criticized Arab society for punishing women for extramarital sexual practices which it considered outrageous and immoral in women while completely ignoring or even tacitly approving of the same thing in men. Critics in Syria were not permitted to evaluate the new novel as freely as they might have because the censor believed that Eve was a sacrosanct figure and should not be a subject treated by writers. See Niqula Haddad, *Hawwa al-Jadida aw Yvonne Monar,* 3rd ed., (Cairo, 1919), p. 115.

74. See *Zenobia* in *al-Jinan* (1871), p. 499, and Najm *al-Qissa fi al-Adab al-Arabi al-Hadith,* pp. 140-146.

75. *Zenobia, Ibid.,* pp. 1, 4, 100, 281, 391, 494, 530-532, 889, and 822, and Najm, pp. 144-146.

76. See *Budur* in *al-Jinan* (1872), and Najm, pp. 146-152.

77. See this novel in *al-Jinan* (1874). See also Najm, pp. 152-154.

78. Najm, *Ibid.,* p. 155.

79. For the testimony of Tal Mahri see Michael the Great, *Chronicle* ed. J. B. Chabot, Book XI (Paris, 1910), Chapter 3.

80. See *al-Jinan* (1871), pp. 165-168, and Najm, p. 239.

81. *Asma, al-Jinan* (1873), p. 826.

82. *Al-Hiyam fi Jinan al-Sham, al-Jinan* (1870), p. 732.

83. *Ibid.,* p. 826.

84. Al-Bustani was not in favor of using *saj,* (rhymed prose). See the addendum to his article "al-'Ajab al-'Ujab," in *al-Jinan* (September 15, 1871), p. 611.

CHAPTER VII: FROM AL-BUSTANI TO JURJI ZAYDAN: FRANCIS MARRASH AND NU'MAN AL QASATLI

1. For the biography and writings of Francis Marrash see Philip Tarrazi, *Tarikh al-Sihafa al-Arabiyya* I (Beirut, 1913), 141-143; Jurji Zaydan, *Tarikh Adab al-Lugha al-Arabiyya* IV (Cairo, 1914), 236-238: Cheikho, *al-Adab al-Arabiyya fi al-Qarn al-Tasi* (Beirut, 1926), pp. 44-48; and Qustaki al-Himsi, *Udaba Halab Dhawwu al-Athar fi al-Qarn al-Tasi 'Ashr* 2nd ed., (Aleppo, 1968), pp. 58-72.

2. For the short biography of Abd Allah and Maryana Marrash see al-Himsi, *Ibid.*, pp. 53-57 and 94-94 respectively.

3. Zaydan, *Ibid.*

4. *Ghabat al-Haqq* (The Forest of Truth) was first published by the Maronite Press in Aleppo in 1865. It was republished in Beirut and also in Egypt by the 'Umran Press in 1922. The latter edition used here was made possible by efforts of Abd al-Masih Antaki, owner of al-'Umran Press. Antaki also wrote an introduction to the 1922 edition.

5. *Ghabat al-Haqq, Ibid.*, pp. 6, 44 and 50.

6. *Ibid.*, pp. 71-78.

7. *Ibid.*, pp. 20-27 and 75.

8. *Ibid.*, pp. 33-41.

9. *Ibid.*, pp. 27-32.

10. *Ibid.*, p. 31.

11. This book was published undated in Beirut. See Tarrazi, *Ibid.,* Zaydan, IV, 237 and Cheikho, 11, 45.

12. Among these two treatises having the same title *Hayy ibn Yaqzan* (The Living One Son of the Wakeful), the first of these treatises was written by the renowned philosopher Ibn Sina (Avicenna, d. 1037). It is a symbolic philosophical tract portraying the conflict between good and evil. The other one, sometimes called *Asrar al-Hikma al-Mashriqiyya* (Secrets of Oriental Wisdom), is by the Muslim Spanish physician and philosopher Abu Bakr ibn Tufayl (Abubacer, d. 1185). In this romance ibn Tufayl tells the story of a child cast on a deserted island where he was nursed by a she-deer. The story portrays the vicissitudes of this child from infancy to manhood and his struggle for survival. But the essential point in the story is that if man is left alone uncorrupted by external human influences he may succeed in fathoming the secrets of the higher world and its dependence on a supreme being. The gist of the story is that the intellect of man derives from the divine intellect. This romance further shows not only the fertility of medieval Islamic thought but that Muslim thinkers were concerned with the concept of man's nature and his undisputed natural rights many centuries before Rousseau wrote. Ibn Tufay's *Hayy*

ibn Yaqzan was first translated into Hebrew in 1349 and into English by Edward Pococke the Son and published in Oxford in 1671. It was also translated into several European languages. Ibn Sina's *Hayy ibn Yaqzan* was published in Leiden in 1899. See Ahmad 'Atiyya Allah, *al-Qamus al-Islami,* I (Cairo, 1966), 181, and Philip Hitti, *History of the Arabs* (London, 1970), p. 582.

13. *Ghabat al-Haqq,* pp. 99-100.

14. *Ibid.,* pp. 84-85.

15. Francis Marrash, *Durr al-Sadaf fi Ghara'ib al-Sudaf* (literally, Pearl Shells in Relating Strange Coincidences), (Beirut, al-Ma'arif Press, 1872).

16. See al-Qasatli's remark at the end of his romance *Riwayat Anis* in *al-Jinan* (1882), p. 382.

17. Nu'man Abduh al-Qasatli, *al-Rawda al-Ghanna fi Tarikh Dimashq al-Fayha,* p. 90, quoted by Shakir Mustafa, *al-Qissa fi Suriyya hatta al-Harb al-Alamiyya al-Thaniya,* p. 97.

18. Al-Qasatli mentions these experiences in his historical romance *Murshid wa Fitna* which appeared serially in *al-Jinan* (1880-81).

19. Nu'man Abduh al-Qasatli, *al-Fatat al-Amina wa Ummuha, al-Jinan* (1880), p. 30

20. *Ibid.,* p. 90.

21. *Ibid.,* pp. 122-123.

22. Nu'man Abduh al-Qasatli, *Riwayat Anis, al-Jinan* (1881-1882).

23. *Ibid., al-Jinan* (1881), pp. 185-186.

24. *Ibid.,* pp. 250-251, 572-573, and 634.

25. *Ibid.,* p. 250.

26. *Ibid.,* pp. 378-379.

27. *Ibid.,* p. 60.

28. *Ibid.,* pp. 62, 153, 159, 255 and 281.

29. For al-Bustani's criticism of Ottoman government officials, see his novel *Zenobia* in *al-Jinan* (1871), pp. 1, 4, 494, and 822. Perhaps for fear of retaliation by the Ottoman censor, al-Bustani's criticism was mostly implicit.

CHAPTER VIII: JURJI ZAYDAN 1861-1914

1. See the autobiography of Zaydan entitled *Mudhakkirat Jurji Zaydan,* ed. Salah al-Din al-Munajjid (Beirut, 1968), pp. 1-20. Portions of these *Mudhakkirat* have been appended to Zaydan's *Tarikh Adab al-Lugha al-Arabiyya,* IV (Cairo, 1914), 325-326. See also, *Mukhtarat Jurji Zaydan,* I (Cairo, 1919), 7-17. Ignaz Kratschkowsky "Zaidan," *The Encyclopedia of Islam,* IV (Leyden, 1934), 1195-6; and Muhammad Abd al-Ghani Hasan, *Jurji Zaydan* (Cairo, 1970), pp. 1-44.
2. See *Mudhakkirat,* p. 53.
3. *Mudhakkirat Jurji Zaydan,* pp. 15-100. The *Mudhakkirat* ends with Zaydan's arrival in Alexandria in October, 1883.
4. See Zaydan, *Tarikh Adab al-Lugha al-Arabiyya,* IV, 325-326; *Mukhtarat Jurji Zaydan,* 1, 14-15; and Muhammad Yusuf Najm, *al-Qissa fi al-Adab al-Arabi al-Hadith,* 2nd ed. (Beirut, 1961), pp. 74-76. For a list of Zaydan's writings see Yusuf Alyan Sarkis, *Mu'jam al-Matbu'at al-Arabiyya wa al-Mu'arraba,* I (Cairo, 1928), 987, and Yusuf As'ad Daghir, *Masadir al-Dirasa al-Adabiyya,* II (Beirut, 1955), 442-446. See also Elias Zakhura, *Mir'at al-'Asr fi Tarikh wa Rusum Akabir al-Rijal fi Misr* (Cairo, 1879), p. 464; Anis al-Khuri al-Maqdisi, *al-Funun al-Adabiyya wa A'lamuha* (Beirut, 1963), p. 516; Abd al-Muhsin Taha Badr, *Tatawwur al-Riwaya al-Arabiyya fi Misr 1870-1938* (Cairo, 1963), pp. 409-410; and Joseph Harb, *Jurji Zaydan Rajulun fi Rijal* (Beirut, 1970), pp. 25-26.
5. See Kratschkowsky, pp. 1195-1196.
6. See *al-Hilal,* V, 24.
7. See Zaydan's introduction to his novel *al-Inqilab al-Uthmani, al-Hilal,* XVI (1908), and his *Tarikh al-Tamaddun al-Islami* ed. Husayn Mu'nis, 1 (Cairo, n.d.), 12; Badr, *Tatawwur al-Riwaya al-Arabiyya,* p. 96; and Najm, *al-Qissa fi al-Adab al-Arabi al-Hadith,* etc., pp. 143-144.
8. See Zaydan's introduction to his novel *al-Hajjai Ibn Yusuf, al-Hilal,* X (1901), and Kratschkowsky, *Ibid.,* p. 1195, who states that "The main value of his (Zaydan's) novels lies in their popularizing of history."
9. See Zaydan's introduction to his novel *al-Inqilab al-'Uthmani, al-Hilal* XVI, and his introduction to *Tarikh al-Tamaddun al-Islami,* ed. Mu'nis, I, p. 12.
10. *Ibid.*
11. See Badr, *Tatawwur al-Riwaya al-Arabiyya,* p. 90, and Najm, *Ibid.,* p. 162.
12. Badr, *Ibid.,* pp. 91-92, and Najm, *Ibid.,* p. 162.
13. See Abd al-Fattah 'Ibada, *Jurji Zaydan,* p. 133, quoted by Najm, *Ibid.,* pp. 159-160.
14. See for example, *Ghadat Karbala, al-Hilal,* IX (1900), 106-107 and 143.
15. See *al-Hajjaj Ibn Yusuf, al-Hilal,* X (1901), 36-40. Cf. Badr, *Tatawwur al-Riwaya al-Arabiyya,* p. 96.

16. This is true of all Zaydan's novels. See for example, *al-'Abbasa Ukht al-Rashid,* where Zaydan gives full description of the city of Baghdad.

17. See Zaydan's *al-Inqilab al-'Uthmani,* (Beirut, n.d.), pp. 3 and 42. Cf. Badr, *Ibid.,* p. 100.

18. See Zaydan's *Armanusa al-Misriyya,* (Beirut, n.d.), and Mahmud Hamid Shawkat, *al-Fann al-Qisasi fi al-Adab al-Misri al-Hadith* (Cairo, 1956), p. 146.

19. See Zaydan's *Ghadat Karbala,* (Beirut, n.d.), and Shawkat, *Ibid.*

20. *See Zaydan's Abu Muslim al-Khurasani,* (Beirut, n.d.); Shawkat, *Ibid.;* and Najm, *al-Qissa fi al-Adab al-Arabi al-Hadith,* p. 184.

21. See Zaydan's *Abd al-Rahman al-Nasir,* (Beirut, n.d.), and Shawkat, *Ibid.,* pp.146-147.

22. See Zaydan's *al-Amin wa al-Ma'mum,* (Beirut, n.d.), and Shawkat, *Ibid.,* p. 147.

23. See Zaydan's *al-Mamluk al-Sharid,* (Beirut, n.d.). pp. 49-50. Zaydan surprises us with even more startling coincidences when he reveals that Jamila, a princess of the Shihabi family in Lebanon, was not known or even recognized by the Amir Bashir ll al-Shihabi (d. 1850) until it was suddenly revealed that Jamila was no other than the princess Salma, thought to have been lost many years ago, and this, despite the fact that Jamila lived in the Amir's palace. *Ibid.*

24. See *al-Hajjaj Ibn Yusuf,* pp. 115-122.

25. See Zaydan's *Fatat Ghassan* II, (Beirut, n.d.), 361-363.

26. See Zaydan's *'Adhra Quraysh,* (Beirut, n.d.), pp. 89-90.

27. See Zaydan's *Asir al-Mutamahdi,* (Beirut, n.d.), pp. 4, 29, and 132.

28. *Ibid.,* p. 28.

29. *Ibid.,* pp. 143-160.

30. Cf. Shawkat, *al-Fann al-Qisasi fi al-Adab al-Misri al-Hadith,* p. 148.

31. See Zaydan's *Seventeenth Ramadan,* (Beirut, n.d.), pp. 5-6.

32. *Ibid.,* p. 7.

33. *Ibid.,* pp. 9-15.

34. See *al-'Abbasa Ukht al-Rashid,* pp. 5-7.

35. *Ibid.,* pp. 7-16. According to Abu al-Hasan al-Mas'udi, al-'Abbasa used Ja'far's mother to arrange for her meeting with Ja'far. Ja'far's mother dressed al-'Abbasa like one of her slave girls and offered her as a present to her son. Not knowing that she was the sister of the Caliph, Ja'far had intercourse with al-'Abbasa, who later revealed her true identity to the Ja'far. Al-'Abbasa conceived from Ja'far a boy who was raised in Mecca. When the Caliph, al-Rashid, discovered that Ja'far had violated his order, he had him beheaded. See al-Mas'udi, *Muruj al-Dhahab wa Ma'adin al Jawhar,* ed. Muhammad Muhyi al-Din Abd al-Hamid, III (Cairo, 1938), 290-292.

36. See *al-Mamluk al-Sharid,* p. 19.

37. *Ibid.,* pp. 23 and 34.

38. *Ibid.,* pp. 23-24.

39. *Ibid.,* pp. 27-31.

40. See *al-Amin wa al-Ma'mun,* pp. 16,17.

41. *Ibid.,* p. 16.

42. *Ibid.,* p. 18.

43. *Ibid.,* p. 17.

44. *Ibid.,* pp. 17-18.

45. See Najm, *al-Qissa fi al-Adab al-Arabi al-Hadith,* p. 161.

46. Cf. Badr, *Tatawwur al-Riwaya al-Arabiyya,* pp. 90-101, where the author insists that Zaydan was only an instructor of history.
47. *Ibid.,* p. 99.
48. See Zaydan *al-Inqilab al-'Uthmani,* (Beirut, n.d.), 99-100.
49. Cf. Najm, pp. 168-169.
50. See Zaydan, *Arus Farghana* (Beirut, n.d.), the front page.
51. *Ibid.,* pp. 38-39.
52. See *Asir al-Mutamahdi,* p. 69.
53. See Zaydan, *Jihad al-Muhibbin* (Beirut, n.d.), the front page.
54. Najm, *al-Qissa fi al-Adab al-Arabi al-Hadith,* p. 77.
55. *Ibid.,* p. 78.
56. Zaydan, *Jihad al-Muhibbin,* pp. 20-22.
57. *Ibid.,* pp. 44-51.
58. See for example, *Jihad al-Muhibbin,* pp. 20-21.
59. Badr, *Tatawwur al-Riwaya al-Arabiyya al-Haditha,* p. 106.
60. For a list of Zaydan books see Abd al-Ghani Hasan, *Jurji Zaydan,* pp. 229-236.
61. See for example, *Shawkat,* pp. 152-154, 165, 171-175, and 186; Badr, pp. 107-111; and Najm, pp. 187-190.
62. Najm, pp. 158-159.
63. See Ignaz Kratschkowsky "Zaidan" *The Encyclopedia of Islam,* IV, p. 1196. Other critics mentioned by Kratschkowsky include Yusuf Tabshi, *al-Burhan fi Intiqad Riwwayat 'Adhra Quraysh* (Cairo, 1900). See also Najm, *Ibid.,* pp. 158-159; Zaydan, *Tarikh Adab al-Lugha al-Arabiyya,* III, 6; and Muhammad Abd al-Ghani Hasan, p. 156.
64. Kratschkowsky, *Ibid.,* pp. 1196.
65. Zaydan expresses his predicament in the introduction to his *Tarikh Adab al-Lugha al-Arabiyya,* III. See also Muhammad Husayn Haykal *Fi Awqat al-Faragh,* 2nd ed. (Cairo, 1968), p. 238, and Muhammad Abd al-Ghani Hasan, pp. 153-161.
66. For this statement by Taha Husayn see *al-Kitab al-Dhahabi li al-Hilal* (Cairo, 1942), quoted by Muhammad Abd al-Ghani Hasan, *Jurji Zaydan,* p. 104.
67. Badr, pp. 107-115.
68. Shawkat, pp. 152-179.

EPILOGUE:

1. Ahmad Hafiz 'Awad, *al-Hal wa al-Ma'al* (Cairo, Musamarat al-Sha'b, No. 4, 1905).

2. On this point see Abd al-Muhsin Taha Badr, *Tatawuur al-Riwaya al-Arabiyya al-Haditha fi Misr* 1870-1938 (The Development of Modern Arabic Novel in Egypt, 1870-1938) (Cairo, 1963), pp. 144-146.

3. See Sir Hamilton A. R. Gibb, *Studies on the Civilization of Islam* (Boston, 1962), Part III; Mahmud Hamid Shawkat, *Al-Fann al-Qisasi fi al-Adab al-Misri al-Hadith* 1800-1956 (Cairo, 1956), pp. 317-333.

4. Muhammad Husayn Haykal's *Zaynab* appeared anonymously in 1912. The author wrote it between April, 1910 and March, 1911 as a law student in Paris. When he returned to Egypt in 1912 to practice law, he was reluctant to publish the novel under his own name, for fear of damaging his professional standing. Thus he chose to have it published as *Zaynab, Manazir wa Akhlaq Rifiyya*, by Misri Fallah (Zaynab, Country Scenes and Manners, by an Egyptian Peasant). Not until 1922 did it appear with the full name of the author. The edition referred to here appeared in 1963. For comments on this novel, see Ali al-Ra'i, *Dirasat fi al-Riwaya al-Misriyya* (Studies in the Egyptian Novel) (Cairo, 1964), pp. 23-55; Shawkat, pp. 220-227; and Badr, p. 157. Of particular interest also is the chapter on this subject by Yahya Haqqi in *Fajr al-Qissa al-Misriyya* (The Dawn of the Egyptian Novel) (Cairo, 1960).

5. Haqqi, pp. 75-76 and 103-106; Mahmud Timur in *al-Adab* VIII (September, 1960), 10-11; Muhammad Husayn Haykal, *Thawrat al-Adab* (The Revolution of Literature) (Cairo, 1965), pp. 8-9.

6. For an interesting discussion of Timur's works and career, see Fathi al-Abyari, *Mahmud Timur wa fann al-Uqsusa al-Arabiyya* (Mahmud Timur and the Art of the Arab Short Story) and, by the same author, *Fann al-Qissa ind Mahmud Timur* (The Art of the Story of Mahmud Timur) (Cairo, 1964).

7. Cf. a radio lecture delivered by Timur in 1960 and published in *al-Adab* VIII (September, 1960), 10-11.

8. For further information see Badr, pp. 233-258.

9. Mahmud Timur, *al-Atlal* (Cairo, 1934). Timur rewrote the work in 1951, altering the structure and adding several chapters, and published it under the title *Shabab wa Ghaniya*. See al-Abyari, *Fann al-Qissa*, pp. 12-17.

10. Haqqi, pp. 84-85.

11. Taha Husayn, *al-Ayyam*, 2 vols., (Cairo, 1929). See Shawkat, p. 229; Badr, pp. 207-303; and Shawqi Dayf, *al-Adab al-Arabi al-Mu'asir fi Misr* (Contemporary Arabic Literature in Egypt) (Cairo, 1961), pp. 284-287.

12. Taha Husayn, *Shajarat al-Bu's* (The Tree of Misery) (Cairo, 1935); al-Ra'i, pp. 140-156.

13. Among those novels are *Ibrahim al-Katib* (1931), *Ibrahim al-Thani* (1943), *'Awdun 'ala Bad* (1943), *Mido wa Shurakahu* (1943), *Thalathat Rijal wa Imra'a* (1944), and *'Almashi* (1944).

14. On this point see al-Mazini, *Ibrahim al-Katib* (Cairo, 1931), Introduction pp. 9-10; Haykal, *Thawrat al-Adab,* pp. 82-87.

15. See al-Mazini, *Qissat Hayat* (A Life's Story) (Cairo, 1961), pp. 32-33, in which the author discusses he was poor, and in adolescense he developed a complex caused by an accident which left him with a limp. Consequently he came to believe that he could not be loved. He developed a deep fear of death when the family lived next to a cemetery. For further analysis, see Ni'mat Fu'ad, *Adab al-Mazini* (Cairo, 1954), p. 68; al-Ra'i, pp. 82-88; Badr, pp. 333-339.

16. Badr, p. 346.

17. Fu'ad, pp. 179, 188 and 192.

18. Dayf, p. 289.

19. Tawfiq al-Hakim, *'Awdat al-Ruh* (The Return of the Spirit), 4th ed., 1 (Cairo, 1957), 141.

20. For an interesting analysis of this and other aspects of *'Awdat al-Ruh,* see al-Ra'i, pp. 98-139, and Badr, pp. 379-397. Shawkat, p. 242, comments briefly on the same subject.

21. Badr, p. 392.

22. Yahya Haqqi *Khutuwat fi al-Naqd* (Steps in Criticism) (Cairo, 1961), p. 101.

23. *Ibid.*

24. 'Abbas Mahmud al-'Aqqad, *Sarah* (Cairo, 1938), p. 53.

25. Al-Ra'i, pp. 55, 68-69.

26. Al-'Aqqad, p. 22; Badr, p. 365; Shawkat, pp. 259-260.

27. Al-Ra'i, pp. 69-70.

28. Shawkat, p. 263.

29. Al-Ra'i, p. 251.

Bibliography

Arabic Sources

Abd Allah, Tawfiq. *Al-Qisas al-'Asriyya.* Cairo, n.d.
Abd al-Raziq, Mustafa. *Muhammad Abduh.* Cairo, 1946.
Abdel-Meguid, Abdel Aziz. *Al-Uqsusa fi al-Adab al-Arabi al-Hadith: Namadhij.* Cairo, n.d.
Abduh, Ibraham. *Tarikh al-Tiba'a wa al-Sihafa fi Misr Khilal al-Hamla al-Faransiyya,* Cairo, 1949.
───────. *Tatawwur al-Sihafa al-Misriyya.* Cairo, 1945.
───────. *Jaridat al-Ahram.* Cairo, 1951.
───────. *Al-Waqa'i al-Misriyya, 1828-1942.* Cairo, 194?.
───────. *Abu Nazzara Imam al-Sihafa al-Fukahiyya al-Musawwara wa Za'im al-Masrah fi Misr.* Cairo, 1953.
───────. *Al-Suhufi al-Tha'ir.* Cairo, 1955.
Abduh, Muhammad and Afghani, Jamal al-Din al-. *Al-Urwa al-Wuthqa,* Beirut, 1909.
Abduh, Tanius. *Diwan Tanius Abduh.* Cairo, 1925.
Abyari, Fathi al-. *Mahmud Timur wa fann al-Uqsusa al-Arabiyya.* Cairo, 1964.
───────. *Fann al-Qissa ind Mahmud Timur.* Cairo, 1964.
Ahmad, Ahmad Sulayman al-. *Dirasat fi al-Masrah al-Arabi al-Mu'asir: al-Masrah al-Shi'ri 1876-1966.* Damascus, 1972.
'Alim, Mahmud Amin al-. *Alwan min al-Qissa al-Misriyya.* Cairo, 1956.
───────. *Ta'ammulat fi 'Alam Najib Mahfuz.* Cairo, 1970.
Ali, Muhammad Kurd. *Khitat al-Sham.* 6 Vols., Damascus, 1925.
'Amara, Muhammad, ed. *Al-A'mal al-Kamila li al-Imam Muhammad Abduh.* Vol. I Beirut, 1972.
Amin, Ahmad. *Zu'ama al-Islah.* Cairo, 1965.
Amin, 'Uthman. *Muhammad Abduh.* Cairo, 1944.
'Aqqad, 'Abbas Mahmud al-. *Sarah.* Cairo, 1938.
───────. *Rijal Araftuhum.* Cairo, 1963.
───────. *Muraja'at fi al-Adab wa al-Fann.* Cairo, 1925.
───────. and Mazini, Ibrahim Abd al-Qadir al-. *Al-Diwan fi al-Adab wa al-Naqd.* Cairo, 1921.
Asad, Nasir al-Din. *Muhadarat 'an Khalil Baydas Ra'id al-Qissa al-Haditha fi Filastin.* Cairo, 1963.
*Awad, Ahmad Hafiz. *Al-Hal wa al-Ma'al.* Cairo, 1904.
*Awad, Louis. *Al-Mu'aththirat al-Ajnabiyya fi al-Arabi al-Hadith.* Cairo, 1962.
───────. *Dirasat fi Adabina al-Hadith.* Cairo, 1961.
───────. *Maqalat fi al-Naqd wa al-Adab.* Cairo, n.d.

'Ayyad, Shukri Muhammad. *Al-Qissa al-Qasira fi Misr: Dirasa fi Ta'sil Fann Adabi.* Cairo, 1968.

'Aziz, Sami. *Al-Sihafa al-Misriyya wa Mawqifuha min al-Ihtilal al-Ingilizi.* Cairo, 1968.

Badr, Abd al-Muhsin Taha. *Tatawwur al-Riwaya al-Arabiyya al-Haditha fi Misr,* 1870-1938. Cairo, 1963.

Badawi, Abd al-Rahman. *Fann al-Shi'r.* Cairo, 1953.

Baydas, Khalil Ibrahim. *Masarih al-Adhan,* Cairo, 1924.

Bishri, Abd al-'Aziz. *Al-Mukhtar.* 2 Vols:, Cairo, 1959.

Bustani, Sa'id al-. *Dhat al-Khidr.* Beirut, 1884.

Bustani, Salim al-, *Asma, al-Jinan,* 1873.

_____. *al-Hiyam fi Jinan al-Sham, al-Jinan,* 1870.

_____. *Budur, al-Jinan,* 1872.

_____. *al-Hiyam fi Futuh al-Sham, al-Jinan,* 1874.

_____. *Bint al-'Asr, al-Jinan,* 1875.

_____. *Fatina, al-Jinan,* 1877.

_____. *Salma, al-Jinan,* 1878-1879.

_____. *Samiya, al-Jinan,* 1882-1884.

Cheikho, Louis. *Al-Adab al-Arabiyya fi al-Qarn al-Tasi 'Ashr.* Vol. 1, 1800-1870 and Vol. 2 1870-1900. Beirut, 1924-1926.

_____. *Tarikh al-Adab al-Arabiyya fi al-Rub' al-Awwal min al-Qarn al-'Ishrin.* Beirut, 1926.

Daghir, Yusuf As'ad. *Masadir al-Dirasa al-Adabiyya.* 2 Vols., Beirut, 1956.

Dawwara, Fu'ad. *Fi al-Riwaya al-Misriyya.* Cairo, 1968.

_____. *'Ashrat Udaba Yatahaddathun.* Cairo, 1965.

Dayf, Shawqi. *Al-Maqama.* Cairo, 1964.

_____. *Al-Adab al-Arabi al-Mu'asir fi Misr.* Cairo, 1961.

Dimashqi, al-Khuri Mikha'il Burayk al-. *Tarikh al-Sham.* 1720-1782. ed. al-Khuri Constantine al-Pasha, Harisa, Lebanon, 1930.

Din, Jalil Kamal al-. *Al-Shi'r al-Arabi al-Hadith wa Ruh al-'Asr.* Beirut, 1964.

Din, Sa'id Taqi al-. *Lawla al-Muhami.* Beirut, 1924.

Disuqi, 'Umar al-. *Fi al-Adab al-Hadith.* Beirut, 1967.

_____. *Muhadarat an Nash'at al-Nathr al-Hadith wa Tatawwuruhu.* Cairo, 1962.

Fu'ad, Ni'mat Ahmad. *Adab al-Mazini.* Cairo, 1954.

Gibran, Faraj. *Qisas an Jama'a min Mashahir Kuttab al-Gharb.* Cairo, 1927.

Ghunaym, Abd al-Hamid. *Sanu Ra'id al-Masrah al-Misri.* Cairo, 1966.

Haddad, Niqula. *Hawwa al-Jadida aw Yvonne Monar.* 3rd ed. Cairo, 1929.

Hakim, Tawfiq al-. *Al-Malik Odib.* Cairo, 1949.

_____. *'Awdat al-Ruh.* 2 Vols., 4th ed. Cairo, 1957.

Hamada, Ibrahim. *Khayal al-Zill wa Tamthiliyyat Ibn Daniyal.* Cairo, 1963.

Hamza, Abd al-Latif. *Adab al-Maqala al-Suhufiyya.* 6 Vols., 2nd ed., Cairo, 1958-1959.

Haqqi, Yahya. *Fajr al-Qissa al-Misriyya.* Cairo, n.d.

_____. *Khutuwat fi al-Naqd.* Cairo, n.d.

Harb, Joseph. *Jurji Zaydan Rajulun fi Rijal.* Beirut, 1970.

Hasan, Muhammad Abd al-Ghani. *Jurji Zaydan.* Cairo, 1970.

Haykal, Muhammad Husayn. *Zaynab.* Cairo, 1963.

_____. *Thawrat al-Adab.* Cairo, 1965.

_____. *Fi Awqat al-Faragh.* 2nd ed., Cairo, 1968.

Himsi, Qustaki al-. *Udaba Halab Dhawu al-Athar fi al-Qarn al-Tasi' 'Ashr.* Aleppo, 1968.

Hunayn, Edward. *Shawqi 'ala al-Masrah.* Beirut, 1936.

Husayn, Taha. *Mudhakkirat Taha Husayn.* Beirut, 1967.

_____. *Al-Ayyam.* 2 Vols., Cairo, 1929.

_____. *Du'a al-Karawan.* Cairo, 1934.

_____. *Shajarat al-Durr.* Cairo, 1935.

_____. *Shajarat al-Bu's.* Cairo, 1935.

_____. *Adib.* Cairo, 1962.

_____. *Hafiz wa Shawqi.* Cairo, 1966.

Ibrahim, Hafiz. *Layali Satih.* ed. Abd al-Rahman Sidqi. Cairo, 1964.

Id, al-Sayyid Hasan. *Tatawwur al-Naqd al-Masrahi fi Misr.* Cairo, 1965.

Inan, Muhammad Abd Allah. *Qisas Ijtima'iyya wa Namadhij min Adab al-Gharb.* Cairo, 1932.

Ishaq, Adib. *Al-Durar.* ed. Awni Ishaq. Beirut, 1909.

Isma'il, Izz al-Din. *Qadaya al-Insan fi al-Adab al-Masrahi al-Mu'asir.* Cairo, n.d.

Jabarti, Abd al-Rahman al-. *Aja'ib al-Athar fi al-Tarajim wa al-Akhbar.* Bulaq, 1297 A.H./A.D. 1897.

Jalal Muhammad Uthman. *Al-Masrah al-Arabi: Dirasat wa Nusus—Muhammad Uthman Jalal.* ed. Muhammad Yusuf Najm. Beirut, 1964.

_____. *Al-Uyun al-Yawaqiz fi al-Amthal wa al-Hikam wa al-Mawa'iz.* Bulaq, 1313 A.H./A.D. 1895.

Jumu'a, Muhammad Lutfi. *Layali al-Ruh al-Ha'ir.* Cairo, 1912.

Jumu'a, Muhammad Kamil. *Hafiz Ibrahim ma lahu wa ma Alayhi.* Cairo, 1960.

Jundi, Adham. *A'lam al-Adab wa al-Fann.* Damascus, 1954.

Jundi, Anwar al-. *Adab al-Mar'a al-Arabiyya: al-Qissa al-Arabiyya al-Mu'asira-Tatawwur al-Tarjama.* Cairo, n.d.

_____. *Al-Kuttab al-Mu'asirun: Adwa ala Hayatihim.* Cairo, 1957.

_____. *Al-Fikr al-Arabi al-Mu'asir fi Ha'rakat al-Taghrib wa al-Taba'ryya.* Cairo, n.d.

Khal'i, Kamil. *Al-Musiqi al-Sharqi.* Damascus, 1948.

Khayrat, Mahmud. *Al-Fatat al-Rifiyya.* Cairo, 1905.

_____. *Al-Fata al-Rifi.* Cairo, 1905.

Khidr, Abbas. *Al-Qissa al-Qasira fi Misr Mundhu Nash'atiha hatta Sanat 1930.* Cairo, 1966.

Karim, Ahmad Izzat Abd al-. *Tarikh al-Ta'lim Fi 'Asr Muhammad Ali.* Cairo, 1938.

_____. *Tarikh al-Ta'lim fi Misr: 'Asr Isma'il.* Cairo, 1945.

_____. *Tarikh al-Ta'lim fi 'Asr Abbas wa Sa'id,* 1848-1863. Cairo, 1946.

Khurshid, Faruq. *Fi al-Riwaya al-Arabiyya: 'Asr al-Tajmi.* Alexandria, n.d.

Khuri, Shakir. *Majma al-Masarrat.* Beirut, 1908.

Kratschkowsky, Ignaz. *Al-Mukhtarat.* 3 Vols., Moscow, 1956.

Mala'ika, Nazik al-. *Qadaya al-Shi'r al-Mu'asir.* Beirut, 1962.

Mandur, Muhammad. *Masrahiyyat Shawqi.* Cairo, 1954.

_____. *Al-Masrah.* Cairo, 1963.

_____. *Fi al-Mizan al-Jadid.* 3rd ed., Cairo, n.d.

——————. *Al-Naqd wa al-Nuqqad al-Mu'asirun.* Cairo, n.d.

——————. *Qadaya Jadida fi Adabina al-Hadith.* Beirut, 1958.

Maghribi, Abd al-Qadir al-. *Jamal al-Din al-Afghani.* Cairo, 1948.

Makhzumi, Muhammad al-. *Khatirat Jamal al-Din al-Afghani.* Beirut, 1931.

Marrash, Francis. *Ghabat al-Haqq.* 2nd ed., Cairo, 1922.

——————. *Durr al-Sadaf fi Ghara'ib al-Sudaf.* Beirut, 1872.

Marzuq, Hilmi Ali. *Tatawwur al-Naqd wa al-Tafkir al-Adabi al-Hadith fi Misr.* Cairo, 1966.

Manfaluti, Mustafa Lutfi al-. *Al-Nazarat.* 11th ed., Cairo, 1954.

——————. *Fi Sabil al-Taj.* Cairo, 1920.

Maqdisi, Anis al-Khuri al-. *Al-Ittijahat al-Adabiyya fi al-'Alam al-Arabi al-Hadith.* Beirut, 1967.

——————. *Al-Funun al-Adabiyya wa A'lamuha.* Beirut, 1963.

Mas'udi, Abu al-Hasan al-. *Muruj al-Dhahab wa Ma'adin al-Jawhar.* 4 vols., ed. Muhammad Muhyi al-Din Abd al-Hamid. Cairo, 1938.

Mazini, Ibrahim Abd al-Qadir. *Sunduq al-Dunya.* Cairo, 1929.

——————. *Ibrahim al-Katib.* Cario, 1931.

——————. *Qissat Hayat.* Cairo, 1961.

Mubarak, Ali. *'Alam al-Din.* 3 Vols., Cairo, 1888.

——————. *Al-Khitat al-Tawfiqiyya.* 15 Vols., Bulaq, A.H. 1304-6/A.D. 1886-8.

Muhammad, Muhammad 'Awad. *Al-Isi'mar wa al-Madhahib al-Isti'mariyya.* 3rd ed., Cairo, 1961.

Mustafa, Shakir. *Muhadarat an al-Qissa fi Suriyya hatta al-Harb al-'Alamiyya al-Thaniya.* Cairo, 1958.

Muttalib, Muhammad Abd al- and Abd al-Mu'ti Mar'i. *Harb al-Basus.* Cairo, 1911.

Muwaylihi, Muhammad al-. *Hadith 'Isa Ibn Hisham Aw Fatra min al-Zaman.* 4th ed., Cairo, 1964.

Najm, Muhammad Yusuf. *Al-Qissa fi al-Adab al-Arabi al-Hadith.* Beirut, 1961.

——————. *Al-Masrahiyya fi al-Adab al-Arabi al-Hadith 1847-1914.* Beirut, 1967.

Naqqash, Salim al-. *Al-Masrah al-Arabi: Dirasat wa Nusus-Salim al-Naqqash.* ed. Muhammad Yusuf Najm. Beirut, 1964.

Nassaj, Sayyid Hamid. *Tatawwur Fann al-Qissa al-Qasira fi Misr 1910-1933.* Cairo, 1968.

Naqqash, Marun al-. *Arzat Lubnan.* ed. Niqula Naqqash, Beirut, 1869.

——————. *Al-Masrah al-Arabi: Dirasat wa Nusus-Marun Naqqash.* ed. Muhammad Yusuf Najm. Beirut, 1961.

Nu'ayma, Mikha'il. *Ab'ad min Moscow wa min Washington.* Beirut, 1957.

——————. *Sab'un: Hikayat 'Umr-al-Marhala al-Ula.* Beirut, 1959.

——————. *Al-Ghirbal.* 7th ed., Beirut, 1964.

——————. al-'Arid, Ibrahim; Timur, Mahmud and Jabbur, Jibra'il. *Fi al-Adab al-Arabi al-Hadith.* Beirut, 1954.

Qabbani, Ahmad Khalil al-. *Al-Masrah al-Arabi: Dirasat wa Nusus-al-Shaykh Ahmad Abu Khalil al-Qabbani.* ed. Muhammad Yusuf Najm. Beirut, 1963.

Qal'aji, Qadri. *Jamal al-Din al-Afghani Dhikrayat wa Ahadith.* Beirut, 1948.

Qara'ali, Bulus. *Al-Suriyyun fi Misr.* Cairo, 1928.

Qasatli, Nu'man Abduh al-. *Al-Fatat al-Amina wa Ummuha, al-Jinan,* 1880.

——————. *Riwayat Anis, al-Jinan,* 1881-1882.

Qassab, Abd al-Muhsin al-. *Dhikra al-Afghani fi al-Iraq.* Baghdad, 1945.

Ra'i, Ali Al-. *Dirasat fi al-Riwaya al-Misriyya.* Cairo, 1964.

Ramadi, Jamal al-Din al-. *Min A'lam al-Adab al-Mu'asir.* Cairo, n.d.

Rafi'i, Abd al-Rahman al-. *Tarikh al-Haraka al-Qawmiyya wa Nizam al-Hukm fi Misr.* 4th ed., Cairo, 1955.

_____. *'Asr Muhammad Ali.* 3rd ed., Cairo, 1951.

_____. *Mustafa Kamal Ba'ith al-Haraka al-Wataniyya.* 4th ed., Cairo, 1962.

Rif'at, Muhammad. *Tarikh Misr al-Siyasi* 2 Vols., Cairo, 1929.

Rifa'i, Shams al-Din. *Tarikh al-Sihafa al-Suriyya.* 2 Vols., Cairo, 1969.

Rizq, Qustandi. *Tarikh al-Musiqa al-Sharqiyya.* Cairo, n.d.

Rida, Muhammad Rashid. *Tarikh al-Ustadh al-Imam al-Shaykh Muhammad Abduh.* Cairo, 1350 A.H./A.D. 1931.

Sabih, Muhammad. *Al-Shaykh Muhammad Abduh.* 2 Vols., Cairo, 1944.

Sa'id, Jamil. *Nazarat fi al-Tayyarat al-Adabiyya al-Haditha fi al-Iraq.* Cairo, 1954.

Sa'id, Nafusa Zakariyya. *Tarikh al-Da'wa ila al-'Amiyya wa Atharuha fi Misr.* Cairo, 1964.

Salama, 'Aziz Abd Allah. *Mukhtarat.* Cairo, 1926.

Sanu, Ya'qub. *Al-Masrah al-Arabi: Dirasat wa Nusus-Ya'qub Sanu (Abu Naddara).* ed. Muhammad Yusuf Najm. Beirut, 1963.

Sarkis, Alyan. *Mu'jam al-Matbu'at al-Arabiyya wa al-Mu'arrabe.* 2 Vols., Cairo, 1928.

Shayib, Ahmad. *Muhammad Abduh.* Alexandria, 1929.

Shawkat, Mahmud Hamid. *Al-Fann al-Qisasi fi al-Adab al-Misri al-Hadith 1800-1956.* Cairo, 1956.

Shayyal, Jamal al-Din al-. *Tarikh al-Tarjama wa al-Haraka al-Thaqafiyya fi 'Asr Muhammad Ali.* Cairo, 1951.

_____. *Rifa'a Rafi' al-Tahtawi.* Cairo, 1958.

Shidyaq, Ahmad Faris al-. *Al-Saq 'ala al-Saq fi ma huwa al-Faryaq.* Vols., Cairo, 1855.

Shukri, Ghali. *Al-Muntami: Dirasa fi Adab Najib Mahfuz.* Cairo, 1964.

_____. *Thawrat al-Fikr fi Adabina al-Hadith.* Cairo, 1965.

_____. *Mudhakkirat Thaqafa Tahtadir.* Beirut, 1970.

Tabshi, Yusuf. *Al-Burhan fi Intiqad Riwayat 'Adhra Quraysh.* Cairo, 1900.

Tahtawi, Rifa'a Rafi' al-. *Takhlis al-Ibriz fi Talkhis Paris.* Bulaq, 1834.

Tajir, Jacques. *Harakat al-Tarjama fi Misr Khilal al-Qarn al-Tasi 'Ashr.* Cairo, 1946.

Tarrazi, Philip. *Tarikh al-Sihafa al-Arabiyya.* 2 Vols., Beirut, 1913.

Timur, Mahmud. *Malamih wa Ghudun.* Cairo, 1950.

_____. *Al-Atlal.* Cairo, 1934.

_____. *Fann al-Qisas.* Cairo, 1948.

_____. *Muhadarat fi al-Qisas fi al-Adab al-Arabi Madihi wa Hadiruhu.* Cairo, 1958.

_____. *Nushu al-Qissa wa Tatawwuruha.* Cairo, 1962.

Toson, 'Umar. *Al-Ba'that al-'Ilmiyya fi 'Ahd Muhammad Ali.* Alexandria, 1934.

Tuqan, Qadri Hafiz. *Jamal al-Din al-Afghani: Ara'uhu wa Kifahuhu wa Atharuhu fi Nahdat al-Sharq.* Jerusalem, 1947.

'Ubayd, 'Isa. *Ihsan Hanim: Majmu'at Qisas Misriyya 'Asriyya.* 2nd ed., Cairo, 1964.

'Umar, Mustafa Ali. *Al-Waqi'iyya fi al-Masrah al-Misri.* Alexandria, 1968.

Yaghi, Hashim. *Al-Naqd al-Adabi al-Hadith fi Lubnan.* 2 Vols., Cairo, 1968.

_____. *Al-Qissa al-Qasira fi Filastin wa al-Urdun* 1850-1965. Cairo, 1966.
Zakhura, Elias. *Mir'at al-'Asr fi Tarikh wa Rusum Akabir al-Rijal fi Misr.* Cairo, 1879.
Zaydan, Jurji. *Mukhtarat Jurji Zaydan.* 2 Vols., Cairo, 1919.
_____. *Tarajim Mashahir al-Sharq.* 3rd ed., 2 Vols., Cairo, 1902-1903.
_____. *Tarikh Adab al-Lugha al-Arabiyya.* 4 Vols., Cairo, 1911-1914.
_____. *Mudhakkirat Jurji Zaydan.* ed. Salah al-Din al-Munajjid. Beirut, 1968.
_____. *Tarikh Riwayat al-Islam,* 5 Vols., Beirut, n.d. These volumes contain
    all of Zaydan's novels.
_____. *Tarikh al-Tamaddun al-Islami.* 5 Vols., ed. Husayn Mu'nis. Cairo, n.d.
Zayyat, Ahmad Hasan al-. *Wahi al-Risala.* 4 Vols., 7th ed., Cairo, 1962.

Western Sources

Adams, Charles C. *Islam and Modernism in Egypt.* Oxford University Press, 1933.
Ahmad, J. M. *The Intellectual Origin of Egyptian Nationalism.* Oxford University
    Press, 1960.
Amin, Osman. *Muhammad Abduh.* (C. Wendell trans.): American Council of Learned
    Societies), Washington, 1953.
Badawi, Zaki. *The Reformers of Egypt.* Totwa, N.J., 1978.
Baignières, Paul De. ed. *! Égypt Satirique.* Paris, 1886.
Boustani, Salaheddine. *The Press During the French Expedition in Egypt* 1798-1801.
    Cairo, 1954.
Brockelmann, Karl C. *Geschichte der arabischen Literatur.* Vols. 2 & 3., Weimar,
    1898-1902.
Cromer, the Earl of. *Modern Egypt.* 2 Vols., New York, 1908.
Haywood, John. *Modern Arabic Literature.* London, 1971.
Heyworth-Dunn, J. *An Introduction to the History of Education in Modern Egypt.* 2nd
    ed., London, 1968.
Gardey, Louis. *Voyage du Sultan Abd-ul-Aziz de Stambul au Caire.* Paris, 1885.
Gendzier, Irene L. *The Practical Visions of Ya'qub Sanu.* Harvard University Press,
    1966.
Gibb, H.A.R. *Studies on the Civilization of Islam.* Boston, 1962.
Hartman, Martin. *The Arabic Press of Egypt.* London, 1899.
Holt, P.M. *Studies in the History of the Near East.* London, 1973.
Hourani, Albert. *Arabic Thought in the Liberal Age* 1798-1939. Oxford University
    Press, 1970.
Hurat, Clement. *A History of Arabic Literature.* Beirut, 1966.
Hurewitz, J.C. *Diplomacy in the Near and Middle East.* Vol. 1, Princeton, New Jersey,
    1956.
Jacob, Georg. *Geschichte des Schattenstheaters.* Berlin, 1907.
Jonquire De la, C. *L'Expédition d'Égypte* 1798-1801. Paris, 1899.
Keddie, Nikki R. "Sayyid Jamal al-Din al-Afghani. A Case of Posthumous
    Charisma?" *In Philosophers and Kings: Studies in Leadership.* ed. Dankwart
    A. Rustow, New York, 1970, pp. 148-179.
_____. *An Islamic Response to Imperialism: Political and Religious Writings of
    Sayyid Jamal al-Din "Al-Afghani."* Berkeley and Los Angeles, 1968.
Kedourie, Elie. *Afghani and Abduh: An Essay on Religious unbelief and Political
    Activities in Modern Islam.* London: Frank Cass, 1966.

Kratschkowsky, I.Y. *Among Arabic Manuscripts.* Leiden, 1953.

Landau, Jacob. *Studies in the Arab Theater and Cinema.* Philadelphia, 1958.

Lane, Edward William. *An Account of the Manners and Customs of the Modern Egyptians,* London, 1895.

Meguid, Abdel-Aziz Abd al-. *The Modern Arabic Short Story.* Cairo, n.d.

Nerval, Gérard De. *Voyage en Orient.* Paris, 1876. An English translation of the same is entitled *The Women of Cairo.* Translated by Conrad Elphinstone. London, 1929.

Nicholson, R. A. *A Literary History of the Arabs.* London, 1907.

Niebuhr, M. C. *Travels Through Arabia and Other Countries in the East.* Trans. Robert Heron, Edinburgh, 1792.

Pérès, Henri. *Le roman et la Littératur* I, Bibliographie des ouvrages, originaux in Annales dr Institute Oriental d, Alger, 111, 1937.

──────────. *Littératue Arabe Moderne: Grands Courants* -Bibliographie, Algiers, 1940.

Regnault, A. *Voyage en Orient: Grèc, Turquie, Égypt.* Paris, 1855.

Roux, Charles F. *Bonaparte Gouverneur d, Égypte.* Paris, 1936.

Urquhart, David. *The Lebanon (Mount Souria): History and Diary.* London, 1860.

Volney, Comte de, Constantine Francois Chasseboeuf. *Voyage en Syrie et en Égypte, pendant les Anées* 1783, 1785. Paris, 1787.

Wahab, Farouk Abdel. *Modern Egyptian Drama: An Anthology.* Bibliotheca Islamica Chicago, 1980.

Articles

Barbour, Nevill. "Al-Manfaluti—An Essayist," *Islamic Culture,* VII (1933).

──────────. "The Arabic Theater in Egypt," *Bulletin of the School of Oriental Studies.* London, 1935-37.

Bustani, Fu'ad Afram al-. "Awwal Masrahiyya bi al-Lugha al-Arabiyya" *al-Shira,* No. 1, Beirut, 1948.

──────────. "Marun Naqqash Walid al-Masrah al-Arabi," *al-Shira* Nos. 1 & 3, Beirut, 1948.

Bustani, Salim al-. "Al-Riwayat al-Khedawiyya al-Tashkhisiyya," *al-Jinan,* 1875.

──────────. "Ruh al-'Asr," *al-Jinan.* July, 1870.

──────────. "Al-Insaf," *al-Jinan.* June, 1870.

──────────. "Al-Ams," *al-Jinan.* October, 1870.

──────────. "Al-Dawla al-'Aliyya," *al-Jinan.* June, 1870.

──────────. "Al-'Ajab al-'Ujab," *al-Jinan.* September, 1871.

Daghir, Yusuf As'ad. "Fann al-Tamthil fi Khilal Qarn," *al-Mashriq,* XLII, 1948.

Gaylani, Ibrahim al-. "Ahmad Abu Khalil al-Qabbani," *al-Mu'allim al-Arabi,* Damascus, 1948.

Hifni, Abd al-Mun'im al-. "Al-Ruh al-Arabi fi al-Adab wa al-Fann," *Adab,* Beirut, No. 7, 1963.

Issawi, Charles. "European Loan-Words in Contemporary Arabic Writing: A Case Study in Modernization," Middle East Studies Spring, 1967, pp. 110-133.

Jundi, Adham al-. "Al-Abqariyya al-Shamikha: Abu Khalil al-Qabbani," *al-Fayha.* Damascus, July, 1952.

Kratschkowsky, Ignaz, "Zaidan," *The Encyclopedia of Islam,* IV (Leiden, 1934), 1195-6.

Landau, Jacob. "Abu Naddara, An Egyptian-Jewish Nationalist," *The Journal of Jewish Studies,* III, No. 1, 1952.

Luqa, Anwar. "Masrah Ya'qub Sanu," *al-Majalla.* Cairo, March 15, 1961.

Menzel, Th. "Khayal-i-zill," *The Encyclopedia of Islam.* II, 1927.

Moosa, Matti. "The Growth of Modern Arabic Fiction," *Critique: Studies in Modern Arabic Fiction,* XI, Minneapolis, 1968.

Naqqash, Salim al-. "Fawa'id al-Riwayat aw al-Tiyatrat," *al-Jinan.* Beirut, 1875.

Prüfer, Curt. "Drama (Arabic)," *Encyclopedia of Religion and Ethics,* 1912.

Semaan, Khalil. " 'Ala Hamish Da'wa al-Su'uba fi Ta'allum al-Arabiyya," *Majallat Majma' al-Lugha al-Arabiyya bi Dimashq* XLII, October, 1967.

Saussey, E. "Une Adaptation Arabe en Paul et Virginie," *Bulletin d'Etudes Orientales,* I, 1931.

Su'ud, Fakhri Abu al-. "Al-Qissa fi al-Adabayn al-Arabi wa al-Ingilizi," *al-Risala,* No. 198, 1937.

Tulaymat, Zaki. "Nahdat al-Tamthil fi al-Sharq al-Arabi," *al-Hilal.* Cairo, April 1939.

Unpublished Dissertations

Dykstra, Darrell J. *A Biographical Study in Egyptian Modernization: Ali Mubarak 1823-1893.* University of Michigan, 1977.

Georgescu, Constantine Juliu. *A Forgotten Pioneer of the Lebanese Nahdah: Salim al-Bustani* (1848-1884), New York University, 1978.

Khoury Nabil A. *Islam and Development in the Middle East: The Thought of Muhammad Abduh.* Sunny, Albany, 1976.

Pelletier, Stephen. *The Print and the Forcing of Islam: The Failure of Liberalism in the Arab Middle East.* University of California, Berkeley, 1976.

Zayyat, Latifa al-. *Harakat al-Tarjama al-Adabiyya min al-Ingiliziyya ila al-Arabiyya fi Misr fi al-Fatra ma Bayn 1882-1925 wa Mada Irtibatuha bi Sihafat hadhihi al-Fatra,* Cairo University, Egypt, 1957.

Index